DISAPPEARING PEASANTRIES?

Disappearing Peasantries?

Rural Labour in Africa, Asia and Latin America

Edited by
DEBORAH BRYCESON,
CRISTÓBAL KAY and JOS MOOIJ

INTERMEDIATE TECHNOLOGY PUBLICATIONS 2000

Intermediate Technology Publications
103/105 Southampton Row, London, WC1B 4HH, UK

A CIP catalogue record for this book is
available from the British Library

ISBN 1 85339 477 7

Typeset by Dorwyn Ltd, Rowlands Castle
Printed in the UK by SRP Exeter

Contents

Preface

THE IDEA FOR this book originated from an international conference on 'Agrarian Questions: The Politics of Farming Anno 1995', held in Wageningen, The Netherlands in May 1995.

On the eve of the millennium, we were drawn together by the common goal of exploring the position of peasantries throughout the developing world. Our editorial work involved frequent meetings to discuss the thematic content of the book, whilst each editor was responsible for selecting the contributions for her or his respective regional specialization. Most papers underwent rewriting with this book in mind, and some chapters were newly commissioned with a view to filling gaps in the collection. We are thankful to the contributors for bearing with us during the long but rewarding editing process.

Significantly, the book's title is posed as a question: Are peasants disappearing? Each editor has a different answer to this question, reflecting our respective disciplinary biases, our regional vantage point, and the state of flux in which peasantries are presently found. Rather than papering over these differences, they are readily apparent in our respective chapters. We believe that this diversity of editorial opinion enhances the analytical content of the book, providing readers with an array of perspectives from which to evaluate the evidence.

The language editing of the entire book was expertly carried out by Diana Kay. We very much appreciate her contribution in making this a more readable text. Financial support for this enterprise was largely provided by the Agrarian Questions Conference Committee at Wageningen, but valuable financial help was also received from the Institute of Social Studies in the Hague and the African Studies Centre in Leiden. We would like to thank them all.

The Editors
The Hague and Leiden
June 1999

About the Authors

Editors

Deborah Fahy Bryceson is a Senior Research Fellow at the African Studies Centre, Leiden, The Netherlands, and was formerly studying and later doing research at the Universities of Dar es Salaam (1972–81) and Oxford (1981–91). Her research activities have concentrated on issues of food marketing, urbanization, gender, rural transport and mobility patterns. She is currently coordinating a research programme focused on rural employment in sub-Saharan Africa.

Cristóbal Kay is Associate Professor of Rural Development at the Institute of Social Studies, The Hague, The Netherlands. He was a researcher at the University of Chile in Santiago (1966–73), Visiting Professor at the Catholic University, Lima, Peru (1979–80), and for many years a Lecturer at the University of Glasgow. He has written numerous articles on the agrarian question in Latin America and is the author of *Latin American Theories of Development and Underdevelopment* and co-editor of *Development and Social Change in the Chilean Countryside*.

Jos Mooij is a Lecturer in Agricultural and Rural Development at the Institute of Social Studies, The Hague, The Netherlands. She has carried out extensive field research in India and is the author of *Food Policy and the Indian State: The Food Distribution System in South India*, recently published by Oxford University Press, New Delhi. Her main research interests are food (in)security, poverty and social security in India.

Contributors

Magdalena Barros Nock is a social anthropologist at the Colegio de la Frontera Norte, Tijuana, Mexico. Her main research interests relate to agriculture and rural development, migration and transnational family enterprises, and the North American Free Trade Agreement.

Chris Bramall is a Fellow and Director of Studies in Economics at Sidney Sussex College, University of Cambridge. His main interests centre on inequality, agriculture, collectivization and the role of the state in China. He is the author of *In Praise of Maoist Economic Planning*, published by Oxford University Press in 1993, and he has recently completed a manuscript on the *Sources of Chinese Economic Growth, 1978–1996* (forthcoming, Oxford University Press).

Jan Breman is Professor of Comparative Sociology at the University of Amsterdam and part-time Professor of Sociology at the Institute of Social Studies in The Hague. He has been Dean of the Centre for Asian Studies Amsterdam and the Amsterdam School of Social Science Research. He has carried out extensive anthropological field work in India (south Gujarat) and Indonesia (Java) on rural and urban labour and has researched on these themes and also from a historical perspective. He has published several books and numerous journal articles.

Robert Buijtenhuijs studied political science and anthropology in Amsterdam and Paris. From 1970 until his retirement in March 1999, he worked as a Senior Research Fellow at the African Studies Centre, Leiden, The Netherlands. His main interests are revolutionary movements and, more recently, democratization in Africa, particularly in Chad.

Carmen Diana Deere is Professor of Economics and Director of the Center for Latin American, Caribbean and Latino Studies at the University of Massachusetts, Amherst, USA. She carried out field research in Cuba under a MacArthur Foundation grant on Collectivization and Decollectivization of Socialist Societies. She is co-author of *Cuba Agraria: Transformaciones Locales en el Siglo XX* (forthcoming, Social Science Press, Havana).

Kees Jansen has a doctorate in the sociology of rural development and is currently a Research Fellow in the Department of Technology and Agrarian Development, Wageningen Agricultural University, The Netherlands. His current research focuses on risk, cultural theory and political ecology in Central America. He is the author of *Political Ecology, Mountain Agriculture and Knowledge in Honduras* (Thela Publishers, Amsterdam, 1998).

Marion Jones is an Assistant Professor in the Department of Economics, University of Regina, Canada. Her current area of interest is the rural Chinese economy, embracing employment generation and factor market rigidities as these relate to Chinese economic growth and the well-being of individuals. She is also involved in interdisciplinary research on sustainable community development in Costa Rica, Chile and southern Saskatchewan.

Karin Kapadia is currently Gender Specialist for South Asia in the Social Development Division of the World Bank. She is the author of *Siva and her Sisters: Gender, Caste and Class in Rural South India* (Westview Press, 1995) and co-editor (with Jonathan Parry and Jan Breman) of *The Worlds of Indian Industrial Labour* and (with Terry Byres and Jens Lerche, forthcoming) of *Rural Labour Relations in India*. She is currently working on a book on rural industrialization, notions of rights and social transformation in India.

John Knight is a Lecturer in Social Anthropology at Queen's University, Belfast. He is a social anthropologist who has carried out field work in Japanese mountain villages and has published widely on the themes of rural depopulation, village revitalization, forestry and wildlife.

Luis Llambí is Chair of the Laboratory of Rural and Agrarian Studies at the Venezuelan Institute for Scientific Research. He is the author of *La Moderna Finca Familiar* (1988) and *La Reforma del Estado en Venezuela: El Sector Público Agrícola y el Proceso de Descentralización* as well as a large number of journal articles. His main research interests are global–local restructuring, state reforms, and the links between rural poverty, agricultural change and the environment in Latin America.

Mahmood Mamdani is A.C. Jordan Professor of African Studies and Director of the Centre for African Studies, University of Cape Town. He is the author of *Citizen and Subject* (Princeton, 1996) amongst other books and articles on African politics and society. He completed his PhD at Harvard University in 1974 and taught at the University of Dar-es-Salaam and Makerere University in Kampala. He is the founding Director of the Centre for Basic Research in Kampala. Mamdani is currently (1998–2001) President of the Dakar-based Council for the Development of Social Research in Africa (CODESRIA).

Kate Meagher has an M Phil in Development Studies from the University of Sussex and taught Rural Sociology at Ahmadu Bello University in Zaria, Nigeria from 1991–97. She is currently based at Nuffield College, Oxford where she is doing doctoral work on informalization and economic restructuring in Nigeria. Her major research interests include cross-border trade, structural adjustment policies and agriculture, trends in rural non-farm activities, the urban informal sector and the progress of informalization, and agricultural biotechnology.

Philip Raikes is an agricultural economist with a long-term general interest in the integration of peasant agricultural production into larger-scale economic circuits. He is presently based at the Centre for Development Research (CDR), Copenhagen, Denmark. His first job was in Tanzania where he stayed until the mid-1970s. He has worked on food security (*Modernising Hunger*, 1988), agricultural extension, credit and marketing. He is currently doing research with colleagues at CDR on the effects of restructuring and deregulation on labour and control processes along selected commodity chains, with special reference to their African ends.

PART ONE: INTRODUCTION

1. Peasant Theories and Smallholder Policies: Past and Present

DEBORAH FAHY BRYCESON[1]

> Day by day, the peasants make the economists sigh, the politicians sweat and the strategists swear, defeating their plans and prophecies all over the world – Moscow and Washington, Peking and Delhi, Cuba and Algeria, the Congo and Vietnam (Shanin 1966: 5).

IN WESTERN INDUSTRIAL culture, the term 'peasant' has been largely associated with a way of life and frame of mind counter to 'modernization'. The three meanings of the word listed in the *Concise Oxford Dictionary* reflect this: '(colloquial) countrymen and countrywomen, rustics . . . (historical) a member of an agricultural class dependent on subsistence farming, (derogatory), a lout, a boorish person'.

Yet in Europe peasant economies and societies have dominated three-quarters of the past millennium. It is only in the most recent 200 years, as the industrial revolution took hold and fanned out to other parts of the world, that peasant populations started losing their determining influence over mass culture. And it is only very recently that they have relinquished their demographic majority worldwide (Cipolla 1962). Their numbers are currently concentrated in the continents of Africa, Asia and Latin America where they continue to lend economic, political and cultural body to their respective nation-states.

Over the past two decades peasants have been slipping from the political and academic gaze. Preoccupation with peasant politics during the 1960s has given way to a reconceptualization of peasants as 'smallholders', rational economic agents seeking material betterment through participation in agricultural commodity production. In this context, the term 'peasant' has taken on the derogatory connotation of its dictionary meaning. Peasants and hippies are relegated to the same dustbin of history. But unlike the ephemeral hippies, peasants' endurance has generated an illustrious body of theoretical literature with relevance to the present day.

The objective of this book is to explore the current nature of peasant labour in Africa, Latin America and Asia. This introductory chapter provides some definitional parameters before outlining the contours of peasant discourse over the past two centuries, asking why western social science enquiry has embraced the topic of peasant transformation in some periods and ignored it in others. Concentration is placed on the post-World War II literature, which is bifurcated into a comparative rural sociological 'peasant' perspective and an economic development approach focused on 'smallholders'.

The main body of the book consists of three sections centred on peasant societies in sub-Saharan Africa, Latin America and Asia, respectively. The introduction to each section reviews patterns of peasant formation and dissolution over time, while the ensuing chapters provide concrete illustrations and discuss current issues surrounding today's peasantries. The concluding chapter contrasts continental experiences and discusses rural policy options.

Peasantries in Formation and Dissolution in World History

Our definition of peasants encompasses four main criteria (adapted from Shanin 1976), namely:

- *farm* – the pursuit of an agricultural livelihood which combines subsistence production with commodity production;
- *family* – internal social organization based on family labour, whereby the family serves as the unit of production, consumption, reproduction, socialization, welfare and risk-spreading;
- *class* – external subordination to state authorities as well as regional or international markets, inferring surplus extraction and class differentiation;
- *community* – village settlement and traditional conformist attitudes and outlook.

The first three criteria are found in one form or another in most definitions of peasantries, whereas the fourth is more controversial. Its emphasis on socio-geographical settlement patterns, related to physical isolation and low mobility, has often been used as the analytical inroad for western-biased labelling of peasantries as 'backward', 'closed' societies. In fact, the isolationist character of the community criterion cannot be overstated without undermining class which clearly posits peasants *vis-à-vis* a wider market and state structures. Thus we prefer to use community with a small subscript c to denote relative physical isolation and local extended family and patron–client relations, which constitute a middle ground between the family and class criteria.

This ffc_c amalgam is our starting point for identifying peasant societies through time and over space. However, 'identifying' peasantries is not a simple taxonomic exercise, whereby rural populations present themselves as perfect embodiments of ffc_c criteria. Peasantries are best understood as the historical outcome of an agrarian labour process which is constantly adjusting to surrounding conditions, be it fluctuations of climate, markets, state exactions, political regimes, as well as technological innovations, demographic trends, and environmental changes. Thus rural populations become peasants by degree and relinquish their peasant status only gradually over time. Peasantries do not adopt fixed forms, a fact that suggests the popular view of peasants as stagnant producers is totally misconceived. In view of their dynamic character, one must ask: When do agrarian producers become peasants? And when do peasants cease to be peasants? There must be definitional boundaries.

It seems relatively easy to draw locational and occupational boundaries. Peasants are resident in rural areas and cultivate the land. But what of segments of rural populations which have a near landless status, who live in the countryside but eke out a subsistence as wage labourers, or engage in a variety of non-agricultural activities, or work in towns on a periodic basis? These are cases when not only necessary but also sufficient factors in the ffc_c amalgam are at issue. Occupational attributes may drop away, as well as the village context, but social characteristics of family and class, combined with reliance on both subsistence and commodity production, are essential. Peasant livelihood involves a changing agrarian labour process that cannot be equated with an agricultural livelihood[2] and rural residence *per se*. Nor must the bulk of peasant production be for subsistence. Family units of production and consumption, political relations with external powers, and combined subsistence and market-oriented production are the more enduring features. Thus, we are not just drawing boundary lines but shading, highlighting and adding texture.

At the outset it is useful to delineate two dynamics that are intimately related but vital to distinguish in discerning peasantries' spatial and temporal incidence, namely:

- *Agrarianization/De-agrarianization*[3] – economic sectoral change arising from expansion and contraction of rural populations that derive their livelihood from agriculture;
- *Peasantization/De-peasantization* – fluctuating populations of rural producers involved specifically in the peasant labour process denoted by ffc_c criteria.

Globally, agrarianization resulted from gradual incremental change. Archaeologists date the beginning of the Neolithic revolution at around 10 000 years ago (Leakey and Lewin 1979). At that time the world's population was estimated to be roughly 10 million people. Between 8000 BCE and 1000 CE, agricultural practices spread slowly worldwide. Population growth was estimated between 0.03 and 0.04 per cent per annum. About 1000 CE, agricultural modes of livelihood were found throughout the populated world with the heaviest preponderance of agriculturalists in Europe and Asia. The population growth rate between 1000 and 1800 CE increased to 0.10 per cent annually. About 80 per cent of the world's population were concentrated in Eurasia on the eve of the industrial revolution (Cipolla 1962).

Over the past two centuries, there has been a global tendency towards de-agrarianization, but de-peasantization cannot be equated with this tendency. Peasantization/de-peasantization fluctuates in association with, but not necessarily in consonance with, de-agrarianization. For example, replacement of peasant agriculture with plantation agriculture is de-peasantization, but not de-agrarianization. Peasantization can be an ongoing phenomenon in specific localities at the same time as de-agrarianization becomes more generalized throughout the world. Somewhat paradoxically, industrialization from 1800 to the present has drawn labour, often peasant labour, out of agriculture while simultaneously having a stimulating effect on the growth of global peasantries. Firstly, the industrial revolution had a dramatic effect on world population growth which jumped to almost 1 per cent per annum on average. Technological breakthroughs in the control of famine and disease emanating from industrial societies spilled over into the largely agrarian continents of Asia, Africa and Latin America, causing population growth rates in peasant societies to accelerate. Secondly, leading industrialized countries, seeking sources of raw materials and market, colonized many parts of the agrarian world, often engendering the formation of peasantries in areas where they had hitherto not been found. Thus, de-agrarianization has exerted both stimulating and braking influences on peasantries globally.

Attempts to discern long-term trends and broad spatial patterns are always hazardous, but especially so in relation to peasantries whose geographical dispersion imparts a highly localized character to each peasantry. There is no way of knowing precisely the percentage of the world's population that can currently be classified as peasants. Extremely crude estimates can be made of agrarian populations, but these need to be followed by the far more difficult task of disaggregating categories of rural producers. According to the World Bank (1998), out of a world population of 5.7 billion, 2.9 billion people live in the rural areas of low- and middle-income countries. In fact many rural dwellers in low- and particularly middle-income countries do not farm, or farm on a strictly commercial basis, so the percentage of peasants within this total undoubtedly falls below 50 per cent. With a worldwide annual urban growth rate of 2.6 per cent, it is fairly safe to assume that peasant populations are decreasing globally. However, this decrease is relative to expanding urban populations and does not necessarily imply an absolute decline in peasant numbers, since rural population growth rates remain high overall in many parts of the world.

First and foremost, peasantries represent a politically constructed agrarian labour process. This book focuses on the economic, political and social factors that underlie peasants' expansion or contraction relative to other organizational forms of agrarian production. Rural agricultural production can be viewed as a field of organizational forms that are in flux (see Table 1.1).

In the process of peasant formation and dissolution, peasant labour emerges from or merges into one of these agricultural production forms. Historical evidence demonstrates that certain patterns of transformation are stronger in one direction than another, e.g. from slave to peasant production units and from peasant to capitalized family enterprise or industrial production units as depicted in Figure 1.1 However, it would be wrong to interpret these organizational changes as linear evolutionary development. There are no fixed formulae or immutable directions of change. Human preferences and behaviour in developmental processes vary widely and continually give rise to new patterns. Tracing the historically contingent processes of peasant formation and dissolution confirm rather than deny the importance of differences in locality, context and human agency.

Figure 1.1 depicts the most likely directions of peasantization/de-peasantization within agriculture. The movement of labour from peasant family farms to urban or rural non-agricultural employment adds additional dynamism, and contributes to the shrinkage of the agricultural sector relative to the industrial and service sectors. This movement represents the convergence of de-peasantization and de-agrarianization. De-peasantization, as historically contingent organizational change within agriculture, combines with de-agrarianization, which over the past two centuries has gained the status of epochal change by virtue of its sustained duration and unmistakable direction. The synergy between the two processes accounts for the rapid, forceful change experienced in so many of the world's peasant societies at present.

Are today's 'disappearing peasantries' primarily the outcome of historically contingent organizational change or of inevitable epochal transformation? Can the viability of peasants' livelihoods and their cultural vitality persist in the post-industrial information age of the twenty-first century, or will the world's remaining peasantries shrink in size to be likened to today's

Table 1.1: Organizational units of agricultural production by scale and type of labour

Degree of tied labour	*Scale of agricultural labour unit*	
	Small	*Large*
More	Domestic slavery	Slave plantation
	Bonded labour	Latifundia
	Peasant family farm	Collective farm
Less	Family enterprise farm	Industrial farm

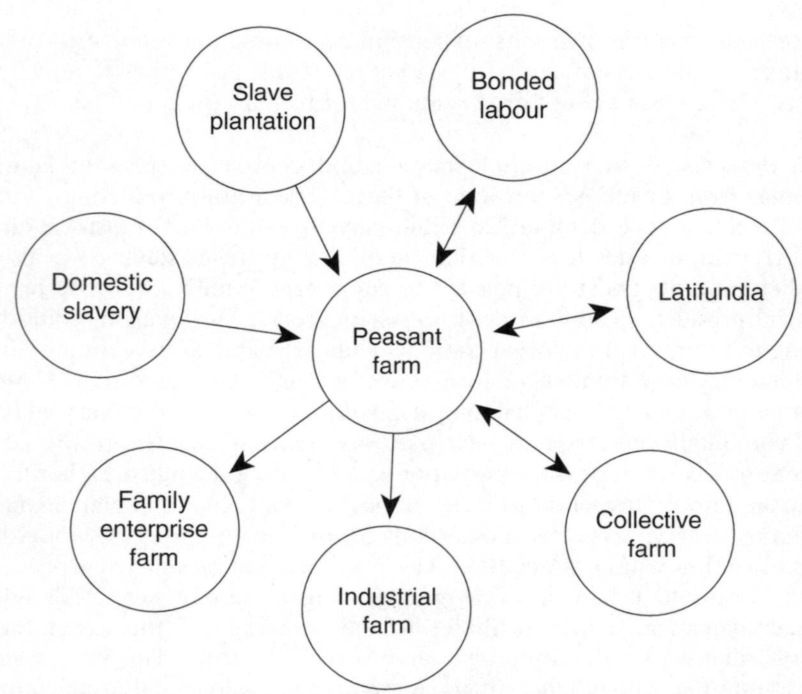

Figure 1.1: Directions of peasantization/de-peasantization vis-à-vis various organizational units within agriculture

vestige hunting and gathering societies – remote curiosities and walking museums of techniques, artefacts and social structures?

Post-modernists tend to dismiss the 'peasantry' as a valid analytical category, viewing it as an integral part of the modernization imperative of western social science development theory with its gratuitous imposition of value judgements regarding the superiority of industrial society. Development theorists are criticized for assuming 'desirable' rural change can be replicated anywhere regardless of labour conditions and contexts. In fact, the dismissiveness of post-modernists and the over-confidence of development theorists both ignore the fact that peasants are still readily discernible, and most significantly that their future is now in question entailing serious welfare consequences for vast numbers of the world's poorest people.

To fathom how this blind spot has occurred, the following sections trace peasant analyses in 'First', 'Second' and 'Third' World social science discourse. The teleological perspective of the literature is readily apparent. Peasants are portrayed as technologically backward and doomed by the forces of modernization and industrialization. Yet peasants have confounded western social science by their enduring presence. Grappling with this paradox has generated a wealth of creative insights.

Classical Origins of the Peasant and Smallholder Literature of the 'First World'

The main western social science disciplines of today, economics, sociology, political science and anthropology, have all been influenced in one way or another by peasant discourses. Most of these discourses have centred on the dissolution of peasantries. This is in part because the historical context in which the western social sciences arose was one of disintegrating peasantries linked to the industrial revolution in western Europe. At the same time, however, peasantries were being formed through the imposition of colonial rule and the expanding world market. The peasant and smallholder discourses to be reviewed in the following section focus on the interface between peasant and industrial populations. Both derive thematic inspiration from the works of the classical political economists which underpin the institutionalization of the western social sciences and the epistemological foundations of the 'first world' as it emerged after World War II. We turn to a brief examination of how Adam Smith, David Ricardo and Karl Marx conceptually understood peasant societies.

Living in the late eighteenth century, Adam Smith observed British trade and colonial conquest expanding abroad while putting out systems were being centralized and scaled up into factory units within the country. His central theme was the role of the technical division of labour in enhancing productivity. Writing before the industrial revolution unleashed the benefits of mechanical invention, it was labour specialization *per se* which he saw as critical to the 'wealth of nations' (Smith 1776). In his view, trade represented the opportunity to increase *in situ* labour specialization to achieve higher productivity.

Smith concentrated on the trade and manufacturing sectors; reference to the agricultural sector was mainly in passing. His countryside was a world of landlords, commercial farmers and wage workers, not peasants. Nonetheless, his basic assumption that the agrarian sector by its very nature was incapable of achieving high levels of labour specialization or productivity influenced subsequent peasant and smallholder literature:

> The division of labour . . . so far as it can be introduced, occasions, in every art, a proportional increase in the productive powers of labour . . . The nature of agriculture, indeed, does not admit of so many subdivisions of labour, nor of so complete a separation of one business from another, as manufactures . . . The spinner is almost always a distinct person from the weaver; but the ploughman, the harrower, the sower of the seed, and the reaper of the corn, are often the same. The occasions for those different sorts of labour returning with the different seasons of the year, it is impossible that one man should be constantly employed in any one of them. This impossibility of making so complete and entire a

separation of all the different branches of labour employed in agriculture, is perhaps the reason why the improvement of the productive powers of labour in this art, does not always keep pace with their improvement in manufactures . . . In agriculture, the labour of the rich country is not always much more productive than that of the poor; or, at least, it is never so much more productive, as it commonly is in manufactures (Smith, 1776: 70–2).

Ricardo (1817), writing some 30 years later, witnessed the industrial revolution and observed the social brakes imposed by landed interests *vis-à-vis* the emerging industrial bourgeoisie. Like the work of Adam Smith, his well-known argument for repeal of the Corn Laws was premised on the importance of specialization to national labour productivity. Any livelihood or profit loss in the agrarian sector arising from cheaper grain imports would be more than compensated by gain in the industrial sector. Ricardo's legacy to western social science was to situate the issues of class and economic sectoral change against the already established concern with improving labour productivity.

Unlike Adam Smith, Ricardo saw the possibility of increasing productivity in farming arising from the application of scientific advances, such as soil fertilization and mechanization, making it possible to reduce labour inputs. His point of reference was capitalist not peasant agriculture. Ricardo was Malthusian with respect to the issue of demographic growth, believing that the growth of the labouring classes outstrips the demand for their labour. The issue of labour absorption was apparent in his desire for the expansion of national wealth through increasing profits of urban-based capitalist industrialists rather than the higher rents of landlords. Viewing the agriculture of other countries where land was not capitalized as extremely backward, Ricardo provided an early rationalization for European colonialism or even the 'good governance' perspective of today's donors:

> In those countries where there is abundance of fertile land, but where, from the ignorance, indolence, and barbarism of the inhabitants, they are exposed to all the evils of want and famine . . . the evil proceeds from bad government, from the insecurity of property, and from a want of education in all ranks of the people. To be made happier they require only to be better governed and instructed, as the augmentation of capital, beyond the augmentation of people, would be the inevitable result (Ricardo 1817: 314).

Marx emphasized the backwardness of peasant economies and politics in the process of 'primitive accumulation' and the evolution of western national democracies (Marx 1850–52, 1867). He dates the disappearance of serfdom and emergence of a free peasantry to the latter part of the fourteenth century. In tracing the gradual dissolution of the English peasantry through a combination of economic and political forces, which undermined their land rights between 1450 and 1750, Marx recognizes that there was an oscillation between expansion and contraction of peasant numbers. The putting out system, which kept people nominally on the land, gave rise to the possibility of peasant inroads depending on market fluctuations and cropping patterns. Stressing peasants' diversification strategies, Marx observed:

> England is at certain epochs mainly a corn-growing country, at others mainly a cattle-breeding country. These periods alternate, and the alternation is accompanied by fluctuations in the extent of peasant cultivation . . . we always find [during the last third of the fifteenth century] that this peasantry turns up again, although in diminished number, and in a progressively worse situation (Marx 1867: 912).

Marx saw the central dilemma facing the peasantry as contracting land access arising not only from the encroachment of landed gentry, but also from its own population growth which led to family subdivisions of land down to unviable units. Even under French freehold conditions, granted by Napoleon Bonaparte, Marx argued that peasantries were doomed.

> Their mode of production isolates them from one another instead of bringing them into mutual intercourse . . . A small-holding, a peasant and his family; alongside them another small-holding, another peasant and another family. A few score of these make up a village, and a few score of villages make up a Department. In this way, the great mass of the French nation is formed by simple addition of homologous magnitudes, much as potatoes in a sack form a sack of potatoes . . . what is now causing the ruin of the French peasant is his small-holding itself, the division of the land, the form of property which Napoleon consolidated in France . . . Two generations have sufficed to produce the inevitable result: progressive deterioration of agriculture, progressive indebtedness of the agriculturist . . . To the four million (including children, etc.) officially recognized paupers, vagabonds, criminals and prostitutes in France must be added five million who hover on the margin of existence and either have their haunt in the countryside itself or, with their rags and their children, continually desert the countryside for the towns and the towns for the countryside . . . an unemployed surplus population for which there is no place either on the land or in the towns (Marx 1850-52: 230–5).

Peasants and the Establishment of the 'Second World'

Classical political economists dealt with peasantries tangentially. It was left to the theorists of the Russian revolution to document the political dynamics and economic logic of peasant societies. Unlike the classical political economists writing about Britain, the Russian theorists had access to first-hand knowledge of peasants who constituted a sizeable proportion of the population. Upon the foundation of rich statistical information and detailed regional studies of peasant production, debate about the 'agrarian question' unfolded (Harriss 1982; Byres 1991, 1996). The central issue remained the peasantry's relationship to industrialization, while the political dimension changed from that of decentralized capitalist expropriation of the rural masses to tactical means by which the socialist movement could recruit peasant support. The leading theorists on peasant societies of the 'second world' were Lenin, Kautsky, Preobrazhensky and Chayanov.

Whereas the classical political economists had treated peasantries as undifferentiated, organizationally or technologically backward producers, Lenin went to great pains to differentiate peasants by income and asset holdings. Peasant strata were related to the degree that they were imbued with the capitalist profit motive and inversely, their socialist revolutionary potential (Lenin 1899). He observed that normally the richest and poorest peasants had the most contact with the market. The former were actively engaged in agricultural commodity markets whereas the latter participated in wage labour markets. The middle peasantry provided for the subsistence needs of their family units and produced a surplus in good years that could be converted to capital. Sometimes they resorted to hiring labour. Lenin saw the middle peasantry as a wayward force in socialist transformation because of their vacillating nature on the border of subsistence and profit-oriented production, and because of the brakes they placed on the development of a home market, given their tendency to be self-sufficient producers (Lenin 1920). In the long run, Lenin favoured large-scale collective and mechanized agriculture, but in the short and medium term he believed that the co-operation of the peasantry was vital in ensuring food supply to the urban-based industrial proletariat.

Lenin expanded on Marx's notion of primitive accumulation, arguing that as a process of capitalist expansion it extended beyond the boundaries of nation states. In *Imperialism: The Highest Stage of Capitalism,* he demonstrated that European colonialism engulfed peasant societies throughout the world, extending capitalist market relations and state power as conditions of existence for non-capitalist peasant production (Lenin 1917).

In contrast to Lenin's focus on peasant differentiation, Kautsky's *The Agrarian Question* (1899) was concerned with the dissolution of peasantries as an unfolding process. Like Marx, he analysed the interface between rural peasant agriculture and capitalist industry, emphasizing the effects of the latter on the former, the reverse of what Marx had done. Kautsky's starting point was peasant households within the context of European feudalism. These family units were perceived as self-sufficient not only in food, but in non-agricultural articles of consumption produced through household handicraft production.

Capitalist urban industry and the creation of a home market undermined peasant households' handicraft traditions, making them reliant on agricultural crop sales for purchasing their non-agricultural needs, and engendering a clear division of labour between town and country as well as peasants' vulnerability to the profiteering of merchant capital. The latter was seen as the catalyst in a process of growing peasant indebtedness and economic differentiation that ultimately led to landlessness for broad masses of the peasantry.

Kautsky dwelt at some length on the actual manifestations of the slide into indebtedness and landlessness (see Chapter 13 in this volume). He observed the decline in household size as youthful members of peasant households were encouraged to migrate and engage in non-agricultural forms of livelihood. This tendency was exacerbated by the introduction of agricultural machinery. On the other hand, as the population emigrated, the family labour force for peak agricultural-season tasks was insufficient, creating an agricultural labour market at specific times of the year. In posing the agrarian question, Kautsky stressed that the dissolution of peasant production is a slow process whereby peasant petty commodity producers co-exist with agrarian and urban industrial capitalism, gradually shrinking over time under the force of urban migration.

In *The New Economics* (1926), Preobrazhensky's concern with the Soviet Union's industrialization led him to see the peasantry as critical for the production of food for the expanding urban working class as well as for export crops to earn hard currency for importing foreign machinery. As a Bolshevik intellectual active in Soviet policy debates of the 1920s, Preobrazhensky argued for 'primitive socialist accumulation', the replacement of merchant capital by state marketing and controlled prices set below world market prices but high enough to provide incentives to peasant production. The surplus could then be channelled to the socialist state's industrialization effort. He shared Kautsky's view of the exploitative nature of merchant capital *vis-à-vis* the peasantry. Local traders were viewed as 'parasites', whose appropriation, contrary to the forces of primitive socialist accumulation, did not lay the basis for industrialization and higher productivity in rural areas. Peasants themselves were seen as nascent capitalists. Preobrazhensky quotes Lenin approvingly regarding the eventual replacement of the peasantry by modern large-scale production.

Chayanov's contribution to Soviet debates, as well as to the literature more generally, was his theory of the peasantry as a particular kind of economy with its own growth dynamic and economic system which could not be equated to an early stage of capitalist development. On the basis of decades of detailed rural survey data, he conceptualized the peasant economy as being made up of family labour farms operating with their own calculus based on subsistence needs rather than profit. Central to Chayanov's theory is the notion of a labour–consumer balance, whereby peasant household effort is determined by a disutility for labour exertion beyond the realization of the household's basic needs for food and shelter or anticipated improvement in their standard of living.

The size and composition of the peasant family were the main determinants of the magnitude of farm output. The size of the family and the ratio of working members to non-working members affected both labour demand and supply of the family farm. Emphasis on family composition led Chayanov to a distinct demographic theory of social differentiation in contrast to the concept of class differentiation that prevailed in the Soviet Union of his time. Peasant household output and land holdings were related to family life cycles. Farm size and output were projected to be small during the initial stage of family development after the reproductive couple married and had small children. As the children grew old enough to contribute to the labour effort output increased, only to decrease as the children reached adulthood and left their natal homes to start their own families.

In opposition to Soviet policies, Chayanov argued that horizontal collectivization of peasant production did not necessarily offer economies of scale. It depended on the nature of farming systems and agronomic conditions. Only areas of extensive cultivation, notably flat, grain-producing areas, could benefit. Peasants could enjoy economies of scale through participation in co-operatives, which afforded vertical integration while continuing to produce on family farms. He maintained that intensive cultivation and livestock breeding was best pursued in peasant family units where work motivation was determined by the labour–consumer balance. He foresaw a problem of declining work incentives and bureaucracy in collectivized agriculture. Not surprisingly, Chayanov's views led to accusations of being pro-*kulak* and a *petit bourgeois* idealizer. He was arrested in 1930 and died in 1939, marking the end of an important chapter in social science discourse about the peasantry.

Peasantries in 'Third World' Development

World War II and the Cold War served to divert the world's attention from peasant economies. Debate about the nature and role of peasant societies in 'modern' nation-states did not revive until the 1960s and early 1970s, benefiting from a growing body of case study material (e.g. Lewis 1951, Wolf 1955, Redfield 1956). Two world wars and one worldwide depression had led to an uneasy awareness of global interdependence despite vast material and cultural differences between nations, reflected in the terms 'First', 'Second', and 'Third' World. Nonetheless it was a time of optimism in which the inequities existing between these three worlds were expected to decline through economic growth. From the mid-1950s to the early

1970s, international prices for primary commodities produced in the Third World were relatively buoyant. Relations between the First World and Third World were slated to be those of co-operation, while First World–Second World relations froze into Cold War wariness.

Peasants had largely vanished in the first world. Vestiges of a peasant past and displays of traditional national dress were transformed into tourist attractions throughout western Europe – hardly symbolic, let alone real. In the Second World, peasantries were waning under socialist policies that favoured collectivization and large-scale state farm production. By contrast, as the Third World neared the end of colonial rule, national head counts revealed peasants to be an overwhelming majority in most countries. Peasant uprisings flared in the decolonization process, further fuelled by neo-colonial designs and super-power rivalry as exemplified by the Vietnam War.

Against this background, two distinct peasant-focused literatures surfaced: firstly, the comparative study of peasantries influenced by economic anthropology and rural sociology; and secondly, a more applied agrarian policy approach associated with the emergence of development economics as a distinct area of study. Nourished by different social sciences, both nonetheless reflected the theoretical legacy of classical political economy and the Soviet discourse about the peasantry.

Formal/substantivist debate of economic anthropologists in the 1950s–60s

The publication of Karl Polanyi's book *The Great Transformation* (1946) revived and updated the classical debate about the dissolving effect of free trade and industrialization on rural producers. Polanyi (1957) and Dalton (1961) went on to draw attention to the differences in the nature of trade and exchange in pre-industrial societies as opposed to industrial capitalist societies. They argued that rural producers evinced a distinct economic logic based on subsistence requirements, reminiscent of Chayanov's earlier work.

Their position was counterpoised by Firth (1967) who stressed that peasants, not unlike people in industrial societies, exercise choice over the allocation of scarce resources. Thus, anthropology could utilize prevailing economic theory to study how peasants organize their production and consumption activities even though they lacked specialized economic institutions such as banks and commodity exchanges. Firth and like-minded theorists (Dewey 1962, Douglas 1963) were labelled 'formalists', who were attempting to break the classification divide between 'primitive' and 'modern' societies as well as the disciplinary divide between economics and anthropology, by applying formal economic concepts to non-capitalist societies. By contrast, 'substantivists' – Polanyi and associates (e.g. Sahlins 1965) – following Durkheim, distinguished economies whose exchange was based on interpersonal relations from economies which had a complex division of labour and markets with impersonal, atomistic, profit-oriented exchange. Their perspective inferred an evolution from simple to complex through economies based on various stages of market development (e.g. Nash 1971).

Formalists disapproved, stressing the similarities between economic systems through universalized principles of resource allocation and exchange. A lively debate ensued. Despite avowed affiliation to one or another camp, positions were not as polarized as they were projected to be. Both sides in one way or another acknowledged the substantivist nature of their subject matter and resorted to the construction of formal ideal types: substantivists idealized types of societies, whereas formalists idealized types of economic transactions. The extent that a transaction matched its ideal type was a question of degree both in non-industrial, peasant societies and in industrialized societies. However, many unwarranted assumptions crept into the study of peasant societies when analytical concepts institutionally relevant to an industrial society were simply transposed to a peasant society (Cohen 1967). Nonetheless, the formalists' position advanced the importance of economic analysis in developing countries, providing a strong rationale for development economists' study of peasants in the guise of 'smallholders'. This debate marked the conceptual pivot for the bifurcation of sociologically oriented peasant studies and the smallholder economic development approach.

Rediscovering peasant societies in the 1960s and 1970s

The formalist–substantivist debate underpinned a renewed interest in peasant societies and economies. By the 1960s anthropologists' search for 'primitive' tribal people untouched by western influence was reaching an impasse. Less exotic peasant societies were nonetheless perplexing. Mass peasant movements evidenced in organizational features of the Vietnam War and China's Cultural Revolution caught the western world's attention. As 'halfway societies', spanning the gap between industrial and tribal peoples, peasantries offered western scholarship a rediscovered terrain. Furthermore, peasants comprised the bulk of the population of the new nation-states arising from western decolonization. When donor agencies and the new nation-states initiated their rural development policies, knowledge of peasant societies gained applied relevance. Rural sociologists directed their analytical energies to studying peasantries as a 'world-wide type of social structure' (Shanin 1976).

In the introduction to his peasant anthology, Shanin (1976) identifies four major theoretical influences on the peasant literature. The first, and the point of entry, was the ethnographic tradition of anthropology which emphasized the 'otherness' of peasant society, recording the pre-industrial character of its rituals, belief systems and social structures as interconnected components of holistic agrarian-based societies (Wolf 1966). The second, and stronger, influence was that of Chayanov (1925). His notion of the family-farm economy was a central axis of the reborn peasant theorists, with respect to an appreciation of peasant economic logic based on subsistence requirements as well as the demographic dynamic of peasant societies related to household labour needs. To some extent the Russian debate was being re-enacted as the third influence, an insistence on Leninist class analysis, sometimes complemented and sometimes contested the Chayanovian perspective. Finally, one could identify the influence of Durkheimian theory of social change that contrasted complex, atomistic industrial societies with simple, interpersonal, non-industrial societies.

A flurry of detailed empirical field studies of peasant societies during the 1960s and early 1970s provided a large body of comparative literature of a highly heterogeneous nature. The label 'rural sociology' used to describe this literature is somewhat misleading since the literature was multidisciplinary with sociology, anthropology and politics strongly represented. Analytically descriptive rather than prescriptive, the literature documented the internal structure of peasantries, as well as their relationships to nation-states, markets and international politics. The former was in many respects a restatement of the Russian theorists' findings. The reborn peasant theorists' original contribution came primarily in the form of documenting peasants' relationship to the outside world, a world that had experienced dramatic change since the 1920s. Scott's (1976) analyses of peasant revolt used the concept of the 'moral economy' to explain peasants' motivations to take up arms to defend their means of subsistence from the larger impersonal forces of the world market and post-colonial capitalist development. This perspective starkly contrasted with the conspiracy theories associated with the Cold War mentality of the time.

The peasant literature contributed to post-colonial dependency theory, viewing the world in terms of centre–periphery relations, a perspective best demonstrated by the Latin American experience (Frank 1969). Pearse (1971) describes the centre's pernicious influence, stressing the receptiveness of the peasants themselves at this juncture in history:

> [E]xpansion of the core of the great industrial (developed) societies . . . [is] . . . the most important single factor in the alterations of rural life and social structure, laying down new conditions in which peasants make their decisions . . . What generally operative principles can be adduced to explain why the traditional peasant decides to change his way of life? The answer seems to be that the alternative to changing his behaviour is a deterioration of his condition, a result of the obsolescence of traditional technical and institutional means. At the same time, new means become available to replace them; and new goals come within the range first of his aspirations, and then of his expectations. This phase marks

> the passage from a static to a dynamic situation . . . Competition for the appropriation of new facilities now takes place, but their distribution is differential because the competitors are unequally equipped for the struggle (Pearse 1971: 70–80).

In contrasting the peasantry as a worldwide social structure relative to capitalist industrial societies, the peasant revivalists – sometimes consciously sometimes inadvertently – drew attention to the diminishing worldwide demographic and political strength of the peasantry, despite the well-publicized peasant resistance of the time.

Marxist rural transformation, modes of production and state/peasantry relations in the 1970s

In the politically charged atmosphere of the 1960s, Marxist influence on peasant discourse surfaced in its own right, providing theoretical insight into the position of peasantries *vis-à-vis* the capitalist world market and post-colonial nation-states. During the 1970s, Indian peasant debates informed by Marxist class analysis were especially prominent, inspired by existing traditions of rural protest as well as Marxist disagreement with prevailing caste-based analyses of rural societies (Banaji 1972). Latin American peasant studies drew on the Marxist literature related to rural transformation and the 'roads to capitalism' in their consideration of the relative strengths of landlord and peasant classes (Kay 1974, 1980; Lehmann 1976).

In sub-Saharan Africa, the debate reflected the less consolidated nature of peasantries. French structuralists took the lead, extending Marxist methodology and theoretical concepts to the analysis of pre-capitalist societies, employing the notion of an 'articulation of modes of production'. Pre-capitalist modes were seen to be linked to the capitalist mode of production through trade, primarily through the slave trade, and later through capitalist re-ordering of local production relations (Godelier 1973, Dupré and Rey 1978, Seddon 1978). Many distinct modes of production were theorized in a debate that spanned all three continents. Kay (1989) summarizes the debate in Latin America (see Chapter 7 in this volume), and Mooij (Chapter 12) points to its leading proponents in Asia (Banaji 1972, Thorner 1982, Patnaik 1990). In Africa, Meillassoux (1972) focused on capitalist penetration of self-sustaining African rural societies. Adopting Chayanov's stress on rural household demographic cycles, he argued that 'reproduction' of the rural domestic community preserved the pre-capitalist society and facilitated its articulation to capital. Capitalist enterprises operated on a low-cost basis, recruiting male labour, paying low wages, and returning workers to their rural homes at the end of the labour contract period (Meillassoux 1981).

A number of labour themes arose in the context of the articulation of modes of production debate. Wolpe (1972) illustrated the importance of the concept of social 'reproduction' of cheap labour power with reference to the South African migrant labour system, while Bundy (1972) drew attention to the creation and then marginalization of South African peasantries resulting from South African state agrarian and labour policies. A consideration of reproduction as well as production patterns merged with a growing interest in gender and the household, generating a profusion of studies on rural peasant women's work in developing countries (e.g. Abdullah and Zeidenstein 1982, Benaria 1982, Deere and de Leal 1982, Bryceson and Vuorela 1984, Croll 1984).

Bernstein (1994) rejected the notion of peasants within an articulation of modes of production, and argued instead their dual class character as 'petty commodity producers' who are both capitalists with direct access to the means of production and workers using their own labour. Exploring the nature of surplus extraction from peasantries, Bernstein (1977) stressed the cheapness of peasant-produced export commodities by virtue of the 'simple reproduction squeeze'. This amounted to peasants' coping strategies in the face of declining terms of trade in the world market. While disassociating himself from Chayanovian 'essentialism', he nonetheless argued that the logic of the peasant household economy was determined by the needs of 'simple reproduction', in other words, subsistence needs rather than profit. A deterioration in market prices for peasant export commodities, rising costs of land or labour, and the effect of rural development schemes encouraging the use of more expensive inputs without guarantees of higher output, caused peasant producers either to intensify their commodity production or to reduce their level of consumption, or both.

A peasant collectivization debate reminiscent of the Soviet debate arose when African socialist development strategies were launched in the 1970s. Inspired by the experience of Chinese peasant collectivization, massive programmes in Tanzania and Ethiopia were implemented to relocate peasants in nucleated settlements with the aim of achieving economies of scale. In the literature documenting these processes, Leninist themes came to the fore, notably peasants' relationship to the modernizing African state and rural class stratification (e.g. Shivji 1975, Dessalegn Rahmato 1984).

The majority of Third world nation-states did not pursue peasant collectivization, whereas most did implement peasant commodity marketing policies to facilitate agricultural modernization and industrialization (Harriss 1982, Hart, et al. 1989, Mooij 1999). Resurrecting Preobrazhensky's primitive accumulation strategy, state marketing agencies were established to extract surplus from peasant commodity production in the form of food for the urban population and foreign exchange earnings from export crops. However, from the mid-1970s onwards and particularly in the most peasant-based economies of Africa, this strategy was increasingly undermined by declining terms of trade for peasant export crops on the world market and by spiralling oil prices. Escalating transport costs embedded in crop outputs from widely dispersed peasant production units were absorbed by state marketing agencies. In the price squeeze, state marketing boards ran up enormous debts with knock-on inflationary effects on national economies as a whole. State-supported industries could not meet production targets. The state–peasantry debate became progressively anti-state as peasant-based national economies came asunder (Williams 1976).

Peasant rationality and autonomy in the 1980s

After two decades of Marxist peasant debate, salient critics emerged from the discipline of political science. Popkin (1980) challenged peasants' affinity to a 'moral economy' in which egalitarian concerns and kinship relations were given precedence. Echoing the formalists of 20 years earlier, he argued that the moral economy approach comprised a romantic view of peasantries that blurred the boundary between individual and community rights. Villages, rife with conflict, necessitated an analytical approach focused on individual decision-making with respect to market opportunities, patron–client relations, entrenched group interests, and trade-offs between private and collective benefits. Using examples primarily from south-east Asia and pre-industrial Europe, Popkin assumed that there are certain individual optimizing as well as risk-taking tendencies that are universal. Rejecting the substantivist notion of peasant structures and behavioural systems, he attacked moral economists and Marxists:

> I have made assumptions about individual behaviour diverging from those of the moral economists. These assumptions have drawn attention to different features of villages and patron–client ties and have led to questions about the quality of welfare and insurance embedded in both villages and vertical patron–client ties. This, in turn, has demonstrated that there is more potential value to markets, relative to the *actual performance level* of these other institutions. Commercialization of agriculture and the development of strong central authorities are not wholly deleterious to peasant society. This is not because capitalism and/or colonialism are necessarily more benevolent than moral economists assume, but because traditional institutions are harsher and work less well than is often believed (Popkin 1980: 462).

The theme of peasant brutishness reaches its apogee with the work of Hyden (1980). Like Popkin, Hyden felt compelled to use terminology derived from Marxist political economy to make his points even though he was reacting negatively to the Marxist tenor of the peasant debate. Arguing that African peasants were misperceived by the modernization paradigm of the west advocated by Marxists and non-Marxists alike, he stressed the ability of peasants to opt out of development programmes of the African state. Whereas many analysts from Marx onwards had emphasized peasant self-sufficiency, Hyden elevated peasant autonomy to a quintessential characteristic. Peasants' ability to retreat into subsistence production was seen as the bane of the modernizing African state. In his view peasants encased themselves in an 'economy of affection' in which kinship and neighbourhood ties overrode all other concerns.

> . . . the economy of affection is primarily concerned with the problems of reproduction rather than production. Work, or improving productivity, is not an end in itself. While in the modern economies – both capitalist and socialist – the leading motto is 'live in order to work, in the economy of affection it is 'work in order to live' (Hyden 1980: 18).

Hyden (1980) constructed a stark duality between a rational state and an irrational peasantry, condoning state force as a means of 'rationalizing' peasant settlement and production. In a later book (Hyden 1983) his position dramatically changed in conformity with the mood of the times. Like Popkin, he strongly endorsed the market as a spur to peasant crop production. His peasant autonomy argument rested on equating peasants' assertion of autonomy with declining export crop production and increasing food production, yet he failed to establish that peasants' increased food output was for subsistence (Kasfir 1986). Available evidence suggests that a great deal of peasant food production was in fact sold in black markets. Hyden attempted to have it both ways, by maintaining that peasants were not market-oriented or price-sensitive but also that their so-called 'retreat into subsistence' was triggered by the declining prices offered by state marketing boards for their export crops.

Approaching peasants from two different directions, Hyden painted a picture of naive, tightly knit, minimum-effort agriculturalists whereas Popkin saw cagey, in-fighting, individual maximizers. Nonetheless, both held the view that peasants were backward relative to producers in capitalist societies. Thus we have come full circle, back to Adam Smith and the advantages of free trade in increasing productivity in a backward rural sector. It is appropriate to turn to the smallholder literature at this point.

Smallholders in Economic Development Policy

Development economics, which emerged as a specialized subdiscipline of economics following World War II, focused on patterns of Third World economic growth. The 1950s offered economists starkly different economic conditions from those that had prevailed during the depression and the war. The global economy was expanding amidst the break-up of the colonial world and being refashioned into independent 'developing countries'. It was an era of optimism, in which development economists carved out an active advisory role for themselves in the policy formulation of new nation-states. The relative weighting of neo-classical and Keynesian influences on the discipline affected individual economists' normative judgements about the positive and negative roles of the state and market in development. However, development economists were united in their strong adherence to a positivist methodology, mathematical data analysis and model-building that had gained sway in the post-war western social sciences. Normative judgements were lodged behind model-building assumptions, hypothesis testing and use of estimated constant variables.

The term 'peasant', although never explicitly rejected by development economists, was generally avoided.[4] Rather 'smallholder' was used to denote rural producers operating on their own account on relatively small farms. In this way, the class and family criteria of the peasantry definition outlined earlier were largely circumvented. Attention was deflected from the fact that rural producers are politically subordinated in state and market relations, or that their work motivation derives from provisioning family subsistence as well as profit maximization. Both of these aspects were not easily amenable to model-building assumptions about rural agents' market-optimizing decisions. Nonetheless, despite the bias against family and class dimensions of peasant societies, the legacy of the Russian peasant debate was evident in the development economics literature.

Smallholders' inferior productivity, i.e. 'backwardness', relative to other sectors of the economy and urban areas, was the starting premise for development economists. The development trajectory was unquestionably that of moving from agrarian to industrial-based national economies.[5] The role of smallholders in economic development was conceptualized along the lines of Preobrazhensky:

> A widespread view . . . is that agricultural progress is necessary in order to supply, firstly, *a surplus of labour* for industry, secondly, *a marketable surplus of food* for industrial workers and, thirdly, *an investible surplus of savings* for urban industry [Streeten's emphasis] (Streeten 1972: 12).

Development economists' visions of peasant smallholders' transitional roles in development were premised on classical concepts of market optimization. Peasant participation in world commodity markets would spur improved agrarian labour productivity and capital investment in agricultural technology. However, in practice their labour optimization and technology acquisition proved to be more problematic than the theory suggested. The following subsections schematically trace development economics' main discourses on smallholder transformation.

Smallholders' commodity export and the 'vent for surplus'

Myint (1958) updated Adam Smith's free trade argument, countering the view that the newly formed nation-states of the Third World were necessarily disadvantaged in the exchange of primary commodities for manufactured goods from industrialized countries in the nineteenth century when so many of them became involved in the export of peasant-produced commodities.

> Firstly, international trade overcomes the narrowness of the home market and provides an outlet for the surplus product above domestic requirements. This develops into what may be called the 'vent for surplus' theory of international trade . . . Secondly, by widening the extent of the market, international trade also improves the division of labour and raises the general level of productivity within the country. This develops into what may be called the 'productivity' theory (Myint 1958: 99).

Myint argued that the employment of surplus resources provided positive benefits to peasant producers largely by virtue of their self-sufficiency in subsistence production.

> . . . we assume that our peasants start with some surplus resources which enable them to produce the export crop *in addition* [Myint's emphasis] to their subsistence production. Here the surplus resources perform two functions: firstly, they enable the peasants to hedge their position completely and secure their subsistence minimum before entering into the risks of trading; and secondly, they enable them to look upon the imported goods they obtain from trade in the nature of a clear net gain obtainable merely for the effort of the extra labour in growing the export crop. Both of these considerations are important in giving the peasants just that extra push to facilitate their first plunge into the money economy (Myint 1958: 99).

Bauer (1954) documented the entry of West African and Malayan peasants into commodity production for the world market, taking a highly polemical stance against what he termed the 'western guilt' syndrome.

> Since the middle of the nineteenth century commercial contacts established by the West have improved material conditions out of all recognition over much of the Third World, notably in South-East Asia, parts of the Middle East, much of Africa, especially West Africa and parts of East and Southern Africa; and very large parts of Latin America . . . Before 1890 there was no cocoa production in the Gold Coast or Nigeria, only very small production of cotton and groundnuts, and small exports of palm oil and palm kernels. By the 1950s these had become staples of world trade. They were produced by Africans on African-owned properties . . . Over this period imports both of capital goods and of mass consumer goods for African use also rose from insignificant amounts to huge volumes. The changes were reflected in government revenues, literacy rates, school attendance, public health, life expectations, infant mortality and many other indicators (Bauer 1981: 71–2).

In contrast to this rosy view of benefits accruing to peasants from their production for the world market, Prebisch (1950) pointed to the 36 per cent decline in terms of trade between primary-producing and industrial countries from 1876 to 1938. The trend was analysed, updated and termed 'unequal exchange' by Emmanuel (1972) and Evans (1975). The underlying assumption of classical political economy regarding the overall benefit of trade was undermined by certain empirical facts of the nineteenth- and twentieth-century world market. As Lewis (1978a) observed, agricultural productivity was higher in industrialized countries than in the so-called 'agricultural countries' resulting in distorted interpretations of 'comparative advantage'.

> It came to be an article of faith in Western Europe that the tropical countries had a comparative advantage in agriculture. In fact, as Indian textile production soon began to show, between the tropical and temperate countries, the differences in food production per head were much greater than in modern industrial production per head (Lewis 1978a: 11).

Third-world trade in agricultural commodities, despite the lower productivity of their agricultural sectors relative to industrial countries, produced many paradoxes. Lewis (1978b) argued that this productivity differential played a part in worsening the Third World's terms of trade because world prices for crops exported by tropical countries declined as the opportunity costs of smallholder labour cheapened. Third-world opportunity costs of labour were reduced by population growth and the importation of cheaper food from industrialized countries. With the substitution of imported food for locally grown staples, more smallholder farmers grew more export crops and, through competition with one another, drove export prices down further in the face of inelastic demand for their exports in the industrialized countries. Nonetheless, despite their disadvantaged trading position, Lewis believed that the world market afforded a means for smallholders to lift themselves out of stagnant subsistence production.

As the above citations indicate, the economic development literature recognized, but debated the extent of, value transfers from peasant commodity production through 'primitive accumulation' on the part of Third-world governments' or international markets' 'unequal exchange'. In so doing, development economists inadvertently affirmed the notion of peasants as a subordinated class. Their proviso, in line with Lewis, was that commodity-producing smallholders were better off than if they had no relations with the market.

Smallholders' labour and 'disguised unemployment'

Somewhat similar to assumptions regarding the existence of a 'vent for surplus' prior to market penetration, development economists hypothesized smallholders' under-utilization of labour, otherwise termed 'disguised unemployment'. For the early development economists such as Nurkse and Lewis, this was seen not as an 'original sin', but an 'original blessing', that could be put in the service of development. In contradistinction to Myint's 'vent for surplus', Nurkse (1953) argued that the concept of 'disguised labour' pertained to densely populated rural areas of the Third World, especially in Asia. It was labelled 'disguised' because the labour was employed in smallholder family units despite zero or near zero marginal output. This was possible because the labour was not paid. All members of the household shared family food supplies regardless of work output. Nurkse attributed this labour waste primarily to poor organization, inefficient tasks and poor transport conditions that could be corrected through agricultural reorganization.

Lewis (1955a) constructed a dual-sector model comprising urban industry and rural smallholding agriculture. The marginal productivity of labour in densely populated rural settlements was reckoned to be zero or near zero, such that a transfer of labour from agriculture to non-agriculture could take place without any reduction in agricultural output. Under these assumptions, rural emigration to urban areas, particularly the industrial sector, was considered beneficial. As Boserup (1990) points out, later economists tended not to make a distinction between the value of rural labour in densely, as opposed to sparsely, populated rural areas. The latter were more prevalent in sub-Saharan Africa. In African peasant agricultural systems, increasing population was being accommodated by expansion into new land or more labour-intensive methods of production. With marginal productivity of rural labour well above zero, emigration was ill-advised.

The linked issue of urban industry's labour absorption capacity came to the fore. Despite concentrated efforts on the part of independent national governments to pursue import-substitution strategies, it quickly became apparent that the supply of labour from rural areas was exceeding the labour demand of urban areas and urban unemployment was not disguised. In its urban unemployed form, the surplus labour posed a visible threat to the political stability of national governments. Conversely, the labour loss experienced by rural areas was reckoned to be large, since the rural migration stream was primarily of youth whose superior education to their parents had been considered an important component of future smallholder agricultural development. Africa, Asia and Latin America were therefore facing a problem of labour displacement manifested in uncontrollable expansion of an urban 'informal sector' (Hart 1973, de Janvry 1981, White 1983, Breman 1994). The theme of the informal sector and impoverishment represented an updated version of Marx's concept of 'surplus population' that indirectly referred to an ongoing process of peasant dissolution.

Technology Transfer and the Staple Food Supply Constraint

According to Lewis (1955b), the productivity of smallholder staple food production is axiomatic to national development and poses its greatest stumbling block.

> In practice in most backward economies the sector which usually responds least well to growth in other sectors, and which therefore acts as a brake on all economic growth, is the agricultural sector producing food for home consumption. This is because, when agriculture is in the hands of small farmers, the introduction of innovations depends more upon government initiative than upon the initiative of private entrepreneurs . . . To increase the output of peasants . . . requires a number of actions which are essentially in the government sphere; above all, considerable expenditure on agricultural research and agricultural extension, as well as expenditures on roads, rural water supplies, agricultural credit facilities, etc. (Lewis 1955b: 281).

In the tropical agricultural countries there has been a bifurcation of countries into those which have and those which have not succeeded in raising their food productivity. Many if not most sub-Saharan African countries and several Latin American countries, despite concerted government efforts during the 1960s and 1970s, experienced relatively stagnant staple food yields. Some governments found it easier to encourage the importation of cheaper food from industrialized countries to feed their urban populations than to have it produced by indigenous smallholders (Bryceson 1990, Fox 1992, Goodman and Watts 1994). In this regard, Boserup (1981) draws attention to the detrimental effect of North American and European governments' agricultural subsidies on Third World peasant food production.

The literature dealing with African stagnation of food productivity tends to blame African governments' over-control of food pricing and inefficient marketing structures, a charge which became one of the central rationales for implementing structural adjustment. More recently, in a liberalized market setting and with the absence of marked improvement in peasant food-production output, the blame has been placed on poor productive infrastructure arising from the disintegration of African governments' financial capability to maintain, let alone extend, rural roads, water supplies and agricultural extension services.

By contrast, several areas of Asia, and to a lesser extent Latin America, have experienced spurts in smallholder food-crop yields connected with land reform and the 'green revolution'. Generally instigated by heavy government involvement in the transfer of technological innovation through improved rural infrastructure and input packages for smallholders, these actions represented the developmental path originally recommended by Lewis.

These promising developments were associated with a more up-beat debate in the development economics literature concerning the relationship between farm size and factor productivity. Berry and Cline's (1979) study of Brazil, Colombia, the Philippines, Pakistan, India and Malaysia showed that the smallholding peasant sector achieved higher production per unit of land than the large farm sector due to the intensity and flexibility of labour based on family units. Cornia's (1985) larger sample of 15 countries, including five African countries, further reinforced the pattern of higher labour intensity and output on small holdings. The findings harked back to Chayanov and had several important policy implications. Firstly, they provided a sound basis for the implementation of Latin American land reform and its frontal attack on large, inefficient *hacienda* agricultural production units (see Chapter 7 in this volume). Secondly, the evidence suggested that the new green revolution technology could generate constant rather than increasing returns to scale in agriculture, making increasing yields of new grain varieties within the reach of small as well as large farmers (see Chapter 12, this volume). Nonetheless, as time elapsed, it became evident that technological advances in agriculture tended disproportionately to benefit large farmers while the position of small farmers was more likely to be weakened by the re-alignment of rural land and labour assets between households and deepening rural class differentiation. Not infrequently, segments of peasant producers experienced labour redundancy culminating in rural out-migration (Byres 1981).

Down to fundamentals: economic rationality of smallholding peasants justified then jettisoned

In the 1960s, the formalist debate in anthropology was mirrored by a debate about peasant rationality in development economics. Colonial notions of a backward-sloping supply curve of labour had already fallen out of vogue. Schultz (1964) argued that peasant smallholders are optimizers in line with principles of neo-classical perfect competition and that their optimization behaviour was observable through price responsiveness, an assumption that increasingly underlined international development agencies' smallholder economic policy recommendations.

Lipton (1968) countered the prevailing view, calling attention to a number of environmental and contextual factors that prevented smallholders from reacting with decisiveness to optimize production. Peasant farmers lack requisite information, the biggest unknown being rainfall – its sufficiency and temporal distribution. Imperfect factor markets, inter-farm variation in output, and rapid changes in the productive environment brought about by local population growth and government policies, all contribute to a high level of uncertainty. Furthermore, peasants' production decisions, intimately bound up with household consumption requirements, bear high costs for those who miscalculate. With such uncertainty, risk management becomes critical. In Lipton's view peasants cannot afford to use an 'optimizing algorithm'. Instead, they individually develop and pursue an array of 'survival algorithms' to suit their circumstances, which explains inter-farm differences.

> Arguments about optimal policies, based on false analogies with the human, rich and risk-cushioned agricultures of the West, do not impress the subsistence farmer. A bad year or two, in an optimal policy sequence, will not prevent the Western farmer from retaining land and other assets sufficient to follow through the sequence; they will ruin the Indian farmer. His first duty to his family is to prevent such ruin; with growing population, fewer and fewer have enough land left for subsequent optimizing experiments. Risk premium is an increasing function of risk and a decreasing function of assets . . . The reduction in family holdings, as India's population grows, will increase the sensible safety-first propensities of the Indian farmer – and probably the annoyance of the agricultural economist who observes them (Lipton 1968: 266).

Replacing or at least augmenting profit maximization with risk minimization puts economic modelling of peasant production functions on a more realistic basis, salvaging the utility of mathematical data analysis in development economics. Furthermore, household survival considerations were to form the basis for subsequent stress on household coping and livelihood strategies in the literature. Development economics was veering towards the view that the smallholder household, rather than individuals within the household, constituted the basic unit of economic decision-making. While accommodating a re-orientation in their units of analysis, development economists showed less willingness to confront the fundamental paradox in Lipton's insights. Lipton's work logically inferred the need for familiarity not only with peasants' production constraints, but also with how they perceive and manipulate the constraints they face, and an understanding of their social agency including shared norms of obligation and reciprocity, as well as contested arenas of power in resource allocation. This could only be achieved through greater rapport between development economists and other social scientists studying non-economic aspects of peasant societies.

The farming systems research approach was a partial response to this need, involving multidisciplinary, location-specific field research which aimed to resolve smallholders' practical production constraints. In actual fact, its multidisciplinarity was more a matter of combining agricultural economics with technical fields such as agronomy and civil engineering, rather than representing the convergence of development economics and more socially based peasant studies. The approach was criticized for its insensitivity to smallholders' perspectives with its top-down orientation to the transfer of technology (Chambers 1983).

Development economics remained relatively aloof from the farming systems' applied, on-farm perspective. Instead the 1970s and 1980s saw the discipline relying heavily on simplifying assumptions[6] to facilitate the mathematical modelling of smallholder production and interpretation of quantitative survey findings in the light of market prices and government policies. The influence of rainfall variation was rarely, if ever, considered, and cultural and social dynamics, less amenable to quantification, were circumvented.

The rise of neo-liberal 'mono-economics' of the 1980s further narrowed the frame of reference in development economics. 'Monoeconomics' (Toye 1995) imputed profit maximization goals to all economic agents regardless of context. Market optimization was elevated to a global imperative in which peasant economic calculation along the lines argued by Lipton became peasant irrationality or market imperfection.

Much of the fine-tuning of Third World macro- as well as micro-development economics theory was being jettisoned by neo-liberalism. In the wake of the oil shocks of the 1970s, rising fuel costs had deeply affected the competitiveness of peasant-produced commodities, given the more dispersed nature of peasant agricultural production units in comparison with the plantation sector and agro-industry. Meanwhile, the long-term price decline for tropical products continued. State marketing agencies were squeezed into ever tighter real margins. International financial institutions, adopting a neo-liberal offensive, blamed Third World government intervention for smallholders' declining producer prices.

The enforcement of structural adjustment programmes and market liberalization policies reduced, if not eliminated, the possibility of Third-world national governments providing producer subsidies and other buffer measures to protect peasant producers from the adverse effects of commodity price decline. The establishment of the World Trade Organisation and the erosion of preferential trade agreements, such as the Lomé Agreement between the European Union and the African, Caribbean and Pacific region, more fully exposed peasants to international market forces. Global markets were not new and they bore predictable consequences for peasant producers sidelined by larger-scale production. Karl Polanyi (1957) had already drawn attention to the labour-dislocating impact of American and Australian grain imports on nineteenth century European peasant farming.

Large-scale European and American agro-industry, itself subsidized, increasingly threatened the smallholder agricultural economies of Africa, Asia and Latin America (McMichael 1995). Historical lessons, however, were not allowed to clutter the neat policy solutions of the Washington Consensus. In proselytizing the idea that free trade in the global market was capable of achieving higher productivity, leading to more goods and services at cheaper prices and eventual welfare gains for all, the inevitability of massive peasant labour displacement on developing-country economies was simply not mentioned (World Bank 1995). The triangular relationship between peasants, states and markets that had occupied the intellectual energies of social scientists for over two centuries was pushed aside. Only markets mattered in the neo-liberal perspective (see critiques of the Washington Consensus by Singh 1996, Singer 1997, Taylor 1997).

Losing Sight of Smallholder Peasants in the Twenty-first Century

This literature review has highlighted some of the western biases that have permeated comparative peasant studies through time. Themes originating in the early classical literature of Smith, Ricardo and Marx and the Soviet debate of the early 1900s have continually reappeared in rural sociology and development economics during the twentieth century. Both intellectual streams see peasant society in linear terms, as materially more 'backward' than industrial society. While the former tends to depict this difference as culturally enriching, development economics has sought to modernize peasant economies through various prescriptive policy measures. In the past decade both discourses have been overshadowed by the force of neo-liberal theories and structural adjustment policies. Despite in-depth awareness of the complexity of peasant societies and economies, neither rural peasant studies nor development economics successfully combated the analytical reductionism of the neo-liberal perspective.

Under the dominating influence of the Washington Consensus, development economists faced a particular quandary. They provided the bulwark of consultants employed by international development agencies. The risk of adverse employment consequences or censure from breaking ranks with their professional colleagues was apparent for those challenging the wisdom of neo-liberalism. By narrowing their analytical gaze, focusing on the micro-level of rural households' coping and livelihood strategies, development economists could circumvent controversy. Policy aims couched in terms of sustainable development aimed to alleviate poverty and lessen the environmental degradation of smallholder farming. Unlike the ambitious quest in the 1970s for 'Third World national development' and transformation of smallholder production, sustainable development of the 1990s was defensive, attempting to stave off worsening conditions for smallholders. It was directed primarily at the household and community rather than the national level. Meanwhile, development economists' industrialization trajectory was quietly sidelined in the face of stagnant and shrinking employment in that sector worldwide. Asia alone, prior to the late 1990s economic recession, could boast significant labour-absorbing industrial growth.

Some development economists have sought more humanistic theoretical traditions in the social sciences as a way to evade neo-liberalism. The French regulation school and convention theory provide a perspective which integrates the analysis of other institutions besides the market and explores symmetrical relationships between people and things which embody human value (Wilkinson 1997). Institutional economics, drawing inspiration from Veblen and Weber, amongst others, places less emphasis on price and resource allocation *per se* and more on organizational aspects of the economy, acknowledging the power relations that underpin market dynamics. Its evolutionary perspective on institutional development roots it firmly in western modernization discourse.

Despite these moderating influences, the methodological divide between development economics and the other more qualitative social sciences has yet to be bridged. Amongst mainstream economists, attempts at being more multidisciplinary tend to be discounted as 'going soft'. Following the behavioural economics of Becker (1976), some have ventured beyond, applying mathematical modelling and simplifying assumptions about economic utility maximization to traditional sociological subject matter such as household relations, educational investment and domestic labour. However, economists themselves criticize this approach for its insidious methodological imperialism (Blaug 1980, Akram-Lodhi 1997, Fine 1997).

Other social sciences, particularly anthropology and rural sociology, have undergone a wave of theoretical scepticism associated with post-modernist thought. Post-modernism rejects western bias in mainstream social science, specifically its meta-narratives constructed on the basis of linear trajectories and dualistic contrasts. Although its critique is primarily directed at the theories of industrial modernization, it nonetheless strikes at the heart of peasant studies that tended to assume linear evolution of 'backward peasant societies' towards 'technologically advanced industrial societies' (Araghi 1995, Long and Long 1992). Peasant theory is on the retreat, withdrawn into post-modernist reflection about discourse, blurred identities and power relations. Post-modernists primarily direct their attention to features of post-industrialization – the production of knowledge rather than goods. Here, too, peasants are sidelined. Few post-modernists notice them and their anomalous position in the information age; those who do, see peasants as a transitional category between town and country, their 'true voices' impossible to capture amidst the din of globalization (Kearney 1996). Actor-oriented approaches, on the other hand, concentrate on the micro–meso level of decision-making and action, and recognize peasants as reactive agents amongst several other categories of local actors (Long 1990). The historical significance and class dimension of peasants' existence is often disregarded by this approach.

So, are peasantries disappearing or are they merely fading from western social science scrutiny? During the 1990s, the salience of peasant theories and development economic concerns with peasant smallholders have certainly dimmed. Concurrently, it can be argued that the implementation of structural adjustment policies and market liberalization worldwide have had a dissolving effect on peasants' livelihoods, as several of the following chapters document.

One could argue that peasants are now more elusive than before. The economic, social and political pressures and opportunities that have befallen them have led many peasantries to diversify into a number of occupations and non-agricultural income-earning avenues. Their relationship to the soil has changed. Multi-occupational, straddling urban and rural residences, flooding labour markets, peasants become definitionally problematic. State and market influences have permeated their societies, and the nature of the peasant family and village community has altered. In a situation of rapid flux, peasants disappear, then reappear as if by some conjuror's trick. The direction of change confuses and its rapid rate affords little time for synchronic analysis. Peasant transitional processes are more complex.

The theoretical challenge is to capture a moving target. This book endeavours to bring peasants back into theoretical and policy debates. 'Rethinking peasantries' is our aim. With this goal in mind, the following chapters document various thematic strands, topical issues and empirical tendencies arising from existing peasant activity in Asia, Africa and Latin America.

Notes

1. I have greatly benefited from the critical comments of my co-editors, but the views expressed in this chapter are mine rather than those of the editorial collective.
2. For example Firth and Yamey (1964: 17–18) do not confine their definition of peasant economy to people primarily engaged in agriculture stating that we 'speak not only of peasant agriculturalists but also of peasant fishermen, peasant craftsmen and peasant marketers, if they are part of the same social system. In any case, such people are often in fact part-time cultivators as well'.
3. 'De-agrarianisation' is defined as a long-term process of (1) occupational adjustment, (2) income-earning reorientation, (3) social identification, and (4) spatial relocation of rural dwellers away from strictly agrarian modes of livelihood (Bryceson 1997).
4. The early work of Schultz (1964) and subsequent work of Ellis (1996) are notable exceptions. Ellis's textbook, *Peasant Economics: Farm Households and Agrarian Development* represents a careful exposition of the theoretical frameworks of rural sociology and development economics. Ellis replaces the term 'smallholder' with 'peasant' throughout the book while focusing on development economists' quantitative models of farm-level decision-making.
5. However, the means to this end was contested during the 1960s and 1970s when the issue of agricultural versus industrial-led development arose in reaction to Mao's revision of Chinese policy towards its peasantry (Singh 1979). This debate was essentially about tactics and timing rather than about challenging industrialization as the development goal.
6. 'The information content of most estimates of peasant allocative efficiency is disappointingly low because they are based on an excessively simple model of microeconomic behaviour and, therefore, an excessively simple concept of efficiency' (Barrett 1997). Also see critiques by Mitra (1976), Lewis (1978b) and Boserup (1998).

References

Abdullah, T. and Zeidenstein, S. (1982) *Village Women of Bangladesh: Prospects for Change*, Pergamon Press, Oxford.
Akram-Lodhi, A.H. (1997) 'The unitary model of the peasant household: an obituary', *Economic Issues*, 2(1): 27–42.
Araghi, F.A. (1995) 'Global depeasantization, 1945–1990', *Sociological Quarterly*, 36(2): 337–68.
Banaji, J. (1972) 'For a theory of colonial modes of production', *Economic and Political Weekly*, 7(52): 2498–502.
Barrett, C.A. (1997) 'How credible are estimates of peasant allocative, scale, or scope efficiency? A commentary', *Journal of International Development*, 9(2): 221–9.
Bauer, P.T. (1954) *West African Trade*, Cambridge University Press, Cambridge.
Bauer, P.T. (1981) *Equality, the Third World and Economic Delusion*, Weidenfeld and Nicolson, London.
Becker, G.S. (1976) *The Economic Approach to Human Behavior*, University of Chicago Press, Chicago.
Benaria, L. (ed.) (1982) *Women and Development: The Sexual Division of Labour in Rural Societies*, Praeger, New York.
Bernstein, H. (1977), 'Notes on capital and peasantry', *Review of African Political Economy*, No. 10, 60–73.
Bernstein, H. (1994) 'Agrarian classes in capitalist development', in L. Sklair (ed.) *Capitalism and Development*, Routledge, London, pp. 40–71.
Berry, R.A. and Cline, W.R. (1979) *Agrarian Structure and Productivity in Developing Countries*, Johns Hopkins University Press, Baltimore.
Blaug, M. (1980) *The Methodology of Economics*, Cambridge University Press, Cambridge.
Boserup, E. (1981) *Population and Technology*, Blackwell, Oxford.
Boserup, E. (1990) 'Agricultural growth and population change', in T.P. Schultz (ed.) *Economic and Demographic Relationships in Development*, Johns Hopkins University Press, Baltimore, pp. 11–24.
Boserup, E. (1998) *My Professional Life and Publications 1929–1998*, Museum Tusculanum Press, Copenhagen.
Breman, J. (1994) *Wage Hunters and Gatherers*, Oxford University Press, Delhi.
Bryceson, D.F. (1990) *Food Insecurity and the Social Division of Labour in Tanzania, 1919–1985*, Macmillan, London.
Bryceson, D.F. (1997) 'De-agrarianisation in sub-Saharan Africa', in D.F. Bryceson and V. Jamal (ed.) *Farewell to Farms*, Ashgate, Aldershot, pp. 3–20.
Bryceson, D.F. and Vuorela, U. (1984) 'Outside the domestic labour debate: towards a theory of modes of human reproduction', *Review of Radical Political Economics*, 16(2 and 3): 4–27.
Bundy, C. (1972) 'Emergence and decline of a South African peasantry', *African Affairs*, 71(285): 369–88.

Byres, T.J. (1981) 'The new technology, class formation and class action in the Indian countryside', *Journal of Peasant Studies*, 8(4): 405–54.
Byres, T.J. (1991) 'The agrarian question and differing forms of capitalist agrarian transition', in J. Breman and S. Mundel (eds) *Rural Transformation in Asia*, Oxford University Press, Delhi, pp. 3–76.
Byres, T.J. (1996) *Capitalism from Above and Capitalism from Below*, Macmillan, London.
Chambers, R. (1983) *Rural Development: Putting the Last First*, Longman, London.
Chayanov, A.V. (1925) *The Theory of the Peasant Economy*, (1966 edition) (translated by D. Thorner, R.E.F. Smith and B. Kerblay). Irwin, Glencoe, Illinois.
Cipolla, C. M. (1962) *The Economic History of World Population*, Penguin, Aylesbury (1979 edition).
Cohen, P. (1967) 'Economic analysis and economic man: some comments on a controversy', in R. Firth (ed.) *Themes in Economic Anthropology*, Tavistock Publications, London, 91–119.
Cornia, G.A. (1985) 'Farm size, land yields and the agricultural production function: analysis for fifteen developing countries', *World Development*, 13(4): 513–34.
Croll, E. (1984) *Changing Patterns of Rural Women's Employment, Production and Reproduction in China*, International Labour Office, Geneva.
Dalton, G. (1961) 'Economic theory and primitive society', *American Anthropologist*, 63: 1–25.
Deere, C.D. and de Leal, M.L. (1982) *Women in Andean Agriculture*, International Labour Office, Geneva.
de Janvry, A. (1981) *The Agrarian Question and Reformism in Latin America*, Johns Hopkins University Press, Baltimore.
Dessalegn Rahmato (1984) *Agrarian Reform in Ethiopia*, Scandinavian Institute of African Studies, Uppsala.
Dewey, A.G. (1962) *Peasant Marketing in Java*, Free Press of Glencoe, New York.
Douglas, M. (1963) *The Lele of the Kasai*, Oxford University Press, London.
Dupré, G. and Rey, P.-Ph. (1978) 'Reflections on the Relevance of a Theory of the History of Exchange', in D. Seddon (ed.), *Relations of Production: Marxist Approaches to Economic Anthropology*, Frank Cass, London, pp. 171–208.
Ellis, F. (1996) *Peasant Economics*, Cambridge University Press, Cambridge.
Emmanuel, A. (1972) *Unequal Exchange: A Study in the Imperialism of Trade*, Monthly Review Press, New York.
Evans, D. (1975) 'Unequal exchange and economic policies: some implications of the new-Ricardian critique of the theory of comparative advantage', *IDS Bulletin*, 6(4).
Fine, B. (1997) 'The new revolution in economics', *Capital & Class*, No. 61, 143–8.

Firth, R. (1967) 'Themes in economic anthropology: A general comment', in R. Firth (ed.) *Themes in Economic Anthropology*, pp. 1–28, Tavistock Publications, London.
Firth, R. and B.S. Yamey (ed.) (1964) *Capital Saving and Credit in Peasant Societies*, Allen and Unwin, London.
Fox, J. (1992) *The Politics of Food in Mexico: State Power and Social Mobilization*, Cornell University Press, Ithaca and London.
Frank, A.G. (1969) *Capitalism and Underdevelopment in Latin America*, Penguin, Harmondsworth.
Godelier, M. (1973) *Perspectives in Marxist Anthropology*, Cambridge University Press, Cambridge (1977 edition translated by R. Brain).
Goodman, D. and Watts, M. (1994) 'Reconfiguring the rural or fording the divide?: capitalist restructuring and the global agro-food system', *Journal of Peasant Studies*, 22(1): 1–49.
Harriss, J. (ed.) (1982) *Rural Development: Theories of Peasant Economy and Agrarian Change*, Hutchinson, London.
Hart, G., Turton, A. and White, B. (ed.) (1989) *Agrarian Transformations: Local Processes and the State in Southeast Asia*, University of California Press, Berkeley.
Hart, K. (1973) 'Informal Income Opportunities and Urban Employment in Ghana', *Journal of Modern African Studies*, 2(1): 61–89.
Hyden, G. (1980) *Beyond Ujamaa in Tanzania: Underdevelopment and an Uncaptured Peasantry*, Heinemann, London.
Hyden, G. (1983) *No Shortcuts to Progress: African Development Management in Perspective*, Heinemann Educational, London.
Kasfir, N. (1986) 'Are African peasants self-sufficient?', *Development and Change*, 17(2): 335–57.
Kautsky, K. (1899) *The Agrarian Question*, Zwan Publications, London (1988 edition).
Kay, C. (1974) 'Comparative development of the European manorial system and the Latin American hacienda system', *Journal of Peasant Studies*, 2(1): 69–98.
Kay, C. (1980) 'The landlord road and the subordinate peasant road to capitalism in Latin America', *Études Rurales*, No. 77, 5–20.
Kay, C. (1989) *Latin American Theories of Development and Underdevelopment*, Routledge, London.
Kearney, M. (1996) *Reconceptualising the Peasantry: Anthropology in Global Perspective*, Westview Press, Boulder, Colorado.
Lehmann, D. (1976) *A Theory of Agrarian Structure: Typology and Paths of Transformation in Latin America*, Centre of Latin American Studies, Cambridge.
Leakey, R.E. and Lewin, R. (1979) *Origins*, Rainbird Publishing, London
Lenin, V.I. (1899) 'The development of capitalism in Russia' in *Lenin Collected Works,* Vol. III, Progress Publishers, Moscow (1974 edition).
Lenin, V.I. (1917) *Imperialism: The Highest Stage of Capitalism*, Foreign Language Press, Peking (1965 edition).

Lenin, V.I. (1920) 'Preliminary draft theses on the agrarian question for the second congress of the Communist International', in *Lenin Collected Works,* Vol. XXXI, Progress Publishers, Moscow (1974 edition).
Lewis, O. (1951) *Life in a Mexican Village: Tepoztlán Restudied*, University of Illinois Press, Chicago.
Lewis, W.A. (1955a) 'Economic development with unlimited supplies of labour', *Manchester School of Economic and Social Studies Bulletin*, 22: 139–92.
Lewis, W.A. (1955b) *The Theory of Economic Growth*, Allen & Unwin, London.
Lewis, W.A. (1978a) *The Evolution of the International Economic Order,* Princeton University Press, Princeton.
Lewis, W.A. (1978b) *Growth and Fluctuations 1870–1913*, Allen & Unwin, London.
Lipton, M. (1968) 'The theory of the optimizing peasant', *Journal of Development Studies*, 4(3): 327–51.
Long, N. (1990) 'From paradigm lost to paradigm regained? The case for an actor-oriented sociology of development', *European Review of Latin American and Caribbean Studies*, No. 49, 3–24.
Long, N. and Long, A. (ed.) (1992) *Battlefields of Knowledge: The Interlocking of Theory and Practice in Social Research and Development*, Routledge, London.
Marx, K. (1850–52) Excerpts from 'The Class Struggles in France 1848–1850' and 'The Eighteenth Brumaire of Louis Bonaparte', in K. Marx and F. Engels, *Selected Works*, Vol. 1, London, Lawrence & Wishart (first published 1852).
Marx, K. (1867) *Capital*, Vol. 1, Penguin, Harmondsworth (1976 edition).
McMichael, P. (ed.) (1995) *Food and Agrarian Orders in the World-Economy*, Praeger, Westport.
Meillassoux, C. (1972) 'From reproduction to production', *Economy and Society*, 1(1): 94–105.
Meillassoux, C. (1981) *Maidens, Meal and Money: Capitalism and the Domestic Economy*, Cambridge University Press, Cambridge.
Mitra, A. (1976) 'The new obfuscators', in A. Mitra (ed.) *Calcutta Diary*, Frank Cass, London.
Mooij, J. (1999) *Food Policy and the Indian State: The Public Distribution System in South India*, Oxford University Press, Delhi.
Myint, H. (1958) 'The classical theory of international trade and underdeveloped countries', *Economic Journal*, 68, June, pp. 317-37.
Nash, M. (1971) 'Market and Indian peasant economies', in T. Shanin (ed.) *Peasants and Peasant Societies*, Penguin, Harmondsworth, pp. 161–77.
Nurkse, R. (1953) *Problems of Capital Formation in Underdeveloped Countries*, Oxford University Press, Oxford.
Patnaik, U. (ed.) (1990) *Agrarian Relations and Accumulation: The Mode of Production Debate in India*, Oxford University Press, Delhi.
Pearse, A. (1971) 'Metropolis and peasant: the expansion of the urban–industrial complex and the changing rural structure', in T. Shanin (ed.) *Peasants and Peasant Societies*, Penguin, Harmondsworth, pp. 69–80.

Polanyi, K. (1946) *The Great Transformation*, Gollancz, London.
Polanyi, K. (1957) *The Great Transformation: The Political and Economic Origins of Our Time*, Beacon, Boston.
Popkin, S. (1980) 'The rational peasant: the political economy of peasant society', *Theory and Society*, 9(3): 411–71.
Prebisch, R. (1950) *The Economic Development of Latin America and its Principal Problems*, Economic Commission for Latin America, United Nations, New York.
Preobrazhensky, E. (1926) *The New Economics*, Clarendon, Oxford (1965 edition translated by B. Pearse, with an introduction by A. Nove).
Redfield, R. (1956) *Peasant Society and Culture*, University of Chicago Press, Chicago.
Ricardo, D. (1817) *Principles of Political Economy and Taxation*, Doubleday, New York (1946 edition).
Sahlins, M.D. (1965) 'On the sociology of primitive exchange', in M. Banton (ed.), *The Relevance of Models for Social Anthropology*, Asia Monographs, 1, pp. 139–236, London, Tavistock Press.
Schultz, T.W. (1964) *Transforming Traditional Agriculture*, Yale University Press, New Haven.
Scott, J.C. (1976) *The Moral Economy of the Peasant Rebellion and Subsistence in Southeast Asia*, Yale University Press, New Haven.
Seddon, D. (ed.) (1978) *Relations of Production: Marxist Approaches to Economic Anthropology*, Frank Cass, London.
Shanin, T. (1966) 'The peasantry as a political factor', *Sociological Review*, 14(1): 5–27.
Shanin, T. (ed.) (1976) *Peasants and Peasant Societies*, Penguin, Harmondsworth.
Shivji, I. (1975) *Class Struggles in Tanzania*, Tanzania Publishing House, Dar es Salaam.
Singer, H.W. (1997) 'The golden age of the Keynesian consensus – the pendulum swings back', *World Development*, 25(3): 293–5.
Singh, A. (1979) 'The "basic needs" approach to development vs the new international economic order: the significance of Third World industrialization', *World Development*, 7(6): 585–606.
Singh, A. (1996) 'Liberalization and globalization: an unhealthy euphoria', paper presented to the conference on *Full-Employment without Inflation*, Robinson College, Cambridge, May, 1996.
Smith, A. (1776) *An Inquiry into the Nature and Causes of the Wealth of Nations*, Doubleday, New York (1946 edition).
Streeten, P. (1972) *The Frontiers of Development Studies*, Macmillan, London.
Taylor, L. (1997) 'The revival of the liberal creed – the IMF and the World Bank in a globalized economy', *World Development*, 25(2): 145–52.
Thorner, A. (1982) 'Semi-feudal or capitalism? Contemporary debate on classes and modes of production in India', *Economic and Political Weekly*, 17(51): 2061–6.
Toye, J. (1995) 'Structural adjustment: context, assumptions, origin and diversity', in R. van der Hoeven and F. van der Kraaij (ed.), *Structural*

Adjustment and Beyond in Sub-Saharan Africa, James Currey, The Hague and London.
White, B. (1983) '"Agricultural Involution" and its critics: twenty years after', *Bulletin of Concerned Asian Scholars*, 15(2): 18–31.
Wilkinson, J. (1997) 'A new paradigm for economic analysis?', *Economy and Society*, 26(3): 305–39.
Williams, G. (1976) 'Taking the part of the peasants: rural development in Nigeria and Tanzania', in P.C. Gutkind and I. Wallerstein (eds) *The Political Economy of Contemporary Africa*, Sage Publications, Beverley Hills, pp. 131–54.
Wolf, E.R. (1955) 'Types of Latin American peasantry: a preliminary discussion', *American Anthropologist*, 57: 452–71.
Wolf, E.R. (1966) *Peasants*, Prentice-Hall, Englewood Cliffs, New Jersey.
Wolpe, H. (1972) 'Capitalism and cheap labour power in South Africa', *Economy and Society*, 1(4): 425–56.
World Bank (1995) *World Development Report 1995: Workers in an Integrating World*, Oxford University Press, New York.
World Bank (1998) *World Development Indicators 1998*, World Bank, Washington, D.C.

PART TWO: AFRICAN PEASANTRIES

2. African Peasants' Centrality and Marginality: Rural Labour Transformations

DEBORAH FAHY BRYCESON

NO OTHER CONTINENT at present is so closely identified with smallholding peasant farming as Africa. The centrality of peasants in both the academic and policy-oriented literature on Africa belies the marginality of African peasants in the terms that really matter, namely their capability to achieve self-destiny. This chapter could have been aptly titled 'African Peasants in the World Economy: Make or Break', for the conscious creation and the ongoing, seemingly unintentional, dissolution of African peasantries within global trade networks has been compressed into hardly more than a century. For most of recorded history, Africa has been a relatively sparsely populated continent. Labour has been at a premium, while land has been plentiful. The appearance and disappearance of peasantries in this context has to be related to demographic as well as to economic and political factors. This chapter provides historical background to the pre-colonial period. It then traces the emergence of African peasantries under European colonialism, their consolidation amidst decolonization and early independent government, and finally the circumstances undermining their existence from the mid-1970s onwards.

Obstacles to Peasant Formation in Pre-Colonial Sub-Saharan Africa

It is abundantly evident that peasant societies existed long before European colonial rule. Peasants' contributions in the form of labour services, cotton exports and tax payments are associated with the Kush culture of the Nile valley, which prevailed between 1000 BCE and 600 CE, in what is now Sudan. Similarly, the Aksum kingdom of the Ethiopian highlands flourished from 100 to 700 CE, utilizing the labour of peasants producing with ox ploughs. However, despite these highly durable examples, available evidence suggests that peasant societies remained exceptional in Africa at large, both with respect to population and geographical coverage.

The emergence of peasant societies capable of generating marketable and taxable agrarian surpluses depends on a suitable combination of factors related to population density, ecology, and technology. It is with respect to the former that Africa has posed the greatest challenges. As a continent of climatic extremes, roughly 10 per cent of its land mass is enveloped in tropical rainforest or coastal mangrove systems with extremely high rainfall and humidity, whilst another 40 per cent is subject to arid conditions. The Sahara Desert has expanded and contracted in size over time, and is currently on the advance. Barring massive irrigation works, the vast expanses of both the Sahara and Kalahari Deserts rule out the possibility of viable agriculture, whereas clearance of rain forest areas requires enormous labour investment. Once cleared, the soils are subject to intense leaching and fertility depletion by heavy rainfall. Savanna, the remaining 50 per cent of the continent's surface area, receives average amounts of rainfall that are more conducive to sedentary agriculture, although rainfall variability from year to year poses an impediment. Only areas of higher altitude with sufficient, predictable rainfall encourage the development of reliable, staple food cropping patterns around which sedentary agricultural systems and agrarian cultures can evolve unthreatened by recurrent episodes of drought.

In view of the harsh environmental context, it comes as little surprise that the prevalence of agrarian modes of livelihood throughout sub-Saharan Africa is relatively recent. It is believed that hunting, gathering and pastoral activities constituted the bulk of sub-Saharan Africans' working lives prior to the southerly expansion of Bantu-speaking people between 1000 BCE and 1000 CE from an area of what is now Cameroon (Andah 1993). Evidence of plants associated with West Africa's forest agriculture date back as far as 3500 years ago (Sutton 1997). Grains such as sorghum and millet were probably domesticated between 2000 and 1000 BCE in West Africa.

The Bantu expansion is identified not with the discovery of agriculture *per se*, but with a tool kit combining technological and social elements capable of catalysing the intensification of agricultural systems and agrarian cultures in local communities. Knowledge of iron-making and plant husbandry was combined with existing livestock keeping and hunting and gathering activities. Organizational features, notably a flexible lineage social structure with strong matrilineal tendencies and pronatalist values, encouraged gender and generational relationships that could accommodate high degrees of spatial mobility and high fertility to counteract the vagaries of the harsh environment (Bryceson 1995).

Although agrarian foundations were laid through most of the arable parts of the continent by 1000 CE, the emergence of peasantries still depended on the build-up of population density and surplus-producing capability. This was a task that only a few kingdoms accomplished during the intervening period prior to the establishment of European rule. Most African kingdoms of this time were established on the basis of trading empires exporting gold or slaves, rather than peasant-produced agricultural commodities (Klein 1980).

External demand for African slaves emanated first from the Arabian Peninsula and then from Europe. The slave trade had a far-reaching effect on the continent's labour supply only after the establishment of European agricultural enterprises in the Americas (Hopkins 1973). Whether the transatlantic slave trade depopulated the continent or merely slowed down population growth is debatable; in any case it posed a barrier to peasant formation (Iliffe 1995). It is estimated that between 11 and 13 million slaves were transported to the Americas between the sixteenth and eighteenth centuries. The number of slaves lost en route, to say nothing of the numbers killed in the course of slave raiding, is subject to much speculation. The slave trade disrupted agricultural innovation and growth of output. Local agrarian communities were subject to the seizure of their most economically active members.[1] Those left behind had to farm in a circumscribed manner under conditions of extreme insecurity – forced to site their settlements in areas easy to defend rather than agriculturally favourable locations, productivity suffered. Losses were only partially compensated by the introduction of several crops that were to become main staple foods, notably maize and bananas. Their spread displaced the drought-resistant but low-yielding, indigenous sorghums and millets. African surplus food production required to feed those involved in the export slave trade was often grown on slave plantations belonging to African élites. In this way the functional need for peasant commodity production was largely precluded.

In 1807 Britain, the principal European actor in the transatlantic slave trade, stated its intention of ending the Atlantic slave trade and in 1838, under missionary pressure, slavery was abolished in the Cape Colony of South Africa. Over the course of the nineteenth century the international slave trade tapered off throughout the continent, and forest and agricultural products began to replace slaves as the continent's main export. Although slavery still existed and in many cases intensified domestically as the possibility of slave export diminished, the tide had definitely turned. When the European scramble for Africa began in the late 1880s, domestic forms of slavery within Africa were destined for replacement as well.

Emerging African Peasantries under Colonial Rule, 1888–1945

Removing technological barriers

Inter-European rivalry spurred annexation of the bulk of the African continent, but it was late nineteenth century technological advance that made the colonial creation of African peasantries feasible. When the Suez Canal was opened, East Africa became relatively accessible to Europe for the first time. Meanwhile, steam ships capable of plying several of West Africa's rivers led European traders to venture much further into the interior.

The technologies to remedy the problems of surface transport were also at hand. Trade in many bulky agricultural commodities had hitherto been ruled out because of the vast distances to cover in a relatively unpopulated continent. Heavy reliance was placed on human porterage unaided by pack animals owing to widespread tsetse fly infestation. Within the first decade of colonial rule, railway construction became a priority. By the 1910s several railways had been built and financed by colonial governments.[2] Transport costs were sufficiently reduced to make the export of African peasant products on the world market viable. Road investment came next. One of the main tasks of colonial district officers was to build roads using corvée labour. Slowly the infrastructure for the long distance transport of commodities to markets and ports congealed.

Transport improvement represented great savings on the labour demands of porterage, but road-building itself brought the labour question to the fore. At the onset of European colonial rule most Africans were agricultural producers with tribal usufruct rights to land, meeting their needs largely on the basis of community self-sufficiency. They had little if any need to seek wage labour. The lack of a labour market and the ban on slavery led colonial officialdom to resort to various forms of forced labour, be it in lieu of tax payment or tied to land tenancy, as a means to secure sufficient labour supplies for infrastructural development. Heavy penalties for labour absconding were promulgated in Master and Servant Ordinances.

Surge in peasant commodity production

European contact with Africa had originally been pursued by overseas traders engaged principally with West Africa, but as colonial penetration proceeded European interests shifted. The actors changed to government officials, missionaries, settlers, large-scale planters and mining firms, and their areas of geographical concentration grew to include Central, East and Southern Africa. A complex mesh of interests was thrashed out between European colonists over access to rural Africans' land and labour.

On the labour question, European mining concerns, large-scale plantations and settler farms seeking to recruit labour usually opposed the large-scale formation of peasantries as they feared this would tie African rural dwellers to their land. The half-way solution was the development of a quasi-peasantry through a process of gender differentiation in which women were obliged to stay on their farms while their men engaged in wage labour on the basis of circular migration. This had the support of labour employers who sought to justify paying 'bachelor wages', which did not cover the full costs of maintaining a worker's family. Out of necessity, male African workers kept one foot in farming and one in wage labour. This pattern was particularly prevalent in East and Southern Africa.

Attracting European investment but little European settlement, West Africa experienced fewer constraints on the development of peasantries.

Peasant production had already begun to surface in the nineteenth century with oil palm exports. New crops such as cocoa gave further impetus. The United Africa Company, the major European investor, resorted to out-grower schemes which thrived on the existence of independent peasantries. The meteoric growth of cocoa in the Gold Coast and Nigeria, and peanuts in northern Nigeria and Senegal, involved large numbers of African peasant producers (Watts 1983). Quite quickly some growers in these peasant societies experienced economic success whilst others were marginalized. Colonial authorities tried to contain this economic differentiation by placing bans on freehold land tenure.

In East Africa, with far less room for manoeuvre, a successful cotton-producing peasantry emerged amongst the Baganda of Uganda (Brett 1973). Elsewhere, European planters and settler farmers pressurized colonial governments to restrict peasant production of such export crops like coffee and tea. When that was not possible, they often managed to persuade the colonial government to agree to dual-tiered pricing systems which ensured that settlers obtained higher prices and protection against the 'flooding of the market' by peasant farmers.

Political tendencies: taxing times

Colonial governments, although relatively thin on the ground in terms of personnel, nonetheless endeavoured to be highly regulatory. The linchpin of the colonial governments' entire political and economic system was taxation. The costs of colonial administration were not to be passed back to the colonizing power. Colonized populations were taxed to cover these costs and to induce African market-oriented activity in the form of peasant commodity production or labour force participation. In a few territories, such as the Nigerian protectorates, the level of trade was sufficient to generate the bulk of tax revenue through custom duties. But in most areas, the low levels of export and commerce generally made some form of direct taxation inescapable. At the outset of the imposition of hut and poll taxes, many colonial governments accepted payment in kind, but the logistical difficulties of in-kind payment led to the enforcement of cash payment quickly thereafter. Even in its cash form, African tax collection was a daunting undertaking given the dispersed nature of rural settlement. Colonial administrations attempted to restructure tribute collection of traditional African élites, converting these élites into their tax-collecting agents, yet allowing them certain leeway to carry on in a 'customary' fashion. So began a two-tiered, highly ambiguous dualism between the customary and statutory realms of 'native administration'.

In non-hierarchical, chiefless societies chiefs were often created. In other more hierarchically structured societies, existing African leadership forms were remoulded to suit colonial governments' bureaucratic norms. The resulting 'native authorities' were compromised powers in all senses.

Politically despotic in character, lacking legitimacy in the eyes of their subjects, they varied enormously in their effectiveness as tax-collecting agencies. Colonial officials manipulated ethnic identities to encourage popular support, a process which had ramifications in the decades to come (see Chapter 5 in this volume).

In the savanna areas of eastern and southern Africa, where male circular migration for European mining concerns and plantations prevailed, quasi-peasantries were maintained through paternalistic colonial strictures. Native authority regulations kept women firmly tied to their rural homelands, while men of an economically active age were largely absent, returning home between labour contracts to renew their rights and obligations to their rural households (Mbilinyi 1989). Constraints placed on African housing in towns made urban areas particularly unwelcoming places for women. Those women who nonetheless ventured forth faced heavy sanctions. Labelled as prostitutes, they were subject to the colonial governments' strenuous efforts to 'repatriate' them to their home areas. Repatriation is an appropriate term given that women were permanent legal minors, being classified as economic dependents under the roof and guardianship of a father, husband or brother by the colonial government and their native authorities. Consequently men, not women, were designated as taxpayers.

Male labour migration and peasant commodity production imposed several strains on the productive capacity of local communities. In addition to the containment of female mobility, native authorities sought to stabilize village life through various bye-laws regarding crop production. In many colonial territories, peasants were obliged to plant food crops in sufficient quantity for household survival before planting export cash crops. In areas of unpredictable rainfall, the cultivation of so-called 'famine crops', such as cassava and sweet potatoes, as well as other famine prevention measures, were enforced by the native authority. When these measures failed, the native authorities were in charge of dispensing famine relief under the direction of the colonial district officer. In this way, African rural producers were drawn full circle into peasant/central governing power relations (Bryceson 1990). Obliged to grow cash crops or sell their labour power to pay taxes, they received colonial state paternalistic 'protection' in return. This indisputably contributed to rural population growth. It is estimated that from the 1920s onwards the population increased measurably. Demographers point to the colonial influence not only with respect to the prevention of death through famine, but also to declining mortality arising from the cessation of inter-ethnic war and the introduction of western preventive and curative medicine (Kuczynski 1948–53).

Tribal mask of peasant relations

The defining feature of a peasantry is often thought to be its relationship to the land. Peasants are subject to the suzerainty of a higher power. It is argued that agrarian producers who cultivate the land under tribal rules of allocation are not peasants (Wolf 1966).[3] Through 'indirect rule' policies, colonial powers attempted to govern via 'tribal' native authorities and to enforce existing procedures of land inheritance and allocation, albeit imperfectly understood, in rural areas not alienated for European settlement (Mamdani 1996). Paternalistic laws aimed to define and safeguard tribal lands and check the development of freehold land tenure. In this way, market relations were extended only to labour and commodities, stopping short of the development of land markets and impeding the development of class formation.

However, when applying the ffc_c definition of the peasantry outlined in this book's Introduction, and when emphasis is placed on the peasantry as a process of formation and dissolution, then the classification of African rural communities as strictly tribal or strictly peasant societies is immaterial. Tribal identities were largely fostered by colonial authorities through the policies of indirect rule. The colonial creation of tribal native authorities and associated land law facilitated the creation of peasantries in a tribal guise.

In many countries, African 'tribal' farmers formed the base of a three-tiered racial society, with European colonial administrators forming the apex and non-European traders, be they Asian or Lebanese, wedged in between. The dualism of statutory and customary law lent flexibility to the system from the perspective of the colonial administration, who were in a position to ordain which set of laws applied where. Native authorities and their customary bye-laws functioned to restrict non-European traders' extraction from peasantries by banning the extension of credit to natives by non-natives, whilst safeguarding the continuous reproduction of peasantries through famine prevention and relief measures which did not pose barriers to colonial economic interests (Bryceson 1980a).

Within the institutional constructs and operational procedures of European colonialism, classic patterns of suzerainty and power over agrarian peasantries evolved. Nonetheless, it must be stressed that the colonial powers' success in asserting control and reproduction guarantees varied in degree from place to place and colony to colony. For example, Watts (1983) stresses that British indirect rule in northern Nigeria never mounted effective famine prevention and relief procedures to reduce the exposure of the Hausa peasantry to the periodic food shortages arising from the semi-arid climate. If anything, the colonial cash-cropping policies increased famine risks in that area.

In effect, much of the anthropological literature in the early part of the twentieth century was concerned with the transition from African 'tribesman' to peasant. For British anthropologists such as Audrey Richards (1939) these were practical considerations resulting in policy recommendations or impact assessments of existing colonial government policy. They centred on the changing loyalties and relational ties of rural people in lineage or clan-based societies as the political hierarchy of the colonial state was superimposed and community transfers, such as tribute to a local chief, were transformed into tax payments. They were also an exploration of the degree of economic restructuring that local agriculturalists could absorb without local rural communities losing their social and political coherence. In other words, the delicate tension between internal and external power experienced by all peasant societies was congealing; farmers sharing a common identity embedded in their agrarian community were linked through colonial state and market mechanisms to global economic and political forces. Colonial policies were directed at spurring peasant participation in the world market, intensifying peasant labour to produce exports, but limiting their involvement in land and capital markets. The colonial bugbears of 'peasant laziness' and peasants' 'backward-sloping supply curve' clearly revealed peasants' awareness of the low returns from commodity market engagement, and their reluctance to supply their labour for non-subsistence work beyond achievement of target incomes to pay taxes or brideprice under the prevailing terms of trade and power relations.

So much of African farming, particularly in the drier savanna areas depended on shifting cultivation, with ratios of fallow to cultivation of any specific land being as much as 20 or even 30 years' land fallow followed by three to four years' cultivation (Allan 1965). Thus with low life expectancies an individual might never 'return' to any land he or she cultivated.[4] As population growth proceeded, fallow periods shortened and farming households developed strong notions of rights over particular pieces of land, although they were generally subject to land allocation by native authorities, rather than owning the land *per se*. Most colonial governments were anxious to prevent the development of land markets and the consequent evolution of landlessness, with the highly notable exception of those zones where European settler land alienation took precedence. Paternalistic colonial intervention came in the form of legislation to prevent African 'native' producers from using their land as collateral in debts, particularly debts incurred with non-African traders. This aimed to preserve 'tribal lands' intact and to curtail the growth of economic differentiation amongst African producers. Land accumulation remained largely in step with the accumulation of household labour, putting strong checks on peasant differentiation.

During the first decades of colonial rule, the wide variety of forms of African lineages and age-grade systems, which had functioned as flexible social organizations for facilitating territorial movement and minimizing risk connected with shifting cultivation, were eroding. Pressure was exerted on the dispersed loyalties and rights and obligations of individuals within lineage structures to consolidate and concentrate loyalties within household units where production, consumption and reproduction activities intersected. The forces contributing to this trajectory were primarily external. The imposition of hut and poll taxes entailed identifying a 'head of household' as the taxpayer; expanding religious conversion to Christianity encouraged the strengthening of more insular household relations; and the growing cash economy led to increased fixed and moveable property ownership of individuals and households compared with larger collective units. Such household relations intersected rather than displaced lineage structures and the various cross-cutting ties created by numerous function-based associations, such as dance and cult groups and production teams.

Gender and age had been the primary basis of economic stratification and labour recruitment in pre-colonial, non-slave society. Thus, women and youth were at the service of male elders in both matrilineal and patrilineal societies. Matrilineal societies tended to be found in more sparsely populated, cattle-less areas, which retained their womenfolk's childbearing capacity *in situ*. As population density and wealth accumulation became more pronounced, women's labour power and fertility became negotiable in exchange for cattle or other forms of moveable property. Islam and Christianity, both based on patriarchal value structures, strengthened patrilineal principles of social organization, causing many matrilineal societies to take on a more patrilineal character (Swantz 1985). Polygamy, on the other hand, proved to be a more formidable foe to Christianity, being a well established form of labour recruitment for male heads of households whose economic success, particularly in peasant cash cropping, depended on expansion of the household labour force.

Polygamy and brideprice payments were sources of great tension between male elders and youth (Isaacman 1993). The polygamous practices of affluent men reduced the supply of marriageable women for young men, forcing the latter to postpone marriage indefinitely. Meanwhile, in many areas, particularly in successful peasant cash crop-producing areas, brideprice payments were escalating. Young men's delayed marriage was reinforced by brideprice systems involving the exchange of cattle for women, in which young men were dependent on their fathers for access to sufficient cattle in order to marry. It was only as cash replaced cattle as a form of payment that young men, particularly those involved in labour migration with access to cash, gained greater leverage in determining when they could marry (Wilson 1977).

Consolidating Peasantries, 1945–80

Awakening political consciousness

World War II marked a watershed in African peasant formation. Unlike World War I, there were no battles waged in sub-Saharan Africa but, as colonies of European powers at war, African economies, particularly those subject to British rule, were forced to restructure and produce 'essential commodities' for the war effort. Peasants experienced conflicting demands as they were pressured to produce particular crops within household production units at the same time as male peasant labour power was being recruited for military service abroad or for domestic plantation and mine work. Most colonial governments operated with skeletal staffs, as European personnel enlisted for the military or were recalled to their respective motherlands. Native authorities were given more rein over increasingly feminized rural communities, suffering severe internal labour shortfalls. Both rural and urban food security became problematic in many colonies as the impact of bad weather combined with rising food demand, associated with rapid urbanization, and declining supply due to labour depletion in peasant food production.

This was a period of widespread agricultural marketing reform. In line with developments in the European powers themselves, state regulation of national food supply was initiated in the form of food marketing boards. Marketing boards to facilitate quality control and crop exports had already been formed for many peasant export commodities in the preceding decades. Food marketing controls, particularly the dual pricing systems which gave African peasants lower prices than those pertaining to 'capitalized' European settler farmers, took on new significance in this period. The racial divides between black, brown and white populations became all the more apparent with this sudden restructuring of colonial economies. As more Africans moved to urban areas, where the racial differences in standards of living were starkly evident, resentments began to simmer. After the war, the return of African troops who had encountered the nationalist movements of south and south-east Asia, meant that the situation was ripe for fundamental change in towns and in the countryside.

Isaacman (1993) argues that African peasant struggles throughout the colonial period were primarily characterized by covert resistance and non-co-operation, 'everyday struggles' to evade tax and increased labour demands from enforced peasant commodity production. It is only when faced with threats to basic peasant subsistence, in the form of land seizure, extortionate taxes or labour demands, that these subtle acts of sabotage give way to overt peasant insurgency. African nationalists, well aware of the need for mass support, devised ways of channelling the accretion of peasants' dislike of colonial rule into popular clamour for national independence. The spread of the African co-operative movement after World War II is illustrative.

The African co-operative movement was fuelled by peasants' growing awareness of price differentials and margins for their crops. In many instances, it was a direct attempt to wrest produce marketing, especially of export crops, away from non-African traders. The charge of underpricing peasants' produce was a rallying cry directed at non-African traders' use of various market ploys to increase profit, such as underweighing with faulty scales, and 'scissors pricing' by which traders charged peasants high prices for consumer goods relative to the prices they offered for peasant-produced crops.

The initial impetus for the spread of co-operatives was economic but, as the movement expanded, its political character gained ascendance. In many ways it served to undermine the power of the native authorities whose gerontocratic leadership was inadvertently challenged by younger men with less parochial outlooks. These were the sons of peasants who had received some primary, or even secondary, education and achieved economic success as peasant cash-crop producers. Frequently, these embryonic élites extended their efforts beyond farming to trade and transport, gaining an economic foothold in a regional town as well as in the countryside. Their business interests pitted them against the formidable strength of the already well established non-native traders. Not surprisingly, these men sought leadership positions within the co-operative movement. Unlike chiefs, who depended on magico-religious claims to legitimize their leadership, they were the elected representatives of their peasant communities, enjoying a local 'big-man status', with the patron–client relations attached to such positions. Despite their local character, they were the natural allies of urban-based African nationalists who needed mechanisms for mass mobilization of the rural peasantries (Bryceson 1990).

Not all nationalist movements coalesced around peasant marketing co-operatives; others were more urban-focused. What is striking about African nationalist struggles continentally is how quickly they developed over the course of the 1950s, and how rapidly their aspirations were achieved. Ghana in the late 1950s was followed in the 1960s by an avalanche of countries gaining independence from Belgian, British and French colonialists. In most of the remaining countries the quest for independence from colonial rule evolved into a protracted, often violent struggle. This was particularly the case in those countries under Portuguese rule or with large European settler populations (Zimbabwe) or extensive mineral wealth (Namibia, South Africa), where European colonial governments held out far longer against African nationalist demands. In most cases, the success of the nationalist cause ultimately depended on winning mass support from the rural peasantries. In some cases this involved mobilizing peasantries for guerilla warfare (Zimbabwe, Namibia, Guinea Bissau, Mozambique, Angola).

Much has recently been written about the yawning gap between African ruling élites and their peasant citizenries. As Buijtenhuijs illustrates in Chapter 6 of this volume, the relationship between African peasants and their political leaders is one of delicate balance and flux. Time and again it is the physical proximity of leaders and their face-to-face accountability to peasant producers which is decisive. The leadership that the peasantry gave birth to was no longer trusted once it moved to the nation's capital city. The peasantry remained largely parochial in outlook, often still subject to conservative, ethnic-bound local chiefs (see Chapter 5 of this volume). The single-party states that were established in many countries in the decade after national independence tended to marshal the support of their respective peasantries quite successfully, usually through pyramidal organizational structures that incorporated peasant leaders at village level.

Economic promise

In the 1950s, peasants' commodity prices increased after a decade-long trough. The inflationary effect of the Korean War and a world commodity price boom gave many African peasantries their first whiff of prosperity. Suddenly peasants could afford to buy radios, bicycles and corrugated iron roofing. Colonial bye-laws, which had forced peasants to grow certain crops, were now redundant as peasants eagerly sought to adopt new cash crops or expand their plantings of already established crops. Income generation extended beyond the target of paying one's taxes and bridewealth.

'Quasi-peasantries' began to disintegrate as plantations and settler farms responded to the worldwide drive for increased capitalization and mechanization. The demand for wage labourers in large-scale agriculture slumped. Colonial officials, mindful of international criticism of the exploitative nature of the bachelor wage system, attempted to 'stabilize the workforce' by replacing male circular migration with permanent employment and a 'family wage' sufficient to cover the costs of residence of an entire domestic unit close by the labourer's place of work. These steps reinforced the capitalists' downsizing strategy, leading to drastic reductions in the total numbers of Africans employed in estate agriculture.

The contraction of the rural labour market was offset by the emerging profitability of peasant agriculture. Many colonial governments, conscious of nationalist pressures, made efforts to upgrade peasant agriculture technically by investing in better marketing facilities, researching improved inputs, improving rural transport, and expanding educational opportunities and health care in rural areas. At independence, these measures had not advanced very far and it was left to the post-colonial governments to 'develop' the rural areas. Many plunged into peasant agricultural 'modernization' with missionary zeal, as Raikes describes in Chapter 3 of this volume. Agricultural research extension programmes developed input packages for peasant smallholders that erred on the side of blanket recommendations and patronising disregard for age-old farming practices, such as intercropping and agricultural plot fragmentation.

In most non-mineral exporting post-colonial African nations, peasant agriculture became the key growth sector during the 1960s. What large-scale trade and industry existed at the time of independence was usually in the hands of non-Africans. African policy-makers, keen to effect Africanization of the economy as rapidly as possible, concentrated on the sector that was overwhelmingly African. Having played such a pivotal role in the achievement of political independence, newly formed African governments were highly responsive to their peasant constituencies. Most government leaders had themselves been born in peasant villages. Peasants' sensitivities were incorporated in tax reform: hut and poll taxes, so deeply associated with colonial overlordship, were largely abolished. Welfare issues came to the fore: food security became a *sine qua non* of post-colonial government policy and emphasis was placed on investments in rural water supply, health and educational facilities.

This orientation had several implications for the role of the state in national economies. Despite improved world market prices for peasant commodities, the peasant production base could not generate the revenues needed to finance such improvements, nor would the market benevolently provision them. The agricultural modernization effort had to be subsidized. The African state, in conjunction with foreign donor contributions, took the lead. State intervention expanded exponentially in the 1960s and early 1970s.

Modernizing peasant agriculture meant subsidizing it in the form of lowered input prices, pan-territorial producer pricing, and lower consumer goods prices. Crop marketing through national crop-marketing boards and decentralized regional and village co-operative structures proved to be increasingly unwieldy. Mismanagement and peculation, associated with local-level patron–client relations within the marketing co-operatives, bloated marketing margins. In the late 1960s many post-colonial governments replaced such institutional structures with parastatal marketing agencies centrally controlled from the capital city.

The principle of national state control reached its apogee in those African countries that adopted ideologies of socialist development, such as Tanzania, Ethiopia and Congo. In Ethiopia's densely populated highlands, land reform became the central rationale for state intervention, whereas in Tanzania it was the least populated rural areas which were the target of government intervention. Here the scattered populations were 'villagized' into rural populations of a critical mass to facilitate the provisioning of rural productive and social services.

From the spectrum of economic development policies pursued by African governments during the early post-colonial years, raising peasant agricultural output stands out. As Raikes argues in Chapter 3 of this volume, this aim was obstructed by the internal contradictions of modernization, notably the costs of the monopoly institutions required to implement (and subsidize) it. Government efforts to capitalize peasant agriculture were also fundamentally flawed by the total dismissal of peasants' knowledge of farming as backward. At the same time, alternative forms of government taxation of peasants were implemented. Peasant produce marketing became increasingly regulated by the state and subjected to various forms of indirect taxation that reduced producer price levels relative to prevailing world market prices.

Rising tax revenues were required for a wide array of purposes which varied in priority depending on government policy orientation. These included (i) the provisioning of social services in the fields of education and health for urban and rural areas to meet the national population's expectations of a rising standard of living; (ii) the expense of urban infrastructure building; and (iii) the drive for economic development through industrialization. All three goals distinguished the post-colonial from the colonial states that preceded them, but it was the latter that most encapsulated the post-colonial state's vision of itself and its development mission. In line with economic thinking of the time, industrialization was viewed as the means by which African nations and their populations would 'catch up' with their former colonial masters and trading partners, the 'developed world'. It was a corollary of this that industrial investment would involve a certain amount of value extraction from the existing foundation of national production, namely the peasantry.

The early independence years spanning the 1960s and early 1970s saw an increase in peasant export-crop production. In some cases, capital and labour investments did result in increasing crop yields. Even more apparent, however, was the expansion of acreage in peasant cash-crop production as increasing numbers of African peasant farmers were incorporated into the cash nexus.

Socio-economic mobility within and beyond African peasantries

African peasants experienced their heyday during these early independence years, with increased agricultural output, rising literacy rates, declining infant mortality, and rapid population growth. Nonetheless, this success generated its own tensions along existing fracture lines of region, age and gender, as well as creating new class fissures.

Peasant export production was not a success everywhere. Much depended on finding a remunerative crop suitable for specific climatic zones that had adequate transport infrastructure. Those areas, usually remote semi-arid areas, which failed to find the right crop fell back in their countries' regional league tables of per capita income and welfare indicators, and sometimes became sources of ethnic tension. Geographically concentrated virtuous cycles of development became ever more prominent as local populations in rural areas with strong cash-crop production invested in the education of their offspring. Sons of peasants in these areas gained positions in the regional and national government bureaucracies, while those in more economically stagnant rural areas faced meagre prospects, be it in cash cropping or non-agricultural employment.

The gender divide was another source of tension. Within the hoe-based peasant societies that dominate sub-Saharan Africa, gender divisions of labour tend to accord women a central role in food production (Bryceson 1995). Muslim-dominated areas where female purdah is practised provide revealing contrasts to the general pattern, as Meagher demonstrates in Chapter 4 of this volume. In the former, cash cropping for sale to the world market expanded primarily on the basis of the notion that export crops belonged to men. This clouded the fact that women, as subordinates to the male household head, were normally co-opted as labourers for the cultivation and harvesting of the crop. It was only at the stage of marketing of household output that men exclusively took over. There is a vast literature on the intensification of African peasant women's working day, their marginalization from agricultural cash earnings, and the ways and means with which they coped (Boserup 1970; Bukh 1979; Dey 1981).

The impact of increasing peasant cash crops on age stratification is difficult to discern. As European-owned plantations and settler farming waned in the face of African governments' policy preference for peasant farming, young African men's rural wage labour options contracted. However, unlike women, they were more strategically placed to seize the fruits of independence. Male elder authority had been dealt a heavy blow with the diminution of chieftaincy systems. Their control of young men's productive capacities through the manipulation of brideprice systems became ever more shaky as brideprice payments became progressively monetarized. Several of the most fertile parts of rural Africa experienced the departure of European farmers. These factors combined to enhance the possibility of young men obtaining a wife and land at an earlier age than had hitherto been the case. In this way, the ranks of cash crop-producing male peasants swelled, further boosted by rising rural fertility rates related to the declining monopoly of older polygamous men on marriageable women.

In many areas of sub-Saharan Africa, particularly the most as well as the least ecologically favoured regions, population densities reached critical levels. Agricultural extension services and the peasants' own efforts to intensify production often could not keep up with the pressure of increasing numbers of people occupying the land. In some areas there were signs of soil degradation. Lineage principles of land inheritance became difficult to reconcile with the reality of contracting land availability, and notions of individual land ownership and land markets surfaced. Conflicting claims and confusion over tribal usufruct and community ownership rights increasingly arose in many peasant communities. The existing blend of formal and informal controls exercised by post-colonial officialdom could not always harmonize differences. Local peasantries often developed informal allocative procedures, which did not strictly accord with 'traditional' customary or modern statutory laws. Contrary to voiced fears, where land titles were introduced (e.g. the Swynnerton Plan of Kenya), rapid economic differentiation and landlessness did not necessarily ensue.

Justification for land claims based on usufruct, the siting of ancestral graves or group membership were still in evidence (Shipton 1992). African lineage-cum-extended families continued to operate as mutual support networks in which the needs of less well endowed relations for accommodation and subsistence could be met in exchange for labour contributions, softening the anticipated consequences of haves and have-nots in African rural societies.

Land constraints and post-colonial governments' rural educational programmes contributed to the increasing willingness of peasant farmers to invest in the education of their children. This had the effect of reducing children's labour input into peasant agriculture both on an immediate day-to-day basis and in the long term, raising the probability that their future working lives would not be spent in peasant agriculture. At first, such investments were primarily focused on male offspring, but over time girls were afforded educational opportunities by some African governments, often prompted by western donors. The introduction of family wage policies after independence gave women a greater chance to migrate from their rural homes. In towns, they gained a foothold in the formal labour force enabling them, like their brothers, to remit income to their rural families. Rural-based parents began to realize returns on the educational investments they had made for their offspring and often encouraged both sons and daughters to migrate in the hopes of future pay-offs (Bryceson 1980b).

In the first decade after independence, many regional peasantries developed dense relational ties with urban-based members of their extended families. Exchanges of goods and services between urban and rural family members were common, both providing mutual support and shifting the consumption patterns and material expectations of African peasantries away from household and community self-sufficiency.

By the early 1970s urban migration rates reached historically unprecedented levels. The first generation of educated youth had enjoyed enormous employment opportunities, to say nothing of their fortuitous inheritance of the reigns of power from the colonial state. Succeeding generations were not so lucky. Their arrival in Africa's burgeoning capital cities exerted enormous urban infrastructural and goods supply pressures. Failing to find employment in the government bureaucracy or embryonic industries, they formed Africa's 'informal sector'. First identified in Kenya by the International Labour Office (ILO 1972), this vaguely defined informal sector mushroomed throughout urban Africa, composed of a bewildering array of different income-generating activities, most of which were unskilled, low-income, makeshift, usually untaxed and sometimes bordering on illegality. These first-generation urban dwellers, the sons and daughters of Africa's rural peasantries, formed the bottom layer of this congealing urban class structure.

Disintegrating Peasantries, 1980–2000

Buckling economic pressures

The euphoria of national independence lasted little more than a decade. Economic indicators of most African countries began falling in the mid-1970s. Interestingly, blame for this state of affairs was placed on the new African urban ruling class. They were seen as pursuing 'urban bias' through policies and institutions, founded on the systematic underpricing of peasant production and value transfers to the urban sector for expensive industrialization efforts and urban consumption levels far in excess of peasants' (Bates 1981). There was nothing new in the notion that urban-based élites were effecting value transfers from rural to urban areas – peasants were by definition subject to such extractive processes. However, it was now argued that such transfers had reached counter-productive proportions and posed disincentives to peasant production. Strongly identified with mismanagement and corruption, African urban élites were seen to be creaming off the surplus for private consumption. Their stewardship of the continent's peasant populations was under fire.

Disillusionment with African ruling elites has to be understood against the background of world market realignments. The meteoric rise in international oil prices in 1973–74 led to economic trauma just at a time when many African governments had assumed virtually full responsibility for their respective national economies and were involved in massive economic experimentation. A subsequent oil price hike in 1979 posed severe problems for the oil-importing countries of sub-Saharan Africa. The continent was heavily biased to road rather than rail transport. In economies based on the agricultural output of peasant cash-crop producers, scattered over vast tracts of land and producing only small amounts of surplus for sale, transport accounted for a large proportion of the agricultural products' total costs at urban centres of food demand and ports for export crop shipment.

High transport costs were also embedded in the expensive crop input improvement packages which African governments increasingly subsidized through deficit financing and over-valuing their national currencies. By the 1980s, after only a few years of implementing crop input programmes, African governments found themselves swamped in debt and forced to appeal to the International Monetary Fund (IMF) and World Bank for help. From this point on, policies and relations with their respective peasant populations were mediated by international capital.

Nigeria, as a major oil-exporting country, followed a different path, as Meagher documents in Chapter 4 of this volume. Awash with the windfall gain of high oil prices, the Nigerian state embarked on a massive spending spree, involving the importation of infrastructural and consumer goods that were primarily used by Nigeria's urbanites. Not surprisingly, rural peasants were attracted to urban areas, and urban growth sky-rocketed in the late 1970s and early 1980s. Peasants' food[5] and cash crop production stagnated. The domestic market for their produce disintegrated as the country's consumption of local staple foods was increasingly undermined by cheap food imports, and the government and traders lost interest in the marketing of peasant cash crops given the far higher returns from the oil export–foreign import economy. In the mid-1980s, when oil price fluctuations were no longer so favourable and Nigerian power politics fanned investor uncertainty, the bubble burst and Nigerian peasants were left with a weak agrarian base and unremunerative urban migration prospects. The Nigerian government implemented a structural adjustment programme that had the contradictory and extremely exceptional twist of banning foreign staple food imports. Thus the more affluent Nigerian peasant farmers successfully moved into grain farming without the threat of foreign competition, under the banner of structural adjustment.

The almost universal implementation of IMF- and World Bank-sponsored structural adjustment programmes in African countries from the mid-1980s, followed by economic liberalization and democratization reforms in the 1990s, caused marked change in the economic and social viability of African peasantries generally. The removal of fertilizer and seed subsidies and government-regulated pan-territorial food pricing undermined peasant production of many food and cash crops, especially in areas with high transport costs. Meanwhile consumer goods inflation and cutbacks in public funding for hospitals, schools and other social services increased peasants' cash needs as they were squeezed between declining agricultural returns and increasing costs of basic needs. This environment of uncertainty induced farmers to search for new, more remunerative activities outside agriculture.

Accelerated growth in the non-farm portion of rural household income coincided with the implementation of structural adjustment (Bryceson 1996). Such income diversification has been conceptualized by peasants and economic analysts as a form of risk management that seeks to achieve a household economic activity portfolio with low covariate risk between activities. By engaging in a range of agricultural and non-agricultural income-earning activities throughout the year, or juggling more than one activity at any one time, peasant household members attempt to compensate for the high risks associated with agricultural price decline, output fluctuations and lack of access to land or credit. In other words, they seek to reduce risks and achieve a continuous earning pattern which covers their day-to-day consumption needs.

Meagher's chapter on northern Nigeria reveals that the process of rural income diversification can fuel the process of rural economic differentiation. Similar patterns are emerging elsewhere. Capital-rich diversifying households, operating on economies of scale in agriculture, can weather the price squeeze and buy the fertilizers necessary to sustain their yields. Through cross-investments between agriculture and non-agriculture, these households manage to expand their activity portfolio and successfully accumulate. Their non-agricultural investments are directed at the higher income-earning activities that require more capital to initiate. By contrast, the majority of peasant households can no longer afford to apply the recommended level of inputs, leading them to experience declining yields. They are generally unable to pursue non-agricultural activities other than those with low entry capital requirements. These are over-subscribed, highly competitive and poorly remunerated.

Implemented in the name of addressing rural–urban bias and creating market conditions for peasant farmers to achieve better prices for their agricultural commodities, structural adjustment and economic liberalization have in fact coincided with sharpened economic differentiation within African peasantries and a movement away from peasant agriculture. As African government controls on land and labour markets are lifted, the classic Marxist paradigm of primitive accumulation gains relevance. Poor peasants' access to land weakens and they are forced into wage labour or petty trade offering exceptionally low returns. Retaining a foothold in subsistence agriculture for as long as they can, they are in effect displaced peasant farmers with no clear sense of direction.

Unravelling social fabrics and political designs

What stands out in the period spanning 1980–2000 is the blurring of social constructs surrounding African peasant life. The major oppositional relationships arising from colonial and post-colonial conceptions of peasant reality become indeterminate and highly contestable. The dichotomies of rural and urban, male and female, elder and youth are challenged by economic exigency as revealed by recent village case studies (Iliya 1998, Madulu 1998, Mung'ong'o 1998, Bank 1999).

The rural–urban dichotomy was central to international financial institutions' rationale for implementing structural adjustment. Urban areas were viewed as privileged havens that existed at the expense of rural peasant areas. As this debate was going on, the relative economic advantages of urban dwellers in most African countries was dissipating under the duress of the international oil crisis. Real incomes of urban formal-sector salaries were sliding into ever smaller fractions of the amount needed to cover the earner's monthly household needs (Bryceson 1993). Income diversification tendencies started in urban areas as formal sector employees gravitated to informal sector pursuits to compensate for the decline in their official earnings. Urban agriculture became a salient feature of most African cities, and closer exchange ties between urban and rural wings of extended families came to the fore as urban dwellers sought more reliable and cheaper supplies of staple foodstuffs from rural relations during the hard times.

Standards of living of rural and urban areas levelled downwards as urban dwellers fell back on agrarian ways and means of making ends meet.

Some urban survival strategies successfully crossed the line to become accumulating strategies. Meanwhile, farmers in rural areas, feeling the effect of subsidy removal, diversified into non-agricultural activities. Income diversification became the *sine qua non* of urban and rural areas. Such diversification required greater mobility to seize business opportunities, especially in trade. Circular migration re-emerged, not in the sense of one to two year contracts away from rural home areas as had prevailed in the bachelor wage system of the quasi-peasantries of old, but in the form of a growing number of rural people commuting back and forth between the city and village. No longer strictly classified as rural or urban residents, they are perhaps best described as a 'neither-here-nor-there' population, living testimony to the blurring of rural and urban categorizations.

Gender differences, so much a part of African peasant conceptions of a 'natural order', and embedded in colonial and post-colonial policies, remarkably have been muted as long-established, ideologically safeguarded household divisions of labour came under severe pressure during the 1980s and 1990s (Mbilinyi 1997, Iliya 1998). The cash crisis in peasant household units forced virtually all able-bodied adults to seek different forms of income-earning. Many peasant women, particularly in East and Southern Africa, hitherto excluded from handling the money derived from cash-cropping and paid work of any description outside the home, have suddenly been projected into the exigencies of finding an income to cover some of their households' basic cash needs. Interestingly they often succeeded while their husbands failed. Despite heavy schedules of domestic labour, they have shown willingness to take on a broader range of work, often of low status and remuneration, in contrast to many men who still cling to the production of unremunerative cash crops. Peasant women often find themselves in the position of having cash to spend on household necessities while their men go empty-handed. Access to capital for business development has been facilitated by rotating credit schemes which build on women's existing strong solidarity networks. Meagher's Hausa case study in Chapter 4 of this volume demonstrates the interactional effects of gender and class. The combined influence of the structural adjustment programme and Hausa women's seclusion practices severely limited poor women's range of involvement in non-farm activities at the same time as pressure increased for them to contribute cash to meet household consumption needs. More affluent women, with capital to invest in non-farm activities and hire labour, were not in such a disadvantaged position.

In non-purdah areas, the economic tilting of gender roles has had far-reaching implications for male patriarchy. With their cash earnings, women are in a position to decide on its disposal, particularly where the man fails to live up to his traditional duties to meet the bulk of household monetary expenses. Tensions between the sexes are unavoidable. Many men, while admitting the necessity of their wives' earnings for household welfare, nonetheless are resentful. Sometimes men have turned to alcohol or wife-beating, or have sought escape by marrying another wife. Female resentment has surfaced as well. Despite peasant women's enhanced cash-earning role, they are still expected to perform all the housework. Their husbands do not volunteer to help with childcare or the arduous tasks of African domestic life, namely water and firewood collection, cooking and cleaning.

Increasingly peasant women no longer see themselves as economic dependants, but as economic supporters with dependants, and some, particularly younger women, are beginning to desire fewer children. The strong pro-natalist orientation that placed such high value on children as a source of labour in African peasant production is losing sway over women's fertility decisions. Countries such as Kenya and Zimbabwe, which had experienced the world's highest recorded birth rates, have seen a turnaround (Lockwood 1995). The AIDS epidemic that began to adversely affect rural Africa in the 1990s has given further impetus to changing attitudes towards fertility.

Generational change has taken very immediate forms. Rural youth, responding to the decline in dependency on male heads, are assuming greater responsibility for their own economic well-being, often at younger and younger ages. Decision-making power over earnings relates to the emergence of a youth subculture, which is more in tune with life in the urban capital or western society generally than with local agrarian norms. Young men in particular are adopting a different set of values, reflected in their expenditure on clothes and music, to those of saving for bridewealth payments or land and cattle purchase. They tend to be the most mobile segment of the village population, often involved in circular migration between their village and urban areas. Their remittance patterns are increasingly subject to criticism from their elders, who expect or rather hope to benefit materially from their offspring's travels. On the other hand many parents, especially those in areas of land pressure, are sanguine, seeing the change as an outcome of their own failure to leave their sons sufficient land to farm on a viable basis (Mwamfupe 1998). Certainly, the inheritance factor figures in village youth's changing career expectations. No longer assuming they will become farmers like their parents, even when lacking the skills or education needed to move into the labour market, youth have gravitated to non-agricultural income diversification, especially petty trade.

With expectations of a better, more remunerative life than that experienced by their farming parents, youth's generally paltry earnings from non-agricultural activities stand in stark contrast to the market liberalization and democratization hype accompanying structural adjustment programmes. The positive pull factor from agriculture that income diversification represents to youth is being transposed into a negative push factor, fuelling their resentment, and in a significant number of cases sowing the seeds of political discontent.

Youthful disillusionment has emerged amidst major African government political restructuring led by the IMF and the World Bank and enforced by loan conditionality of a united front of international bilateral and multilateral donor agencies. In their bid to rid the continent of 'rent seeking', multi-party democracy was quickly introduced into one African country after another. As Mamdani argues in Chapter 5 of this volume, this often had a destabilizing rather than a democratic effect on national politics. New parties proliferated, bereft of substantive issues, in a climate where IMF/World Bank conditionality gave no scope for African policy-makers and politicians to voice independent policy initiatives. In the glare of the international media and the donor country's election monitors, party activists mobilized support by actively or inadvertently fanning the old ethnic divides of colonial indirect rule. Such ethnic identities span rural and urban areas, and offer easy rationalizations for the widening economic gulfs between different groups of people under economic liberalization. In peasant communities, the divides have become more apparent as land and labour markets have become more pronounced. 'Outsiders' from other ethnic groups are entering rural areas and acquiring land titles, and operating commercial operations on the basis of hired labour. Ethnic-based 'haves' and 'have-nots' are rapidly congealing.

In this unstable climate, political tensions can and sometimes do break into civil disturbances and even war. Rwanda provides the most tragic example. With the highest rural population densities in Africa and extremely limited off-farm opportunities (von Braun et al. 1991), ethnic genocide led to the death of more than a million people, mostly peasants. The list of civil wars in sub-Saharan African countries during the late 1980s and 1990s has mounted: Angola, Burundi, Congo, Zaire, Liberia, Sierra Leone, Guinea Bissau, Chad, Sudan and Somalia. Other countries, such as Cameroon and Kenya, have experienced rising levels of ethnic tension. It is pertinent to note that these violent conflicts often originate in peasant rural areas – peasants bear the brunt of the fighting. Over protracted periods of time, they have endured restricted movement to their fields to farm, pillaging and fear of rape and torture. The perpetrators are mainly bands of young men, most from peasant backgrounds. As Buijtenhuijs (Chapter 6 of this volume) observes, unlike the liberation freedom fighters of the 1960s, few have a strong ideological motivation for fighting. In effect, being a soldier offers an alternative livelihood to farming and proves to be highly lucrative when combined with looting and living off local peasantries.

Famine is a concomitant of war. The widespread famines which have reached world headlines over the past decade have almost all been associated with war zones or civil strife, notably those occurring in Sudan,

Somalia and Rwanda. African peasantries are both literally and figuratively dying in these instances. The sheer magnitude of the relief effort has prompted some western donors to rethink their donor strategies putting more emphasis on conflict resolution and humanitarian relief, often at the expense of economic development assistance (de Waal 1997). Increasingly, western donor attitudes are characterized by the view that African nations must be left to find their own way. Whatever way this is, all the signs seem to indicate that peasant societies and economies will face further marginalization.

From Labour Shortage to Labour Glut: African Peasant Redundancy in the Global Economy

It has been argued in the Introduction to this volume that peasantries represent a dynamic labour process that is bounded by the defining criteria of class status and family units combining subsistence and commodity production. From the late nineteenth century, colonial states took measures to encourage the growth of peasantries and their production of what were to become the continent's major export crops, namely coffee, cocoa, tea, groundnuts and cotton. Post-colonial governments in the 1960s, backed up by western donor funding, elaborated this strategy by implementing development programmes which aimed materially to improve peasant agricultural output and living standards. However, since the mid-1970s African peasantries have faced declining farming prospects. Accelerated class differentiation within and outside the peasantry have acted as an erosive force on their economic coherence. Associated social pressures have blurred the internal structure of African peasant families, altering long-standing gender and generational roles. In the process, peasant communities have become far more open to external cultural and political influences, some with strong destabilizing tendencies.

Currently, as agri-business and intense competition engulf world agriculture, international markets increasingly bypass the commodities produced by African peasantries. Furthermore, the peasant labour reserve that was on tap for colonial commerce and industry is no longer of strategic utility to investors. African peasant labour is an anachronism and even a nuisance in the face of the industrialized countries' own politically unacceptable rates of unemployment. In the non-industrialized countries of sub-Saharan Africa, peasants continue to produce food to feed the burgeoning urban towns, but only just. They frequently cannot compete with the far cheaper grain imports which economic liberalization policies have introduced.

African peasant response is, as always, dynamic. As active agents in the de-agrarianization process, they are seeking alternative forms of livelihood to farming. This involves both distress and discovery. Certainly, more sympathetic and sensitive African government and donor policies could facilitate the balance tipping in favour of the latter. In the meantime, peasant community identities and increasingly dispersed social networks continue to inform the economic, political and cultural destiny of the African continent.

Notes

1. The slave trade selectively seized people of the economically active ages between 15 and 30. Two-thirds of the slaves seized for the Atlantic slave trade were men, whereas the trans-Saharan slave trade involved more women (Hopkins 1973; Inikori 1997).
2. South Africa to Bulawayo in 1897, Mombasa to Lake Victoria in 1901, Senegal to Niger in 1905, Lagos to Kano in 1912 and Dar es Salaam to Lake Tanganiyka in 1914 (Iliffe 1995: 204).
3. Another perspective is provided by Fallers (1961) who expressed reservations about the degree of peasantization in Africa. Fallers argues that lack of cultural differentiation between 'high' and 'folk' cultures, arising from the relative absence of literary religious traditions and rural–urban dichotomies, resulted in 'proto-peasantries' rather than full peasantries.
4. African peasant farming has historically been very land-extensive, raising the question of how 'sedentary' it is. It is significant to note that some analysts classify African pastoralists as 'peasants' (Painter 1997), and stress that the rural population of the arid Sahelian zone had to be very geographically mobile as well as occupationally flexible in combining farming, pastoralist and craft pursuits to sustain their livelihood. In this book, we have opted, in accordance with commonly held views, to restrict the term 'peasantry' to those who are 'farmers', pursuing plant husbandry in a bounded zone, though not necessarily on specific plots of land passed down from generation to generation. Thus nomadic herders are excluded from the definition. Nonetheless, it must be recognized that in many semi-arid areas, the boundaries between peasant farmers and nomadic herders can be blurred.
5. Nonetheless, grain farming in northern Nigeria responded positively to the surge in demand arising from the Sahelian famine in Niger and Chad as well as government fertilizer subsidy schemes. Cross-border trade during the late 1970s and early 1980s created a stratum of medium- and large-scale grain farmers (Meagher 1993).

References

Allan, W. (1965) *The African Husbandman*, Oliver & Boyd, Edinburgh.

Andah, B. (1993) 'Identifying early farming traditions of West Africa', in T. Shaw, P. Sinclair, B. Andah and A. Okpoko (eds) *The Archaeology of Africa: Food, Metals and Towns*, Routledge, London.

Bank, L. (1999) 'No visible means of subsistence: rural livelihoods, gender and deagrarianization in the Eastern Cape, S. Africa', *De-Agrarianisation and Rural Employment Programme Working Paper*, Afrika-Studiecentrum, Leiden and Institute of Social and Economic Research, Grahamstown.

Bates, R. (1981) *Markets and States in Tropical Africa: The Political Basis of Agricultural Policies*, University of California Press, Berkeley.
Boserup, E. (1970) *Women's Role in Economic Development*, George Allen & Unwin, London.
Brett, E.A. (1973) *Colonialism and Underdevelopment in East Africa*, Heinemann, London.
Bryceson, D.F. (1980a) 'Changes in peasant food production and food supply in relation to the historical development of commodity production in pre-colonial and colonial Tanganyika', *Journal of Peasant Studies*, 7(3): 281–311.
Bryceson, D.F. (1980b) 'The proletarianization of women in Tanzania', *Review of African Political Economy*, No. 17, 4–27.
Bryceson, D.F. (1990) *Food Insecurity and the Social Division of Labour in Tanzania, 1919–1985*, Macmillan, London.
Bryceson, D.F. (1993) *Liberalising Tanzania's Food Trade*, James Currey, Oxford.
Bryceson, D.F. (1995) *Women Wielding the Hoe: Lessons from Rural Africa for Feminist Theory and Development Practice*, Berg, Oxford.
Bryceson, D.F. (1996) 'Deagrarianization and rural employment in sub-Saharan Africa: a sectoral perspective', *World Development*, 24(1): 97–111.
Bukh, J. (1979) *The Village Woman in Ghana*, Scandinavian Institute of African Studies, Uppsala.
de Waal, A. (1997) *Famine Crimes: Politics and the Disaster Relief Industry in Africa*, James Currey, Oxford.
Dey, J. (1981) 'Gambian women: unequal partners in rice development projects?', in N. Nelson (ed.) *African Women in the Development Process*, Frank Cass, London, pp. 109–22.
Fallers, L.A. (1961) 'Are African cultivators to be called "peasants"?', *Current Anthropology*, 2(2): 108–10.
Hopkins, A. (1973) *An Economic History of West Africa*, Longman, London.
Iliffe, J. (1995) *Africans: Story of a Continent*, Cambridge University Press, Cambridge.
Iliya, M. (1998) 'Income diversification in the semi-arid zone of Nigeria', paper presented at the Workshop on Income Diversification in Nigeria, Centre for Research and Documentation, Kano, September.
ILO (1972) *Employment, Incomes and Equality: A Strategy for Increasing Productive Employment in Kenya*, International Labour Office, Geneva.
Inikori, J.E. (1997) 'Slave trade: western Africa' in J. Middleton (ed.) *Encyclopedia of Africa South of the Sahara*, Charles Scribner's Sons, New York, pp. 88–94.
Isaacman, A.F. (1993) 'Peasants and rural social protest in Africa', in F. Cooper, F.E. Mallon, S.J. Stern, A.F. Isaacman and W. Roseberry (eds) *Confronting Historical Paradigms: Peasant Labor and the Capitalist World System in Africa and Latin America*, University of Wisconsin Press, Madison.

Klein, M. (1980) *Peasants in Africa: Historical and Contemporary Perspectives*, Sage, Beverly Hills.
Kuczynski, R.R. (1948–53) *Demographic Survey of the British Colonial Empire*, Oxford University Press, Oxford.
Lockwood, M. (1995) 'Development policy and the African demographic transition: issues and questions', *Journal of International Development*, 7(1): 1–23.
Madulu, N.F. (1998) *Changing Lifestyles in Farming Societies of Sukumaland*, De-Agrarianisation and Rural Employment Programme Working Paper, Afrika-Studiecentrum, Leiden and Institute of Resource Assessment, Dar es Salaam.
Mamdani, M. (1996) *Citizen and Subject*, Princeton University Press, Princeton.
Mbilinyi, M. (1989) 'Women's resistance in "customary" marriage: Tanzania's runaway wives' in A. Zegeye and S. Ishemo (eds), *Forced Labour and Migration: Patterns of Movement within Africa*, Hans Zell, London, pp. 21–54.
Mbilinyi, M. (1997) 'The end of small-holder farming?', paper presented at the Tanzania Gender Network Programme Seminar, Dar es Salaam, August.
Meagher, K. (1993) *Nigeria, Granary of Niger?: The Implications of Cross-Border Trade for Food Security in Nigeria and Niger*, Integration through Markets in the Sub-Region, Niger–Nigeria Interaction, CILSS/Club du Sahel/Cinergie.
Mung'ong'o, C. (1998) *Coming Full Circle: Agriculture, Non-Farm Activities and the Resurgence of Out-Migration in Njombe District, Tanzania*, De-Agrarianisation and Rural Employment Programme Working Paper, Afrika-Studiecentrum, Leiden and Institute of Resource Assessment, Dar es Salaam, November.
Mwamfupe, D. (1998) *Village Land, Labour and Livelihoods in Rungwe and Kyela Districts, Tanzania*, De-Agrarianisation and Rural Employment Programme Working Paper, Afrika-Studiecentrum, Leiden and Institute of Resource Assessment, Dar es Salaam, November.
Painter, T.M. (1997) 'Peasants: western Africa', in J. Middleton (ed.) *Encyclopedia of Africa South of the Sahara*, Charles Scribner's Sons, New York, pp. 374–7.
Richards, A.I. (1939), *Land, Labour and Diet in Northern Rhodesia: An Economic Study of the Bemba Tribe*, Oxford University Press, Oxford.
Shipton, P. (1992) 'Debts and trespasses: land, mortgages, and the ancestors in western Kenya', *Africa*, 62(3): 358–88.
Sutton, J.E.G. (1997) 'Agriculture: Beginnings and Early Development', in J. Middleton (ed.) *Encyclopedia of Africa South of the Sahara*, Charles Scriber's Sons, New York, pp. 13–17.
Swantz, M.-L. (1985) *Women in Development: A Creative Role Denied*, C. Hurst & Co, London.
von Braun, J., de Haan, H. and Blanken, J. (1991) *Commercialization of Agriculture under Population Pressure: Effects on Production, Consumption and Nutrition in Rwanda*, Research Report No. 85, International Food Policy Research Institute, Washington, D.C.

Watts, M. (1983) *Silent Violence: Food, Famine and Peasantry in Northern Nigeria*, University of California Press, Berkeley.
Wilson, M. (1977) *For Men and Elders: Change in the Relations of Generations and of Men and Women among the Nyakyusa-Ngonde People, 1875–1971*, International African Institute, London.
Wolf, E.R. (1966) *Peasants*, Prentice-Hall, Englewood Cliffs, New Jersey.

3. Modernization and Adjustment in African Peasant Agriculture

PHILIP RAIKES

It is a commonplace that, within the Third World, sub-Saharan Africa has suffered the most severe impoverishment, deprivation and socio-political breakdown during the past two decades. Though this seems generally true, it depends in part on what this is taken to mean – something on which agreement is notoriously difficult to reach. Moreover, variation between countries and their regions is enormous, as between social groups and classes, age cohorts, genders and seasons.

Just as commonplace, but thoroughly deceptive, are statements that per capita food and agricultural production have declined steadily for the past two decades and that this derives from a combination of stagnant technology and all-too-dynamic population growth. Food production data for tropical Africa are too inaccurate and biased to be quoted with confidence, but it is less the empirical assertion than the over-simplified causality which misleads. No one could seriously doubt that rapid population growth is among the many problems facing tropical Africa or that productivity needs to increase faster. But to make this combination the basic or only cause of food insecurity is wrong.

This chapter looks at how structural adjustment in Africa has affected agricultural modernization, the general line of thinking which has underlain agricultural policy directed at smallholding peasants in Africa, and elsewhere, for the past half century or so. Although modernization ideology underlies most thinking on agriculture by international financial institutions (IFIs)[1] and donors, it makes demands for the development of a state and parastatal sector which are in conflict with the aims and requirements of adjustment. Internal inconsistency arises as structural adjustment implementation removes the conditions for modernization policies, while positing itself as a vehicle for modernizing peasant agriculture.

Trends in African Peasant Agriculture

In one sense there is no such thing as 'African agriculture'. Apart from differences in climate, soils and techniques of production which dwarf those experienced in Europe, agricultural sectors vary enormously in structural terms between and within different countries. In most countries, peasant smallholdings account for the bulk of production and typically include two-thirds or upwards of the total population, notably its poorest sections. However some African countries have agricultural sectors dominated by farms and ranches of up to several thousand hectares, often foreign-owned and usually at least as mechanized as 'northern' agriculture. Nonetheless, even in these areas, most of the rural population is normally composed of households living on very small patches of land.

Part of peasant production provides for household subsistence needs, but virtually all households are also involved with markets. Many cannot survive from own-farm agriculture, so family members also engage in wage labour, petty trading and artisanal activities to earn a living and spread risk. Risk-spreading also involves cultivating a network of kinship and other relations to improve access to resources and provide security for times of need. Such networks tend to be strongly patriarchal (though women often have their own separate networks), integrated into local politics and marked by patron–client linkages.

Markets abound but not 'the market', since most of them are affected by personal and patronage ties, not to mention political links, whether local or larger scale. Local politics in turn usually combine both 'traditional' authorities and 'modern' ones, like those of state bureaucracies, including agriculture. Obviously enough, the power balance between them varies enormously, as does the quality of relations, which can vary from rivalry to close complicity.

Most African rural societies are not particularly egalitarian, control over resources and political power being concentrated in a minority of households and their heads. Social differentiation is often less institutionalized and stable than in other parts of the world, but not necessarily less important. The impression of limited differentiation arises partly from the fact that the same extended family may contain the most powerful people in an area and the poorest, though these poor people may at least have superior access to loans or assistance in time of urgent need.

Men own or control most land and other resources, while women do much of the work, especially in the production and processing of food crops. While it is convenient to refer to the household as the basic productive and consumption unit, this can be misleading, as many households function as only partially linked sets of sub-units based on gender or age. There is usually some degree of labour specialization between men and women concerning both crops and tasks, while in some cases, groups of men or women from different households work together on a reciprocal or co-operative basis.

Population and Technology

A widely propagated myth about African agriculture is that it has been technologically static for decades, if not centuries, and that it is being left hopelessly behind by population growth and by the march of progress elsewhere. In fact, African farming techniques are everywhere in transition towards greater intensity, under pressure from population increase and from the expansion of cash-crop production and related accumulation of larger holdings. The intensity of technology tends to lag behind what is required, but invariably there has been change. Nonetheless, the incomes of the poorest peasants are falling and insecurity of food supply is rising. On average, land is more abundant in Africa than in other continents, but most Africans have only very small plots and an increasing number are landless.

A century ago, the vast majority of all rural households in Africa practised shifting cultivation, in which the soil was cultivated until fertility fell or weed growth increased too much then left until fertility recovered. When population density was low, this was an effective way of using household labour which, together with fire and simple hand tools, was by far the most important input into farming. Several crops were often inter-planted on the same plot, either simultaneously or in sequence, keeping the ground covered for as much of the year as possible to reduce the erosive impact of wind and rain, and make use of the complementary nutrient requirements of different crops.

Over large parts of tropical Africa, women did the major part of crop labour, while men (in the non-tsetse fly areas) concerned themselves with livestock. For the most part such households were scattered or grouped in small villages where there was quite limited exchange of produce or specialization. Artisanal products, including metal wares, were produced, but except in a few regional centres those who engaged in such production also produced much or most of their own food needs. Should this sound like an idyllic golden age, the impression is unintended and misleading. Such societies were subject to droughts and famines, outbreaks of disease and attacks from enemies. By no means least, huge swathes of the continent were subject to the ravages of the slave trade.

From the late nineteenth century, most of Africa was colonized by different European powers. Local ruling groups, from informal gatherings of village elders to royal courts, were profoundly changed in being subordinated to external rule. Almost all experienced a diminution in their capacity to ensure their subjects' food security in times of shortage – but also in their capacity to wage war. Most colonial regimes imposed requirements for men to work on colonial plantations or roads and railways, or made the cultivation of certain (usually export) crops compulsory. While the wages for such labour were almost invariably too low to provide full household subsistence, combined with household food production by women, they did sometimes allow accumulation of livestock or land.

Since the early years of the present century, African rural populations have increased by four to five times. Fallow periods have been progressively shortened, and in many places completely disappeared. In most parts of the continent, cash crops have been introduced, and other crops dropped to save space or labour time. In short, in less than one century local farming systems have undergone changes which took hundreds of years in European agriculture. Even if food production has not fully kept pace with population growth, this is very far indeed from the standard picture of static technology. Furthermore, recent population figures indicate that rates of growth have peaked and are beginning to decline, though demographic momentum will keep populations rising for decades to come.

Diversified Patterns of Accumulation

The largest farming units in tropical Africa are usually foreign-owned, and the next largest owned by urban dwellers. But even among local inhabitants of rural areas there is considerable difference between households in terms of income and power. Moreover, the benefits from development projects and other external interventions are usually captured by the wealthy and politically influential, even when they are advertised as 'small-farmer' or 'poverty-oriented'. Thus economic and social differentiation in peasant communities has generally increased with growth and development. But there are characteristic strategies of African peasant households, whether for accumulation, reproduction or sheer survival, which seem to stretch from top to bottom of the income and social scales.

One of the most notable of these is the diversification of investment, whether this be of tangible resources, or of time, effort and technical or social skills. This is basically a means to avoid or cope with risks, ranging from drought, changes in market prices and government policy to civil war. Resources are kept as mobile as possible which, apart from their higher rates of return, favours investment in transport and trading rather than in production. This encompasses all social strata. The rich man has a job, political appointments and contacts, is involved in transport, trading and hotel business, as well as having a scattering of farms and being a member of committees which enhance his access to resources and influence. He may well be a respected elder, involved in clan or family, school or church, and the professional or political affairs of his community. At the other end of the income scale, a poor woman struggling to survive will also be involved in many different activities and networks, as well as working on 'her own' food-crop plot.[2] Besides looking after children, collecting wood and water, and other household chores, she will probably try to earn money by selling farm produce, prepared food, alcoholic drinks or handicrafts. Furthermore she may also collect forest products for home use or sale, and be involved in one or more groups for co-operative work and/or savings, whether as part of an extended family structure or through other organizations such as churches.

Work by Berry (1985) shows that while diversification and the cultivation of networks and patron–client relations improve the relative security of those involved in them, they do so at significant costs. They limit the type of specialization which generates technical efficiency and, by setting different corporate groups in political competition with each other for access to resources, may reduce security and predictability within the society as a whole. The heaviest price is paid by those excluded from such networks, such as widows, witches or low-status labour migrants from poor areas.[3]

Given the considerable socio-economic differentiation of African rural areas, the term 'peasant' is used to describe a huge variety of different types and sizes of household. The boundary between peasants and non-peasants can be hard to draw, when the same extended family contains professionals and politicians at one end and destitutes at the other. It is common to divide peasants into 'rich', 'middle' and 'poor', but the dividing line between them is necessarily arbitrary. One could consider those involved in accumulation as rich peasants, those who are more or less able to reproduce existing conditions and living levels as 'middle' and those who are losing land or otherwise moving downwards as 'poor'. But this raises as many problems as it solves, including that it is usually only possible to tell *ex post* (and often years or decades *ex post)* into which category a household fits. A related tendency sees middle peasants as more stable and 'authentic' peasants, and since the definition implies a balance between hiring in labour and working for others, it is widely assumed that middle peasants do little of either. In fact, it is just as common for them to do both, in some cases with men working for wages most of their lives and sending back remittances for both consumption needs and farm investment to a *de facto* female-headed household.

Given the extent of diversification of activities and the wide range of ways of achieving family reproduction, one could question whether the processes discussed here should be referred to as 'de-peasantization' or as the enforced extension of peasant survival strategies under pressure of impoverishment. True, this process does seem to be leading to the breakdown of many kinship/locality networks, but so long as at least parts of a family have some rural basis in farming I would see them as remaining peasants.

Agricultural Modernization

If 'agricultural modernization' simply meant that using modern inputs, such as fertilizers and insecticides, can help intensify agriculture and increase its productivity, I would have no argument with it. But for most agricultural modernizers it is taken to imply far more, being associated with a theory of 'traditional' and 'modern' agriculture, about processes of change and how to achieve them, building on a simplified version of Weber's traditional–modern dichotomy. Significant among the assumptions is that modern agriculture is simply and absolutely better than the traditional because it is scientifically based, while traditional cultivation is primordial and irrational. This implies that the optimal approach to farm improvement should be to replace these outworn methods with modern ones, rather than build on what there is by integrating new methods. So peasant agricultural methods, cultures, cognitive processes and social structures are reduced to 'traditional barriers to change'. It is not hard to see how colonial racism gave a further twist to this viewpoint, which implies that the people in question may have to be forced to innovate 'for their own good'.

Modernization theory aims both to analyse and to accelerate the change process, which it sees generally as the diffusion of innovations from areas, institutions and individuals with higher levels of modern technological skills to those with lower levels. Its ideas on how to achieve this come from (radio-inspired) communications theory, aimed at optimizing transmission of a message from a source, via a medium to a receiver. Strength and clarity of signal and redundancy (repetition) improve reception; noise and resistance in the medium inhibit it. By analogy, messages concerning agricultural innovation should be shorn of 'unnecessary' discussion and explanation (noise), reduced to simple commands, stated loudly and clearly (strength) and repeated often (redundancy).[4] For communications theory, the content of the message is not at issue; its concern is solely with accuracy of transmission so the correctness of extension messages is taken for granted. Combined with the assumed superiority of the modern, this leaves no space in the theory for an incorrect message or for rational rejection of advice.[5] Rejection is seen only in terms of irrational resistance to change, which is to be overcome by strengthening the signal or increasing redundancy, repeating the message loudly and clearly in command form, and often with punishment for failure to obey.

This set of assumptions exaggerates the benefits of using modern inputs in (among others) the following ways.

- *Confusing technical and economic efficiency.* Fertilizers usually increase crop yields, but not necessarily by enough to cover the cost of the fertilizer. Remarkably, extension personnel frequently fail to ensure that this is the case.[6]
- *Narrow focus.* Much extension advice focuses on single crops and on specific activities in producing single crops, i.e. applying fertilizer to maize. But most African peasants grow a wide range of crops for different markets and uses, and many are also involved in wage-labour trading, transport or other economic activities, not to mention cultivating social contacts which are often economically important for getting access to resources or to ensure help in case of misfortune. Any of these

may give 'returns' which outweigh those of recommended innovations, and pre-empt the resources or labour time which a recommended innovation would use.

- *Research practice*. This sometimes exaggerates the expected benefits of innovations, by overlooking experimental results from years with poor rainfall, valuing fertilizers at the subsidized or tax-free prices which state research stations pay, or omitting labour costs paid out of the general research station budget. Most African extension services advise farmers to use more fertilizer on maize than its price will bear, on the basis of experiments done years ago, under research station conditions and an entirely different (pre-adjustment) price regime.

All the above are exaggerated by characteristics of the means of transmission.

- *Hierarchy*. Government departments of agriculture, which dominate the extension process, are hierarchically structured, with information passed down from superiors to subordinates and accepted without question. This is progressively simplified and 'squared off' as it passes downwards to allow for differences in education, to eliminate doubt and ambiguity, and to turn advice into orders. The net result is that peasant farmers receive bald commands about when to plant and at what spacing, when to weed, and what inputs to apply when. Any competent farmer knows that advice always needs adjusting for specific circumstances. There is no point in applying pesticide six times if there is no pest problem; nor in applying irrigation water if it is raining; nor in planting on December 20th if it has not rained for several months. Yet top-down extension has advised and even enforced such stupidities and worse.
- *Class*. Extension personnel at lower levels owe their social superiority over the peasantry to their education and training, which makes them unwilling to discuss matters of science on an equal basis with 'ignorant' peasants.

These factors combine to create a system of generating and spreading agricultural innovations which is subject to serious biases, and predisposed to ignore local ideas and methods except as objects of criticism. The classic example is inter-planting (of different crops in the same field), widely held by colonial extension services to be a pernicious practice representing the sloppiness of the African personality, and to be discouraged or stamped out. More recently it has simply been ignored by most extension workers. Yet many studies have found it highly beneficial, reducing erosion and the need for manual weeding by keeping the soil covered more of the time, increasing total output through better use of soil nutrients, and maintaining soil fertility. Such practices should be considered in framing fertilizer recommendations, but very seldom are. Quite the reverse: peasant farmers are often encouraged not to interplant fertilized maize with beans, a practice which could save on costs by synthesizing atmospheric nitrogen.

Some may feel that the above presents a biased picture of current modernization theory and practice.[7] During the past two decades, the number and influence of those who focus on the needs of peasant farmers and welcome their participation in setting agendas and contributing knowledge has increased considerably, especially among those who work under the rubric of 'farming systems'. However, these are still a minority and where it really matters – in formulating and implementing agricultural extension policy – hard-line modernizing thought still prevails. In any case, the modernizing institutions which have dominated policy for peasant agricultural development in Africa for decades were formed under the full force of hard-line modernization thinking.

Colonial Institutional Foundations and Early Modernization Policies

The colonial state played an all-important role in shaping African rural economies, but one which varied both between crops and territories, and over time. In early colonial days, wherever there was significant white settlement, Africans were forbidden to produce both export crops (as alternative income sources might reduce the supply of wage labour) and crops produced by settlers for domestic markets (for the same reason, as well as to prevent peasant competition from reducing prices). Where there were no settlers, export-crop production was 'encouraged' by direct force, or by imposing taxes to be paid in cash. This required the co-operation of a local élite of chiefs and native authorities, who were repaid by being helped rather than ordered to produce for the market. They were also sometimes provided with inputs, equipment and credit. Peasant export-crop production in early colonial Africa was overwhelmingly based on expanded labour input rather than purchased inputs, and chiefs, whose job included provision of labour (often by force) for settler farms and local public works, were well placed to expand and accumulate by making use of such labour themselves.

At this stage, the institutional requirements were fairly simple: a Department of Agriculture to generate ideas and innovations, and native authority extension personnel to diffuse and enforce them. In the process, innovations became rigid bye-laws, enforced by extension agents as agricultural policemen, subverting both the quality of advice and the relation between extension agents and peasant farmers. Markets were mostly private and input supply negligible. But requirements to direct product flows (for example away from where they could compete with whites in settler colonies) meant that most markets were controlled by state marketing boards.

From 1945 onwards a fundamental change gradually emerged in the basis of output expansion, from enforced extra labour to modernization based on input use, and this much increased the scope and complexity of the institutions required. With the mechanization of white settler agriculture, chronic labour shortage was replaced by chronic surplus, removing one reason to exclude Africans from commercial agriculture. In any case, approaching independence in many countries implied the reverse: the need to develop a class of wealthier African farmers to act as a dynamic force economically and a conservative force politically. Secondly, a rapid and accelerating worldwide increase in the use of improved seeds, fertilizers and pesticides made input-based modernization an increasingly central part of the repertoire of agricultural advisors, from universities to local extension officers. This required an expanded institutional structure to handle input supply and provision of credit.

While this may sound like a welcome shift from coercion to scientific advance, the reality was less impressive. Most of the innovations had been developed outside Africa and adapted for African soils and climate. But few saw any need to adapt for local peasant farming, since modernization saw no virtue in 'traditional' practices and worked solely for their replacement. This reinforced and was reinforced by coercive relations between agricultural extension 'policemen' and peasants and kept the quality of advice low. But while formerly mistakes had 'just' wasted peasant time and effort, now they could also cost them money spent on (or borrowed for) inputs. Meanwhile the disparity in treatment between chiefs and commoners persisted in a new form. A wealthy minority of 'progressive farmers' were treated as individuals and supplied with advice, cheap inputs and credit – as against the arbitrary treatment of most peasants, who were either ignored or subjected to campaigns for the achievement of one or more desired innovations, which were usually highly simplified in conception and often imposed through force.

It was thus in marketing systems that the major institutional changes occurred. Modernization involved use of inputs and their delivery to farmers, and it was widely assumed that 'traditional conservatism' would inhibit their adoption unless provided cheaply and/or on credit. Private traders in rural Africa were seldom interested in opening new markets for low-value and bulky products such as fertilizers, still less in providing them on credit. Not only did customary tenure exclude the pledging of land as collateral, but most British colonies had enacted Credit to Natives (Restriction) Acts which achieved their purpose by making the debts of Africans legally uncollectable.

In this situation the only available security for loans to peasants was a lien on the crop for which input loans were given. This in turn could only work at all under monopoly control of markets and if repayment could be organized through 'deduction-at-source' before crop proceeds were paid out. Monopoly over marketing was also seen to be necessary because it made it possible to cheapen inputs and credit (and fund losses from non-repayment) through cross-subsidy from crop prices. Without monopoly the reduction in product prices would drive producers to seek alternative markets.[8] Thus the central mechanisms by which modernizers hoped to improve African peasant agriculture all depended on monopoly control of marketing, and since they involved grants, subsidies and costs of infrastructure, distribution and extension, the state, parastatal corporations or boards and state-regulated co-operatives were inevitably involved.

Modernization in Expansion, Sclerosis and Decline: 1960s, 1970s and post-1980

Most of the elements of parastatal marketing, criticized by the IFIs and assumed to derive from rent-seeking, were deliberately introduced during the colonial period as necessary elements of modernization policy. Colonial marketing systems were less notorious for corruption and high costs than they later became, partly because this was not studied at the time and because arbitrary use of force and wasted peasant time do not show up in the account books. But it also has to do with the scope and pace of operations. The greater the number of activities linked by cross-subsidy, the harder it is to maintain accounting control, while the more external funds flow through the system, the greater the incentive to misappropriate them. So the limited extent of colonial agricultural spending should itself have made control easier to exert.

As concern to expand agriculture grew after independence, and as different donors came in with offers to fund modernization projects, the size, scope and complexity of programmes increased, and with them the chances for misappropriation. Independence also increased the scope for arbitrary political interventions, with senior politicians or state officials ordering parastatals or co-operatives to provide inputs or credit to individuals, schemes or villages, despite their previous failure to pay or repay. Worst of all, things went totally awry during periods of grandiose political 'transformation', where the language of the battlefield (campaigns for this, operations for that) dominated the development discourse, and resources were deployed with military wastefulness. Similar problems arose with large bursts of donor aid, as shown by the experience of the 1970s.

Most African countries achieved independence in the 1950s or 1960s. Almost all increased state spending rapidly, to make up for excessive colonial parsimony and a disastrous lack of infrastructure and trained persons. Thus many countries faced serious budget and foreign-exchange constraints by the early 1970s. In 1973 the Sahel reached the final year of a multi-year drought, and many countries of eastern Africa were also suffering food shortages, while US wheat sales to the USSR had helped to triple world grain prices. Events thus pushed the issue of food security to centre stage.

Also in 1973, the OPEC oil-price rise shifted the terms of trade and petro-dollar recycling set off the mid-1970s monetary boom. This hugely increased aid inflows and lending to African countries, relaxing the budgetary constraints which might otherwise have slowed the growth of imports and public spending. Spending on agricultural development also rose rapidly, and many countries were awash with projects and programmes to attack food insecurity and poverty by spreading modern agriculture to peasants. Large amounts of money chasing limited projects and local institutional capacity aggravated the worst aspects of the system described above. The combination of increased but wasteful spending and a shift of focus to food crops actually reduced levels of export-crop production, largely failed to improve official urban food supplies, and increased indebtedness at all levels.

It must be stressed that this episode combined internal and external factors. Local states made many of the decisions and expanded their parastatal monopolies to (try to) accommodate the increase in projects. But their shape and size was every bit as much decided by donors and their consultants, who usually designed the programmes and always had the final say on funding. Thus in Tanzania, the World Bank was involved in several export-crop promotion campaigns, directed through parastatal 'authorities', a number of investments in export-crop processing, input credit, fertilizer supply and a major food-production project, all directed through monopoly parastatal 'authorities'. The food-crop programme, like a similar donor-funded one in Zambia, used transport equalization subsidies to draw peasants from the furthest reaches of the country into production for the official national market. This increased deliveries from new areas, but since the same price structure pushed maize from closer consumption centres onto black markets, this increased total deliveries hardly at all. But total costs increased massively – and in line with programme 'success', as old production areas close to consuming areas were replaced by others at much greater distance.[9]

By 1979–81, excessive investment and activity on all fronts (industry, agriculture, infrastructure) had massively overstretched African state and parastatal capacity, leading to major losses and inefficiency, with large and growing budget and foreign exchange deficits. In 1979–81 real interest rates multiplied by ten to fifteen times, while terms of trade for main exports fell sharply, and the debts incurred were transformed into the debt crisis. This period also saw a sharp turn in IFI and other donor policies against state and parastatal intervention in the economy, thus turning on the institutions they had spent the past ten years building up.

Structural Adjustment to the 'Rescue'

Very roughly, one can distinguish two phases of structural adjustment. The first followed the World Bank-sponsored Berg Report (World Bank 1981), took most of the 1980s, and focused on devaluation, cuts in state expenditure and tighter control over parastatals. The second, from the late 1980s, focused on privatization or closure of public sector institutions and encouragement of an 'enabling environment' for private enterprise. Some have seen the second as a relaxation of conditionality. But it seems rather to embody more radical and irreversible changes. Institutions which no longer exist can hardly revert to old ways.

In the first phase, devaluation and reduced marketing margins were intended to increase export-crop producer prices and so exports, thus reducing the trade gap and improving debt-servicing capacity. Cuts in state spending would reduce the revenue gap, the public borrowing requirement and the rate of inflation. This assumed increased export-proceeds, despite abundant evidence that terms of trade were falling. Furthermore, a continent-wide effort to increase total exports would accelerate the decline by further saturating markets for products facing inelastic demand.

In fact, there was little increase in agricultural exports from tropical Africa. But large increases from elsewhere in the south, and shifting demand patterns in the north, meant continued terms-of-trade decline. Devaluation aimed to offset this by raising prices in local currency, but this often failed to reach through monopoly marketing systems to producers. Part arose from parastatal inefficiency and corruption, but some was related to adjustment itself. Devaluation and interest-rate increases hugely increased their debt-service costs, while some governments 'finessed' conditionality by removing subventions to parastatals for loss-making activities without removing their obligation to perform them (transport equalization and/or subsidy, input subsidies whose cost rocketed with devaluation).

Ironically enough the large increases in aid which usually followed a structural adjustment agreement themselves tended to undercut financial controls, at least for the institutions receiving the aid. By the end of the 1980s, after several years of following IFI adjustment conditionality, the most obvious macro-economic change in most tropical African countries was further increased indebtedness as a proportion of GDP and of debt service as proportion of exports. There was also evidence of declining incomes among the poorest groups and of further deteriorating social services. Statistical sources emanating from the World Bank and IMF show increased growth in agricultural production from 1986–90. Much of this seems to have been weather-related, and most does not come from the export products which were the primary focus of policy, but from various food crops, for which production estimates contain a significant element of guesswork (Gibbon and Raikes 1996).

The IFIs attributed the failure to achieve better results almost solely to resistance to structural reform on the part of rent-seekers in the state and parastatal sectors. No doubt this was one important factor, though with real wages often below a half or even quarter of their late 1970s levels 'rent' is hardly the appropriate word for what those at lower levels were seeking.

Others, myself included, would start by noting that parastatal inefficiency and corruption were hugely multiplied by the mid-1970s aid boom, and see the reasons for failure in the first phase to expand export-crop production as deriving in part from the combination and sequencing of adjustment policies themselves. More generally, these plans for agriculture were built on the fatal inconsistency of trying to achieve rapid modernization, while dismantling the institutional structure on which it was based.

The focus of adjustment in the second phase shifted from specific measures to institutional changes, which largely meant closing or privatizing what remained of the state marketing sector. Sheer necessity dictated that loans were made financially softer and debt service increasingly rescheduled, but political conditionality hardened, especially as regards the need to be seen to accept the supremacy of the private sector and market. Many countries are in the position that they can 'get by' so long as their compliance with structural adjustment keeps the aid flowing and ensures that debt service is rescheduled on favourable terms. Without these they would rapidly fall into economic disaster.

In terms of agricultural policy, this has meant removing parastatal monopolies and often either closing them down or selling them (or their components) off to private enterprise. Increasingly the removal of subsidies started or mooted under phase one is completed. Combined with devaluation, this has enormously increased the price of inputs such as fertilizers and chemicals, which must be imported. This is not necessarily a problem for export-crop producers, since devaluation also increases product prices. But it has much reduced the use of fertilizer on maize, whose price in most cases will no longer bear the cost of previous levels of application. There are only a few signs that research and extension agencies are responding to this major change with revised recommendations.[10]

With regard to agricultural exports, the record is mixed and increasingly hard to read at all, as it is yet harder to get accurate figures in today's decontrolled marketing than it was before. It does seem that, in some cases, private marketing channels are handling increasing amounts of produce, though at the cost of some loss of quality (Raikes and Gibbon 1998). Quality premia on world markets seem to be increasing, and Africa's loss of world market share for many exports in recent years seems to arise as much from relative price/quality decline as from slower output growth. But more generally, spiralling indebtedness is in most cases way beyond the capacity of even rapid increase in export-crop revenues, while most countries cannot even cover current imports.

Structural Adjustment versus Agricultural Modernization

In both phases, structural adjustment has increasingly, but apparently unintentionally, undercut the whole agricultural modernization model. The

Berg Report (World Bank 1981) went on at great length about the inefficiency of agricultural marketing parastatals but did not link this to project spending and agricultural policy, since by focusing on the proportional decline in investment to agriculture during the 1970s it missed the huge increase in absolute spending. It thus recommended both cutting state and parastatal expenditure and increasing development spending on agriculture, ignoring the fact that almost all development programmes for agriculture were not only designed for and directed through parastatals, but involved instruments which depended on their monopoly status. Thus austerity and parastatal cuts usually overrode investment expansion.

Similar cuts affected ministries of agriculture and left many field personnel 'grounded' for lack of transport and materials – except where there were donor projects and funds. With devaluation, donor funds became steadily more important and influential at all levels, from national policy to the 'topping-up' of salaries for state officials involved with projects. But at the same time adjustment conditionality severely limited the scope of policy initiatives, since almost all involved some form of subsidy, and these were increasingly outlawed under IFI conditionality. State and donor projects had been implemented through monopoly parastatal marketing agencies because this allowed input credit to be 'secured' through deduction-at-source and cross-subsidization of inputs from producer prices, two of the central mechanisms of input-based modernization. The World Bank and other donors had been clear enough about that when they sponsored the programmes in the 1970s. A few years later, obsessed with rent-seeking as the basis of state control, they seemed not to notice that closing parastatals and eliminating subsidies meant the end of agricultural modernization in its existing form. Of course, this action has not meant its complete demise, since some donors do continue to include grants and subsidies of various sorts – notably the unintended sort, as when credit is poorly secured and not repaid – but the incidence of large-scale innovation and input-supply projects has clearly declined. This is much to be welcomed. There is little doubt that these projects achieved little (and sometimes more harm than good) at tremendous cost. What is less clearly positive is the closing of a number of other public-sector supply channels since, for example, there has been no rush of private business to supply agricultural inputs to 'backwater' areas. But it may be better to be without them altogether than to be bound to them by monopoly – and it is not always clear that they could operate without either monopoly or donor subvention.

This has all meant a major redefinition of agricultural policy, though in many respects an inadequate and inconsistent one. In recent years, much of the focus has been on how the private sector would provide marketing services at much lower cost. It is probably generally true, though by no means always so, that overall marketing margins are lower and also that a significant proportion of this results from competition and elimination of unnecessary costs. But private traders will only supply inputs at higher costs, and credit (if at all) at very much higher rates. Most programmes for the 'improvement' of input credit under adjustment turn out to be for closing down state institutions to allow prices and interest rates to rise enough to attract private enterprise, or for turning them into commercial banks with market interest rates and requirements for land as collateral, which preclude peasants and all but a small wealthy minority from using them.

The new situation requires a flexibility in thinking about alternatives, which has not been shown by either neo-liberals or modernizers, and least of all by those who tie themselves up in adherence to both of these incompatible dogmas. Many of the former programmes were unsustainable without subsidies, and some would have been even without inefficiency and corruption in implementation, because they were based on presentations of research results which over-estimated returns to inputs and so over-recommended them. There is little point in calling for high levels of input use when returns to producers do not warrant it. What are needed are means to achieve better effects from smaller doses through integrating them with use of organic and green manures, crop rotations, intercropping and other means to increase available nutrient supply. Similarly, lower and less toxic doses of chemicals (or even none at all) can achieve the same impact as higher ones, when used with particular patterns of crop combination or segregation, natural insecticides or biological control. Some, though certainly not all, of the techniques needed can be found in or adapted from local knowledge, most particularly including experiments by peasant farmers with different combinations of 'local' and 'modern' on their own farms.

It is not at all clear where the accumulation, adaptation and rediffusion of such knowledge is to come from. State extension services are ever more starved for funds and transport, and most of their field personnel are quite narrowly trained, focusing on modern input use at high levels. Few have either the skills or the disposition for learning from peasants and integrating useful aspects of their farming methods. Nor is there any encouragement from above for them to do so. One of the most discouraging trends is the spread, under adjustment conditionality, of the World Bank's training-and-visit extension model to increasing numbers of African countries. Not only is this top-down and rigid, without space for any transmission of knowledge up the scale, it is far too expensive for most African countries with their decimated agricultural budgets.

All signs are that most World Bank thinking goes in the opposite direction, seeking to re-establish modernization programmes through the private analogue of parastatal programmes: contract farming schemes. One sees many positive references to contract-farming and its scope for developing peasant agriculture. One can argue about the relative merits and demerits, but for practical purposes it does not seem to matter much. Over a decade after most African countries embarked on, or were pushed into, structural adjustment, the number and coverage of contract-farming schemes in Africa remains minute, and recent growth still less. Foreign capital seems relatively uninterested in setting up such schemes in Africa – and the vast majority of the few existing schemes are situated near to ports, capital cities and airports, in the best infrastructure the continent has to offer (and not infrequently involve white commercial farmers). The chances that contract farming will be the means to develop the less-favoured rural areas of Africa, where most of the people live, are slightly better than that pigs will fly, but not much so.

Conclusions

Modernization was always a problematic basis for developing African peasant agriculture, since it both neglected and rejected local production systems, while trying to force pieces of a modern farming system into them. On the other hand, its assumption of the necessary superiority of modern methods led to an exaggeration of their benefits and non-economic recommendations. On top of this, it required and generated an expensive and cumbersome series of institutions and transfer payments to operate the mechanisms which its theory said were necessary to persuade peasants to innovate.

But the extremes of parastatal development from the mid-1970s to the mid-1980s were not a necessary concomitant of 'state-centred development', but rather the result of a specific conjunction of events – the most important of which, like the OPEC oil-price rise and the rise of the Eurodollar market which helped transform this into a monetary (and aid) boom, occurred outside Africa and were linked less to the post-war Keynesian system than to its breakdown. However caused, though, the damage to African economies, their agricultural sectors and agencies of modernization was probably irreparable.

This leads to serious problems about what should replace modernization as the basis of state and donor agricultural policy. A fairly sensible policy in agricultural and micro-economic terms, as sketched above, would require huge amounts of unavailable skills and labour time, and it is hard to see who would pay for it. But perhaps more relevantly, unless the major donors and state institutions can be persuaded to see that traditional modernization is dead, they will presumably continue trying to revive the carcase with hidden subsidies and grants, and probably waste money on private-enterprise agricultural projects in the same way they once did with parastatal ones.

Notes

1. International financial institutions, a term used to cover both the World Bank and International Monetary Fund (IMF).

2. Given women's limited access to land, this will often be part of her husband's farm if she is married, or rented land if she is a widow or unattached.
3. Widows are often excluded from land-holding by male-dominated tenure institutions. By reputation, this makes them 'hungry' for the husbands of other women and so vulnerable to witchcraft accusations.
4. A false analogy is thus implied between resistance in radio systems (a property of the medium) with the 'resistance to change' supposedly shown by 'traditional people' (a response of recipients not a property of media, involving rejection of the content of the message, which is irrelevant for communication theory).
5. Not merely hypothetical: during the 1970s in Tanzania, I heard farmers criticized as 'traditional' for 'opportunistic' pesticide use, now recognized by most authorities as superior to blanket dosage on economic and ecological grounds (slower growth of pest resistance).
6. My first introduction to this came from noting the many fertilizer recommendations from the Tanzania extension service (and its foreign advisors) whose expected yield did not cover the cost of the fertilizer.
7. Criticism of modernization theory and related extension advice does not imply that 'local' knowledge is necessarily correct, still less that it should be accepted without critical scrutiny.
8. In practice large amounts were diverted in any case. But the adjustment-related removal of parastatal monopolies under adjustment has made it virtually impossible for them to collect debts for input credit.
9. This effect of transport equalization is well known, especially to neo-liberals, so it is odd that in Tanzania the World Bank started a programme entirely dependent on them and supported it until the late 1980s, despite its failure to improve urban food supply (Raikes 1988, Gibbon and Raikes 1996).
10. In 1995, the Kenya Agricultural Research Institute (KARI) produced revised fertilizer recommendations, reflecting price changes and estimates of climatic risk. Selected results show dramatic reductions: of 14 recommendations, nine were reduced to zero and most others by over half (*Daily Nation*, 20 April 1995).

References

Berry, S. (1985) *Fathers Work for their Sons*, University of California Press, Berkeley and Los Angeles.

Gibbon, P. and Raikes, P. (1996) 'Structural adjustment in Tanzania, 1986–1994' in P. Engberg-Pedersen, P. Gibbon, P. Raikes and L. Udsholt (eds) *Limits of Adjustment in Africa*, James Currey, London.

Raikes, P. (1988) *Modernizing Hunger*, James Currey, London.

Raikes, P. and Gibbon, P. (1998) 'The current restructuring of African export crop agriculture in a global context', paper presented to a Conference on Africa and Globalization, University of Central Lancashire, Preston, 24–26 April.

World Bank (1981) *Accelerating Development in Sub-Saharan Africa* (also known as the Berg Report), Washington, D.C.

4. Veiled Conflicts: Peasant Differentiation, Gender and Structural Adjustment in Nigerian Hausaland

KATE MEAGHER

THE IMPACT ON PEASANT differentiation of pro-peasant capitalist development strategies, such as the promotion of improved agricultural input packages and structural adjustment programmes, is more complex than theory predicts. The various peasant-friendly policies are refracted through political and class structures of the societies concerned, as well as through gender relations within the household. The way in which these policies and the structures through which they are mediated affect the process of differentiation vary widely, not only from society to society, but also within a given society, depending on class, ethnic and gender relations and the cultural practices of a given group.

In Africa, analyses of peasant differentiation tend to gloss over stark variations in forms of agricultural organization, gender roles and cultural practices. This tendency is most striking in the analysis of gender relations. The current orthodoxy presents a highly dualistic picture of African agriculture, in which women produce 'subsistence' food crops and men dominate export- or 'cash'-crop production. Gender analyses of the impact of adjustment policies on agricultural production and resource allocation tend to be carried out within this framework (Palmer 1988, Lele 1991).

This chapter undertakes to challenge the current orthodoxy by considering the ways in which variations in gender roles in agriculture influence the impact of structural adjustment policies and the mediation of differentiation processes within the household. The analysis focuses on the Hausa of northern Nigeria, an ethnic group which, contrary to the norm among African peasantries, has a comparatively low rate of female participation in agriculture, food-crop or otherwise. While the Hausa are unusual in this regard, they constitute nonetheless a politically and numerically important peasantry, with a population numbering roughly ten million in northern Nigeria alone. In addition, the unusual structure of, and internal variations in, agrarian gender relations among the Hausa provide an opportunity to highlight the variable ways in which gender relations mediate the impact of structural adjustment on peasant differentiation.

At the level of male agricultural actors, peasant differentiation among the Nigerian Hausa has become increasingly pronounced since the 1970s, owing to a combination of 'urban-biased' economic policies which have undermined peasant agriculture, and the introduction of improved input packages which have tended to favour large-scale farmers. The imposition of Nigeria's Structural Adjustment Programme (SAP) in 1986 has done little to alter this trend. Proclaimed as a policy package designed to favour small-scale agriculture, structural adjustment has tended to have the opposite effect in the context of northern Nigeria. Large increases in grain prices have significantly increased the profitability of food-crop farming, but rising production costs progressively restrict such profits to those who can afford the necessary inputs and labour. Among the Hausa, the dominant ethnic group in northern Nigeria, the impact of these policies has been to intensify tendencies toward differentiation. In the struggle to keep up with the rising cost of farming, small-scale farmers are increasingly involved in a process of 'de-agrarianization' taking the form of diversification into a range of non-farm activities (Bryceson and Jamal 1997). Better-off farmers, who are better able to benefit from structural adjustment incentives, show the reverse tendency: a rising share of agriculture in total income.

Within the context of structural adjustment, Hausa women have experienced a different pattern of pressures and incentives from their male counterparts. On the one hand, their agricultural participation is more severely limited by disadvantageous access to land, labour and capital, and is therefore more vulnerable to rising production costs. Moreover, the widespread practice of female seclusion bars a large proportion of Hausa women from direct participation in agriculture, concentrating their income-generating opportunities heavily in the area of non-farm activities. On the other hand, structural adjustment has brought with it a variety of institutional initiatives oriented toward increasing female participation in agriculture and cottage industry. These include the Better Life programme, the Women in Agriculture programme and a variety of non-governmental initiatives.

What has been the impact of these contradictory forces on the role of Hausa women in agriculture? Does the impact of structural adjustment on women intensify or moderate the tendencies toward differentiation and de-agrarianization affecting male members of rural households? How have traditional practices, such as female seclusion and male-dominated patterns of control over land and labour, been affected by the pressures and opportunities created by SAP?

These questions will be addressed through an examination of a variety of published studies, as well as the author's own published and unpublished field data collected at various times between 1990 and 1995 in rural Katsina, Kano and Bauchi States in northern Nigeria. The analysis will focus on the impact of the current policy and institutional environment on women's access to land, labour and capital, mediated through the ideological context of women's roles and the distributional relations within the household. Specific attention will be paid to the influence of cultural/religious and class differences on the economic responses of various categories of Hausa women.

Theoretical Perspectives: Gender and Peasant Differentiation

In the context of northern Nigerian agriculture, the differentiation debate has followed essentially classical lines. On the one hand are those who argue that the social structure of the Hausa peasantry is inherently flexible and resistant to differentiating pressures (Hill 1972, Matlon 1977, Clough and Williams 1987). While it was recognized that there was significant inequality among peasant households, the fragmentation of property at the death of a wealthy peasant, the low technical level of agriculture, the unruliness of the farm labour system, and the heavy social expenditure required of the wealthy prevented any enduring forms of accumulation. At the same time, the relatively easy access to land, access to additional income through agricultural wage labour, and the persistence of various forms of social assistance within rural communities were seen to limit the degree of impoverishment of weaker households. Exploitation emanating from predatory urban élites (Hill 1972, Clough and Williams 1987), and the introduction of technical improvements in agriculture (Matlon 1977) were seen as the only threats to the stability of the peasant social structure.

On the other side of the debate are those who argue that the northern Nigerian peasantry have been subjected to intensifying forces of differentiation as a result of the intervention of the colonial and post-colonial state. Colonial interventions in the form of taxation, cash-crop production and urban food provisioning led to increasing commercialization of peasant life combined with increased pressures on the reproduction of peasant households (Watts 1983, Shenton 1985). In the context of the increased commercialization of food production during the Nigerian oil boom, these processes of polarization and class formation were intensified (Beckman 1987). It is argued that widening differences in wealth and life chances were increasingly being passed down from generation to generation, and that the communal safety mechanisms of the rural social structure have been eroded by the penetration of capitalist relations.

On both sides of the debate, only scant reference is made to the role of gender in these processes, given the lack of female participation in agriculture among the Muslim Hausa majority. Hill (1977) and Matlon (1978) emphasize the significance of female incomes in household reproduction despite the constraints of seclusion, suggesting that the economic role of women mitigates against forces of differentiation. Matlon notes an inverse relationship between levels of female involvement in income-generating activities and the overall income status of households, and concludes that women from poorer households increase their levels of employment to compensate for inadequate male incomes. On the other side of the debate, Watts (1983) argues that the withdrawal of female labour from farm work as a result of seclusion aggravates the serious labour constraint of poor households, a constraint which is unlikely to be compensated for by the limited incomes women are able to generate from within the confines of seclusion. Moreover, women's financial assistance to their husbands was normally made in the form of short-term credit, for which full repayment was expected. The economic role of women is therefore seen to reinforce the process of differentiation.

In the context of economic crisis and adjustment, the economic role of women in rural Hausaland has generally become more pronounced as male incomes come under intensifying economic pressure. What are the implications of crisis in the wider economy, combined with increasing household demands on women's resources, for women's income-generating opportunities and levels of female participation in agriculture? Faced with the contradictory forces of intensified economic pressure and increased institutional support for rural women, do women's economic activities contribute to limiting the forces of differentiation, or are women themselves increasingly subject to such forces? These issues cannot be resolved by theory alone; they require a concrete analysis of the complex reality revealed by the differing responses of Hausa women.

Rural Hausa Women: Theory versus Reality

Dualistic notions concerning the role of women in African agriculture are inappropriate for analysing the situation of rural Hausa women, where there is no issue of 'female' food crops and 'male' cash crops. Since the mid-1970s, grain has been the major cash crop as well as being the staple food of the Nigerian Hausaland, and all crops are commonly cultivated by either sex. In addition, there are wide variations in the gender division of labour encountered among the Hausa, none of which involves the relegation of women to the production of non-commercial crops. There are sharp differences between the Muslim and non-Muslim Hausa (including both pagan and Christian), and even among the Muslim Hausa.

Women from the non-Muslim Hausa, who constitute only about 15 to 20 per cent of the Nigerian Hausa population, participate in most operations on the household farm and also farm on their own account. Non-Muslim Hausa women do not normally inherit land; access to land is largely through husbands, who allocate plots to their wives. Certain fixed periods during the week are allotted for women to work on their own farms (Hill 1972, Jackson 1984). Beer brewing and some marketing of crops constitute women's major income-generating activities. Unlike Muslim women, non-Muslim Hausa women have fairly heavy obligations for the maintenance of the household.

Muslim Hausa women have, on the whole, more control over land and personal incomes than non-Muslim women, but less freedom of movement and therefore greater restrictions on their ability to participate in farming.

During the past century, the practice of female seclusion has been on the increase among the Hausa, restricting the mobility of women from marriage, which normally takes place at puberty, until after child-bearing age (Watts 1983, Jackson 1984, Imam 1993). Despite their physical restrictions, secluded women traditionally enjoy considerable economic autonomy. In accordance with Islamic ideology, men are responsible for providing food, clothing and basic cosmetics for the household. Women's incomes are largely for their own use, although they normally provide at least part of the mid-day meals for themselves and their children, dowry for their daughters, and assistance with household purchases if their husbands are unable to bear the full burden (Jackson 1984, Simmons 1990, Imam 1993). Muslim women can and do inherit land, although the practice of seclusion makes it more difficult for them to claim and use their land directly.

Female seclusion is practised in varying degrees among the Muslim Hausa. The practice is relatively strict in nucleated villages in the southern part of Hausaland, and much looser in dispersed hamlets in the south and in both hamlets and villages in the far north (Jackson 1984, Imam 1993).[1] In both villages and hamlets throughout Hausaland, there is frequently a small but significant proportion of women of childbearing age who are not in seclusion at all, often as a result of extreme poverty (ibid.).

Officially, secluded women do no farm work, except threshing, which can be done inside the house. However, even in the areas where full seclusion is practised, there is considerable dispute as to the extent of participation in farming operations. Watts (1983) and Hill (1972) suggest that strict seclusion, involving abstention from on-farm work, has become 'almost universal' in rural Hausaland; other studies indicate a limited participation of Muslim Hausa women in field operations such as harvesting (Jackson 1984, Simmons 1990, Imam 1993). These various activities may be performed on the household farm, where they are usually remunerated, and on other farms as wage labour. Fully secluded women may also farm on their own account, though this must be done through the agency of family or hired labour, even if the land is within a woman's village of residence.

Although in certain circumstances fully secluded women may participate in farming, they are predominantly engaged in non-agricultural activities. Their principal income-generating activities involve petty commodity production and petty trade, which can be carried out easily from within the home. Procurement of raw materials and the circulation of goods are carried out with the aid of husbands and children. The raising of fowls and small livestock is also done by women, but is normally undertaken as a means of savings rather than income generation (Simmons 1990).

The looser form of seclusion practised in more dispersed settlements and in the far north of Nigeria gives women relatively greater freedom to participate in agriculture. Loosely secluded women perform a wider range of operations in the fields, and frequently farm on their own account, although they depend on considerable assistance from family or hired labour (Jackson 1984, Meagher, unpublished fieldnotes 1990–1). The produce from such women's farms is for their own use, for sale or for gifts at ceremonies. These women also engage in petty snack production and petty trade, which are important sources of funding for their agricultural activities.

Structural Adjustment and Institutional Support Programmes

Nigeria's SAP, introduced in 1986, has significantly altered the structure of economic incentives which had developed during the 1970s. A central aim of the programme was to shift the terms of trade in favour of agricultural production, using a combination of orthodox and unorthodox adjustment measures, including the devaluation of the naira, the liberalization of agricultural marketing, the gradual removal of subsidies on agricultural inputs, the imposition of import bans on wheat, rice, maize and barley, and the creation of a range of incentives for irrigated agriculture.

Attempts were also made to increase incentives for women's agricultural production and processing activities. In recognition of the failure of macroeconomic policies to address the specific needs of women, a number of governmental and non-governmental programmes have been created with the broad objective of 'empowering' rural women in the agricultural development process. The two major state-run initiatives are the Better Life Programme[2], set up in 1987 by the wife of then President Ibrahim Babangida, and the Women in Agriculture programme, begun in 1989 and operating through special units within the state-run agricultural development projects. The central aim of these programmes is to integrate rural women into the national development process, largely by improving women's access to land and credit and by disseminating gender-appropriate technologies for agricultural production and food processing. The Better Life Programme was credited with the mobilization of women into more than 8000 co-operatives nationwide and with the large-scale distribution of improved planting materials and agricultural processing equipment (UNIFEM 1994).

A number of international and local non-governmental organizations (NGOs) have mounted similar programmes oriented towards enhancing women's capacity for agricultural production and income generation. Among these are the UNDP 'Strengthening of Extension' project, the ILO 'Women in Health and Development' project and a programme of co-operation between UNICEF and the Nigerian government (UNIFEM 1994). Local initiatives include the Country Women's Association of Nigeria (COWAN) started in 1982, and the Development Exchange Centre in Bauchi State, started in 1987. These organizations focus on the provision of training, credit and health programmes, and the dissemination of appropriate rural technologies for women's income-generating activities.[3]

Common to all of these programmes is the organization of women into co-operatives for the operation of group farms or the provision of credit or equipment. Despite being ideologically oriented towards the promotion of women's participation in agriculture, the majority of these programmes emphasize income generation through cottage industries and agricultural processing, thereby encouraging diversification into non-agricultural activities. Either way, the thrust of these programmes is to boost female incomes and thereby mitigate the forces of differentiation stimulated by structural adjustment.

Shifting Terms of Trade and Differentiation

The process of differentiation in rural northern Nigeria has been under way for decades, and has been particularly pronounced since the 1970s. In the context of the grain-based agricultural system of the Nigerian Hausa, differentiation among male farmers is most effectively measured by the use of hired labour, since land is relatively plentiful and many poorer farmers suffer from an inability to cultivate the land that they have effectively, rather than from a shortage of land (Mustapha 1990).[4] Small-scale farmers also tend to have less land than large-scale farmers but, more critically, they have less access to family and hired labour and are consequently characterized by lower levels of production and commercialization of agricultural produce. The heavily interventionist agricultural strategies and urban-biased development policies of the 1970s combined to intensify rural differentiation, turning sectoral terms of trade against agriculture and further weakening the access of small-scale farmers to labour and inputs (Beckman 1987).

While SAP has succeeded in shifting the sectoral terms of trade back in favour of agriculture, production and consumption terms of trade within food-crop agriculture have continued to turn against the bulk of small-scale farmers in northern Nigeria.[5] In the face of devaluation and the removal of input subsidies, production costs and the cost of living have tended to rise faster than annual average producer prices for food crops (see Table 4.1). The benefits of structural adjustment have been restricted largely to better-off farmers, who are able to withhold crop sales until late in the season, or have the capital to sell their produce for higher prices in high-value urban, industrial or border markets (Meagher 1993). Within this context, income from non-farm activities has become vital to the majority of farmers for gaining access to labour, fertilizer and other inputs, as well as playing an increasingly important role in access to food (Lennihan 1994, Meagher 1994, Meagher and Mustapha 1997).

Table 4.1: Selected producer and consumer price indices in northern Nigeria (1985 = 100)

Year	*Fertilizer (market price)*	*Labour* (daily rate)*	*Grain† (producer price)*	*Rural consumer price index*
1986	128	–	53	–
1987	–	–	61	–
1988	194	–	173	182
1989	306	–	179	273
1990	256	220	174	293
1991	–	–	330	328
1992	767	600	536	471

* Rates for Kano State only.

† Refers to average annual wholesale price from major rural bulking markets in Northern Nigeria.

Sources: Agricultural Projects Monitoring and Evaluation Unit (APMEU), unpublished grain price data; Central Bank of Nigeria (1988–92), *Annual Report and Statement of Accounts*; Egg and Igue (1993); Katsina Agricultural Development Authority (KTARDA), (1990–92) *Quarterly and Annual Reports*; Meagher, fieldnotes, 1991.

Overall, the impact of SAP on male livelihood strategies varies according to socio-economic status and agro-ecological conditions. In the main grain-production zones of the Guinea and Sudan savanna, the share of non-farm incomes in the total incomes of male household heads has increased among small-scale farmers, and decreased among large-scale and irrigated farmers. Owing to their high levels of commercialization and their access to high-value produce markets, the latter are in the best position to benefit from the agricultural incentives created by SAP. While non-farm activities have become more important in the total incomes of small-scale farmers, rising input and living costs leave them with less to invest in these activities, confining the majority to a range of low-income enterprises. Large-scale farmers, by contrast, have been able to diversify into a more lucrative range of non-farm activities. In the grain-deficit areas of the far north, the share of non-farm incomes is extremely high among both small- and large-scale farmers, and appears to be increasing. This, however, is due as much to ecological factors as to the pressures of structural adjustment (Meagher and Mustapha 1997).

The impact of these trends on the livelihood strategies of rural women, and on their role in the process of differentiation, must consider how the pressures and opportunities of SAP affect women's own agricultural and non-agricultural activities, as well as how these changes are mediated through economic and ideological forces operating within the household. The question to be examined below is how the forces at work affect the income-generating strategies and capacities of different categories of Hausa women, and how changes in women's income generation affect the overall processes of differentiation.

Changing Access to Land, Labour and Capital

The impact of SAP on the economic activities of Hausa women has been extremely uneven. Despite the limitations of seclusion, the macro-economic incentives of SAP combined with the institutional support of women-oriented agricultural programmes have created real opportunities for increased female involvement in agricultural production. Interviews with staff of the Nigerian Agricultural Commercial Bank (NACB), the Institute for Agricultural Research and the Kano agricultural development programme (KNARDA) indicate that in Kaduna, Kano and Sokoto States, better-off Muslim and non-Muslim women are taking up irrigated farming, especially rice and tomato production (see also Lennihan 1994). Under the auspices of Better Life, UNICEF, COWAN and other organizations, secluded as well as unsecluded Hausa women are starting up group farms, which they manage through a combination of hired, family, and personal labour (IAR 1994).

At the same time, other aspects of SAP are negatively affecting women's agricultural participation, most notably in the area of rising input and labour costs. An understanding of the impact of these changes on various categories of Hausa women requires an examination of how the interacting forces of structural adjustment, women-oriented agricultural assistance programmes and structures of resource allocation within the household have affected women's access to land, labour and capital.

Access to land

The question of women's access to land under SAP is complex. It is conventionally argued that in African societies women do not inherit land, and their access is restricted largely to use rights conferred by their husbands. Under SAP, it is believed that women's access to land is eroded by increased male demand for land (Mikell 1984, Palmer 1988). In the case of both the Muslim and non-Muslim Hausa, however, women's access to land does not appear to have been affected as negatively as expected. While rising profits have increased the demand for land among wealthier male farmers, the rising cost of production has limited the ability of small-scale farmers to cultivate the land they already have. Evidence from Kano, Kaduna and Katsina States indicates an increased tendency of small-scale farmers to rent out or mortgage land they can no longer afford to farm (Meagher 1991; Meagher and Ogunwale 1994). This suggests that, at least among small-scale farmers, women's access to land is not likely to come under serious stress as a result of male demands on household land resources.

In part because of this situation, women's access to land outside the household appears to have improved. A small survey of non-Muslim women conducted in 1995 in a village in south-western Kano State indicates that they have no difficulty renting land, or, in the case of wealthier women, even buying land, if they find the allocations from their husbands inadequate. Field studies (Lennihan 1994) and interviews with relevant officials indicate that in the tomato-growing areas of Kaduna State, and on irrigation schemes in Kano and Sokoto States, better-off Muslim women are gaining access to irrigated land by renting from husbands or others, or by seeking official allocations in their own right. However, only fairly wealthy rural women have the means for land purchases or the procurement of irrigation plots. Rental fees for upland farms have remained more modest, but are still beyond the means of many poorer Hausa women.

Available evidence suggests that, among better-off Muslim women, access to land through inheritance has improved marginally under SAP. Various studies of Muslim Hausa communities report figures ranging from 11 to 43 per cent of women who claim to own land (Ross 1987, Meagher 1991, Imam 1993). In the past, Muslim women tended not to take possession of inherited land, leaving it instead in the care of their male kin, their deferred claims giving them certain rights to assistance from their male kin for consumption or capital expenditure, as well as an ongoing right to a share in the produce of that land (Jackson 1984, Ross 1987). Under SAP, however, the tendency for women to claim inherited land appears to be increasing, although this trend is largely confined to better-off women who have the resources and the social clout to assert their claim to inherited land. When claimed, however, such land is rarely farmed by the women themselves; it is normally given to the husband to farm for a share of the produce or a monetary rent, given to children to farm, or rented out to others (Ross 1987, Meagher, unpublished fieldnotes 1990–91).

Overall, access to land appears to have improved for both better-off Muslim and non-Muslim women, who have the resources to rent, purchase or exercise their claim on inherited land. By contrast, poorer Hausa women's access to land remains highly constrained by low incomes and the cost of access to land, whether this be by purchase, rental or the enforcement of inheritance claims.

Control and sale of labour

The ability of women to control labour, both their own and that of others, has been unevenly affected by SAP. While the ideological pressures of seclusion have tended to limit the demands Muslim Hausa men are able to make on the labour of wives, Muslim women have experienced a decline in control over the labour of husbands and children for their own economic activities, and are in some cases forced to sell their own labour in order to meet increased household responsibilities.

Among Muslim women, there is little evidence of women being forced out of seclusion by increased male labour demands, even among poorer households. While secluded women from poorer households may participate somewhat more in husbands' and household farming activities, these have tended to stay within the traditionally acceptable range of agricultural operations such as harvesting and threshing.

Evidence from the 1995 survey of non-Muslim Hausa women suggests that, in their case as well, SAP does not appear to have significantly increased the burden of labour demands on husbands' or household farms. In contrast to Jackson's (1984) observations on the Kano River irrigation project in the 1970s, there has been no reduction in the traditional number of days allotted to women to work on their own farms. One woman even claimed that the number of days had actually increased from two to three. These trends may be related to non-Muslim women's heavy responsibilities for household provisioning. Non-Muslim women in this area of Kano State are expected to provide the household with all its grain needs throughout the dry season, as well as having a general obligation to help their husbands out with additional household expenses.

While Hausa women do not appear to be subject to a significant increase in male demands on their agricultural labour, their access to labour has been restricted by the increased use of children's labour on men's and household farms. Rural women in general, and secluded women in particular, are especially dependent on the labour of husbands and children, both for farming and for non-farm activities (Jackson 1984, Palmer 1988). In the face of rising labour costs, the labour of husbands and children is increasingly diverted to the household farm (Meagher and Mustapha 1997). Among poorer households, the rising cost of living is also creating pressures for sending children out as *almajirai* (koranic students), or marrying off daughters as early as possible in order to have fewer mouths to feed. These pressures to get children out of the house may be counterbalanced by the decreasing ability of rural households to afford the costs of education, and the reduced capacity of young men to afford marriage costs. Either way, SAP has tended to increase the tension between women's and men's economic interests regarding the deployment of children.

Under the pressures of rising agricultural labour costs and a growing tendency to shift the financial burden of household maintenance onto women, there has been an increase in both the demand for and supply of female agricultural wage labour. In Kano and Kaduna States, women could earn about N20 daily (25 US cents) in 1994, approximately one-third to half of the male agricultural wage. Women are increasingly employed by large-scale farmers for a limited range of planting, harvesting and threshing tasks (Lennihan 1994, Meagher, unpublished fieldnotes 1994). In most parts of northern Nigeria, however, the greater use of female wage labour does not appear to represent a breakdown in seclusion practices. In areas of strict seclusion, female wage labourers are made up predominantly of women past child-bearing age and pastoral Fulani women, neither of whom are subject to seclusion (Lennihan 1994, Meagher and Mustapha 1997). Throughout most of Hausaland, the bulk of wage labour continues to be supplied by male migrants from drier parts of northern Nigeria, as well as from the Niger Republic (Lennihan 1994).

An exception to this pattern appears to arise on irrigation projects. Staff of the NACB, and those involved in agricultural development projects and irrigation schemes confirm that, on the Kadawa (Kano State) and Gusau (Sokoto State) irrigation projects, Muslim women of child-bearing age perform a wide range of operations, especially in irrigated rice production. Transplanting, weeding, harvesting and threshing are performed almost exclusively by women. The extremely high wages available on the irrigation schemes have certainly contributed to this situation. In 1994, women could earn N60 to N70 per day as wage labourers on rice farms, which, although only about one-third of the male wage, was three times the rate offered outside the irrigation schemes for female agricultural labour, and considerably more than they could earn from most of their traditional non-agricultural activities.

Access to capital

Women are, on the whole, more vulnerable than men to high input and labour costs, owing to their more restricted access to capital and household labour (Guyer and Idowu 1991, Moore and Vaughan 1994). This holds even more for Muslim Hausa women, most of whom are dependent on hired labour for most field operations. As a result, among fully secluded women, only those from better-off households are able to engage in wet-season farming on their own account, despite the availability of relatively inexpensive land for rent. In the case of semi-secluded and non-Muslim women, who traditionally farm small plots during the wet season, entry into the more profitable dry-season farming is also limited to women from the upper stratum of households.

These financial constraints on women's own-account farming have been intensified by the rising costs of production under SAP. For women as well as men, farming is increasingly dependent on access to lucrative non-farm activities with which to fund input and labour costs. However, SAP has also increased the capital costs of most of the non-farm activities available to women. A study conducted in two villages in Kano and Katsina States found that the wives of small-scale farmers have been forced to cut down production in their non-farm activities, or even abandon them altogether, as a result of rising input costs and declining demand (Meagher 1991). This further constrains access to agricultural inputs and labour among women who farm on their own account.

At the same time, women confront a growing burden of financial demands. Faced with declining production and consumption terms of trade in agriculture, Muslim and non-Muslim men are shifting an increasing proportion of household expenditures onto their wives. In the case of the Muslim Hausa, this trend is in contravention of Islamic practice (Meagher 1991, Imam 1993). Islamic ideology has succeeded in masking this process, partially by an increasingly liberal notion of wives' 'personal' expenditures, and partially by the rise of an ideology of 'pitching in', which presents as intermittent and temporary something that is increasingly becoming the norm. Muslim as well as non-Muslim women are also increasingly beset by demands from their husbands for both production and consumption credit.

These various financial demands are tending to eat into the capital and assets of poorer women, further limiting their ability to engage in lucrative or capital-intensive activities whilst simultaneously pressing them to generate more income by whatever means possible. This is leading to an increasingly desperate process of diversification, in which women from poorer households are being concentrated into a relatively narrow range of low-cost, low-income activities such as wage labour and petty snack production. The more lucrative activities, such as rice-husking, groundnut oil extraction or retail trade are increasingly restricted to better-off households, in which husbands are more able to assist with capital, and which are more able to meet their own obligations for household provisioning.

Much has been made of the importance of women's co-operative networks in coping with economic stress. For a variety of reasons, however, indigenous co-operative structures among Muslim Hausa women are much less common than in other Nigerian ethnic groups. Even traditional rotating credit groups, known in Hausa as *adashe*, are largely confined to women from the same household. Wider social networks of friends and relatives, cemented by ceremony attendance and exchanges of visits and gifts, can also be an important source of assistance in times of stress. Evidence from various Hausa villages suggests that these structures are weakening under the pressures of structural adjustment. In Kano, Katsina and Bauchi States, women's *adashe* are breaking down, largely because of the inability of members to keep up their payments (Meagher 1991, Imam 1993). Financial stress has also forced women from poorer households to cut down on ceremony attendance and visits to relatives living outside their village of residence, resulting in a contraction of their social networks (Meagher, unpublished fieldnotes 1990–91; Meagher and Mustapha 1997).

Within this context, the activities of women-oriented development programmes have become crucial. While women's local co-operative structures have been undermined by SAP, women's development programmes provide access to credit and other resources necessary for engagement in any meaningful level of income generation, agricultural or otherwise. However, the combination of relatively narrow indigenous women's co-operative structures, their weakening by SAP, and the tendency of many of these women's programmes to operate through local government structures, has led to the formation of a plethora of poorly rooted women's co-operatives, often dominated by the wives of the village elite. This is particularly true of the former Better Life co-operatives, which are often characterized by the monopolization of resources at the top, and the exclusion or marginalization of less-privileged women (*National Concord*, 5 August 1991; IAR 1994).

The contribution which these programmes have made to increasing women's involvement in own-account farming also demands qualification. In many cases, the operation of a group farm is necessary to qualify for assistance (IAR 1994). While performance varies, participation in farm work is often lax, and yields correspondingly low. It is common practice in northern Nigeria for loans obtained to be divided among the members for the pursuit of individual income-generating activities (Vonkat 1994, IAR 1994). In addition, the dominant focus on income generation and appropriate technologies has tended to encourage greater concentration of resources on the promotion of non-farm activities, such as agricultural processing activities and cottage industries. This is particularly true among the Muslim Hausa, where the role of farming in women's income generation is already very minor.

The net result is that capital from these women's organizations is tending to reinforce existing patterns of differentiation and income generation. Despite their agrarian and 'grassroots' rhetoric, they are tending to channel resources into the hands of the village élite, and to reinforce the process of diversification into non-agricultural activities.

Conclusions

Among both Muslim and non-Muslim Hausa women, the pattern of pressures and opportunities created by SAP appears to reinforce rather than mitigate wider processes of rural differentiation. While access to land does not appear seriously to constrain women's income-generating opportunities under structural adjustment, increasing constraints on access to labour and capital have severely limited the economic options of poorer women. In addition, pressures to bear an increasing proportion of the cost of household maintenance fall most heavily on women from poorer households, further undermining their control of resources. Among better-off households, women have greater access to lucrative non-farm activities, and are less beset by demands for household provisioning, leaving them better able to take advantage of the lucrative opportunities available both within and outside agriculture.

The institutional initiatives targeted at rural women have tended to reinforce rather than alter these tendencies of differentiation and continued de-agrarianization among the bulk of rural Hausa women. By channelling resources into the hands of élite women and focusing more on the promotion of income generation through non-agricultural activities, these programmes do little to improve the access of the majority of women to the agricultural opportunities for improved income generation created in the context of SAP.

In general, the broad parameters of the traditional gender division of labour have not been significantly altered by the economic context created by SAP (Geisler 1993). Among the Muslim Hausa, increasing pressures on male access to agricultural labour have not, on the whole, undermined the practice of seclusion, even in poorer households. In the face of high agricultural production costs, the agricultural 'opportunities' available to the majority of women if they emerge from seclusion are household and wage labour, both of which are less remunerative than most non-agricultural activities available to secluded women. Similarly, better-off Muslim women who can afford to farm on their own account can also afford to remain in seclusion and hire labour to farm for them, avoiding any sacrifice of social status. It is only on the irrigation schemes, where agricultural wages are significantly higher than other income-generating alternatives, that Muslim women are moving outside the traditional bounds of seclusion, even against the wishes of their husbands. By the same token, non-Muslim women have not, on the whole, been subject to increased male demands on their land and labour or to any significant erosion of their role in household agricultural production.

It is, in fact, as much on the level of reproduction as on the level of production that the pressures of differentiation are feeding through to both Muslim and non-Muslim Hausa women. Structural adjustment has neither economically marginalized Hausa women nor enhanced their ability to compensate for the pressures of differentiation on male incomes. Instead it has created a situation in which those women who are least able to benefit from the economic opportunities of SAP are those who most bear the increasing burdens of household reproduction created by SAP. Precisely as a result of their increasing importance in household income generation, women are reinforcing, rather than counteracting, the forces of differentiation acting on male members of their households.

Notes

1. Hill (1972: 24) relates variations in the practice of seclusion to varying levels of the water table. The higher water table in southern Hausaland allows wells to be dug inside compounds, while women farther north must fetch water from village wells or boreholes. Although this fails to explain variations in seclusion practices between nucleated and dispersed settlements, which relate more to economic and ideological issues (Imam 1993: 153ff.), it does suggest a logic to the declining practice of seclusion as one moves north.
2. This is now known as the Family Economic Advancement Programme (FEAP) under the wife of the current Head of State.

3. Training and income-generation programmes are normally undertaken in a manner which is compatible with seclusion in order to reduce the risk of community resistance to women-oriented development programmes. Seclusion does not prevent women from joining co-operatives, dealing with extension agents, or participating in agricultural ventures, so long as appropriate standards of decorum are observed. This normally means women calling on or employing labour to carry out field operations for them.
4. This indicator is not useful for Hausa women since, owing to the constraints of seclusion, many Muslim women, who are not particularly well-off, hire virtually all the agricultural labour they use.
5. Production terms of trade refer to the relationship between output prices and production costs, including labour and fertilizer. Consumption terms of trade refer to the relationship between output prices and the rural cost of living.

References

Beckman, B. (1987) 'Public Investment and Agrarian Transformation in Northern Nigeria', in M. Watts (ed.) *State, Oil and Agriculture in Nigeria*, Institute of International Studies, Berkeley, California.

Bryceson, D.F. and Jamal, V. (eds) (1997) *Farewell to Farms: De-agrarianisation and Employment in Africa*, Ashgate Publishing, Aldershot.

Clough, P. and Williams, G. (1987) 'Decoding Berg: the World Bank in rural northern Nigeria' in M. Watts (ed.) *State, Oil and Agriculture in Nigeria*, Institute of International Studies, Berkeley, California.

Egg, J. and Igue, J. (1993) *Market-Driven Integration in the Eastern Sub-region: Nigeria's Impact on its Immediate Neighbours*, Synthesis Report, INRA/IRAM/UNB.

Geisler, G. (1993) 'Silences speak louder than claims: gender, household, and agricultural development in southern Africa', *World Development*, 21(12): 1965–80.

Guyer, J. and Idowu, O. (1991) 'Women's agricultural work in a multi-modal rural economy: Ibarapa District, Oyo State, Nigeria' in C. H. Gladwin (ed.) *Structural Adjustment and African Women Farmers*, University of Florida Press, Gainsville.

Hill, P. (1972) *Rural Hausa: A Village and a Setting*, Cambridge University Press, Cambridge.

Hill, P. (1977) *Population, Prosperity and Poverty: Rural Kano 1900 and 1970*, Cambridge University Press, Cambridge.

Imam, A. (1993) ' "If you won't do these things for me, I won't do seclusion for you": local and regional constructions of seclusion ideologies and practices in Kano, northern Nigeria', PhD thesis, University of Sussex.

IAR (1994) *Report on Pre-Technology Survey, Ganjuwa Local Government Area, Bauchi*, Institute for Agricultural Research//UNICEF Series 1, Zaria, Nigeria.

Jackson, C. (1984) *The Kano River Irrigation Project*, C. Overholt, M.B. Anderson, K. Cloud and J.E. Austin (series eds) *Women's Roles and Gender Differences in Development: Cases for Planners*, Kumarian Press, West Hartford, Connecticut.

Lele, V. (1991) 'Women, structural adjustment and transformation: some lessons and questions from the African experience', in C.H. Gladwin (ed.) *Structural Adjustment and African Women*, University of Florida Press, Gainsville, Florida.

Lennihan, L. (1994) 'Structural adjustment and agricultural wage labour in northern Nigeria: a preliminary research note', paper presented at the 37th Annual Meeting of the African Studies Association, Toronto, Canada, 3–6 November.

Matlon, P.J. (1977) 'The size distribution, structure and determinants of personal incomes among farmers in the north of Nigeria', PhD thesis, Cornell University.

Matlon, P.J. (1978) *Income Distribution and Patterns of Expenditure, Savings and Credit Among Farmers in the North of Nigeria*, Occasional Paper, No. 96, Department of Agricultural Economics, Cornell University.

Meagher K. (1994) 'Parallel trade and powerless places: research traditions and local realities in rural northern Nigeria', paper presented at the 37th Annual Meeting of the African Studies Association, Toronto, Canada, 3–6 November.

Meagher, K. (1993) *Nigeria, Granary of Niger?: The Implications of Cross-Border Trade for Food Security in Nigeria and Niger*, Integration through Markets in the Sub-Region, Niger-Nigeria Interaction, CILSS/Club du Sahel/Cinergie.

Meagher, K. (1991) *Priced Out of the Market: The Impact of Liberalization and Parallel Trade on Smallholder Incomes in Northern Nigeria*, MacNamara Research Fellowship Report.

Meagher K. and Mustapha, A.R. (1997) 'Not by farming alone: the role of non-farm incomes in rural Hausaland', in D.F. Bryceson and V. Jamal (eds) *Farewell to Farms: De-agrarianisation and Employment in Africa*, Ashgate Publishing, Aldershot.

Meagher K. and Ogunwale, S. (1994) *The Grain Drain: The Impact of Cross-Border Grain Trade on Agricultural Production in Northern Nigeria*, Research Report for IRAM/INRA/LARES Project on the Eastern Sub-Market (Nigeria and neighbouring countries).

Mikell, G. (1984) 'Filiation, economic crisis, and the status of women in rural Ghana', *Canadian Journal of African Studies*, 18, 1: 195–218.

Moore, H.L. and Vaughan, M. (1994) *Cutting Down Trees: Gender, Nutrition, and Agricultural Change in the Northern Province of Zambia, 1890–1990*, Social History of Africa Series, Heinemann, London.

Mustapha, A.R. (1990) 'Peasant differentiation and politics in rural Kano: 1900–1987', PhD thesis, St Peter's College, Oxford.

Palmer, I. (1988) *Gender Issues in Structural Adjustment of Sub-Saharan African Agriculture and Some Demographic Implications*, Population and Labour Policies Programme, Working Paper No. 166, World Employment Programme, November.

Ross, P. (1987) 'Land as a right to membership: land tenure dynamics in a peripheral area of the Kano close-settled zone', in M. Watts (ed.) *State, Oil and Agriculture in Nigeria*, Institute of International Studies, University of California, Berkeley.

Shenton, R.W. (1985) *The Development of Capitalism in Northern Nigeria*, James Currey, London.

Simmons, E.B. (1990) 'Women in rural development in northern Nigeria' in O. Otite and C. Okali (eds) *Readings in Nigerian Rural Society and Economy*, Heinemann, Ibadan.

UNIFEM (1994) *Community-Based Commodity Approach to Food Security with Women: Draft Project Document*, UNIFEM, Lagos, Nigeria.

Vonkat, J. (1994) 'Experiences of work with women groups', in Role of Women in Agriculture with Focus on Farm Tools and Related Technologies, Conference Proceedings, Institute of Agricultural Research, September.

Watts, M. (1983) *Silent Violence*, University of California Press, Berkeley.

5. The Politics of Peasant Ethnic Communities and Urban Civil Society: Reflections on an African Dilemma

MAHMOOD MAMDANI

THE LATE NINETEENTH century 'scramble for Africa' marks the last great wave of European colonization. The target of the 'scramble' was the land mass between the Sahara and the Limpopo. To these equatorial African colonies late colonialism brought a host of lessons from previous colonizing experiences, particularly those of nineteenth-century Asia. The core lesson favoured a different articulation of power in the colonial state: a distinctive dualism between modern and customary law, civil and traditional society, rights and custom, town and country, and crucially between citizens and subjects. The bifurcated nature of power was reflected in the contrast between a civil power claiming to guarantee civilized rights for a racialized citizenry, and a customary power ('native authorities') claiming to enforce an ethnicized 'custom' on 'native' subjects. The British, who pioneered this dualism, described it benignly as 'indirect' as opposed to 'direct' rule. Its kernel – the division between a racialized rights-bearing citizenry and an ethnicized, largely peasant, rightless subject population – came to be incorporated and reproduced by every colonial power in equatorial Africa. The French called it 'association' to distinguish it from the earlier policy of 'assimilation'. The South Africans, the last to incorporate the lessons of British indirect rule, called it separate development: *apartheid*. The division between the racialized citizen and the ethnicized subject was sharpest where immigrant settler populations achieved self-rule and independence. It is in this sense that apartheid South Africa epitomized not so much an exception to the African colonial experience as the generic form of the colonial state in Africa.

This chapter seeks both to illuminate the legacy of the African colonial state and to examine the two major trajectories forged by post-independence regimes as they sought to reform the state. Bequeathed such a distinctive political legacy, what would an adequate agenda for democratization in post-independence Africa have looked like? I argue that democratization would have required coming to terms with the dualization of power that distinguished between full citizen and peasant subject. As such, it would have required simultaneously detribalizing the Native Authority and deracializing civil power as starting points in an overall programme of reform of the state and society.

The Colonial State and Indirect Rule

The colonial state was in every instance a historical formation. Yet despite differences in setting, its structure came to share certain fundamental features. Just as they learnt from earlier experiences, so colonial powers borrowed from one another in a process of trial and error. Everywhere, the organization and reorganization of the colonial state were in response to a central and overriding question, generally referred to as the 'native question'. Briefly put, how can a tiny and foreign minority rule over an indigenous peasant majority?

To this question, there were two broad answers: direct and indirect rule. In the African context their main features, and the contrast between them, are best illustrated by the South African experience. Direct rule, the main mode of control attempted over 'natives' in the eighteenth and early nineteenth centuries, is best exemplified by the Cape experience. The basic features of indirect rule, on the other hand, are best illustrated by the experience of Natal in the second half of the nineteenth century.

Direct rule was based on the presumption of a single legal order. That order was formulated in terms of received colonial ('modern') law. Its other side was the non-recognition of 'native' institutions. The vision of direct rule was based on an equality of rights in a multi-racial society, but 'uncivilized' peasants were excluded from the ranks of the equal in civil society. Nor did the equality of civil rights mean a similar political equality, for political rights were grounded in the ownership of property. The resulting vision is best summed up in Cecil Rhodes's famous phrase, 'equal rights for all civilised men'.

The social prerequisite of direct rule was rather drastic. It involved a comprehensive sway of market institutions: the appropriation of land, the destruction of communal autonomy, the defeat and dispersal of 'tribal' populations, and the creation of subject peasant populations. Given that background, direct rule meant the reintegration and domination of 'natives' in the institutional context of semi-servile and semi-capitalist agrarian relations.

In contrast to this, indirect rule came to be the mode of domination over a 'free' peasantry. Here, land remained a communal – 'customary' – possession. The market was restricted to products of labour, only marginally incorporating land or labour itself. Peasant communities were reproduced within the context of a spatial and institutional autonomy. Their leadership was either selectively and ethnically reconstituted as the hierarchy of the local state, or freshly constituted and imposed where none had existed, as in the 'stateless societies'. Here, political and civil inequality were grounded in a legal dualism. Alongside the received law, customary law regulated non-market relations, in land, in personal (family) affairs and in community affairs. In South Africa, the dominance of mining over agrarian capital in the late nineteenth century posed afresh the question of reproduction of autonomous peasant communities which would regularly supply male, adult, single migrant labour to the mines.

In a colonial context, direct rule was necessarily unstable. Its claim to a single legal order and an equality of rights in a multi-racial context was premised on a massive exclusion of 'natives' (the 'uncivilized') from the regime of civil power and civil rights. Those excluded experienced direct rule as a centralized despotism. In contrast, indirect rule was premised on an inclusion of this colonized majority in a regime of customary power. Grounded in the local state as an ethnically defined native authority, customary power spoke the language of tradition, not of rights. Its claim was not to guarantee rights but to enforce tradition. Those incorporated in the regime of customary power experienced indirect rule as a decentralized despotism.

A century earlier, direct rule had been *the* mode of colonial rule. It embodied the claim to be a civilizing mission, the reverse side of which was a wholesale condemnation of local tradition and custom as backward. To civilize was to modernize, and to modernize was to Westernize. As the civilizing mission ran into resistance, the colonizing power – in particular, Britain in nineteenth-century India – was compelled to seek local allies. Thus began a protracted process of thinking through 'tradition' analytically, and separating its authoritarian from its popular strands. The construction of a customary law, whereby authoritarian strands in tradition formed the building blocks of a legal regime disciplining 'natives' in the name of 'tradition', began in India, not in Africa. However, in India this measure came mainly in the aftermath of the great 1857 rebellion, too late to affect the form of land tenure in the colony. The scope of the customary, defined in a religious idiom, was thus restricted to personal law. In Africa, by contrast, the scope of the customary was broadened, most importantly to include land. While the starting point of differentiating two forms of power, one civil and the other customary, lay in earlier colonial experiences, the process of constructing a full-blown bifurcated power culminated in the equatorial African colonies in the twentieth century.

Not surprisingly, indirect rule came to be *the* form of colonial rule. While its basic features were sketched in the colony of Natal during the second half of the nineteenth century, it was elaborated by the British in equatorial Africa in the early twentieth century – by Lugard in Nigeria and Uganda, and Cameron in Tanganyika – then emulated first by the French after World War I, the Belgians in the 1930s and finally the Portuguese in the 1950s. At the same time, indirect and direct rule, customary and civil power, ceased to be thought of as alternatives. While indirect rule became the mode of governing the countryside, towns were subject to direct rule.

Indirect rule was mediated rule. It meant that colonial rule was never experienced by the vast majority of the colonized as rule directly by others.

Rather, the colonial experience for most 'natives' was one of rule mediated through one's own. As Jan Smuts, the South African Prime Minister, emphasized in his Rhodes lecture at Oxford in 1929, 'territorial segregation' would not solve the 'native problem'; 'institutional segregation' was needed (Smuts 1929: 76–8, 92). For the colonial order to be stabilized, the 'natives' would have to be ruled not just by their own but through 'native institutions'. Indirect rule was grounded less in racial than in ethnic structures. Through the combination of a state-sanctioned, ethnically defined 'custom', enforced by a state-appointed, ethnic, customary (Native) Authority, the colonial power attempted to salvage and to build creatively upon the authoritarian strand in 'native' tradition. As such, it tried to turn a growing racial contradiction into an ethnic one.

The African Form of the Colonial State: A Bifurcated Apparatus

The legal dualism characteristic of indirect rule juxtaposed received (modern) law alongside customary law. Modern law regulated relations entered into by 'non-natives', whether with one another or with 'natives'. Customary law, on the other hand, governed relations amongst natives only.

Customary law was said to be 'tribal' law. A tribe or an ethnic group was in turn defined by colonial authorities as a group with its own distinctive law. Referred to as custom, this law was usually unwritten, especially in non-settler contexts. Its source was the native authority, those in charge of managing the local state apparatus, and this native authority was supposedly the traditional tribal authority. In this arrangement, the source of the law was the very authority that administered the law. This meant the absence of a rule-bound authority. Despite the persistent fantasy of colonial powers, particularly Britain and France, that their major contribution to the colonized was to bring them the benefits of the rule of law, there could be no rule of law in such an arrangement. For customary justice was administratively driven. It could not be otherwise in a situation where judicial and administrative authority were fused in the same agency.

The functionary of the local state apparatus was everywhere called the 'chief'. One should not be misled by the nomenclature to think of this as a hangover from the pre-colonial era. The chief was not only a person who had the right to pass rules (bye-laws) governing persons living under his domain, he also executed all laws, and was the administrator in 'his' area, in which he settled all disputes. The authority of the chief thus placed in a single person all moments of power: judicial, legislative, executive and administrative. The administrative justice and the administrative coercion that were the sum and substance of his authority lay behind a regime of extra-economic coercion, a regime that breathed life into a whole range of compulsions: forced crops, forced sales, forced contributions, and forced removals.

The creation of an all-embracing world of the customary, the defining feature of late colonialism in equatorial Africa, had three notable consequences. Firstly, the African colonial experience was marked by force to an unusual degree. Where land was defined as a customary possession, the market could only be a partial construct. Aside from the market, force was the only way of driving land and labour out of the world of the customary. The day-to-day violence of the colonial system was embedded in customary native authorities in the local state, not in civil power at the centre. Custom came to be the language of force. It masked the uncustomary power of native authorities. Not surprisingly, the outlawing of the use of direct force in British colonies after the First World War, and in French colonies after the Second, did not affect the use of direct force by native authorities. Considered a customary practice – since its source was the customary authority – it was exempt from any prohibition in modern civil law. Colonial despotism was highly decentralized.

The locus of customary power was the local state: the district in British colonies, *la cercle* in French colonies. Unlike civil power which was organized on the principle of differentiation, customary power was organized as fused power. Those who enforced custom also defined custom in the first place. Custom, in other words, was state-ordained and state-enforced, but not in the sense that custom was always defined 'from above'. The customary was often the site of struggle. Custom was the outcome of a contest between various forces, not just those in power or its on-the-scene agents. The institutional context in which this contest took place, the terms of the contest and its institutional framework, were heavily skewed in favour of state-appointed customary authorities. It was a game in which the dice were loaded.

The second consequence of creating an all-embracing state-enforced custom was to give 'tradition' a markedly authoritarian content. We need to remember that there were several traditions, not just one, in the late nineteenth-century African context. The tradition which colonial powers privileged as the customary was the one with the least historical depth, that of nineteenth-century conquest states. At the same time, this monarchical, authoritarian and patriarchal notion of the customary most accurately mirrored colonial practices. In this sense, it was an ideological construct.

Finally, more than any other colonial subject, the African peasant was contained in a world of state-enforced custom, not as a racialized 'native' but as an ethnicized 'tribesperson'. Since customary law was defined as the law of the tribe, and a tribe in turn as a group with its own customary law, there was not one customary law for all natives, but roughly as many sets of customary laws as there were said to be tribes. Dame Margery Perham, a semi-official historian of British colonialism, claimed that the genius of British rule lay in seeking to civilize Africans not as individuals but as communities (Perham 1967: 65, 145). More than anywhere else, the African colonial experience embodied a one-sided opposition between the individual and the group, civil society and community, rights and tradition.

Indirect rule, grounded in a legal dualism and the colonial construction of an administratively driven form of justice called customary law was the antithesis of a rule of law. It was, rather, legal arbitrariness. Indirect rule was the form of the state that framed the social life of the 'free' peasantry.

The Anti-colonial Revolt

The form of rule shaped the form of revolt against it. This meant that ethnicity ('tribalism') was simultaneously the form of colonial control over 'natives' and the form of revolt against it. It defined the parameters of both the native authority in charge of the local state apparatus and of the revolt against it. Indirect rule at once reinforced ethnically bound institutions of control and exploded them from within.

Ethnicity was a feature both of power and of resistance. Its two contradictory moments involved both social control and social emancipation. Consequently, it does not make sense to embrace ethnicity uncritically nor to reject it one-sidedly. Everywhere, the local apparatus of the colonial state was organized either ethnically or on a religious basis so that during the colonial period it is difficult to find a single major peasant uprising which was not either ethnically or religiously inspired. This is because the anti-colonial struggle was first and foremost a struggle against the hierarchy of the local state, the ethnically organized native authority which claimed an ethnic legitimacy. Although the cadres of the nationalist movement were recruited mainly from urban areas, the movement gained depth the more it was anchored in the struggle of peasantries pitted against the array of native authorities which shackled them. One needs only recall Nkrumah's 'verandah boys' and Cabral's 'boatmen', and militant nationalist movements such as the CPP in Ghana, TANU in Tanganyika, RDA in Guinea, and PAIGC in Guinea-Bissau, to realize that the key to a militant anti-colonial movement was the forging of a progressive link between town and country.

After independence, there was a dramatic shift in the political focus of the nationalist leadership, away from the local to the central state apparatus, and away from democratizing local state apparatuses to deracializing civil society in the towns.

History of Actually Existing Civil Society

In current debate, civil society is presented as an agenda for change. By contrast, my focus is on civil society in its actual historical formation, i.e. actually existing civil society. The history of civil society in colonial Africa is laced with racism, for civil society was first and foremost the society of the colons who were urban citizens rather than rural peasants. In addition, civil society was primarily a creation of the colonial state. The rights of free association and free publicity, and eventually of political representation, were rights of citizens under direct rule, not of subjects under indirect rule. In other words, the colonial state was Janus-faced. One side, the state that governed citizens, was bounded by the rule of law and an associated regime of rights; the other side, the state that ruled over peasant subjects, was a regime of extra-economic coercion and administratively driven justice.

The first historical moment in the development of civil society involved the colonial state as the protector of the society of the colons. Not surprisingly, therefore, the struggle of subjects was both against the 'tribal' authorities in the local state and against civil society. The latter was particularly acute in the settler colonies, where it often took the form of an armed struggle. Its best known theoretician is Frantz Fanon. This second moment saw a marked shift in the relation between civil society and the state. This was the moment of the anti-colonial struggle, which was at once also a struggle of the embryonic middle and working classes for entry into civil society. That entry, that expansion of civil society, was the result of an anti-state struggle. Its consequence was the creation of an indigenous civil society, a process set in motion by the post-war colonial reform. But this was a development of limited significance. It could not be otherwise, for any significant progress in the creation of an indigenous civil society required a change in the form of the state. It required a deracialized state.

Independence, the birth of a deracialized state, was the context of the third moment in this history. Independence deracialized the state, but not civil society, although the independent state played a key role in the struggle to deracialize civil society. The key policy instrument in that struggle was what today is called 'affirmative action' and what was then referred to as 'Africanization'. The politics of Africanization were simultaneously unifying and fragmenting. It involved the dismantling of racially inherited privilege, unifying the victims of colonial racism. However, it divided that same majority along lines that reflected the channels of actual redistribution: regional, religious, ethnic, or even just familial. The focus on corruption in the literature of post-independence Africa has served to detach the redistributive tendency, and thereby to isolate and to decontextualize it through ahistorical analogies that describe it as the politics of patrimonialism or prebendalism, or so on. The effect has been to caricature the practices under investigation and to make them unintelligible.

The politics of affirmative action were marked by a sharp ideological shift in the language of contest. With independence, the defence of racial privilege could no longer be expressed in the language of racism. Confronted by a deracialized state, racial privilege not only receded into civil society, but defended itself in the language of civil rights, particularly individual rights and institutional autonomy. To indigenous ears, the vocabulary of rights rang hollow, a lullaby for perpetuating racial privilege. In opposition to this rights-based discourse, indigenous demands were formulated in the language of nationalism and social justice. The result was a breach between the discourse on rights and that on power: while the language of rights appeared as a fig-leaf for privilege, power appeared as the guarantor of social justice and redress.

This is the context of the fourth moment in the history of civil society. This is the moment of the collapse of indigenous civil society into political society. It is the moment of the marriage between technicism and nationalism. It is the time when social movements were demobilized and political movements were infiltrated by the state. The absorption of civil into political society in the post-independence period took place in the heyday of state nationalism. On the one hand, there was a deep division in civil society, a division along racial lines: while racially acquired privilege spoke the language of rights and autonomy, the state claimed to be the beacon of social justice and appeared as the cutting edge of the struggle to deracialize civil society. On the other hand, deracialization was not simply the harbinger of corruption and private accumulation. It also led to an impressive degree of social progress, particularly in the fields of education and health, and especially when set against comparable figures for the colonial period.

This trajectory came to a close with adverse international economic trends in the mid-1970s. The lack of an attempt to democratize local state apparatuses turned into a failure to mobilize a truly national effort to reform international relations of dependency. As a result, adverse trends in the changing international context were more or less mechanically translated into a deepening fiscal crisis of the state. In one country after another, it led to a widespread surrender to an international regime of financial discipline in the form of structural adjustment programmes, against African urban and rural peasant interests.

It is in this context that the middle and working classes rediscovered the language of rights. That rediscovery is central to the development of what came to be referred to as 'pro-democracy movements' in the late 1980s. While these movements herald the rights-based agenda of a re-awakened civil society, at the same time they underline the limits of a civil society-bound perspective: for they lack an agenda of reform of the customary power subjugating the peasantry, the power that is the core institutional legacy of the indirect rule state. The initiative to reform customary power, as we shall see, still remains in the grasp of a re-articulated, reborn, state nationalism.

Post-independence Reform

The post-independence struggle tended towards deracialization but not democratization. In the case of the 'conservative' African states, this is self-evident. The hierarchy of the local state apparatus, from chiefs to native authorities administering customary law, continued after independence. It was reproduced unproblematically, as part of tradition. The chief remained the enforcer of this peculiarly authoritarian version of tradition, fusing its legislative, executive, judicial and administrative moments. In this context, even if the central state was reorganized as a representative parliamentary democracy, the local state continued to function as a decentralized despotism. For the fact remained that the same peasants who could elect their representative in parliament had little choice about who would be their chief wielding despotic power over them in the local context.

In a country where urban areas were administered through electoral civic order and rural areas through appointed chiefs, the impact of multiparty electoral democracy turned out to be flawed. An arrangement which limited meaningful choice to a minority – citizens in urban areas and chiefs in rural areas – was obviously biased. But this electoral system, in which the winning party would both represent citizens in urban civil society and be the master of peasant subjects it ruled through appointed chiefs in rural areas, turned out to be explosive.

Chiefs understood this fact well: none could underplay the importance of delivering 'their' peasants to their party. In time, this localized oppression contaminated the whole political system. Not only did the chief claim to represent 'his' people, he claimed it as a traditional ethnic right and he barred entry to 'his' area to all who would not go through him. Electoral contests in rural areas immediately took on an ethnic flavour as political parties took on the ethnic tag of the chiefly authority they came to ally with.

An electoral democracy where peasants were left as a rightless mass under an hierarchy of chiefs inevitably led to a double corruption. Firstly, the city came to be linked to the country through patronage, and secondly, these ties took on an ethnic flavour as chiefly authority was organized along ethnic lines. The conveyor belt for this institutionalized patronage was the political party system. The switch that linked the two forms of corruption was the election: it simultaneously set in motion the machinery of patronage and triggered ethnic tensions.

The Legacy of the Single Party

The alternative to a customary power, a countryside run through a hierarchy of chiefs, was the single party. Alongside Ghana and Guinea, Tanzania came to symbolize the most radical attempt to deal with the political legacy of colonial rule by dismantling the institution of chiefship. In all three countries, a militant anti-colonialism linked urban-based nationalists to varied peasant struggles against chiefship and its corruption of tradition. The inheritor of that experience was the single party.

At one level, the single party was a way to contain the social and political fragmentation reinforced by ethnically organized native authorities. At another level, the militants of the single party came to distrust democracy, by which they understood an electoral reform that left chiefship intact in the rural areas and so confined civil society to urban areas. A democratic link between the urban and the rural was in their eyes synonymous with an ethnically based system of privilege that linked chiefly power in rural areas with urban-based civil organizations. They understood the single party, although a solution imposed from above, to be preferable to this colonial corruption.

The accent in the 'radical' African states was on change, not continuity. In some instances, a constellation of ethnically defined customary laws was done away with as a single customary law transcending ethnic boundaries was codified. The result was to develop a single country-wide customary law applicable to all peasants regardless of ethnic affiliation, functioning alongside a modern law for urban dwellers. While custom no longer corresponded to ethnicity as in the colonial period, the divide between customary and modern law did reproduce and reinforce the division between town and country. Despite the overwhelming accent on change, there was an important continuity with colonial practices: in as much as these 'radical' regimes shared with colonial powers the conviction to effect a 'revolution from above', they ended up intensifying the administratively driven nature of justice. What had happened was a change in the title of the functionaries of that justice, from chiefs to cadres. But it was a change in nomenclature without a fundamental change in the organization of power. While the bifurcated state that was created with colonialism was deracialized – in some cases, even de-ethnicized – it was not democratized.

In urban areas, the single party tended to depoliticize civil society. The more it succeeded, the more it came to be bureaucratized. The centre of gravity shifted from the party to the state, while the method of work came to rely more on administrative coercion than political persuasion. In the words of Fanon, militants of yesterday turned into informers of today. The attempt to reform localized despotism turned into a centralized despotism. There were cadres of the single party unleashing compulsion in the language of 'revolution' and 'development'.

The reaction to the legacy of the single party came in two waves in the 1980s. The first came to be known as the pro-democracy movement. From Francophone countries in West Africa (Benin, Niger, Ivory Coast, Mali) to Anglophone countries in the East (Kenya, Sudan, Zambia), the pro-democracy movement tended to be urban-centred. It was guided by the perspective that democracy equals multi-party competition and majority rule through electoral representation. Wherever the multi-party reform took root, the results were disappointing. In the absence of a democratization of power in the rural areas, urban-based political parties were forced to deal with ethnically organized chiefly hierarchies in the countryside. In the process, parties tended to turn into so many ethnically organized coalitions. While usually less coercive than the single-party variant, its bitter fruit was ethnic conflict.

The second response to the legacy of the single party has come in the form of a rebirth of radical nationalism. It is the great virtue of the second generation of radical nationalists in Africa not to have one-sidedly dismissed the legacy of militant nationalism (and its child, the single party) but to have critically incorporated that experience in a re-worked programme. The continuity lay in the conviction that without dismantling ethnically organized chiefly power it would not be possible to check tendencies to political fragmentation strengthened by colonial indirect rule. The difference lay in the recognition that this dismantling could not be from above and by force; it would have to be from below and through popular support.

As one would expect, this lesson was drawn in not one but several countries, beginning with the early Gaddafi, Sankara, and the early Rawlings. But it is in Uganda under Yoweri Museveni that the lesson was underlined with the full force of a comprehensive reform: the introduction of village-based councils and committees, called resistance councils and committees (RCs). The RC system separated powers which had hitherto been fused in the chief. Legislative power now belonged to a council of all village adults, whereas executive power lay with a committee elected by the village council. The chief was turned into a simple administrative officer, paid, hired and fired like any other member of the civil service – except that he was accountable to popular organs. 'The first function of the RC', said the Report of the 1987 Commission of Inquiry into Local Government, 'is that of a "watchdog": it is to resist any tendency on the part of state officials towards abuse of authority or denial of the rights of the people'.

Versions of Democracy: Representation and Participation

These two broad reform movements have been characterized as multi-party and representative on the one hand, and non-party and participatory on the other. If one thought of democracy as representative, the other championed it as participatory. If one saw the countryside as the real problem, the other saw the city as symptomatic of corrupting tendencies. While the focus of the multi-party reform was on democratizing the centre, that of non-party reform was on the local and the rural.

Such a comparison, however, misses an important point: the originality of the radical nationalist contribution. For while the movement for multi-party reform is literally content to translate democracy as a turnkey project from western manuals, it is the great merit of second generation radicals to have come to grips with a key political legacy of Africa's colonial experience: the recognition that the real and enduring political legacy of colonial rule in Africa goes beyond the racial effrontery of alien rule to local despotisms that are institutionalized and legitimized as so many customary forms of power. These customary forms of power are still at issue.

To appreciate the radical nationalist contribution is not to argue that it is free from dilemmas. It is exemplified by the non-party option put forth by Museveni and the National Resistance Movement in Uganda, which is likely to be emulated in neighbouring Democratic Republic of Congo (former Zaire). The radicals' great success has been the rural and the local; their great dilemma continues to be the urban and the central. For this very reason, they are often tempted to pit rural against urban areas, arguing that the participatory aspect of democracy is its truly popular aspect, whereas its representational side is really meant for selfish élites, who can be safely ignored for they are a small minority. Or, in a different version of the same argument, a multi-party democracy may be good for Europe which is urban and class-divided, but not for Africa which is rural, and where class divisions are incipient since people tend to live in village communities as peasant producers tilling land which is not yet fully commoditized.

Urban areas may be small, particularly in Uganda which at around 10 per cent has one of the lowest proportions of urban dwellers in Africa. However, Africa is urbanizing at a rate second to none globally. The population of Kinshasa, the capital of the neighbouring Democratic Republic of Congo, is estimated at between 5 to 7 million (around 15 per cent) of a total population of roughly 40 million.

To take into account the most dynamic features of the African reality is to recognize that African countries are not just villages or towns, but both; not just rural peasant communities or class-divided urban areas, but both. It highlights the limits of both the 'pro-democracy' multi-partyists who offer representation without participation and the second generation radicals who champion democracy as participation without representation. It is a context requiring democracy in both its participatory and its representative aspect. How to marry the two is the first challenge facing Africans today.

The second challenge stems from a more universal lesson, one underlined by political crisis in different contexts. How many revolutionary governments have begun with genuine mass support, often primarily peasant support, and ended as repressive isolated regimes? How many governments used the fact of popular support to avoid the question of power, of putting in place a constitutional mechanism for a change in government? Is there not a shared lesson in the experience of the Communist Party in the former Soviet bloc and the single party in post-independence Africa, both of which held regular elections but neither of which allowed rival political organizations? Is not the lesson that a political system which does not guarantee the right of opposition – the right to organize as an opposition – can be neither stable nor self-sustaining? Ironically, the second-generation radicals in power now are not averse to championing a regime of rights, but only in its most individualistic version, thereby avoiding the question of power. How to join the question of rights to that of power in the overall discourse on democracy is Africa's second challenge today.

The legacy of colonial government ruling localized peasant populations through ethnicized and despotic forms of power legitimized as the continuation of tradition has stunted the growth of vibrant civil societies in African states. Peasant producers can no longer be circumscribed as tribal subjects, nor can African states function with ethnic units as their local authorities and political constituencies. This time warp is giving way at the seams.

References

Perham, M. (1967) *Colonial Sequence, 1930 to 1949*, Methuen, London.

Smuts, J.C. (1929) *Africa and Some World Problems* (including the Rhodes Memorial Lectures Delivered in Michaelmas Term, 1929) Clarendon Press, Oxford.

6. Peasant Wars in Africa: Gone with the Wind?

ROBERT BUIJTENHUIJS

> We speak of peasants, but the term 'peasant' is very vague. The peasant who fought in Algeria or China is not the peasant of our country. It so happens that in our country the Portuguese colonialists did not expropriate the land. . . . Telling the people that 'the land belongs to those who work on it' was not enough to mobilise them, because we have more than enough land. We had to find appropriate formulae for mobilising our peasants. . . . We could never mobilise our people simply on the basis of the struggle against colonialism. . . . Instead we use a direct language that all can understand:
> 'Why are you going to fight? What are you? What is your father? What has happened to your father up to now? What is the situation? Did you pay taxes? Did your father pay taxes? What have you seen from those taxes? How much do you get for your groundnuts? Have you thought about how much you will earn with your groundnuts? How much sweat has it cost your family? Which of you have been imprisoned? You are going to work on road-building: who gives you the tools? You bring the tools. Who provides your meals? You provide your meals. But who walks on the road? Who has a car? And your daughter who was raped – are you happy about that?' (Cabral 1969: 128).

From the 1960s until the mid-1980s peasant wars were a topic of deep interest to social scientists. Alavi's (1965) seminal article on 'Peasants and revolution', which identified the 'revolutionary potential' of different categories of peasants, was followed by Wolf's (1973) trend-setting book *Peasant Wars of the Twentieth Century*. In Africa south of the Sahara, Barnett's (1973) booklet *Peasant Types and Revolutionary Potential in Colonial Africa* and Welch's (1978) article on 'Obstacles to "peasant wars" in Africa' are just two examples of the expanding literature of the time.

Most case studies of African rural protest movements classified their subject matter as peasant wars. Thus the Mau Mau revolt in Kenya (Barnett and Njama 1966, Buijtenhuijs 1971); the anti-colonial uprising in Zimbabwe (Ranger 1985); and the Agbekoya uprising in western Nigeria (Beer 1976) were seen to be generated by peasants expressing their ties with the soil and as taking forms which displayed the organizational advantages and limitations of peasant communities.

However, peasant wars have now faded from the world stage, or at least from western social science literature, and especially from academic discourse on Africa south of the Sahara. How should we explain this change? Have peasant wars indeed become extinct, or have social scientists revised their paradigms so that what would formerly have been categorized as peasant wars are now seen in other terms? This chapter seeks to answer these questions.

Principled versus Predatory Wars

The perception of African peasant wars was undoubtedly influenced by the literature on movements elsewhere. The recent experience of peasant mass rebellions in Asia was highly influential. In the 1960s Mao became a cult figure on western university campuses, and anti-war demonstrations against US involvement in Vietnam played on the fact that rural peasants were being bombarded by an industrial power whose technological advantage bordered on the obscene.

On the African continent, decolonization unfolded in fits and starts and national liberation movements sprang up in those countries where colonial powers were reluctant to leave. The social origins of the leadership of these movements were highly variable but their followers consisted primarily of peasants. The rationale for peasants joining were undoubtedly complex. Amilcar Cabral, leader of Guinea Bissau's PAIGC, was adamant that material reasons held sway:

> Keep always in mind that the people are not fighting for ideas, for the things in anyone's head. They are fighting . . . for material benefits, to live better and in peace, to see their lives go forward, to guarantee the future of their children. National liberation, war on colonialism, building of peace and progress – independence – all that will remain meaningless for the people unless it brings a real improvement in conditions of life (confidential memorandum from Amilcar Cabral to the PAIGC membership dated 1965, quoted by Davidson 1969: 122).

Whatever reasons the peasant rank and file may have had for joining an African national liberation movement, liberal and radical western observers interpreted their actions largely in terms of popular struggles for nationhood, what might best be termed 'just wars'. This view was supported by documented cases of colonial government repression which turned hesitant peasants into determined rebels, as exemplified by Kenya's Mau Mau (Barnett and Njama 1966) and the 1961 Northern Angolan insurrection (Davezies 1965, Buijtenhuijs 1996).

As national liberation movements became more dependent on guerilla warfare tactics, the concept of a 'just war' was extended to the notion of a 'people's war'. Amilcar Cabral, Africa's foremost spokesman and strategist for waging a people's war, explained:

> When the African peoples say in their simple language that 'no matter how hot the water from your well, it will not cook your rice', they express with singular simplicity a fundamental principle, not only of physics, but also of political science. We know that the development of a phenomenon in movement, whatever its external appearance, depends mainly on its internal characteristics. We also know that on the political level our own reality – however fine and attractive the reality of others may be – can only be transformed by detailed knowledge of it, by our own efforts, by our own sacrifices (Cabral 1966: 74).

The peasants' role in the war effort was that of supplying combatants, nurturing them, and feeding and hiding them as and when circumstances required. This symbiotic relationship with the peasants was not compatible with the liberation movement sacrificing means for ends. The promise of political freedom at some future date was not enough. The movement was judged on its ability to extend egalitarian relations in an immediate temporal and spatial sense as well as on its ability to deliver freedom from foreign oppression at some future date.

Women in particular were called on to nurture, feed and hide combatants, and in most cases, such as in the Mau Mau revolt, they responded eagerly. Although the proportion of women amongst the forest fighters never exceeded 5 per cent of the total, they dominated what was wrongly called the 'passive wing' of the Mau Mau, i.e. the urban and village networks which supplied the fighters with food, clothing, medicines and sometimes weapons. By way of illustration, Kikuyu prostitutes in Nairobi were said to require bullets when delivering their services to African members of the armed forces. More generally, several British colonial administrators were convinced that women were among the most 'fanatical' adherents of the movement and took the Mau Mau oath in great numbers.

Much later, during the 1970s, when western preoccupations became strongly focused on gender relations, attention was drawn to the liberation movements' ability to redress traditional patriarchal attitudes and practices amongst the peasantry. Young women in Guinea Bissau and Mozambique, desirous of escaping oppressive customs such as forced marriage, polygyny and lack of divorce rights, joined the PAIGC as combatants (Manceaux 1975, Urdang 1979). In Zimbabwe, ZANU activists actively sought to enforce more egalitarian relations in peasant households:

> Women's articulated demands were for their husbands to stop beating them and cease drinking . . . From all accounts, the guerrillas then punished the husbands by beating them. . . . For a brief period, wives acquired control over their husbands (Kriger 1992).

By the mid-1970s, peasant wars throughout Africa had gained significant ground and had achieved national independence in the ex-Portuguese colonies of Guinea Bissau, Angola and Mozambique, as well as in Zimbabwe and Namibia. The optimism of this era arose from the belief that illiterate African peasants with a just cause or, in other words, 'a small people with a big cause' would succeed, achieving the seemingly impossible goal of national independence despite the great technological and financial advantages of the colonial governments. South Africa remained the stark exception. It was the only sub-Saharan African country which no longer had a significant peasant population and whose industrialized status had significantly raised the stakes of African majority rule.

The concept of a 'people's war' peaked in southern Africa, and it was here too that it began to turn sour. The death of Samora Machel, the leader of Mozambique's national liberation movement, FRELIMO, marked a turning point. His death was linked to sabotage on the part of the South African government and increased counter-insurgency inside Mozambique through its support for Renamo.

In the early 1980s a new phenomenon of 'predatory war' emerged in Africa. This refers to insurgent movements whose objectives are not, or not solely, to drive incumbent rulers out of power and form a new government, but rather to secure by force of arms the economic resources in those areas which combatants control. These resources include agricultural produce or cattle (Somalia) and, in the more 'sophisticated' cases, minerals such as diamonds and gold.

Although peasants may still be the main participants in these forms of insurgency, they are not a form of social protest by peasants *per se*. In many cases the rebellion is not identified with any political message nor does it represent the interests of identifiable social classes or categories. Rather, violent rebellion becomes an occupational career in and of itself for the combatants. Although involving peasants, and in cases such as Liberia or Somalia (where child-soldiers are numerous) the sons and daughters of peasants, their motivations are not those of peasants fighting for their livelihoods or for control of land. In fact, as the rebellion unfolds, peasant interests are progressively undermined. The combatants live off the land at the expense of the remaining genuine peasantry, extracting road and market tolls, taxes, and forced political contributions from them. In some cases, namely those of Liberia, Sierra Leone and Chad in the 1980s, the countryside was emptied of people, who fled for protection and survival to urban areas or across international borders.

The cases of Liberia and Somalia are the best documented and most dramatic examples of a predatory war (Reno 1993, 1995, Richards 1995, Ellis 1995, Marchal and Messiant 1997, Compagnon 1999). The degree of violence and detrimental impact on the rural population, as well as the flamboyant manner and dress of the youthful combatants, captured world media attention. However, this chapter draws on the Chadian experience to demonstrate the differences between the two generations of African civil wars. Although less well known than the Liberian case, it illustrates well the evolution of rural protest from that of a 'principled' to a 'predatory' form of war.

Evolution of the FROLINAT's Peasant War in Chad

Civil war broke out in Chad as early as 1965 and continues intermittently to this day. All sources confirm that the early years of struggle of the Chadian rebels, who rose up against the country's independent government primarily as peasants and secondarily as Muslims, were particularly harsh (Buijtenhuijs 1978). Banding together in the movement called FROLINAT, most rebel fighters were malnourished and inadequately armed, as reported in a letter dated 24 May 1971 from Goukoiruni Weddeye, one of the movement's military commanders, to Abba Sidick, the then Secretary-General of FROLINAT in 1971:

> At the moment, all three detachments are being fed through collection and by the local population, which as you should know is all rather meagre. One of the detachments has gone eight days without any food (not even dates), drinking water and the dried fruit of the *doum* palm tree. In such conditions, needless to say, fighting or even defending themselves is out of the question.

Tellingly, the very first FROLINAT fighters in 1966–67 were called 'the thin ones of Ibrahima Abatcha' (the movement's founder and first Secretary-General). Thus, initially, a high degree of conviction was necessary to become a rebel for the material gains were almost non-existent.

However, this situation changed radically in 1977 when, with geopolitical designs, Libya's Colonel Qadafi gave his backing to the FROLINAT rebels and started supplying them lavishly with arms, food and other goods. With these sophisticated weapons, including artillery and ground-to-air SAM 7 rockets, the rebels easily defeated the government's ill-equipped and poorly motivated army, establishing themselves permanently as the rulers of vast areas of northern and eastern Chad. At this point, war became an industry, a career and a way of life, as much for the grassroots fighters as for the movement's leaders.

> Factionalism in Chad has become a full-time occupation which involves only a small part of the population. . . . The use of foreign sponsors on a wide scale supports an entire politico-military class which lives off the war and its dividends. . . . At that level, aspirations of 'national reconciliation' become less than obvious (Triaud 1985).

Grassroots fighters were transformed into 'professional' soldiers who embraced the revolution as a career opportunity. Given the conditions in

Chad in the late 1970s, such a choice could be seen as the optimal way to ensure both immediate well-being and future prospects. Conversely, rural communities had to bear the brunt of a very heavy 'revolutionary' fiscal policy. Arbitrary acts, perpetrated by armed young men with scant regard for the law or traditional moral codes, became the order of the day. During this period of anarchy, the main objective of Chad's 'revolutionary' armed factions was to control as much territory as possible in order to tax the local rural communities. Commenting on the situation in eastern Chad in the early 1980s, Doornbos notes:

> It is my impression that Chad's eastern rebels' only preoccupation since 1978 has been ensuring their day to day survival and fighting neighbouring rebels. An attack from the outside can have the effect of reducing the territory where they rule over the *masakin*, the common people (Doornbos 1982).

Gone forever was the FROLINAT of the early days which advanced the claims of peasant communities and whose members behaved as 'bandits of honour', not as outright gangsters. Alongside the collapse of discipline with respect to the peasantry, there was also a breakdown in FROLINAT's chain of command. The movement gradually disintegrated into various factions without any central command, who sometimes co-operated, sometimes fought each other. This splintering of the movement arose primarily over the question of how much Libyan aid was acceptable, and was exacerbated by ethnic tension. Over the years, the FROLINAT rebellion ran full circle, evolving from a genuine peasant revolt against a powerful, urban-based, non-Muslim, African élite into a predatory warlord movement. But its longevity is exceptional. Most rural revolts are not so enduring.

More generally, African rural movements have tended to be short-lived. Most movements which were active from the 1950s to the 1970s corresponded to the 'principled war' model of the early FROLINAT years. For example, the Mau Mau revolt in 1952 and the anti-colonial uprising in Cameroon which began in 1955 showed no evidence of the leadership or rank-and-file pursuing violent rebellion for the sake of private profit. The anti-colonial uprisings in the Portuguese African territories during the 1970s also belong to the category of genuine peasant revolts, although some factors were already present which would later transform them into predatory wars, as illustrated by Jonas Savimbi's UNITA movement in Angola.

The anatomy of the 'principled' peasant war involved a symbiotic relationship between combatants and peasant cultivators in which it was understood that soldiers were materially supported in the here and now in the cause of peasant victory. External sponsorship – especially where generous – was seen as an intrusion which, in the absence of careful control, could short-circuit the local synergy between peasant and soldier. The guerilla fighters who received training abroad and acquired sophisticated weapons were often able to conquer large tracts of land which extended beyond their home territories. In so doing, they sometimes gained access to valuable economic assets (such as diamonds in the case of Sierra Leone and Angola, or cattle in the case of Somalia), control of which fuelled warlordism.

Such riches were not part of the rural protest movements of the 1960s and earlier. The colonial peasant revolts such as Kenya's Mau Mau and the Cameroonian UPC did not receive any foreign assistance. For the individual fighters, revolution meant economic sacrifice rather than betterment. Amilcar Cabral in Guinea Bissau, Agostino Neto in Angola and Samora Machel in Mozambique received foreign funds and weapons, mainly from the Soviet Union and other East European countries, but these leaders were motivated by nationalist aspirations and sufficiently committed to their cause to keep outside assets in check. By contrast, this was no longer the case amongst the new generation of post-colonial military rebel leaders, such as Liberia's Charles Taylor. Predatory wars became a common feature of politics in several African countries. Indeed, these armed insurrections had few characteristics in common with the earlier peasant wars. This explains in part why the concept of 'peasant wars' disappeared as an analytical category from academic discourse.

New or Old Paradigms?

However, this is only part of the explanation. The other part relates to the emergence of new paradigms in western social science with quite different ways of interpreting social phenomena. In the wider context of the fall of the Berlin wall and the disintegration of the Soviet Union, neo-Marxism and other related analyses were put on the defensive. Class analysis generally, and peasant wars more specifically, ceased to be fashionable topics in academic circles. This does not mean that peasant wars, or peasant conflict, disappeared entirely from African reality, but that scholars interpreted them in other terms.

In current debate, important conflicts in Africa are most often seen as 'tribal' or 'ethnic' wars, especially in the media. There has been a revival of interest in the question of ethnicity, as in the decolonization period of the 1950s when African rural dwellers were yet to be identified as peasants. Civil strife in rural areas is no longer depicted as 'peasant' in nature but is analysed in terms of ethnic affiliation and ethnic alliances. Peasant conflict is not thereby eliminated but merely ignored by social scientists.

This can be illustrated by the recent spate of extremely bloody conflicts in Ruanda and Burundi. For the non-specialist, who flicks through what has been written on these civil wars, it would appear that these are tribal, involving Tutsi and Hutu tribesmen who are bent on ethnic cleansing. Ethnicity is undoubtedly an important aspect of the Ruanda–Burundi conflicts but one should not overlook another key dimension. At the outbreak of conflict, these countries had the highest recorded rural population densities in Africa and there were few off-farm economic opportunities for the rural surplus population. Land had become an increasingly scarce asset in a situation where peasants formed the overwhelming majority of the population. Tutsi and Hutu combatants vie not only for political power at the central state level, but also for more material causes at the local level in the hills (*collines*) (de Lame 1996). The age-old peasant concern with land stares social scientists in the face. Thus, these civil wars are as much peasant wars as they are ethnic wars, and would undoubtedly have been analysed as such by an earlier generation of social scientists, such as Alavi or Wolf.

The similarities with the Mau Mau are striking. In the early 1950s the Mau Mau uprising was primarily interpreted as an uprising of Kikuyu tribesmen, only later being reclassified as a peasant rebellion. Ironically, the early 1990s have witnessed the revival of ethnic interpretations of rural land conflict. In the wake of political liberalization, conflicts between local Kalenjin and new immigrants, mainly of Kikuyu origin, erupted in the Rift Valley province, the former 'White Highlands'. To limit the effects of political contestation, it is argued that Kenya's President Daniel arap Moi played on the ethnic sentiments of his fellow Kalenjin to drive the 'foreigners' out of an area he considered to be his home base, and whose votes he needed for the first multi-party presidential elections held in 1992. But this is not the whole story as argued by Médard:

> These ethnic conflicts should be related to clearly expressed territorial claims corresponding to both preoccupations about land and electoral considerations. To obtain land and to circumscribe political contestation are the two faces of the same strategy, and, in the case of Kenya, they should not be conceptually separated. There is practically no arable land available any more. And in order to find arable land, the only solution seems to be to create a space for oneself, even if this entails driving out already established groups (Médard 1996).

The continuation of peasant war can be illustrated in Chad as well. Over the past 15 years, the difficult co-habitation of agriculturalists and herdsmen, especially in the southern provinces, has emerged as one of the country's main problems. Following the severe droughts of the 1970s and 1980s, northern nomadic herdsmen made more frequent and long-lasting incursions in the southern *préfectures* to find grazing and water for their cattle. This phenomenon gained momentum from 1982 onwards, when Hissein Habré, an ex-representative of the northern FROLINAT rebellion, seized power by force of arms (Buijtenhuijs 1987). Many of these herdsmen are now permanently settled in the south, leading to frequent clashes with local peasants over the damage which cattle cause to their crops.

Until recently, most social scientists analysed this friction in terms of north–south regional conflict and as a cultural and ethnic problem (Buijtenhuijs 1995). However, this perspective has to be linked to the issue of access to land and water in a situation of growing rural population density as well as the introduction of new competing agricultural crops:

> Although the increase of manioc production has permitted a partial solution to the food problem of the cotton areas, this crop represents for the Arab and Peul herdsmen the main obstacle they encounter during their journeys. It is their nightmare. Indeed manioc whose cultural cycle covers a year or even more is permanently there [blocking their passage] (Arditi 1992).

A similar situation has occurred in the eastern part of Chad:

> . . . very often, especially around Abéché, the agriculturalists clear land about anywhere without taking into account the traditional passage ways of the herdsmen. Occupying pastures, they limit the movements of the herds on the move and block . . . the passages of the herdsmen. Finally, water-points where the nomads traditionally water their cattle are also occupied by sedentary agriculturalists who cultivate all around. Ten years ago, there were no villages between Goz-Beida and Am-Timan. Today, there are villages everywhere and the herdsmen can't get through (Authosserre, French expert on pastoralism, quoted by Bérassidé 1997: 5).

Conclusions

Wars conducted in rural areas of Africa are on the increase. There is no doubt they are changing in nature, in terms of both their organization and the objectives of the combatants. Social scientists have reverted to seeing their underlying motivation in terms of ethnic chauvinism or individual pecuniary gain. Yet to believe that predatory war is the whole story is to believe in the pendulum swings of human nature. From the euphoria of western social scientists cheering peasants' 'principled wars' for national freedom and social equality, we now have social scientists despairing about the depths of depravity exhibited in the civil strife of rural Africa. A comparison between the social science literature of the early 1970s and that of today, 35 years later, gives the impression that peasants, who once succeeded in achieving the politically impossible, have now sunk to unthinkable depths of social degradation. Perhaps the truth is less dramatic and more enduring: peasant communities have struggled to secure viable means of livelihood then and now, and their struggle has intensified and taken on more desperate forms over time.

References

Alavi, H. (1965) 'Peasants and revolution', in R. Miliband and J. Savile (eds) *The Socialist Register 1965*, Merlin Press, London.

Arditi, C. (1992) *Etude régionale des stratégies différenciées des éleveurs d'Afrique centrale: Le Tchad*, République du Tchad, Ministère de l'Elevage et de l'Hydraulique pastorale, September.

Barnett, D.L. (1973) *Peasant Types and Revolutionary Potential in Colonial Africa*, LSM Press, Richmond BC, Canada.

Barnett, D.L. and Njama, K. (1966) *Mau Mau from Within: Autobiography and Analysis of Kenya's Peasant Revolt*, Monthly Review Press, New York and London.

Beer, C.E.E. (1976) *The Politics of Peasant Groups in Western Nigeria*, Ibadan University Press, Ibadan.

Bérassidé, G. (1997) 'Almy Bahaïm: une approche pragmatique', *N'Djaména Hebdo*, No. 269, February.

Buijtenhuijs, R. (1971) *Le mouvement 'mau mau': Une révolte paysanne et anti-coloniale en Afrique noire*, Mouton, Paris-La Haye.

Buijtenhuijs, R. (1978) *Le Frolinat et les révoltes populaires du Tchad, 1965–76*, Mouton, Paris-La Haye.

Buijtenhuijs, R. (1987) *Le Frolinat et les guerres civiles du Tchad (1977–1984): La révolution introuvable*, Karthala, Paris.

Buijtenhuijs, R. (1995) 'La situation dans le Sud du Tchad', *Afrique contemporaine*, No. 175, July-September, 21–30.

Buijtenhuijs R. (1996) 'The rational rebel: how rational, how rebellious? Some African examples', *Afrika Focus*, 12(1–3): 3–25.

Cabral, A. (1966) Address delivered to the first Tricontinental Conference of the Peoples of Asia, Africa and Latin America, Havana, January.

Cabral, A. (1969) *Revolution in Guinea: An African People's Struggle*, Stage 1, London.

Compagnon, D. (1999) *Ressources politiques, régulation autoritaire et domination personnelle en Somalie: le régime de Siyaad Barre (1969–1991)*, Karthala, Paris, (in press).

Davezies, R. (1965) *Les Angolais*, Editions de Minuit, Paris.

Davidson, B. (1969) *The Liberation of Guiné: Aspects of an African Revolution*, Penguin, Harmondsworth.

Doornbos, P. (1982) 'La révolution dérapée: la violence dans l'Est du Tchad (1978–1981)', *Politique africaine*, No. 7, September, 5–13.

Ellis, S. (1995) 'Liberia 1989–94', *African Affairs*, 94, 375: 165–97.

Kriger, N. (1992) *Zimbabwe's Guerilla War: Peasant Voices*, Cambridge University Press, Cambridge.

Lame, D. de (1996) *Une colline entre mille ou le calme avant la tempête, Transformations et blocages du Rwanda rural*, Musee Royal de l'Afrique centrale, Tervuren.

Manceaux, M. (1975) 'Les femmes du Mozambique', *Mercure de France*.

Marchal, R. and Messiant, C. (1997) *Les chemins de la guerre et de la paix, Fins de conflits en Afrique orientale et australe*, Karthala, Paris.

Médard, C. (1996) 'Les conflits "ethniques" au Kenya: une question de votes ou de terres?', *Afrique contemporaine*, No. 180, October–December, 62–74.

Ranger, T. (1985) *Peasant Consciousness and Guerilla War in Zimbabwe: A Comparative Study*, James Currey, London.

Reno, W. (1993) 'Foreign firms and the financing of Charles Taylor's NPFL', *Liberian Studies Journal*, 18, 2: 175–87.

Reno, W. (1995) 'The Reinvention of an African Patrimonial State: Charles Taylor's Liberia', *Third World Quarterly*, 16, 1: 109–20.

Richards, P. (1995) 'Rebellion in Liberia and Sierra Leone', in O. Furley (ed.) *Conflict in Africa*, I.B. Tauris, London.

Triaud, J.-L. (1985) 'Le refus de l'Etat: l'exemple tchadien', *Esprit*, No. 100, April.

Urdang, S. (1979) *Fighting Two Colonialisms: Women in Guinea-Bissau*, Monthly Review Press, New York.

Welch, C.E. Jr (1978) 'Obstacles to "peasant wars" in Africa', in A.K. Smith and C.E. Welch Jr (eds) *Peasants in Africa*, Crossroads Press, Wathom, Massachussetts, pp. 121–30.

Wolf, E.R. (1973) *Peasant Wars of the Twentieth Century*, Faber and Faber, London.

PART THREE: LATIN AMERICAN PEASANTRIES

7. Latin America's Agrarian Transformation: Peasantization and Proletarianization

CRISTÓBAL KAY[1]

Introduction

This chapter provides an overview of the main transformations in Latin American rural economy and society, and particularly of its peasantry, from the colonial period to the present. It is argued that the various modes of integration of Latin America into the world system have had a major influence, but that this external impact varied according to the particular internal characteristics of each Latin American country and region. The emphasis in this introductory chapter is on the general characteristics and historical trajectory of Latin America's agrarian transformation as a broad framework within with to place the subsequent case studies.

The history of the Latin American peasantry is dramatic. European conquest in the late fifteenth and early sixteenth centuries decimated the indigenous population and forced many to abandon agriculture for work in the gold and silver mines. The subsequent formation of large landed properties led to the settlement of tenants on the estate, alongside the surrounding independent peasant communities engaged in subsistence agriculture.

The transformation of the Latin America peasantry has evolved within the two-fold context of changing internal relations of production on large landed estates and the shifting integration of Latin American agriculture into the world economy. Agriculture, and notably plantation agriculture, initially played a leading role in the emerging world economy of the seventeenth and eighteenth centuries. Ships from Europe brought African slaves to the region and returned to Europe with their cargo of tropical products: the well-known triangular trade. A second wave of integration into the world economy occurred in the last decades of the nineteenth century when exports of wheat, meat, sugar, coffee and tobacco went to feed Europe's growing urban and industrial population. A third and currently ongoing process of globalization of Latin American agriculture is characterized by the growth of new commercial enterprises producing non-traditional agricultural exports (such as soya beans, fruit and vegetables) for the rich countries of the north.

After briefly tracing the colonial legacy, the subsequent sections of this chapter are organized chronologically to discuss the consolidation of a variety of landlord–peasant relations from the independence period until the 1930s, the emergence of import-substituting industrialization process from the 1940s to the 1970s, the agrarian reforms of the 1960s and 1970s, and the emergence of neo-liberalism and export agriculture in the 1980s. The chapter concludes by reflecting on the future of the peasantry within the current process of globalization and briefly introduces the following chapters of this Latin American part of the book.

The Colonial Legacy

At the time of the Spanish conquest, Latin America was dominated by two major empires, the Aztecs and the Incas. Within these empires, three types of land existed: land whose produce was destined for religious ceremonies; land which belonged to the state; and community land. Community members not only worked for their own subsistence but also worked on a rotating basis on state and religious lands.

During the early Spanish colonial economy, based on gold and silver mining, food requirements were initially met by tributes in kind exacted from the communities. Later, large agricultural enterprises developed on former state and church lands which the Spanish Crown had expropriated from the Aztecs and Incas and awarded to the conquering Spanish élite in return for their services. As urban markets expanded, these large estates, later known as *haciendas* or *latifundios*, increasingly encroached on community land and diversified production from livestock to cereals and other food crops.

The main problem facing large estates was the shortage of labour as the conquest had decimated the native population.[2] Until the early eighteenth century, labour requirements were mainly met through the imposition of a variety of servile obligations on indigenous communities and/or by using slave labour. Over time, however, labour relations on the *hacienda* changed. During the first half of the eighteenth century many servile relations were legally abolished and landlords began to settle part of the floating population on their estates. Landowners were particularly keen to attract experienced agriculturalists and pastoralists from the indigenous communities by offering a variety of rental, sharecropping and tenancy arrangements. *Haciendas* also increasingly attracted some seasonal workers by offering payments in money and in kind. During the nineteenth century landlords attempted to secure a more permanent wage labour force through a labour recruitment system known as debt peonage. By offering advance payments or loans, workers soon became indebted and were thus compelled to continue working on the estate.

In some tropical or semi-tropical parts of Latin America (Brazil, parts of Peru, Ecuador and Colombia, Central America and the Caribbean), plantations were the dominant agricultural enterprise. Unlike the *hacienda*, which produced a variety of crops for the domestic market[3], plantation agriculture was export-oriented and monocrop (sugar, coffee, tobacco, cotton and cacao being the most important). Plantation agriculture was mainly a legacy of the Portuguese colonization, Brazil being the largest producer and exporter of sugar in the Americas by far until overtaken by the Caribbean in the 1820s. Plantations were large-scale and relied on African slave labour for much of the colonial period.[4] Plantations generated valuable foreign exchange and attained a higher degree of capitalization than the *hacienda*, especially where the crop required some processing, as in the case of sugar.

In addition to the *hacienda*[5] and the plantation, a third type of agricultural enterprise in the colonial economy was formed by the indigenous community. While plantations and *haciendas* were owned by private individuals (the landlords) or by institutions (such as the church), indigenous communities had communal property rights over their land, part of which was cultivated by individual households and part communally. A variety of communal and reciprocal labour arrangements existed between peasant households, making wage labour non-existent or very rare. Production was mainly for self-consumption and any surplus went to local and regional markets, rather than for export.

The Consolidation of Estates: From Independence to the 1930s

After political independence, which most Latin American countries had achieved by the 1820s, agriculture became more widely integrated into the world market. The century from 1830 to 1930 can be considered the golden age of the *hacienda*: a period of oligarchical domination in which the landed élite, in alliance with the merchant class, controlled the levers of economic and political power.[6]

Landlords responded to the growing profitability of export markets by expanding their estates. This usually meant encroaching on peasant community land or colonizing new areas, often displacing local communities in the process. With the increasing overseas demand, some landlords began to take direct control of the estate's production process, leading to a more centralized type of *hacienda* than had existed in the past.[7]

The additional labour required to meet export demand was obtained by a variety of means. Most commonly, more tenants were settled on the estates but with smaller leases and higher labour services than before. Conditions for existing tenants worsened as they had to work more days for the landlord, receiving in return a small payment or incipient wage. This proto-wage was well below that paid to seasonal wage labour, as tenants also received a subsistence plot. Estates also settled more sharecroppers who, in return for a plot of land, gave a proportion of their harvest to the landlord. In some regions, plantations employed indentured labour, largely from Asia, or relied on labour contractors to recruit labour from indigenous communities. Indeed, some plantation owners in Peru purchased *haciendas* in the highlands with the specific purpose of securing seasonal labour for their plantations on the coast. Debt peonage was also a common way of attracting and retaining labour on the estates.

In sum, the last decades of the nineteenth and the first decades of the twentieth century saw a number of developments. A more centralized *hacienda* gained a foothold in commercially oriented areas, such as central Chile and the cereal and livestock zones of Argentina and Mexico, whilst the decentralized or rentier *hacienda* continued to dominate elsewhere. Secondly, plantations developed in the tropical lowlands and coastal areas of Peru and Ecuador, recruiting labour from highland peasant communities. Thirdly, in the sugarcane zones of north-east Brazil, Colombia and the Caribbean, slave plantations gave way to the capitalist plantation. Fourthly, in south-east Brazil and the pampas of Argentina, where labour was scarce, commercial agriculture developed with European immigrant labour, attracted by the prospect of becoming independent commercial farmers.[8]

Import-substitution-industrialization: 1940s to 1970s

After the second world war, the adoption of an 'import-substitution-industrialization' (ISI) development strategy by many Latin American governments reversed the former emphasis on agricultural exports. This new inward-looking strategy stressed industrialization and the development of an internal market for domestic industry. The state played a leading role in this process through such measures as protectionism, cheap credit, the building of infrastructure and establishment of key enterprises such as steel.

The fact that agriculture was given less preference than industry during this period has led some authors to argue that it was discriminated against. While this may be true in general, this discrimination did not affect all groups evenly. Large agricultural producers often received compensation in the form of highly subsidized credits, cheap imports of agricultural machinery and inputs, and special technical assistance programmes which encouraged the modernization of large farms. Government policy towards agriculture was clearly biased against peasants and rural workers (Kay, 1981).

During the early post-war period, Latin America had one of the most unequal agrarian structures in the world. Although characterizations of the agrarian structure as being sharply divided between the large-scale *latifundio* and small-scale *minifundio* can be overdrawn, there were clearly vast differences between the two sectors. In 1960 *latifundios* comprised roughly five per cent of farm units but owned about four-fifths of the land; *minifundios* comprised four-fifths of farm units but had only five per cent of the land (Barraclough 1973: 16). The middle-sized farm sector was relatively small.

This bi-modal structure encompassed a wide variety of peasants[9], ranging from agricultural workers who owned smallholdings (*minifundistas*); those who had usufruct rights to land through a tenancy (sharecroppers, share-tenants[10] or labour-service tenants[11]); and those who were landless.[12] In 1969 an estimated quarter of the total active agricultural work force were landless (proletarians) and three-quarters had access to land. Of the latter, two-thirds were independent peasant farmers ('external' peasantries) and a third were tenants ('internal' peasantries).[13] Slightly over half of the independent peasant farmers were *minifundistas* (semi-proletarians) and the remainder were formed by larger or richer peasant farmers whose household members did not need to seek outside employment (Barraclough 1973: 19–23). With respect to employment, half the agricultural labour force worked on peasant plots, mainly as unpaid family workers. Large estates employed less than one-fifth of the total agricultural labour force but accounted for 90 per cent of the total hired labour force (ibid.: 22).

This *latifundio–minifundio* agrarian structure was inefficient. While *latifundios* under-utilized land, *minifundios* were wasteful of labour. Not surprisingly, while labour productivity was much higher on *latifundios* than on *minifundios*, the reverse was true for land productivity. Average production per agricultural worker was about five to ten times higher on *latifundios* than on *minifundios*, while production per hectare of agricultural land was roughly three to five times higher on *minifundios* (ibid.: 25–7).[14] Given that much rural labour was unemployed or under-employed and land was relatively scarce, it was more important from a developmental perspective to raise land productivity than to increase labour productivity. The economic inefficiency of this agrarian structure, combined with growing social and political unrest in the 1960s and 1970s, placed agrarian reform on the agenda.

Agrarian Reform: The Demise of The Hacienda

The timing and scope of agrarian reform varied throughout Latin America. Early agrarian reforms had taken place in Mexico in the 1920s and in Bolivia in the early 1950s. However, the main spate of agrarian reform took place in the 1960s and 1970s, in the aftermath of the Cuban revolution. Land reforms in Chile, Peru, Ecuador and Colombia were followed by those in Nicaragua and El Salvador in the late 1970s and early 1980s. Only in Argentina has agrarian reform been completely absent. In Brazil landlords succeeded in thwarting any significant agrarian reform, but minor land redistribution has taken place since the restoration of democratic rule in the mid-1980s.

With respect to the amount of land expropriated, the agrarian reforms in Bolivia and Cuba were the most extensive, expropriating about four-fifths of the country's agricultural land. In Mexico, Chile, Peru and Nicaragua almost half of agricultural land was expropriated, and in Colombia, Panama, El Salvador and the Dominican Republic between one-sixth and a quarter (Cardoso and Helwege 1992: 261). A smaller proportion of agricultural land was affected by agrarian reform in Ecuador, Costa Rica, Honduras and Uruguay. In Venezuela about one-fifth of the land was affected by agrarian reform, but almost three-quarters of this had previously belonged to the state and was largely in areas to be colonized. Thus Venezuela's agrarian reform was mainly a colonization programme.

Cuba, Bolivia and Mexico had the highest proportion of peasants and rural workers who became beneficiaries under the agrarian reform. Roughly three-quarters of agricultural households in Cuba and Bolivia were incorporated into the reformed sector, while in Mexico it was under half. In Nicaragua, Peru and Venezuela the proportion of beneficiaries was about one-third, in El Salvador a quarter, and in Chile a fifth. In Panama, Colombia, Ecuador, Honduras and Costa Rica, about a tenth of agricultural families benefited from land redistribution (Cardoso and Helwege 1992: 261, Dorner 1992: 34). In other countries the proportion was even lower.

Collective and co-operative forms of organization were more common in the reformed sector than one might expect, given the dominant capitalist context of Latin America.[15] Nevertheless, the enduring influence of the pre-reform structure on future organization, and particularly the degree of capitalist development and proletarianization attained by the agricultural labour force, is clearly evident (Kay 1988a). For example, in Peru where decentralized, rentier-type *haciendas* had predominated in the highlands, about half the agricultural land of the reformed sector was cultivated on an individual basis. By contrast, in the more commercially oriented haciendas of Chile and El Salvador the corresponding figure was about a fifth, and in Cuba, where plantations had prevailed, it was insignificant.[16]

The impact of agrarian reform on the peasantry has been correspondingly varied. In some instances, such as Peru and Nicaragua, peasants succeeded in pushing the agrarian reform process further than intended by governments or redirected it in line with their interests.[17] In many Latin American countries, however, peasants were not in a position to extend expropriation or to prevent landlords from blocking or reversing the process. In most countries agrarian reform remained limited in scope in terms of land expropriated and peasant beneficiaries. Despite an explicit commitment to agrarian reform and peasant farming, governments were either too weak to implement a substantial agrarian reform, or had the underlying intention of promoting capitalist farming (de Janvry 1981; Thiesenhusen 1995).

Nevertheless, agrarian reforms did provide an important stimulus to institution-building in the countryside. Rural trade unions, co-operatives and associations integrated the peasantry into the national economy, society and polity, and many peasants, on receiving a land title, felt themselves to be citizens for the first time. Agrarian reform hastened the demise of the landed oligarchy and subsequently the full commercialization of agriculture.

Neo-liberalism and the New Export Agriculture

Since the 1980s the major force shaping Latin American rural economy and society has been the resumption of an outward-oriented development strategy. The debt crisis of the 1980s and the adoption by most Latin American countries of structural adjustment programmes stimulated agricultural exports, which have been growing much faster than agricultural production for the domestic market, reversing the earlier trend during the ISI period. Capitalist farmers had already begun in the 1970s to switch to non-traditional agricultural exports (NTAEs) such as soya, which is used for cattle feed and other purposes.

Neo-liberal land policies abandoned the previous focus on expropriation, emphasizing instead privatization, decollectivization, land registration and land titling.[18] Legislation has been introduced in some countries to facilitate the break-up of indigenous communities and the sale of their land. Chile was the first to initiate decollectivization in the 1970s, followed more gradually by Peru since 1980, Nicaragua since 1990 and Mexico and El Salvador since 1992. Whilst some expropriated land has been returned to former owners (particularly in Chile), most has been subdivided into family farms known as *parcelas* and sold to members of the reformed sector (now known as *parceleros)*. Those unable to secure a parcel have swelled the ranks of the rural proletariat. Although this process of parcellization initially increased the land area of the peasant farm sector, a proportion of *parceleros* could not keep up their repayments or finance their farm operations, and subsequently sold part or all of their *parcela* to the capitalist farm sector, especially in Chile (Jarvis 1992).

The introduction of neo-liberal policies strengthened the development of commercial capitalist farms, using new technology and supplying fruit, fruit juice and vegetables, as well as wood and wood products, to North American, European and Japanese markets. Capitalist farmers have reaped the benefits of this thriving NTAE business, having the resources to respond relatively quickly to neo-liberal trade and macro-economic policy reforms. For peasant farmers, the export market is too risky and the new technology is too expensive. The available technology is also inappropriate for small-scale agriculture and the inferior soils of peasant farming. Nevertheless, through contract farming with agro-industrial businesses, some small-holders are engaged in production for export or for high-income domestic urban consumers.

Changing social composition of the peasantry

The emergence of modernizing capitalist farms geared to the export market has been accompanied by a structural shift in the composition of the agricultural labour force. While some peasants have evolved into 'capitalized family farmers' or 'capitalist peasant farmers' (Llambí 1988), many have become 'proletarians in disguise'. Although formally owning a small-holding, in practice they are completely dependent on agri-business, earning an income similar to that of rural wage labourers. Others have become 'semi-proletarians', whose principal source of income stems from the sale of their labour power rather than from the household plot. Finally, a significant proportion of peasants have been 'openly' and fully proletarianized, having been displaced from markets through shifting consumer tastes, cheap and subsidized food imports, competition from agri-business, and technological obsolescence, among other factors.

This shift to wage labour has gone hand-in-hand with the growth of temporary and seasonal wage labour. In many countries permanent wage labour has declined, even in absolute terms, while in almost all countries temporary labour has greatly increased. While two decades ago two-thirds of wage labour was permanent and one-third was temporary, these proportions have now been reversed in countries such as Brazil and Chile (Grzybowski 1990: 21).

The growth of temporary labour is particularly evident in those Latin American countries whose agro-industries participate in the export of seasonal fruit, vegetables and flowers. Temporary workers are generally paid on a piece rate basis, are not usually entitled to social security benefits, and have no employment protection. This casualization of labour has extended employers' control over labour by reducing workers' rights and increasing flexibility. In addition, this expansion of the temporary labour force has been accompanied by a marked gender division. Agro-industries largely employ female labour as women are held to be more readily available for seasonal work, to be more careful workers, to have lower wage expectations, and to be less organized than men (Barrientos et al. 1999). Any permanent employment, however, tends to be the preserve of men. Although generally employed in low-skilled and low-paid jobs, for many young women these jobs represent an opportunity to earn an independent income and to escape (at least partially and temporarily) from the constraints of a patriarchal household (Stephen 1998).

An additional dimension to the growth of temporary wage labour concerns the geographical origin of the workers so employed. An increasing proportion of temporary workers come from urban areas, being recruited by labour contractors. This indicates both the ruralization of urban areas, as a result of high rates of rural–urban migration, as well as the urbanization of rural areas with the mushrooming of rural shanty towns, thereby blurring the urban–rural divide. Furthermore, rural residents have increasingly to compete with urban labourers for agricultural work, and vice versa, leading to more uniform labour markets and wage levels.

While neo-liberal policies have transformed Latin America's agriculture they have not resolved the problems of rural poverty, exclusion and landlessness. The potential benefits of clearly defined property rights may be substantial, given that about half of rural households lack land titles, but the economic and socio-political context conspires against small farmers (Vogelgesang 1998). Evidence so far suggests that all that has been achieved is 'modernizing insecurity'. While major agrarian reforms, especially of a collectivist kind, are unlikely to recur, resolving the agrarian problem in Latin America still requires changes in the unequal and exclusionary land tenure system.

The Future of the Peasantry

The internationalization of Latin America's agriculture, the demise of the *hacienda* system and the increasing dominance of capitalist farming are having a profound impact on the peasantry.[19] The long-debated question of whether the peasant economy can survive has been given new urgency by neo-liberalism.[20]

Clearly, the peasant household farm sector has not experienced a unilinear decline and is still a significant sector of Latin American rural economy and society. Indeed, the parcellization of the reformed sector in Chile and Peru, and more recently in Nicaragua, significantly expanded the peasant sector. However, these exceptions might prove to be temporary. It is estimated that by 1980 peasant agriculture in Latin America comprised four-fifths of farm units, and possessed a fifth of total agricultural land, over a third of the cultivated land, and over two-fifths of the harvested area (López Cordovez 1982: 26). The peasant economy accounted for almost two-thirds of the total agricultural labour force, the remaining third being employed by capitalist farms. Furthermore, peasant agriculture supplied two-fifths of production for the domestic market and a third of the production for export.

Yet if the Latin American peasantry is far from disappearing, its relative importance for agricultural production is declining. According to de Janvry et al. (1989b) the Latin American peasantry faces both a land squeeze and an employment squeeze. Given that any land acquired has not kept pace with the increase in numbers, the average size of peasant farms has fallen. This fragmentation of the peasant sector mainly affects the small peasantry (*minifundistas*) who comprise about two-thirds of peasant farm households. Their average farm size fell from 2.1 hectares in 1950 to 1.9 hectares in 1980. The remainder of the peasant sector retained an average farm size of 17 hectares, partly through the implementation of redistributive land reforms (de Janvry et al. 1989a: 74). Nor have employment opportunities kept pace with the growth of the peasant population. In addition, peasants face increased competition from urban-based workers for rural employment, as mentioned earlier.

This 'double squeeze' on the peasant economy has led many peasants to migrate. While in 1980 65 per cent of Latin America's population was urban, this increased to 75 per cent in 1995 (IDB 1997). Peasants have also responded by seeking alternative off-farm sources of income (such as seasonal wage labour in agriculture) and/or non-farm sources of income. In many Latin American countries over a quarter of the economically active agricultural population currently resides in urban areas, and the proportion of the economically active rural population engaged in non-agricultural activities is rising, reaching over 40 per cent in Mexico and averaging about 25 per cent in others (Ortega 1992: 129). Thus non-farm employment, is expanding faster than farm employment in rural Latin America.

The process of semi-proletarianization is the dominant tendency currently unfolding among the Latin American peasantry. An increasing proportion of total peasant household income originates from wages. Income from own-farm activities often accounts for under half the total (de Janvry et al. 1989a: 141). The small peasantry (*minifundistas*), who comprise two-thirds of all peasant households, are best characterized as semi-proletarian, as between two-fifths and three-fifths of their household income is derived from off-farm sources, principally from seasonal agricultural wage employment on large commercial farms and estates (ibid.: 63). However, this process of semi-proletarianization is less marked in those few Latin American countries where agrarian reforms significantly increased peasant access to land.

In sum, most of Latin America's peasantry appears to be stuck in a state of permanent semi-proletarianization. Their access to off-farm sources of income, generally seasonal wage labour, enables them to cling to the land, thereby blocking their full proletarianization. This process favours rural capitalists as it eliminates small peasants as competitors in agricultural production and makes them available for employment as cheap labour. Semi-proletarianization is the only option open to those peasants who wish to retain access to land for reasons of security and survival, or because they cannot find alternative permanent productive employment, either in the rural or urban sector.

It is the modernized capitalist farmers, often linked to agro-industrial and international capital, who are setting the pace and controlling the direction of Latin America's agrarian developments. This they can only do within the limitations imposed by the relative decline of agriculture in the national economy and its subordination to the penetrating processes of trade liberalization and globalization. Current schemes of economic integration, such as the North American Free Trade Agreement (NAFTA) between the USA, Canada and Mexico, may offer new possibilities for capitalist farmers and agro-industries but are likely to have deleterious consequences for peasant farmers.

What then are the prospects for a peasant path to rural development? Access to capital, technology, knowledge and information systems, as well as to domestic and foreign markets, is becoming increasingly important in relation to access to land in determining the success of an agricultural enterprise. Although some peasants have gained access to land through agrarian reform, this by no means secures their future development. A viable peasant road to rural development ultimately raises questions about the political power of the peasantry and their allies. For a peasant path to rural development to succeed would require a major shift away from the current emphasis on liberalization, a development which at present appears unlikely. This does not mean that the neo-liberal project has gone unchallenged by peasants. Indeed, the peasant rebellion in Chiapas, Mexico at the beginning of 1994, has come to symbolize the new character of social movements in the countryside in Latin America (Harvey 1998).[21]

More immediately, the key for the future development of peasant farmers lies in enhancing their market competitiveness. In view of the dynamism of the export sector, those governments and NGOs concerned with promoting the development of peasant farmers have sought to shift the production pattern of peasant farmers so as to extend to them the benefits of this lucrative agricultural export boom. However, experience has been rather mixed. In their analysis of the impact of NTAE growth on smallholders and rural labourers in Paraguay, Chile and Guatemala, Carter et al. (1996: 45) found that only in the case of Guatemala was there a broadly based growth due to positive land access and employment effects. In Paraguay the reverse was true, resulting in exclusionary growth. The Chilean case had elements of both: the employment effect was positive but the land access effect was negative as the shift to NTAE worsened the access of peasants to land (see also Gwynne and Kay 1997, Murray 1998).

Conclusions

Latin America's rural economy and society have been transformed in recent decades as a consequence of the widening and deepening of capitalist relations in the countryside, and agriculture's present integration into the world economy. This form of modernization has benefited a small heterogeneous group of agro-industrialists, capitalist farmers, and some capitalized peasant households. For most of the peasantry and the rural labourers, employment conditions have become temporary, precarious and 'flexible'. In addition, some landlords have lost out, especially in countries where more radical agrarian reforms were implemented or they succumbed to competition following liberalization.

The following four chapters address different aspects of this agrarian transformation. Carmen Diana Deere's contribution (Chapter 8), based on a unique retrospective survey and life histories, provides a new historical interpretation of Cuba's peasantry and rural workers. The Cuban case is of particular significance for its continued search for a socialist path within a global, neo-liberal world.

Magdalena Barros Nock (Chapter 9) analyses the changes which have taken place in Mexico's rural economy, and particularly the *ejido*, under neo-liberalism. Mexico is an important case study for its recent move towards economic integration with the USA and Canada, through the NAFTA agreement.

Like Barros Nock, Llambí (Chapter 10) focuses on neo-liberal and structural adjustment policies. He analyses the impact of globalization on Latin America's 'new ruralities' and argues for 'bringing peasants back' into social analysis. Drawing on a case study of Venezuela, he analyses the interlinkages between the local, national and supranational forces shaping the rural economy and society. His theoretical analysis will interest those seeking to overcome the limitations of the globalization approach to rural transformations.

Kees Jansen's contribution (Chapter 11) discusses the impact of structural adjustment and neo-liberal policies on peasant differentiation and the environment in Central America. He carefully examines different interpretations of this impact and finds them all wanting, although not to the same degree. His main empirical material comes from Honduras, but his theoretical analysis is of wider relevance to those interested in environmental and peasant issues.

Notes

1. I am grateful to Deborah Bryceson and Jos Mooij for commenting on this chapter.
2. According to some estimates the population of Mexico fell from almost 17 million in 1532 to 1 million in 1605 (Chonchol 1994: 56).
3. However, at some times and places *haciendas* also produced for export, especially when world market conditions were favourable.
4. Brazil had the largest number of slaves in the Americas. An estimated 3.5 million slaves were brought to Brazil, almost 40 per cent of the total number of slaves shipped from Africa to the Americas (Chonchol 1994: 95).

5. In Argentina *haciendas* were known as *estancias*, vast estates of tens of thousands of hectares, largely located in the fertile *pampas*.
6. Only in Mexico during the revolution of 1910–17 was the landlords' dominance successfully challenged. However, it was not until Cárdenas (1934–40) that the *hacienda* system was finally weakened.
7. In the more decentralized *hacienda*, landlords were mainly rentiers, leasing out over half their land to peasant-tenants in return for a rent in kind or money. Tenants thus accounted for most of the *hacienda*'s production and little, if any, wage labour was employed. Under the centralized *hacienda*, the landlord extended the area under his direct control, the landlord enterprise, and leased out between a quarter and a third to tenants. In this case tenants mainly provided labour services for the landlord but some seasonal wage labour was recruited during the harvest period.
8. A useful analysis of Latin America's agrarian system during this period is provided by Duncan and Rutledge (1977).
9. I am using the term peasant here in a broad sense to refer to all those who derive a livelihood from working a plot of land, be it owned or rented, or who are employed as a rural worker for a wage. In this broad sense, peasants include small, landed proprietors, tenants and agricultural wage workers. For a discussion of the conceptualization of the peasantry, see Chapter 1 in this volume.
10. Share-tenants or sharecroppers hand over part of their crop to the landlord as rental payment for the use of the land. There are a great variety of share-tenancy arrangements. In a common arrangement half of the tenant's production goes to the landlord.
11. Labour-service tenants reside on the estate and their remuneration includes the right to a plot of land in return for working on the landlord's farm or enterprise.
12. Landless workers, or the agricultural proletariat, usually live on smallholdings or in neighbouring villages or towns, and work either full-time or seasonally on other farms. Some landless workers are permanent migrants having no fixed address.
13. For a discussion of the terms 'internal' and 'external' peasantries see Kay 1974.
14. The data reflect the situation during the 1950s or very early 1960s.
15. An important explanation for this statist and collectivist character of Latin America's most important agrarian reforms lies in an economic rationale. Governments feared that subdividing large landed estates into peasant family farms might affect economies of scale and thereby reduce output, and especially foreign exchange earnings. Furthermore, a collective reformed sector avoided subdivision costs, allowed more direct government control over production and marketing, and could foster internal solidarity. In those countries pursuing a socialist path of development, such as Cuba, Allende's Chile, and Nicaragua under the Sandinistas, a collectivist emphasis was also underpinned by political and ideological factors. In some cases collective forms of organization were regarded as transitory as in Chile and El Salvador. As beneficiaries gained entrepreneurial and technical experience a gradual process of decollectivization was envisaged.
16. One feature of Cuba's agrarian reforms (1959 and 1963), which is not often mentioned, is the fact that Castro's government greatly extended peasant proprietorship, giving ownership titles to an estimated 160 000 tenants, sharecroppers and squatters. Before the revolution peasant farmers had numbered only about 40 000 (Ghai et al. 1988: 10, 14). Cuba's agriculture was dominated by sugar plantations and the agricultural labour force was largely proletarian. It was not until almost two decades after the revolution that the Cuban leadership launched a campaign for the co-operativization of peasant farmers. They were

encouraged to form agricultural and livestock production co-operatives (CPAs), having resisted joining state farms, and within a decade over two-thirds of all peasant farmers had done so. CPAs were clearly out-performing state farms (Kay 1988b), eventually leading to their transformation into a new sort of producer co-operative, a process which is still ongoing (see Deere, Chapter 8 in this volume).

17. For example, peasant communities in Peru, which had largely been excluded from land redistribution, later gained direct access to land from the reformed sector. In Nicaragua peasants succeeded in pressurizing the Sandinista government to adopt a less state-centred agrarian reform policy than the one which had privileged state farms since 1979. After 1984 some reformed enterprises were transferred directly to peasant beneficiaries in either co-operative or individual ownership (Enríquez 1991: 91–2).
18. A powerful symbol of the neo-liberal winds sweeping through Latin America is the change to Article 27 of Mexico's Constitution. A new agrarian law passed in 1992 allows the sale of land of the reform sector.
19. The term peasantry is used here in a narrow sense to refer only to those rural workers who own, rent or have access to land which they cultivate with unpaid family labour, thereby constituting a peasant economy. This definition excludes agricultural wage workers.
20. The fate of Latin America's peasantry has long been the subject of disagreement between those who argue that the present phase marks the end of the peasantry (the *descampesinistas* or de-peasantists) and those who stress the resilience, vitality and relative importance of the peasant economy (the *campesinistas* or peasantists) (Feder 1979, Goodman and Redclift 1981, Hewitt de Alcántara 1984). The *descampesinistas* or *proletaristas* (proletarianists) argue that the peasant form of production is economically unviable in the long run and that the peasantry as petty commodity producers will eventually be eliminated. They stress that capitalist development enhances the process of differentiation among the peasantry, ultimately transforming the majority into proletarians. Only a few will become 'peasant capitalists' and even fewer will become capitalist farmers. This approach is influenced by classical Marxist writers on the agrarian question, such as Lenin and Kautsky. The *campesinistas* reject the view that the wage relation is being generalized in the countryside and that the peasantry is disappearing. They argue that the peasantry, far from being eliminated, is persisting and even being reinforced. Thus they view the peasantry as mainly petty commodity producers who are able to compete successfully with capitalist farmers in the market rather than viewing them as sellers of labour power and being subjected to processes of socio-economic differentiation. This peasantization approach has certain affinities with the neo-populist tradition of Chayanov and his contemporary followers such as Shanin. There are intermediate positions, such as in the case of 'Chayanovian Marxism' (Lehmann 1986).
21. During the past decade the peasantry has re-emerged as a significant force for social change not only in Mexico but in Brazil, Ecuador, Bolivia, Paraguay, Colombia and El Salvador. In Brazil, where land inequality is particularly acute (Veltmeyer et al. 1997: 181), the landless rural workers movement of the MST has spearheaded over one thousand land invasions or take-overs of estates demanding their expropriation. A variety of peasants have been involved in these occupations, but mainly rural semi-proletarians or proletarians, such as wage workers, squatters, sharecroppers and tenants. Through direct action they had succeeded in pressurizing the government into settling over 120 000 families on land by 1994 (Petras 1998: 192).

References

Barraclough, S. (1973) *Agrarian Structure in Latin America*, D.C. Heath, Lexington, Massachusetts.

Barrientos, S., Bee, A. Matear, A. and Vogel, I. (1999) *Women and Agribusiness: Working Miracles in the Chilean Fruit Export Sector*, Macmillan, London.

Cardoso, E. and Helwege, A. (1992) *Latin America's Economy: Diversity, Trends, and Conflicts*, MIT Press, Cambridge, Massachusetts.

Carter, M.R., Barham, B.L. and Mesbah, D. (1996) 'Agricultural export booms and the rural poor in Chile, Guatemala, and Paraguay', *Latin American Research Review*, 31, 1: 33–65.

Chonchol, J. (1994) *Sistemas Agrarios en América Latina*, Fondo de Cultura Económica, Santiago.

de Janvry, A. (1981) *The Agrarian Question and Reformism in Latin America*, Johns Hopkins University Press, Baltimore.

de Janvry, A., Marsh, R. Runsten, D. Sadoulet, E. and Zabin, C. (1989a) *Rural Development in Latin America*, Instituto Interamericano de Cooperación para la Agricultura (IICA), San José de Costa Rica.

de Janvry, A., Sadoulet, E. and Wilcox Young, L. (1989b) 'Land and labour in Latin American agriculture from the 1950s to the 1980s', *Journal of Peasant Studies*, 16, 3: 396–424.

Dorner, P. (1992) *Latin American Land Reforms in Theory and Practice*, University of Wisconsin Press, Madison.

Duncan, K. and Rutledge, I. (1977) 'Introduction: patterns of agrarian capitalism', in K. Duncan and I. Rutledge (eds) *Land and Labour in Latin America*, Cambridge University Press, Cambridge, pp. 1–20.

Enríquez, L.J. (1991) *Harvesting Change: Labor and Agrarian Reform in Nicaragua, 1979–1990*, University of North Carolina Press, Chapel Hill.

Feder, E. (1979) 'Regeneration and degeneration of the peasants: three views about the destruction of the countryside', *Social Scientists*, 7(7): 3–41.

Ghai, D., Kay, C. and Peek, P. (1988) *Labour and Development in Rural Cuba*, Macmillan, London.

Goodman, D. and Redclift, M. (1981) *From Peasant to Proletarian: Capitalist Development and Agrarian Transformations*, Basil Blackwell, Oxford.

Grzybowski, C. (1990) 'Rural workers and democratisation in Brazil', in J. Fox (ed.) *The Challenge of Rural Democratisation*, Frank Cass, London, pp. 19–43.

Gwynne, R.N. and Kay, C. (1997) 'Agrarian change and the democratic transition in Chile', *Bulletin of Latin American Research*, 16(1): 3–10.

Harvey, N. (1998) *The Chiapas Rebellion: The Struggle for Land and Democracy*, Duke University Press, Durham, North Carolina.

Hewitt de Alcántara, C. (1984) *Anthropological Perspectives on Rural Mexico*, Routledge & Kegan Paul, London.

IDB (1997) *Economic and Social Progress in Latin America: 1997 Report*, Johns Hopkins University Press, Baltimore, for the Inter-American Development Bank (IDB), Washington, D.C.

Jarvis, L.S. (1992) 'The unravelling of the agrarian reform', in C. Kay and P. Silva (eds) *Development and Social Change in the Chilean Countryside*, CEDLA, Amsterdam, pp. 189–213.
Kay, C. (1988a) 'The landlord road and the subordinate peasant road to capitalism in Latin America', *Etudes rurales*, No. 77, 5–20.
Kay, C. (1988b) 'Cuban economic reforms and collectivisation', *Third World Quarterly*, 10(3): 1239–66.
Kay, C. (1981) 'Political economy, class alliances and agrarian change in Chile', *Journal of Peasant Studies*, 8(4): 485–513.
Kay, C. (1974) 'Comparative development of the European manorial system and the Latin American hacienda system', *Journal of Peasant Studies*, 2(1): 69–98.
Lehmann, D. (1986) 'Two paths of agrarian capitalism, or a critique of Chayanovian Marxism', *Comparative Study of Society and History*, 28(4): 601–27.
Llambí, L. (1988) 'The small modern farmers: neither peasants nor fully-fledged capitalists?', *Journal of Peasant Studies*, 15(3): 350–72.
López Cordovez, L. (1982) 'Trends and recent changes in the Latin American food and agricultural situation', *CEPAL Review*, No. 16, 7–41.
Murray, W.E. (1998) 'The globalisation of fruit, neo-liberalism and the question of sustainability: lessons from Chile', *European Journal of Development Research*, 10(1): 201–227.
Ortega, E. (1992) 'Evolution of the rural dimension in Latin America and the Caribbean, *CEPAL Review*, No. 47, 115–36.
Petras, J. (1998) 'The political and social basis of regional variations in land occupations in Brazil', *Journal of Peasant Studies*, 25(4): 124–33.
Stephen, L. (1998) *Women and Social Movements in Latin America*, University of Texas Press, Austin.
Thiesenhusen, W.C. (1995) *Broken Promises: Agrarian Reform and the Latin American Campesino*, Westview Press, Boulder, Colorado.
Veltmeyer, H., Petras, J. and Vieux, S. (1997) *Neoliberalism and Class Conflict in Latin America*, Macmillan, Basingstoke and London.
Vogelgesang, F. (1998) 'After land reform: the market?', *Land Reform*, No. 1, 20–34.

8. Towards a Reconstruction of Cuba's Agrarian Transformation: Peasantization, De-peasantization and Re-peasantization

CARMEN DIANA DEERE[1]

Introduction

The story of the Cuban agrarian reform – like that of most socialist agrarian reforms – is usually told as one story, based on a macro-periodization derived from changes in state agricultural policy. The manner in which agrarian reforms are carried out at the local level, and the heterogeneous outcomes of these reforms, are rarely addressed in a comparative framework. The main argument of this chapter is that, just as socialist agriculture never coalesced into a single organizational model among socialist countries, the processes of agrarian transformation and reform vary locally, reflecting different initial conditions and the roles of local actors.

The history of Cuba's socialist agrarian transformation is often summarized as consisting of four moments or phases: (i) the initial 1959 agrarian reform law which proscribed the latifundia and significantly expanded the number of property-owning peasants; (ii) the 1963 agrarian reform law which resulted in the expropriation of farms over 67 hectares in size; (iii) a period of consolidation of the state farm model in the late 1960s/early 1970s, which included incorporating peasant lands to state farms through either their rental or sale; and (iv) the mid-1970s policy reversal which gave rise to production co-operatives as an alternative form of organization of socialist agriculture. The recent 1993 decision to convert the huge state-farm sector into production co-operatives constitutes the beginning of a fifth new period in Cuba's socialist trajectory, one resulting from the difficult conditions characterizing the 'Special Period' which emerged after the demise of the socialist trading bloc in 1989.

This chapter focuses on how Cuba's socialist agrarian transformation was conditioned by the capitalist legacy upon which it was constructed. The objective is to illustrate the interaction of national state policy with the many factors influencing the heterogeneous outcomes of socialist agrarian policy at the local level: in particular, the pre-reform land tenure and rural class structure and peasant–state relations. Drawing on a retrospective survey of 475 agricultural workers (representative of state farm wage workers, production co-operative members and individual farmers in the early 1990s), life histories, archival data, and interviews, this chapter attempts to reconstruct the process of agrarian transformation in three municipalities of Cuba.

The first two sections explore the conditions which supported the creation of a sizeable independent peasantry in the western region of the country. It is argued that the different modalities under which the production of sugarcane developed and the class relations with which it was associated largely explain why the main beneficiaries of the agrarian reform were located in this region. The subsequent section describes the consolidation of the state-farm sector in the late 1960s and early 1970s and how, in the central region of the island in particular, this expansion was at the cost of the peasantry. The chapter then focuses on the post-1975 decision to collectivize individual peasant producers through the formation of production co-operatives (*Co-operativas de Producción Agropecuaria*, CPAs) and takes this movement up through the beginning of the Special Period. Here it is argued that the co-operative movement has been most successful in the western region of the country, precisely because this region had a larger peasant base upon which to draw. Finally, it is argued that the rather radical decision taken by the Cuban leadership in 1993 to privatize, in a collective fashion, the huge state-farm sector is largely explained by this historical trajectory. That is, the decision to support the further development of production co-operatives, rather than to turn to family or capitalist farming – as most of the former socialist societies did in the 1990s – was path-dependent.

In terms of the main theme of this book, the story of Cuban socialist agrarian transformation can be retold as one of peasantization, de-peasantization, and re-peasantization – the latter, albeit, in a collective fashion. However, to re-emphasize the central argument of the chapter, regional differences often outweigh national-level trends.

Cuba's Agrarian Structure prior to 1959

At the time of the 1959 revolution, Cuba was the classic agro-export economy. One product, sugar, made up 81 per cent of its total exports; moreover, it was heavily dependent on one country, the USA, for over two-thirds of its exports and imports (Seers et al. 1964: 19–20). Its agrarian structure was characterized by the dominance of large sugarcane plantations and cattle *haciendas*, with many of the former in the hands of US capital. Its class structure was dominated by the presence of a large, landless proletariat, which far exceeded the number of property-owning peasants.

Indicative of the degree of land concentration is the fact that in 1946 farms smaller than ten hectares constituted 39 per cent of the total number of farms, but held only three per cent of the nation's farmland. On the other hand, less than eight per cent of the total number of farms held over 70 per cent of the farmland, with farms greater than 500 hectares in size holding 47 per cent (Cuba 1951: 84). This highly unequal distribution of landholdings was largely an early twentieth century phenomenon, associated with the accelerated growth of sugar production and sugar *latifundia* between 1890 and 1925.

The three municipalities in which our field work was based span the three natural regions of Cuba and reflect the different stages in the development of sugar production – which spread from the western to the eastern part of the island over the nineteenth and early twentieth centuries. The municipality of Güines is located in the western province of La Havana; Santo Domingo in the central province of Villa Clara (formerly Las Villas); and Majibacoa in the eastern province of Las Tunas (formerly part of Oriente). The three are also broadly representative of Cuba's main agricultural rubrics: sugarcane, livestock, and mixed cropping of grains, root crops and vegetables.[2]

Common to both the western and central regions of Cuba was that, by the time of the abolition of slavery in 1886, sugar production was increasingly characterized by the separation of sugarcane production from milling and by the growth of the *colono* system of cane production. Whereas the former was a response to new technological developments, the latter was facilitated by heavy Spanish immigration to Cuba in the 1860s to 1890s. The new modality which developed in the western and central regions was for immigrant Spanish workers and others to be leased land by the *centrales* (company-owned sugar estates), paying a cash rent which was deducted from the *colono*'s sale of cane to the mill at harvest time. The mill owners often provided the *colonos* with the necessary credit for planting, cultivating and harvesting the cane.

In the eastern part of the island sugarcane production for export was not developed until after the US occupation of the island in 1898. The primary economic activity was cattle-raising, coupled with lumber production. This part of Cuba was still largely covered with vast native hardwood forests. All this changed between 1899 and 1916 as US capital built six large and modern *centrales* in the region of Las Tunas. In contrast to the western part of the country, the expansion of cane cultivation in the east did not foster the development of a yeoman peasantry. Rather, the American mills favoured renting land to entrepreneurs of the professional strata – lawyers and engineers, for example – or to the rural petty bourgeoisie who then worked their cane farm with the use of wage labour.

According to the *Anuario Azucarero* (1939) the average *colonia* (as the sugarcane farms were called) in Güines consisted of around 40 hectares, whereas in the region of Las Tunas it comprised 252 hectares. Thus in Güines the typical *colonia* could be worked by family labour, relying on wage labour only for the harvest. In contrast, the large *colonias* of Las Tunas depended upon wage labour for most operations. In the early decades of the century this labour was largely imported from Jamaica and Haiti, particularly for the harvest period.

In all three municipalities the expansion of sugarcane production led to the growing concentration of land. By 1939 the two mills of Güines held 39 per cent of the land of the municipality; the three mills of Santo Domingo controlled 25 per cent; and the six giant mills of Las Tunas held 56 per cent of the land of this province.[3]

The 1946 Agricultural Census provides an approximation of the relations of production which characterized the pre-revolutionary period and of how these differed in the three municipalities (Cuba 1951: 84, Table 8). Firstly, in terms of the distribution of farms by size, smallholdings (those less than 10 hectares) were much more prevalent in Santo Domingo (37 per cent) and Las Tunas (38 per cent) than in Güines (26 per cent), as were large *haciendas* or *latifundia*. Las Tunas, in particular, is a classic example of *minifundia–latifundia* bipolarity, with 4 per cent of its farms larger than 500 hectares in size, compared with the national figure of 1 per cent.[4]

Güines was characterized by a very different size distribution of farms. The largest concentration (39 per cent) was in medium-size farms (between 10 and 24.9 hectares), a characteristic farm size of the 'yeoman' peasantry. Güines also had the largest share of farms (28 per cent) in the 25 to 74.9 hectare range compared to either the national average (14 per cent) or the other two regions.

The above trends are captured by the data on average farm size: 29 hectares in Güines, 56 hectares in Santo Domingo and 100 hectares in Tunas. But part of the difference in average farm size relates to the relative prevalence of cattle ranching in the three municipalities. In Güines, 47 per cent of the farmed area was dedicated to crop production and 43 per cent to pastures. By contrast, in Santo Domingo and Tunas only 21 per cent of the farm area was dedicated to crops and 60 per cent to pastures.

Turning to land tenure, less than one-third of the nation's farms were worked by their owners (Cuba 1951: 88, Tables 3 and 10). In Güines and Santo Domingo, even fewer farms were farmed directly by their owners. By contrast, in Las Tunas, 51 per cent of farms were worked by their owners, as was a majority of total farmland. Nonetheless, there was tremendous heterogeneity among owner-operated farms, which ranged from *minifundia* to large cattle *haciendas* following the bipolarity in size distribution noted earlier.

At the national level, the overwhelming number of farmers (accounting for 41 per cent of the nation's land) were tenants, comprising *arrendires*[5] (30 per cent of the land), sharecroppers (6 per cent), squatters (3 per cent) and *sub-arrendires* (2 per cent of the land). Güines and Santo Domingo follow this trend. In both cases, the share of farms and farmland worked by *arrendires* exceeded the national average. In Las Tunas more farms were either sharecropped (15 per cent) or held by squatters (13 per cent) than rented by *arrendires* (11 per cent), although the latter had access to a much greater share of the total farmland (22 per cent) than the former (3 per cent).

In all three municipalities, *arrendire* arrangements tended to be associated with cane farming whereas sharecropping characterized grain, root crops and vegetable production. The predominance of cane *arrendires* in Güines as compared with Majibacoa, in particular, supports the earlier analysis regarding the different modalities under which sugarcane developed in the western and eastern regions of Cuba.

The preponderant place of the agricultural proletariat within the economically active population (EAP) in agriculture is often considered to be a distinguishing feature of Cuba on the eve of revolution. According to the 1953 census, agricultural wage workers comprised 61 per cent of the agricultural EAP (Pollitt 1977). As Pollitt has argued, this may be an overestimation since 'landless' wage workers often had access to a small plot of land for self-provisioning.

Retrospective survey data are helpful in distinguishing the three regions in terms of class relations. Table 8.1 illustrates the predominant form of access to land of the parents of the 475 agricultural workers surveyed by us in the three municipalities.[6] As can be seen, the greatest number (31 per cent) were landless prior to the 1959 agrarian reform, backing Pollitt's claim that the 1953 census figure of landlessness is an overestimation. Nonetheless, 20 per cent of those surveyed did not know or remember whether their parents had access to land or in what form of tenancy, while fewer than 2 per cent reported their parents to have been squatters. When we followed up on this question with life histories, it became apparent that access to land was a very precarious process, with numerous families having passed through multiple stages of being landless, then squatters who were subsequently evicted, sometimes then becoming sharecroppers until evicted once again.

Given the seasonal nature of wage work on the plantations, most landless wage workers continually attempted to gain access to a small parcel of

Table 8.1: Form of access to land before the Cuban agrarian reform

Form of access to land	*Güines (n = 158)*	*Santo Domingo (n = 158)*	*Majibacoa (n = 159)*	*Total*
Arrendire	30.4	17.7	6.9	18.3
Sharecropper	6.3	–	13.2	6.5
Squatter	–	1.9	3.2	1.7
Landless	21.5	38.6	32.1	30.7
Property	15.2	16.5	32.7	21.5
N.I.*	26.6	25.3	11.9	21.3
Total	100.0	100.0	100.0	100.0

Total sample, parents of interviewees (in percentages).
* No information.
Source: 1991 Agricultural Household Survey of the University of Havana.

land for self-provisioning, by whatever means. In Majibacoa it was a fairly common practice for landless households to live on the estates and *colonias* where they were wage workers, particularly if they were permanent wage workers. There they would be given a small plot, rent-free, to farm for their own self-provisioning. These workers tended to consider themselves among the landless, and to report themselves as such in the survey.[7] Obtaining a permanent job on one of the *colonias*, which entitled the worker to year-round work, was so prized that these positions were often sold.

In Güines landless agricultural workers were more likely than in Majibacoa or Santo Domingo to live in the municipal capital and to pursue non-agricultural sources of employment during the 'dead season' (the sugar harvest lasted only four months or so a year). Santo Domingo and Majibacoa continued to be much more rural than Güines up to the current period, and landless workers more dependent on agricultural employment.

The survey data also confirm how few rural households owned land, only 21.5 per cent of the sample. *Arrendires* (18 per cent) appear more prevalent than sharecroppers (6.5 per cent), but there were striking differences by region. In Güines, the greatest number of families of today's agricultural workers were *arrendires* (31 per cent) before the 1959 agrarian reform. In Santo Domingo the landless predominated (39 per cent); in Majibacoa the sample was equally divided among those who owned property and those who were landless prior to 1959.

Majibacoa appears as the municipality where peasant landowners were relatively more numerous prior to 1959, perhaps because a sugar mill was not built in this zone until after the revolution. Thus, this municipality did not suffer a process of land concentration at the behest of the sugar plantations. But here, as elsewhere, there was a high degree of semi-proletarianization among the property-owning peasantry. Most peasants migrated both near and far to the *colonias* to seek work during the 3–4-month-long cane harvest.

As will be seen below, differences in pre-revolutionary class structure and land tenure in the three municipalities studied had a significant influence on the outcome of Cuba's agrarian reform at the local level.

Cuba's Agrarian Reforms of 1959 and 1963

The first agrarian reform law of May 1959 limited the size of all landholdings to 401 hectares. It also guaranteed all tenants – whether *arrendires*, sharecroppers, or squatters – the right to the land which they worked directly. The October 1963 agrarian reform law reduced the maximum size landholding still further to 67 hectares.

In comparing the implementation of the first and second agrarian reforms in the three municipalities, it is apparent that the local agrarian reform commissions of the National Institute of Agrarian Reform (INRA) had considerable discretion in applying the various decrees. In some cases, the largest landowners were expropriated in their entirety; in others, the size of their holdings was simply reduced to comply with the legal ceiling. Even greater variation was probably introduced by the 1963 agrarian reform law, with the lands of some medium-scale farmers expropriated entirely, while others were allowed to maintain one farm under the 67 hectare limit. These variations suggest that local politics played an important role in the implementation of the agrarian reform laws. Moreover, pre-existing relations of production also influenced the various outcomes of the agrarian reform process.

The agrarian reforms of 1959 and 1963 ended up affecting the greatest number of farms in Santo Domingo. The great majority were expropriated because they had been leased out and, thus, were not worked directly by their owners. However, there were numerous cases of landowners who had directly worked at least a portion of their lands being expropriated. The more drastic application of the agrarian reform laws in Santo Domingo was partly explained by its geographical proximity to the Escambray Mountains, the scene of considerable anti-revolutionary activity between 1959 and 1964. A number of armed bands carried out acts of sabotage here, burning cane fields and vehicles, and sporadically taking over various small towns, leading to armed confrontations with the local militia. Peasants and landlords suspected of collaborating with the armed bands had their lands expropriated in their entirety.

The 1959 decree, which made every squatter, tenant and sharecropper owner of the land which they had previously worked, is estimated to have benefited some 110 000 households nationally (MacEwan 1981: 56–7). Given the predominance of tenancy arrangements in Cuba's pre-revolutionary agrarian structure, the number of property-owning peasant households almost tripled. After the 1963 reform, some 154 000 peasant households held 26 per cent of the area in farms, while another 3 per cent was held by non-peasant households (Trinchet 1984: 22–3).

Our retrospective survey of 475 agricultural households indicates that the families of 35 per cent of Cuba's 1991 agricultural labour force benefited directly from the agrarian reform, receiving land as private property. The regional differences were marked (see Table 8.2). The greatest proportion of beneficiaries, 42 per cent of those interviewed, were located in Güines, where *arrendire* arrangements predominated prior to 1959. The fewest were found in the municipality of Santo Domingo (29 per cent), followed by Majibacoa (32 per cent).

The greatest number of beneficiary families are found among those who today constitute the peasantry, fully 68.5 per cent of these households having been beneficiaries. This figure supports the contention that Cuba's landed peasantry was largely created by the revolution. Moreover, 41 per

Table 8.2: Beneficiaries of Cuba's agrarian reform

Municipality	*Households in which interviewee or parent had title to land*		*Amount of land titled (hectares)*
Güines	65	41.8% (*n* = 158)	19.23 (*n* = 64)
State wage worker	14*	16.7% (*n* = 84)	17.51 (*n* = 13)*
Co-operative member	19	59.4% (*n* = 32)	20.17 (*n* = 19)
Peasant	32	76.2% (*n* = 42)	19.40 (*n* = 32)
Santo Domingo	46	29.1% (*n* = 158)	12.93 (*n* = 44)
State wage worker	18	17.8% (*n* = 101)	9.79 (*n* = 16)
Co-operative member	9	29.0% (*n* = 31)	19.47 (*n* = 9)
Peasant	19	73.1% (*n* = 26)	12.47 (*n* = 19)
Majibacoa	51	32.1% (*n* = 159)	7.30 (*n* = 49)
State wage worker	27	26.7% (*n* = 101)	5.33 (*n* = 25)
Co-operative member	12	35.3% (*n* = 34)	10.51 (*n* = 12)
Peasant	12	50.0% (*n* = 24)	8.19 (*n* = 12)
Total			
State wage worker	59	20.6% (*n* = 286)	9.58 (*n* = 54)
Co-operative member	40	41.2% (*n* = 97)	17.11 (*n* = 40)
Peasant	63	68.5% (*n* = 92)	15.16 (*n* = 63)

* The totals of the number of state wage workers reporting that they or their parents were beneficiaries differ from the number reporting the amount of land titled, as not all interviewees remembered the precise amount of land which their families received.
Source: 1991 Agricultural Household Survey of the University of Havana.

cent of today's co-operative members belonged to families who were beneficiaries of the reform. A not insignificant number of current wage workers on state farms, 21 per cent, were either agrarian reform beneficiaries themselves or belonged to families who were beneficiaries.

Of the 162 households who were beneficiaries of the reform, the great majority (55 per cent) had previously been *arrendires*, followed by sharecroppers (17 per cent) and landless wage workers (9 per cent). In both Güines and Santo Domingo the overwhelming number of beneficiaries (over two-thirds) were previously *arrendires*. In contrast, in Majibacoa sharecroppers dominated (37 per cent) followed by *arrendires* (22 per cent) and the landless (18 per cent).

While the predilection of agrarian reform administrators in Güines to benefit the cane *arrendires* seems justified by the pre-revolutionary pattern of land tenancy, in Santo Domingo it seems as if this group was especially privileged, given their relatively lower representation in the rural class structure. Moreover, agrarian reform administrators in Santo Domingo were far less generous than they were in Majibacoa with landless rural workers and those with unstable access to land.

The relatively large number of landless households who were agrarian reform beneficiaries in Majibacoa may be related to the fact that this municipality was much more rural than the other two, and that many of the 'landless' tended to live on the farms where they worked as wage workers, as noted earlier. In most cases, they were ceded the self-provisioning plot which they farmed, subsequently leading to the creation of an agricultural proletariat composed of 'semi-peasants'. In contrast, in Güines and Santo Domingo it is much less likely in the 1990s for state wage workers to have access to any land at all.[8]

It is also worth noting the relatively large amount of land which the beneficiaries received through the reform. The mean was 13.74 hectares, approximately equal to the traditional Cuban land measure of a *caballería* (equal to 13.43 hectares). As seen in Table 8.2, families who today are co-operative members or peasants received the largest farms. Moreover, the former sugar tenants of Güines received much larger farms (19.23 hectares) than beneficiaries in Santo Domingo (12.93 hectares) or Majibacoa (7.30 hectares). The smaller mean farm size of beneficiaries in Majibacoa is again explained by the presence of a large number of landless wage workers who were titled to their self-provisioning plots.

In all three municipalities some peasant farmers were affected negatively by the agrarian reform. In Majibacoa, three peasant interviewees lost some land as a result of the reform and in Santo Domingo, one household lost some land. Most of these cases concerned families who owned between 27 and 40 hectares and who sharecropped or rented some land to other peasants. In the reform, their tenants were deemed beneficiaries of the land which they worked, but they retained the land they themselves worked directly.

Only in Villa Clara were a good number of peasants totally expropriated for being involved in counter-revolutionary activity, which centred in the Escambray mountains of the province. In the municipality of Santo Domingo, two households sampled in 1991 (currently wage workers) lost all their land, presumably for this reason. The period of counter-revolutionary activity left a mark upon the Communist Party (PCC) in Villa Clara, which continued to ride rough-shod over the peasantry throughout this decade.

In contrast, in Majibacoa, where there was no counter-revolutionary activity, no peasant households were expropriated totally and the agrarian reform process showed considerable flexibility. There were even cases of peasants who owned over 67 hectares not being affected by the 1963 agrarian reform law.

One of the debates in the literature is over the extent to which the Cuban revolution initially attempted to collectivize the peasantry. In the early years of the reform, the Socialist Party of Cuba did in fact attempt to persuade agrarian reform beneficiaries to pool their land to form production co-operatives (known then as *sociedades agropecuarias* or agricultural societies) but these never received much government support. By 1963, on the eve of the second agrarian reform law, they were discouraged, primarily for political reasons, to reassure the peasantry that their right to individual private property was not in jeopardy.

Most peasants became members of peasant associations which constituted the base-level organization of ANAP (National Association of Small Producers) after it was formed in 1961. The peasant associations evolved at different paces within the three municipalities to emerge as credit and service co-operatives (CCSs), taking on juridical form for purposes of receiving credit as a group and purchasing means of production jointly. These were the base units for state agricultural planning of peasant production. From 1963 onwards, peasants were required to sell the bulk of their production to the state procurement agency, *Acopio*, on the basis of contracted quotas.

The Consolidation of the State Farm Sector (late 1960s and early 1970s)

Given the predominance of sugarcane plantations and large cattle *haciendas* in Cuba's agrarian structure, their expropriation under the first agrarian reform resulted in the state holding 40 per cent and the private sector 60 per cent of the land in farms in late 1959. Three years later, in early 1963, the state sector had grown to 52 per cent. After the second agrarian reform was implemented, in October 1963, the state held 71 per cent of the nation's farmland (Trinchet 1984: 24).

Precise data on the growth of the state sector at the municipal level are difficult to come by, as the agrarian reform was implemented through 'agricultural development zones' which encompassed several municipalities. In what was to become the current municipality of Güines, land initially was not so concentrated in state hands, given the large number of *arrendires* who were beneficiaries of the reform. We estimate that approximately 34 per cent of the land in this zone passed to the state after the first agrarian reform, and 50 per cent after the second reform. In 1992 the private sector held 26 per cent of the land in farms, and the state sector 74 per cent.[9]

On the other hand, in Majibacoa, where there were fewer agrarian reform beneficiaries, the state sector would eventually hold 81.5 per cent of the land in farms.[10] In Santo Domingo, which had the fewest beneficiaries as well as prior peasant proprietors, the state sector came to hold 84.2 per cent of the farmland.[11] The degree of concentration of agricultural land by state enterprises in both municipalities exceeded the national average of 74.3 per cent (CEE/AEC 1989: Table VIII.3).

The main change arising from the nationalization of Cuba's plantations and *haciendas* was that the state now guaranteed agricultural workers year-round employment, ending the pattern of seasonal unemployment which had caused so much misery in the past. In the early years of the reform, the state farms also concentrated on diversifying production, both to deepen food import substitution and to generate employment (Seers *et al.* 1964: Ch. 3). By the time that Cuba returned to its primary focus on sugar production for export in 1964, there was a relative labour shortage in agriculture, the product of the many new opportunities which were opened up for rural workers with the revolution, ranging from access to education to military service (Pollitt 1979).

The tendency during the 1960s was towards the consolidation of state enterprises into larger and larger enterprises. Cuban planning became increasingly focused on specialization, and what were termed 'specialized plans' and 'integral plans' were developed in cane, dairy, vegetable and citrus production. The specialized plans attempted to determine the production of state farms along with that of private farmers. In contrast, the integral plans attempted to encourage private farmers to either rent or sell their lands to the state if they were situated on lands adjacent to the expanding state enterprises, and to encourage these peasants to become state wage workers.

ANAP's self-criticism of the period supports the argument that peasants were sometimes forced to lease their land to the state under duress. According to Martín Barrios (1987: 81–4), a member of the ANAP national committee at the time, 'although Fidel had stressed that this [incorporation into state farms] had to be a gradual process, based on persuasion . . . many state functionaries, in their desire to carry out the plan, substituted the necessary discussion for the bureaucratic method of *ordeno y mando* (order and rule)'.

The integration of peasant lands into state enterprises, nevertheless, was also based on material incentives. The state built modern communities on the state farms, communities which included modern housing with electricity, water and sewer systems, a primary school, a health post and a day care centre. Priority access to the housing units – which were rent free – was given to peasants who rented their land to the state.

Between 1967 and 1971 at least 24 500 peasant farms nationally were integrated into the state farms, while additional private land was purchased by the state as a result of the death of the owner, old age, or a lack of heirs willing to work the land (Martín Barrios 1987: 94).[12] Here again, our field work illustrates the process and how its implementation differed: while it fostered a process of de-peasantization in all three municipalities, this was most severe in Santo Domingo which already had the slimmest peasant base.

It is in Santo Domingo that the process of incorporating peasant lands into state plans appears to have been carried out with the greatest degree of coercion. Numerous peasant households were forced to rent their lands to the state when it was decided to convert the *Granja Sabino Hernández* into an integral *Plan Viandero Manacas* in 1967, expanding this large enterprise to some 1616 hectares. Some peasants were forced to rent or sell their land to one of the three sugar plants; others were forced to sell their land and move to a new community when the zone where their farm was located was targeted for the construction of a major dam. Overall, Santo Domingo's agricultural households were the most negatively affected by state intervention, with 11 per cent of those interviewed having been expropriated or having sold or rented land to the state. In interviews, they also seemed the most disgruntled over having lost access to land at the behest of state plans.

It is evident that in the late 1960s the Cuban leadership expected the private sector to disappear as peasants abandoned independent production for the security and modern production conditions of state farms. Little was done, therefore, to modernize private farming, which continued to rely on the ox plough and family labour while state farms mechanized. Despite their relative neglect, private producers benefited greatly from the rural development emphasis of revolutionary policy. During the 1960s thousands of rural schools and health posts were built, along with roads and rural electrification. This maintained a certain amount of trust in the state on the part of private producers, even while it became increasingly apparent that most peasants had no intention of becoming integrated into the state enterprises or of becoming wage workers (Deere et al. 1992).

The Co-operative Movement from the mid-1970s

Growing awareness that most peasants would not voluntarily turn over their land to the state and that the private sector needed modernizing, combined with the desire to control this sector more fully, finally led the Cuban leadership to reconsider the role of production co-operatives. Thus, in a major speech in May 1974, Fidel Castro argued that there were two paths to a socialist agriculture: state farms and collectivization (Martín Barrios 1987: 126–27, 138). Collectivization, or the formation of production co-operatives, was to take place by peasants voluntarily pooling their private property in response to material incentives. At the First Congress of the Cuban Communist Party in 1975, the 'Thesis on the Agrarian Question' was adopted. This stressed that the collectivization process was to be gradual and based on the voluntary decisions of peasants, with the rhythm of the process being dependent on the demonstration effect of successful production co-operatives (ibid.: 128).

The peasant association, ANAP, was made responsible for promoting the new production co-operatives, the CPAs, and at its 1977 national congress it officially adopted collectivization as its goal. Between 1977 and

1982, 1416 CPAs were constituted nationally, with ten CPAs organized in Majibacoa and nine each in Santo Domingo and Güines.

A decade later, in 1991, production co-operatives were a much more important social and productive force in Güines, where CPA members constituted 16 per cent of the agricultural economically active population. In Santo Domingo they constituted only 4 per cent, and in Majibacoa 6 per cent. Moreover, whereas in Güines the CPAs held 46 per cent of private-sector land, in Santo Domingo they held 40 per cent, and in Majibacoa only 37 per cent. As we will demonstrate, the CPAs have also been much more successful in Güines than in the other two municipalities, partly because of their natural and infrastructural endowment and partly because of the composition of their membership.

While the CPAs were initially formed by peasants who pooled their own means of production, by 1991 the majority of members were non-peasants in Majibacoa and Santo Domingo. In Majibacoa the largest number of members, 44 per cent, were agricultural wage workers prior to joining. Similarly, in Santo Domingo former agricultural workers constituted 32 per cent and industrial wage workers (many from the sugar industry) 16 per cent, resulting in the CPAs having a relatively large proletarian base. In contrast, the majority of co-operative members in Güines, 62.5 per cent, were individual peasant farmers prior to joining a CPA.

The proportion of members who belong to families who pooled land to form the CPA is highest in Güines, 72 per cent, and lowest in Santo Domingo, 39 per cent. This is an important variable for explaining the commitment of the membership to the success of the co-operative as well as the different productive outcomes of the CPAs.

The average amount of land pooled was 17.3 hectares. It was much larger in Güines and Santo Domingo than in Majibacoa, where the average amount pooled was only 7 hectares. The value of land and other means of production contributed to the production co-operative was also highest in Güines, averaging 4062 pesos. In Santo Domingo, where the average amount of land contributed was similar to Güines, the mean value was only 3032 pesos, reflecting both poorer quality land and the fact that peasants were much more capitalized in Güines and had other means of production to contribute to the co-operatives besides land.

The CPAs in all three municipalities have been able to build new, modern agricultural communities, although housing construction has lagged somewhat behind in Santo Domingo and Majibacoa as compared to Güines. The general practice is for CPA members to purchase their homes over a 20-year period. If they leave the co-operative, their mortgage payments are considered as the equivalent of rent and they lose their right to eventual ownership, a factor promoting stability in co-operative membership.

The co-operatives in Majibacoa and Santo Domingo have experienced far greater difficulties than their counterparts in Güines. Many CPAs went into excessive debt in the early 1980s, purchasing more equipment than they needed or investing in costly irrigation systems. In addition, some CPAs suffered from severe management problems and were consequently merged with other, better managed CPAs. In some cases these fusions caused the merged CPA to be unprofitable for a number of years, much to their membership's dissatisfaction.

Survey data for 1991 indicate that in Güines all the co-operative members interviewed earned a profit distribution in that year as compared with only 71 per cent in Santo Domingo and 79 per cent in Majibacoa. Most significant was the difference in the level of profits generated by the CPAs in the three municipalities. The average profit distribution in Güines of 2535 pesos was ten times that of Santo Domingo (246 pesos), where the average profit distribution was the lowest. In Majibacoa the average profit distribution in 1991 was 410 pesos.[13]

The level of profit distribution in Güines was slightly higher than the average level of the advance (or implicit wage) which co-operative members pay themselves over the course of the year. The average level of the advance was also highest in Güines as was the implicit value of the food subsidy, the latter measured as the difference between the price co-operative members pay for the products the CPA sells them from the self-provisioning effort and the retail price of these products.

The value of the food subsidy is quite high in all three municipalities, ranging from 866 pesos in Majibacoa to 1018 pesos in Güines. This indicates the high degree of self-provisioning generated by the co-operatives, one of the main accomplishments of the CPAs. A number have been able to forego the ration card for many products, including CPAs dedicated primarily to cane production. In contrast, self-provisioning efforts on the state farms in 1991 were comparatively meagre; the implicit subsidy of self-provisioning purchases ranged from 33 pesos in Santo Domingo to 71 pesos in Majibacoa. Undoubtedly in that year CPA members were eating a more abundant, varied and higher-quality diet than state wage workers, a difference that was exacerbated after 1992.

Overall, the average income of 5800 pesos of co-operative members in Güines from their work in the CPA was almost double the average income of those in Santo Domingo (3239) and in Majibacoa (3061). The profitability of the Güines co-operatives can be attributed not only to their more favourable initial conditions – better land and greater access to irrigation as well as location – but also to the fact that the CPAs in this municipality are much more peasant-based. This in turn is related to the fact, noted earlier, than in Güines there were more agrarian reform beneficiaries than in the other municipalities. Moreover, the Güines CPAs are characterized by a much higher share of peasants who pooled land, bringing large numbers of family members into the CPAs with them. The extremely strong family ties among the membership appear to have committed them to the successful outcome of the co-operative venture.

An indicator of the success of the co-operative movement in general is that in all three municipalities the mean, net household income of co-operative members (6643 pesos) exceeds that of state wage workers (4902 pesos), a difference which is statistically significant. This income difference is particularly marked in Güines where the net household incomes of co-operative members (8619.5 pesos) were the highest of the three municipalities.

In all three regions the highest net household incomes were reported by peasant households (an average of 7898 pesos). However, the difference in the average household income between co-operative members and peasants was not statistically significant. This suggests that the process of collectivization has not severely restricted the income-generating possibilities of those peasants who pooled their land compared with those who did not. However, peasant household income levels have been underestimated as self-provisioning production has been valued at official prices; in 1991 prices on the black market in foodstuffs were considerably higher. Moreover, peasants often tend to under-report what they produce for self-provisioning. These factors lead us to qualify the conclusion that peasant income-generating possibilities have not been adversely affected by collectivization: rather, in comparison with those peasants who only sell their production to the state at official prices, peasants who have pooled land do not appear to be at a disadvantage.

One of the main results of the 1991 Agricultural Household Survey was to reveal the extent of the increase in agricultural workers' living standards since 1959. In the survey of agricultural wage workers undertaken by the Catholic University in 1959, these workers only earned 25 per cent of the average per capita national income in that year (ACU 1972). According to the 1991 survey, state agricultural wage workers earned 74 per cent of this same measure. If the incomes of all agricultural households (including those of peasants and co-operative members) are pooled, they earned 89 per cent of the average per capita national income (Deere et al. 1995).

The CPAs and State Farms in the Special Period, 1989 onwards

Our field work in the three municipalities suggests that the production co-operatives have fared relatively well under the harsh conditions of the Special Period, providing one of the explanations why, after 34 years of viewing state farms as the 'superior' mode of socialist production, the Cuban leadership decided to co-operativize the state farms in September 1993.

Firstly, membership of the production co-operatives in Majibacoa and Santo Domingo has begun to stabilize, although more so in Majibacoa than in Santo Domingo. In Güines the problem is that too many people are eager to join the CPAs, particularly state farm workers. The CPAs do not want too many additional members and are quite selective about whom they admit, generally preferring to add family members. Since membership implies permanent, year-round employment and a commitment to pay the basic 'advance', the CPAs prefer to rely on temporary wage labour during peak periods. The attractiveness of the CPAs in all three regions in the current period is largely due to the high level of self-provisioning which they offer their members. Moreover, with growing unemployment in the cities as a result of the economic crisis, more rural youth are opting to remain in the countryside, and prefer to work on the CPAs than on the state farms.

Despite shortfalls in inputs during the depth of Cuba's economic crisis in early 1992, CPAs in Havana province increased their deliveries to the state of root crops, plantain and vegetables by 17 per cent compared with the same period in 1991.[14] The Güines CPAs were able to increase or at least sustain production levels while using fewer inputs, primarily by bringing more land into food production. There were also plans to transfer land from state farms to the very best mixed cropping co-operatives. According to a functionary of the Ministry of Agriculture, the planned transfer of land indicates that the co-operative sector was finally recognized as being much more productive than the state sector in terms of root crop and vegetable production.

In terms of the cane co-operatives in Güines, yields have fallen drastically since 1990, mainly because of the lack of fertilizers. The 1992–93 harvest was characterized by a 40 per cent drop in supplies of chemical inputs compared with 1990. Notwithstanding the fall in yields, these CPAs continue to be profitable.

All seven CPAs in Majibacoa were profitable for the first time in 1993. In 1991 two CPAs had been on the brink of disintegrating as a result of poor management and excessive debt burdens. In Santo Domingo, several CPAs continued with economic difficulties, but their problems were dwarfed by those facing the state farms, particularly as CPAs provided at least adequate self-provisioning products to their members.

In sum, in our field work in these municipalities during 1993 it was clearly apparent that the CPAs were more successful than the state farms in adjusting to the shortage of modern inputs. Moreover, there was growing recognition among state-farm managers that the CPAs were much more efficient and productive than the state farms. Although the state farms had been experimenting with various new forms of decentralization and worker incentives for several years, the new schemes had not reversed falling production trends.[15] This was the context for the subsequent decision to form basic units of co-operative production (UBPCs) on the state farms.

The UBPCs emulate the CPAs in that members are owners of their means of production (except for land) and of what they produce, with any profits to be distributed among the membership. Where they differ most from the CPA model is that land remains under state ownership; the UBPCs obtain it under long-term leases, rent-free. They also differ from the CPAs in that up to 1996 the UBPCs remained subordinated to the state enterprise from which they emerged; the UBPCs must negotiate their production plans with the state enterprises and the latter are responsible for provisioning them with inputs.

Although it is still too early to judge the performance of the UBPCs, they face several challenges if they are to be as successful as the private-sector CPAs. The membership of the UBPCs is almost exclusively proletarian, whereas the most successful CPAs have a strong peasant base. Whether former wage workers will adopt the peasants' work ethic and love for the land, and develop a sense of ownership, remains to be seen. In other words, the success of the UBPCs is likely to depend on whether wage workers can submit themselves to a process of re-peasantization.

The success of re-peasantization within the UBPCs will surely depend on the degree to which the UBPCs gain relative autonomy from the state enterprises. Too much state control undermines member participation in decision-making and certainly retards the process of members developing a sense of ownership and motivation to increase production. Another lesson from our historical analysis is the importance of flexibility on the part of the state so that the UBPCs are able to develop in accordance with local conditions and aspirations.

Conclusions

The history of Cuba's agrarian transformation in the twentieth century – both capitalist and socialist – has been marked by tremendous regional differences. Under capitalist development, agrarian transformation was largely at the behest of private capital, and the search for land suitable for cane production. While sugarcane came to dominate the economies of the three municipalities studied here, their land tenure and rural class structure differed. The greatest difference was that cane production in Güines was largely carried out by peasant *arrendires*, whereas the cane *colonias* of Santo Domingo and Majibacoa were the domain of urban-based entrepreneurs who were often *arrendires*, but who relied on wage labour. Consequently, whereas in the west the expansion of sugarcane production fostered a yeoman peasant class, in the east the modality under which US-owned plantations developed stunted its formation. The main feature of the peasantry in this latter region was its insecurity with respect to land tenure.

After the revolution, state socialist policy became the 'guiding hand' in regional agrarian transformation. Nonetheless, the pre-revolutionary agrarian structure influenced the manner in which the agrarian reform was carried out in each region. The large number of peasant *arrendires* in Güines resulted in this municipality having the largest number of beneficiaries. In Santo Domingo and Majibacoa, where the landless and/or peasant landowners were more predominant, relatively more land ended up being concentrated in the state sector. Moreover, the role of the peasantry in the counter-revolutionary movement generated an 'anti-peasant' mentality among the Party in Santo Domingo, resulting in many more peasants being affected negatively by state agrarian policy in the decade of the 1960s than in the other two regions. In general, if the initial policy of the revolution was re-peasantization, over the next decade it became de-peasantization.

The larger private sector in Güines compared to the other two municipalities also resulted in the collectivization process of the late 1970s and early 1980s being more successful there than in the other two regions. More peasants had been beneficiaries of agrarian reform and many more peasants pooled land to form production co-operatives, bringing to the co-operatives a large number of family members. All these factors contributed to the cohesion of the CPAs and, together with more advantageous natural and infrastructural conditions, resulted in a much more successful co-operative movement.

While not all production co-operatives have performed as well as those of Güines, the CPAs in general were much better able to withstand the difficult conditions of the Special Period than the state farms, leading to the decision to co-operativize the latter. As argued above, the success of the UBPCs is likely to depend on whether a process of re-peasantization is achieved.

As we have attempted to demonstrate in this paper, socialist transformation and specifically the way in which state policy was implemented at local level was never homogeneous. Rather it was 'path dependent', interacting with such factors as the natural environment and infrastructure, previous land tenancy and class relations, and local peasant–party relations, to produce heterogeneous outcomes.

Notes

1. This chapter draws on collaborative field research carried out by the author with the Rural Studies Team of the University of Havana from 1991 to 1996. It summarizes some of the main findings of Deere, Pérez, Torres, García and González (forthcoming). The author would like to thank her fellow team members for comments on previous versions, and The John D. and Catherine T. MacArthur Foundation for financial support of this research.
2. The three municipalities were also chosen to be representative of the different levels of development attained in the pre-revolutionary period. Güines, as one of the better-endowed regions of the country in terms of natural resources

(fertile land, average rainfall, rivers and drainage) and location, was among the most prosperous municipalities of rural Cuba. Majibacoa was amongst the poorest in the country. Santo Domingo represented a mid-point in terms of these factors.

3. Calculated on the basis of data from *Anuario Azucarero* 1939 and 1959, and the current land surface of the three municipalities.
4. Majibacoa did not become a municipality until 1976. As the larger share of its area belonged to the municipality of Victoria de Las Tunas, the data for this latter municipality are taken as a proxy.
5. *Arrendires*, or *arrendatarios*, together with *sub-arrendires* or *sub-arrendatarios* refer to cash renters or sub-renters. They could be farmers of any size and spanned the spectrum of crop type. However, they were generally, if not exclusively, associated with the sugar sector, in which case they are called *colonos*. Land rent was usually deducted from the price they were paid for the cane. Small *colonos* usually had around 1 caballería (13.43 hectares) and large *colonos* (in the eastern part of the country) well over 10 caballerías in cane production.
6. The methodological aspects of the 1991 Agricultural Household Survey of the University of Havana are described by Deere *et al.*, 1993. The sample was drawn to be representative of the three main sectors in Cuban agriculture today: state wage workers, members of production co-operatives, and peasant farmers. We use the term 'agricultural workers' to include members of all three sectors.
7. In the 1946 Agricultural Census (Cuba 1951), Las Tunas appears as the municipality with the largest share of squatters. While squatting was undoubtedly more common in the eastern region of Cuba than in the more densely populated western region, our survey suggests that many of these 'squatters' may have had the landlord's permission to farm a small usufruct plot if they were permanent workers. Nonetheless, the frequent stories of peasants being dispossessed from such usufruct parcels in the 1940s and 1950s attest to the insecurity of tenure facing all those who did not own land.
8. In Majibacoa, state wage workers had access to an average 1.48 hectares of land in the 1991 Agricultural Household Survey. In contrast, the mean for Santo Domingo was 0.36 and for Güines 0.08 hectares.
9. Comité Estatal de Estadísticas, Güines, *Uso de la Tierra*, 31 December 1992.
10. Dirección de Administración Urbana, Majibacoa, *Balance de la Tierra*, 31 December 1990.
11. Dirección de Administración Urbana, Santo Domingo, *Balance de Tierra*, 31 December 1992.
12. Trinchet (1984: 28) puts this figure at 30 000 peasant households. Under the terms of the initial agrarian reform law, peasant property can be inherited but only sold to the state.
13. See Deere et al. (1995) for a detailed discussion of the generation of household income in the state, co-operative and peasant sectors.
14. The province of Havana was the initial focus of the National Food Programme, a programme which was re-oriented in 1991 towards achieving self-sufficiency in most foodstuffs for the city and province of Havana. See Deere (1993) for a detailed description.
15. See Deere et al. (1994) for a description of the changes introduced on the state farms between 1990 and 1993.

References

ACU (Agrupación Católica Universitaria) (1972) 'Por qué reforma agraria?', reproduced in 'Documentos: encuesta de trabajadores rurales 1956–57', *Economía y Desarollo*, No. 12, 188–213.

Anuario Azucarero de Cuba (1939–62) La Habana: Ed. Cuba Económica y Financiera, various issues.

CEE/AEC, (various years) *Anuario Estadístico de Cuba*, Comité Estatal de Estadísticas, Havana.

Cuba, República de (1951) *Memoria del Censo Agrícola Nacional, 1946*, P. Fernández y Cia, Havana.

Deere, C.D. (1993) 'Cuba's national food program and its prospects for food security', *Agriculture and Human Values*, 10(3): 35–51.

Deere, C.D., Meurs, M. and Pérez, N. (1992) 'Toward a periodization of the Cuban collectivization process: changing incentives and peasant response', *Cuba Studies/Estudios Cubanos*, 22: 115–49.

Deere, C.D., González, E., Pérez, Niurka and Rodríguez, G. (1993) *Household Incomes in Cuban Agriculture*, Working Paper Series No. 143, Institute of Social Studies, The Hague.

Deere, C.D., Pérez, N. and González, E. (1994) 'The view from below: Cuban agriculture in the Special Period in peacetime', *Journal of Peasant Studies*, 21(2): 194–234.

Deere, C.D., González, E., Pérez, N. and Rodríguez, G. (1995) 'Household incomes in Cuban agriculture: a comparison of the state, co-operative, and peasant sectors', *Development and Change*, 26(2): 209–34.

Deere, C.D., Pérez, N., Torres, C., García, M. and González, E. (forthcoming) *Cuba Agraria: Transformaciones Locales en el Siglo XX*, Editorial de Ciencias Sociales, Havana.

MacEwan, A. (1981) *Revolution and Economic Development in Cuba*, Macmillan, London.

Martín Barrios, A. (1987) *La ANAP: 25 Años de Trabajo*, Editorial Política, Havana.

Pollitt, B. (1977) 'Some problems in enumerating the "peasantry" in Cuba', *Journal of Peasant Studies*, 4(2): 162–80.

Pollitt, B. (1979) *Agrarian Reform and the 'Agricultural Proletariat' in Cuba, 1958–66: Some Notes*, Occasional Papers No. 27, Institute of Latin American Studies, University of Glasgow.

Seers, D., Bianchi, A., Jolly, R. and Nolff, M. (1964) *Cuba: The Economic and Social Revolution*, University of North Carolina Press, Chapel Hill.

Trinchet O. (1984) *La Cooperativización de la Tierra en el Agro Cubano*, Editorial Política, Havana.

9. The Mexican Peasantry and the *Ejido* in the Neo-liberal Period

MAGDALENA BARROS NOCK

Introduction

Mexican agrarian structure has undergone important changes over the past few decades. In the 1960s and 1970s the economic model adopted was based on direct state intervention and protectionism, known as 'import substitution'. The modernization of agriculture aimed to increase self-sufficiency in basic grains, with the development of a domestic market. In the 1980s and 1990s a neo-liberal economic model was set in motion, the main characteristics of which are an end to commercial protection by joining the North American Free Trade Agreement (NAFTA), the abolition of subsidies, the privatization of state enterprises such as the Mexican Fertilizer Company (FERTIMEX) or the restriction of the activities of state enterprises such as the National Basic Foods Company (Conasupo), the withdrawal of guaranteed prices for agricultural produce with the exception of maize, and the privatization of land, water and natural resources such that their use is determined by the market.

The objective of this chapter is to analyse the impact of neo-liberal policies on the peasantry, with special reference to the *ejido* sector. The chapter starts by briefly reviewing the main historical trends of Mexico's rural development, paying particular attention to state intervention and the *ejido* sector. It then analyses the impact of three main neo-liberal policies – the privatization of the *ejido*, the withdrawal of subsidies and the reduction of credit, and the free market – on those *ejidos* which produce grains, and assesses their prospects of shifting to fruit and vegetable production for the international market. Finally the question of whether small- and medium-scale peasants can benefit from NAFTA is discussed.

Defining the *Ejido* Sector

The *ejido* is a system of land tenure created by the agrarian reform implemented in Mexico after the 1910 Revolution. It has an economic role as a production unit. Its members (*ejidatarios*) are peasants who live from the land and are subject to a specific organizational model. All *ejidatarios* have access to land, but rather than owning it they only have the right to work on it and benefit from its production. Although the *ejido* was created with the objective of giving peasant households a means of subsistence, *ejidatarios* and their families have increasingly seen the need to supplement their income with off-farm activities and in many cases with seasonal migration.

At present there are roughly 26 006 *ejidos* in Mexico and 2 900 000 *ejidatarios*. *Ejidos* are concentrated in the centre-south region of the country, which is Mexico's most populated area and where most peasant *minifundia*[1] are also found. There are far fewer *ejidos* in the north of the country, where the government prioritized private land tenure and where the largest irrigation systems are concentrated. In total the *ejido* sector covers 95 million hectares. *Ejido* land can be farmed individually (97 per cent), each *ejidatario* farming a piece of land, or collectively (3 per cent) by all members of the *ejido* (INEGI 1990: 78).

The *ejido* authorities act as intermediaries between the state and the *ejido*, giving them a position of power within the *ejido*. The general assembly is the arena where issues concerning the *ejido* are discussed and decisions taken, the most important issue being land. Decisions are supposedly arrived at democratically by all members, and all *ejidatarios* are obliged to attend the general assembly. However, attendance varies among *ejidos* and many are controlled by internal power groups. All *ejidatarios* elect a *comisariado ejidal*, with a president, secretary and treasurer, and a vigilance committee. Resources, credit and incentives provided by the government are channelled through the *ejido* via numerous intermediate organizations. With respect to the distribution and management of credit, peasants are organized into small groups according to the kind of credit and produce grown. These groups are related to the state bank (Banrural) and the state programme for development (FIRA). Infrastructure is constructed and managed in association with the *ejido*.

When analysing the *ejido*, one has to take into account the political as well as the economic factors which have influenced its development. The state has intervened strongly in the *ejido*. After setting up the *ejido* system, the state attempted to organize the peasantry and, in many cases, to control and influence any independent organization which emerged. In this way, the state has absorbed important sectors of the peasant movement.

Peasant organizations have changed over the decades. On the one hand, organizations demanding the redistribution of land have been systematically repressed, thereby losing much of their force and power (Paré 1991: 31, 36). On the other hand, in the 1980s new organizations emerged which are more interested in modernizing production and participating actively in government planning (Myhre 1994). During the past 20 years the number of peasant organizations at regional and national levels has increased significantly. For instance, in 1981 there were 237 *ejido* unions but by 1989 that number had doubled. Most of these were founded by the government, but others arose independently.

By the 1980s, the character of peasant organizations and their demands had been transformed. The medium-sized landholders became leaders of the peasant movement whose demands were diverse and heterogeneous. Organization is no longer based on type of land tenure, that is the *ejido* sector versus the private sector, but is now mixed and based on common objectives. Independent peasant organizations have been able to create horizontal structures at regional and national levels. Their discourse and demands tend more towards negotiation and conciliation than to confrontation and the demand for land (Gordillo 1985). Up to 1991, the constitution prohibited the renting or selling of *ejido* land, although this practice was common in most *ejidos*. *Ejido* land could only be inherited by kin. The *ejido* structure offered *ejidatarios* certain benefits, such as access to government credit without having to mortgage their land.

It is important to emphasize that the *ejido* sector is not homogeneous. Land use varies as follows: 21.4 per cent is devoted to agriculture, (of which 83.7 per cent is rainfed and 16.3 per cent irrigated), 57 per cent to cattle grazing, 17.3 per cent is forest and jungle, and 4.3 per cent has other uses, such as urban plots. Two-thirds of *ejidos* produce maize[2] as their main crop, which is grown both for family consumption and for the market. Maize is the main staple in Mexico and is mostly produced on *ejidos* where *minifundia* dominate. Following maize in importance is sorghum (grown by 6.42 per cent of all *ejidos*) and beans (4.4 per cent of *ejidos*) (Morett 1991: 69–70).

There are some highly productive *ejidos*, with resources, infrastructure and agro-industries. Whilst fruit and vegetable agro-industrial production is dominated by transnationals, some small and medium *ejidatarios*, the 'élite' of the *ejido* sector, who have irrigation, have been able successfully to produce fruit and vegetables and interact and negotiate with foreign companies and state employees (Barros Nock 1998). Nevertheless, the majority of *ejidos* are poor, located on marginal land, and have few possibilities for capital accumulation. Many do not even produce enough for their own subsistence. In effect, most of the *ejido* sector is submerged in a structural crisis.

Historical Development of the *Ejido* Sector

In the 1930s the countryside was engulfed by clashes between peasants and *latifundistas*.[3] Drastic changes in the country's economy were called for, and it was during the Cárdenas regime that the basis of Mexico's modern industrial and agricultural sectors was laid by means of agrarian reform. Rural development was pursued in order to make agriculture, particularly peasant agriculture, more productive and responsive to the needs of the industrial sector. By improving the economic situation of the rural peasantry, the internal market was expected to expand. However, large landholdings stood in the way of this objective.

An important component of Cárdenas' agrarian reform concerned land distribution. The rural land tenure structure was made up of *ejido* communal land and small-scale peasant private property. Collective *ejidos* were promoted on expropriated *hacienda*[4] land. These *ejidos* did not represent a socialist tendency but were the result of an economic rationale which stressed that *haciendas* should not be subdivided but should be retained as efficient units of production, especially those which produced for the export market or provided raw materials for industry (Morett 1991: 24). The *Ejido* Credit Bank was created to finance highly remunerative commercial crops produced on collective *ejidos.* It also provided technical assistance required to recover initial investments. In this sense the bank fulfilled the functional role previously played on the *haciendas* by hired managers (Hewitt de Alcántara 1976).

Approximately 18 million hectares were redistributed. At the end of the Cárdenas presidency, almost half of the arable land (57 per cent of which was irrigated) was in the hands of *ejidatarios.* The *ejido* sector comprised 40 per cent of the economically active population and accounted for 43 per cent of agricultural and forest produce (Morett 1991: 25). The number of landless labourers fell from 68 to 36 per cent of the rural workforce (Hewitt de Alcántara 1976).

Peasants incorporated into the collective *ejidos* represented approximately 20 per cent of land reform beneficiaries. Machinery and equipment were not widely distributed with the land as *hacienda* owners usually retained the means of production.[5] Credit was made available mainly to the collective *ejidos*, to the detriment of *ejidos* where land was sown individually. The state did not intervene in the marketing system and the number of intermediaries increased. This meant that, although the *ejido* was strongly supported by the state[6] during this period, most families could not live exclusively from the land (Morett 1991: 25). Nonetheless, the *ejido* provided the state with a political clientele as well as an economic reserve from which to draw in the development process (Goodman and Redclift 1981: 190).

Cárdenas' Party of the Mexican Revolution (later to become the PRI: Revolutionary Institutional Party) sought the affiliation of worker and peasant organizations. Patronized by the government, *ejidatarios* were organized into a national association called the Peasant National Confederation (CNC) which was integrated into the power structure of the state. Cárdenas initiated a populist tradition in Mexican politics. Mexican populism originates in the state's need to prove its revolutionary heritage, notwithstanding the contradiction between its support for subordinate groups and furthering the development of a capitalist system.

By the end of 1940 the peasant movement was thwarted and the pressure for land decreased. According to Escarcega and Botey (1990: 10) most of the 12 million adult male rural inhabitants had access to land. As a result, in subsequent decades the government was able to direct attention to large private landowners without fearing a strong peasant reaction.

Liberalism and the green revolution (1940–70)

The path of development pursued by Cárdenas was abruptly abandoned. In the 1940s and 1950s there was a marked decrease in the amount of land expropriated and redistributed by the government. In almost 20 years over 15 million hectares were distributed to 527 115 peasants, but this was less than what Cárdenas had distributed in 5 years. In the 1960s, rising pressure from unemployed landless peasants meant that land redistribution increased again. Nevertheless, most of this land was of poor agricultural quality, or was only redistributed on paper, such that there are still *ejidos* waiting to receive land. The state promoted large-scale commercial farming, relegating the *ejido* sector to subsistence agriculture. Large-scale landowners benefited from new irrigation systems financed by the state and various incentives which encouraged a new concentration of land. By contrast, small landowners and the *ejido* sector were subject to repeated subdivisions, creating smaller and smaller plots.

During the 1940s the green revolution, involving high-yielding seeds, chemical herbicides, insecticides and fertilizers, water control, and genetic research, affected Mexican agriculture. Between 1956 and 1966 agricultural production increased at an average annual growth rate of 7.1 per cent, compared to 3.5 per cent between 1930 and 1946 (Rello 1985: 20–1). This period has been referred to as the 'Mexican miracle'. However, the main beneficiaries were the large landowners. The application of these inputs increased the differences between the commercial sector and the subsistence sector formed by peasant *ejidos* and *minifundistas*.

The role played by agriculture in the process of industrialization was determined by this dual nature of the agricultural sector. The large, commercial farm sector provided the foreign exchange to finance imports of intermediate and capital goods for industrial development, whilst the traditional sector, which had benefited less from the green revolution, supplied cheap food to the internal market. This sector also provided an important supply of cheap migrant labour, thus helping to keep wages low (Hewitt de Alcántara 1976; Goodman and Redclift 1981; Harriss 1982). This differentiation was also reflected inside the *ejido* sector, between those few *ejidos* which had more resources and access to credit and markets and the many impoverished small *ejidos* which lacked the technical, financial and organizational means to make their land productive. Sharp inequalities in income distribution thereby resulted.

This situation jeopardized the *ejido*'s capacity to accumulate capital. For many years, prices of agricultural produce were frozen or increases were minimal in relation to the continuous rise in prices of agricultural implements and inputs. Credit for medium- and long-term investments were rarely given to the *ejidos*. Nor was credit available for the creation of small rural industries. The result was that small and medium landholders were not able to capitalize. Credit became a means of keeping the *ejidatarios* from starving and of controlling increasing unrest (Hewitt de Alcántara 1976: 8–15).

This situation had several consequences. Firstly, migration to the cities in Mexico and to the USA increased. Secondly, as agricultural output lagged behind urban demand, food shortages were met by increasing imports of staple food. Mexico thereby was no longer self-sufficient in food production. By 1970 the agricultural annual growth rate had dropped to 0.2 per cent (Hewitt de Alcántara 1976: 11).

By the end of the 1960s, the government was faced with rising social discontent among the rural and urban population. Industry and commercial agriculture had not absorbed as much labour as government planners had anticipated, and the subsistence sector was not able to provide a livelihood for peasants and their families. The growing population pressed for land redistribution and *minifundismo* spread in the rural areas. The government responded to growing unrest in the rural areas by increasingly repressing *ejidatarios* and landless peasants trying to obtain land. Peasant organizations were threatened and the collective *ejidos*' capacity for independent local initiative and control of resources was undermined. Members were denied access to credit and, in some cases, leaders were assassinated. The need to maintain political stability and public order clearly shaped the priorities of the following government.

The neo-agrarian period (1970–82)

At the beginning of the 1970s the economic and political crisis in the countryside forced the government to review its agrarian strategy. A series of state policies, which aimed to recuperate previous growth rates while avoiding the negative effects of past policies, were implemented. Comprehensive public expenditure on social welfare and deficit financing via foreign debt characterized the government's activities. The government once again supported the *ejido* sector, hoping thereby to defuse the increasing discontent in the rural areas. Credit to the rural areas and to the *ejido* sector was increased significantly. The participation of the government in producer organizations also increased, institutionalizing and strengthening the corporatist structure of the state.

By the mid-1970s almost 17 million hectares of land had been redistributed, affecting some of the most highly productive commercial farms in the north. Collectivization was again on the agenda but with the purpose of precluding the division of highly productive farms and the partitioning of land. Collective *ejidos* were expected to produce staple foods, thus contributing to the nation's food self-sufficiency. Special government institutions were created to give support to collective *ejidos*, and those *ejidos* which accepted collectivization were given special concessions.

This programme of change did not succeed as expected, for several reasons. It did not originate from the *ejidatarios* themselves, but rather was imposed by the government. *Ejidatarios* demanded effective control over their land, yet the decision-making process was mainly in the hands of the government through its control of credit and subsidies. Furthermore, resources were scarce and co-ordination between government institutions weak (Morett 1991: 30). Thus state policies benefited only a minority of *ejidos*, mainly those located in highly productive areas.

With the revenues from the oil boom at the end of the 1970s, the government implemented a comprehensive development programme in the *ejido* sector. Known as the Mexican Food System (SAM), its main objective was to restore food self-sufficiency. A large amount of capital was invested in the countryside. Soon after SAM was implemented, production increased dramatically, yet the resources for it came from international credit given to Mexico. When the price of oil dropped, resources were withdrawn and agriculture sank into an even greater crisis than before. It was not possible to capitalize so quickly a sector which had been drained of resources for so long.

At the end of the 1970s and beginning of the 1980s, the government embarked on a new path. The Law for Agrarian Development opened the *ejido* to private capital, by promoting joint ventures. The law, however, was extremely bureaucratic and was not therefore widely referred to by peasants or potential investors. Meanwhile land redistribution to peasants fell drastically to only 179 939 hectares and food supply for the population became a problem (Rello 1985; Calva Tellez 1988). Thus at the start of the 1980s Mexico was faced with a huge debt, and a financial and productive crisis in the rural areas. Under pressure from the International Monetary Fund (IMF) full-blown neo-liberal strategies were adopted in subsequent years.

Neo-liberal Policies and the Free Market (1982 onward)

The neo-liberal strategy is based on structural adjustment policies advocated by the IMF and the World Bank to reduce the state's role in the economy and encourage competitiveness in the world market. This strategy gives full support to private capital, and involves allowing agricultural produce prices to fall in line with the international market, dismantling state enterprises, reducing subsidies and price control over agro-products, and separating policies aimed at increasing productivity from those alleviating poverty and rural development (Robles and Moguel 1990: 10). The goal of food self-sufficiency has been abandoned, and agriculture is expected to turn to the international market to earn much-needed foreign currency. Furthermore, special attention is being paid to the export of fruit, vegetables, flowers and livestock, which peasants are not accustomed to producing.

When Mexico became a signatory to the General Agreement on Tariffs and Trade (GATT) in 1986, restrictions on the export and import of produce and import quotas were reduced. Mexico's membership of NAFTA is based on the premise that Mexico has comparative advantages over the USA and Canada, especially with regard to fruit and vegetable production. Mexican peasants are expected to shift from producing grains to fruit and vegetables, and to compete successfully on the international market. Traditional agricultural exports, such as sugar, are being replaced by off-season fruit and vegetables, horticultural produce and speciality crops, in order to take advantage of the expanding fresh food and luxury produce markets. Mexican agriculture is increasingly becoming part of the global economy, participating in international circuits of production and consumption.

In accordance with these neo-liberal lines, the government is currently implementing changes in the agrarian structure to enable private capital, whether national or international, to invest in agriculture. A key factor in this is the change in the Constitution which now allows the privatization of *ejido* land, giving private capital security and access to land.

The impact of neo-liberal policies on the Ejido *sector*

In the 1980s and the beginning of the 1990s, a lively debate took place in Mexico on the role of the *ejido* at local and national levels. Some, such as Morett (1991), Rello (1985) and Warman (1975, 1991) viewed the *ejido* exclusively as an instrument of state control, a formal structure with no content and no potential for efficient agricultural production. Others, such as Gordillo (1987, 1991) and Myhre (1994), argued that the *ejido* could become an important political and economic tool for organizing agricultural producers in Mexico. The more the *ejidatarios* control the production and marketing of their produce, and the greater the say they have in decision-making, the more the *ejido* becomes a strong organization for peasant representation. The more the *ejido* is subject to decision-making by outsiders, the more it functions as a mechanism of control.

Ejidatarios throughout Mexico have reacted to neo-liberal policies in very diverse ways. The following sections examine more closely the impact of three main neo-liberal policies on *ejidatarios*: privatization, the reduction in subsidies and credit, and the development of the free market.

The privatization of the Ejido

As mentioned above, in anticipation of NAFTA membership, the Mexican government modified the Constitution in 1991 and permitted the privatization of the *ejido*. This change reversed the *ejido* principle of communally held land and brought an end to land redistribution. Members of each *ejido* can now decide in a general assembly whether they want to continue as they are or become private landowners (Salinas de Gortari 1991). Other changes related to the right of *ejidos* to use their land as collateral for the purposes of obtaining credit, amongst others. The *ejido*, either as an *ejido* or as a number of private properties, is now allowed to engage in different forms of association with private national and international capital. Agrarian courts have been created in order to resolve disputes relating to plot boundaries, land ownership and delayed proceedings.

Since the implementation of these constitutional changes, economic differentiation within the *ejido* sector has increased. Between 1990 and 1994 the distribution of land in the *ejido* sector altered. The smallest farms, which fell below subsistence level, have been abandoned and their owners have migrated. Their land has been absorbed by middle-sized and large farms as part of a process of consolidation of the *minifundio* into larger farms. Similarly, common pastures which used to be devoted to grazing have now been re-assigned to cultivation as rainfed land (de Janvry et al. 1997: 31–6). These reforms have increased the land market as land rental transactions increased, even on *ejidos* where land sales had not taken place. One reason for the slow pace of change in land-tenure patterns is the lack of stable non-farm income-generating opportunities outside the *ejido*. Whilst the majority of *ejidatarios* supplement their income with non-farm activities, given their instability, they are reluctant to sell their land. The privatization of *ejido* land has paved the way to the alienation of the property rights of collectives and associations in favour of individual owners, and worsened the situation of the rural poor (de Teresa and Ruiz 1996; Scott 1996).

Reduced subsidies and credit

In the past, official agricultural credit was provided with a technological package (seeds, agrochemicals and cultural practices). Subsidized loans at below-market rates and access to cheap state-produced or state-regulated inputs were the norm. Banrural, the main official credit institution, usually persuaded its clients to sell their harvest to Conasupo, the state food-purchasing and distribution company, thus facilitating its hegemonic market position (Myhre 1994: 41, Rello 1985). In the least well-off *ejidos* credit was used to bring some income into the household, particularly when money was scarce before the harvest.

Nowadays credit has been reduced significantly. Between 1988 and 1994 the number of borrowers fell from approximately 800 000 to 224 000. The government expected foreign investment to increase as a result of the changes in the Constitution, but in 1990 official foreign investment in agriculture amounted to less than 1 per cent of total foreign investment in Mexico (Stanford 1996: 149). A survey carried out by de Janvry *et al.* (1997: 103) found that only 30.5 per cent of households had access to some form of credit. While the availability of credit to agriculture increased during the years analysed, that to the *ejido* sector declined. The resulting serious liquidity crisis hindered the *ejidos'* ability to respond to reforms by shifting to high-value crops with comparative advantages in an open economy (ibid.: 103).

At the same time, production costs have increased. Prices of capital goods such as tractors and agricultural implements, and of inputs such as fuel, fertilizers, insecticides and hybrid seeds, have risen considerably. This has led to a decline in their use by farmers, especially in the *ejido* sector. For example, there were 162 533 tractors at the end of 1981 but this had fallen to 161 470 in 1987 (Calva Tellez 1988: 38–42) and to 110 428 in 1991 (INEGI 1997: 169). A national survey carried out in 1991 found that less than half of the *ejidos* (46.4 per cent) used tractors. De Janvry et al. (1997) come to the conclusion that there was either no change or a decline in the employment of machinery in the *ejido* sector between 1990 and 1994. Tractors have been replaced by labour, and where *ejidatarios* cannot hire labour, this means an increase in the use of family labour.

The state's participation in input and product markets, through guaranteed prices and a vast infrastructure for marketing and storage, has also been modified. Two state enterprises which produced inputs, the National Seed Company (PRONASE) and the Mexican Fertilizer Company (FERTIMEX), have been affected by reforms which allow private producers to participate and compete in the market (de Janvry et al. 1997: 18–19). The inflation suffered in Mexico has been exacerbated by the radical withdrawal of government subsidies from agriculture. Public expenditure for the rural areas decreased in 1986 to half the amount spent in 1981.

With respect to infrastructure, the construction of water projects and the maintenance and management of irrigation districts used to be in the hands of the National Water Commission. In the 1990s these districts were turned over entirely to consumers, a development which has meant a reduction of the investment in irrigation infrastructure. The budget allocated to the Ministry of Agriculture and Water Resources (SARH) decreased by 74 per cent between 1981 and 1987 (Calva Tellez 1988: 38–42) and by 34 per cent between 1991 and 1995 (INEGI 1997: 151).

The impacts of high input costs and of scarce access to credit, technology and high-yield seeds are seen in the changes in land use. From 1990 to 1994 there was a considerable expansion in land devoted to corn cultivation: intercropped corn on rainfed land increased during this period by 67 per cent and monocropped corn on irrigated land increased by 64 per cent. These increases reflect the lack of productive alternatives and the constraints faced by *ejidatarios* in shifting to crops with higher value-added (de Janvry et al. 1997: 62).

The free market and fruit and vegetables

Given these conditions, is it possible for the *ejido* to shift from grains to producing high-value fruit and vegetables? The production and export of non-traditional products, such as melons, tomatoes, brussel sprouts, broccoli and baby corn, have increased during the past two decades. The production of fruit and vegetables is very heterogeneous. Fruit and vegetables are grown throughout Mexico. In 1991 horticulture accounted for only 2.7 per cent of cultivated land and contributed 14.31 per cent of its total production value (Gómez Cruz et al. 1992: 114). The production of fruit and vegetables has steadily increased, almost quadrupling in the past 20 years. The main cause is an increase in the national consumption of fruit and vegetables.

Most fruit and vegetable production is labour intensive, providing employment for approximately 17.5 per cent of the total labour force employed in agriculture. Fruit and vegetables account for almost 40 per cent of agricultural exports (Gómez Cruz et al. 1992: 341). While the export of grains such as beans, rice and maize has been negligible in the past five years, the export of fruit and vegetables has increased significantly. Productivity has also increased more quickly for fruit and vegetables than for other crops such as maize and rice. This high productivity is the result of the adoption of modern technological packages mainly by the northern states of Mexico, where production is geared to the international market, and where North American capital finances and markets most of the export production (ibid).

The participation of the *ejido* sector in the overall national production of fruit and vegetables is small. Only 28 per cent of total fruit and vegetable production in 1991 came from the *ejido* sector, and *ejido* yields are lower than yields on private property (Marsh and Runsten 1996: 173). Only approximately 3 per cent (841) of *ejidos* grow fruit and vegetables. Of these *ejidos,* 282 produce horticultural products. We are not considering here those *ejidos* which grow sugarcane, which account for 3.9 per cent of the total *ejido* sector. Popular crops for the domestic market are usually grown on *ejidos* which are totally or partially irrigated. Some 30 per cent of the *ejidos'* irrigated land is cultivated with fruit and vegetables. Although the number of families producing fruit and vegetables increased from 14.1 percent in 1990 to 17.3 percent in 1994 (de Janvry et al. 1997: 139), this increase is much lower than the government anticipated.

Ejidatarios who produce for the international market usually cultivate small plots of land of one or two hectares. Those *ejidos*, and small private landholders with irrigated land who export their production, usually work under production contracts with transnational companies, although some export their produce directly. Most technological packages from the USA are implemented through production contracts, processing industries or the Mexican associates of these companies. Peasants who cannot afford such modern and expensive technological packages, and who cannot thereby attain the quality standards required by the international market, produce for the domestic market.

One of the most significant obstacles for peasants in participating in the fruit and vegetable agri-business is finance. The average investment required to produce one hectare of melons ranges from US$500 to 700. Lack of financial resources forces many peasants to negotiate disadvantageous production contracts with brokers and even have dealings with brokers of dubious reputation. The availability of credit for fruit and vegetables from Banrural has been irregular, to say the least. One of the main reasons for this irregularity has been the discrepancy between national policies and peasants' real needs.

The main recipient of Mexican fresh and processed fruit and vegetables is the USA. In 1990, 85 per cent of total exports went to the USA and 10 per cent to Canada. There is a constant demand for Mexican winter fruit and vegetable production. Mexican producers have to respond to a fluctuating market, but the flexibility of peasants in producing fresh fruit and vegetables is limited in many ways. Their dependence on foreign capital and the perishability of the produce itself are two major constraints. Land use has to be planned months ahead, based on previous market trends, and *ejido* peasants lack adequate and up-to-date information. The market for perishables is difficult because of seasonal changes in supply, the need for fast and technologically equipped transportation from the packing plant to the market, and hourly changes in prices at the border.

Agricultural and agro-industrial exports are governed by internationally standardized technological requirements. Notwithstanding NAFTA, one of the main problems facing producers is the manipulation by the USA of non-tariff barriers. All Mexican exports to the USA are inspected by the US Department of Agriculture, and must pass through certified packing stations, a procedure which frequently increases costs for farmers.

Peasants left out of the accumulation process

For many peasants, life still consists of working on the land at the beginning of the rainy season and then, once the land has been sown with maize and beans, migrating in search of employment. Other household members (mainly women and children) are left to harvest the crop. This pattern tends to repeat itself year after year. Migrants send back money regularly to their families for subsistence and if possible to improve their homes, purchase agricultural implements, or start up off-farm activities. Migration increased in the late 1980s and 1990s when women also started to migrate, either with their husbands or by themselves. This growing migration is explained both by the networks built up in the USA which facilitate travel and settlement, and by the increasing hardship suffered by peasants given the lack of work opportunities in Mexico.

During the past few decades there has been an increase in migration to other cities of the country and to the USA. Most international migration stems from the centre and north of the country. There are whole communities in which each family has at least one member who has migrated to the USA once in their lifetime. There has also been an increase in US migration by members of indigenous communities. Migration to other cities in Mexico is mainly from the southern states of the country. Many communities survive through a combination of subsistence agriculture and migration.

Standards of living differ markedly between those peasants with irrigation and those with only rainfed land. *Ejidatarios* with irrigation who are able to produce, pack and export their produce can afford to educate their children and even send them to university or technical colleges. By comparison, those with only rainfed land can only afford primary schooling and very occasionally secondary schooling for their children. Peasants with irrigation have more stable and better paid off-farm activities, such as working as garage mechanics or in small stores or restaurants, whilst those without are restricted to taking in washing, sewing or selling food in the street, often undertaken by women. Housing, food and clothing of the two groups also differ. In general the standard of living of those participating in the fruit and vegetable business is higher.

Women and the free market

When the men alone used to migrate, it was the women who tended the fields, but even so the men were the ones considered to be the farmers. The persistence of this ideology has to do with how changes take place in small towns. Women have less mobility, and the boundaries defining women's identity are stronger. Traditional patriarchal values have tended to mean that women have fewer economic alternatives than men for securing a degree of independence from their families and for increasing their room for manoeuvre.

Nevertheless, the nature and social evaluation of women's work is changing. Fruit and vegetable production and the construction of packing plants has changed many aspects of women's lives, especially in agro-industrial regions. The economic mobility of women has increased over the past few decades. Women now participate in production and marketing at all levels. This change is clearly seen in the increasing feminization of the labour force. Studies have shown that approximately 75 per cent of the labour force in the fruit and vegetable packing plants are women (Barros Nock 1998). However, women are paid less than men and their working conditions are inferior. Furthermore, their labour is seen as flexible so that employment can vary from a 40-hour week to a couple of hours a day, depending on the work available. Women do not usually know in advance how many hours they will work each day, and therefore do not know for certain how much they will earn. In addition, they do not have access to benefits, such as medical insurance, attached to stable jobs. This pattern is reinforced by the fact that women are considered to be the economic dependants of males. Multiple identities are given to women as daughters, mothers and wives who, as such, are not in need of a full salary.

Is NAFTA a real alternative for peasants?

The adoption of neo-liberal policies has exacerbated the impact of globalization in the rural areas. The abrupt reduction in state resources earmarked for agriculture has deepened the rural crisis, especially for peasants in the *ejido* sector. The unilateral commercial openings towards the USA and Canada, since NAFTA, have had negative effects for the *ejido* sector. *Ejidos* which mainly produce grains have not been able to compete with the high-technology and subsidized agricultural production of the USA. In the past decade Mexico has tripled its import of basic grains. The same applies to fruit and vegetables, where peasants not only have to compete with US producers but with large landowners in Mexico and other countries.

As mentioned earlier, the privatization of the *ejido* was mainly intended to make Mexico's rural areas attractive to foreign investors. Nevertheless, several case studies have shown that foreigners are not keen to bear the risks involved in owning land, preferring to work with production contracts and to be free to move should these prove unprofitable. Mexico cannot change the objectives and dynamics of foreign companies, but it could develop policies to strengthen the peasants' bargaining position *vis-à-vis* foreign companies (Barros Nock 1998).

The Mexican government has argued that Mexico has comparative advantages over the USA and Canada in fruit and vegetable production. When analysing comparative advantages we have to consider the fact that there is no such thing as a free market. Markets are experienced differentially with respect to the availability of information, financial resources, inputs and communication infrastructure.

With respect to whether peasants from the *ejido* sector can switch to fruit and vegetable production, the answer is largely negative. Peasants cannot respond quickly to market fluctuations, and even *ejidatarios* with irrigation have tended to shift to corn rather than fruit and vegetables. Large amounts of capital are needed and transnational corporations are not generally interested in working with small-scale farmers. Without the support of the state, the prospects for small-scale farmers in small communities appear rather grim.

Conclusions

Neo-liberal policies have reduced the peasants' ability to accumulate capital, sharpened economic differentiation inside the *ejido*, and increased the concentration of land. However there is still a large peasant sector. This can be explained in part by the lack of options of the workforce outside the agrarian sector. This persistence has also to do with the development of reproductive strategies which tend to retain a link with land and to reproduce the bases of communal organization. Even though agricultural production has ceased to guarantee the reproduction of a large number of peasants, it has not been abandoned. Rather, it has been supplemented by the implementation of other economic activities – sub-employment and migration to the cities and the USA – which have become indispensable for the reproduction of the peasant household. The diversification of economic activities has also been furthered by the incorporation of family members, mainly women and children, into the economic sphere and the migration cycle. In this way changes have taken place both in the internal organization of the family as well as in the socio-economic and cultural spaces which they inhabit (de Janvry et al. 1997; Barros Nock 1998).

The forces which influence the dynamics of the reproduction of the peasant population are diverse and multiple. On the one hand, market forces and the withdrawal of the state from peasant agricultural production tend towards the dissolution and dispersal of agrarian society. On the other hand, the strategies adopted by families in their daily struggle for survival are constructed around kin and social relations deriving from their link to the land (de Janvry et al. 1997). For most *ejidatarios* the land is still their base, the refuge whence family members derive a series of strategies and complementary activities. In this sense peasants are reacting to and participating in processes of globalization by acquiring new characteristics and adapting to changing circumstances.

Rurality can no longer be defined solely in opposition to the urban. The old definitions which regarded the rural strictly in relation to land are changing. Globalization has increased the movement of people, goods, services, information, news, products and money, and thereby the presence of urban characteristics in rural areas and of rural traits in urban centres. The implementation of social adjustment policies has brought detrimental social consequences in terms of education, health, housing, working conditions and culture. For many Mexican peasants poverty is not a new condition but the worsening of their pre-existing situation.

Notes

1. *Minifundia* are very small pieces of land. *Minifundistas* refer to those peasants who own, on average, between three hectares and half a hectare. They may belong to an *ejido* or have land in private property.
2. Banrural, the main official credit institution, gives preference to basic grains in order to increase national food supply. Since the 1970s the state has used the *ejido* as the country's barn. Maize and bean production for popular consumption was supported by, if not imposed on, the *ejido* sector. This has largely been achieved by giving maize producers priority in the allocation of credit.
3. *Latifundistas* are large landowners with extensive landholdings, which could range from thousands to even hundreds of thousands of hectares, many of which were left uncultivated.

4. *Haciendas* existed before the Revolution in 1910. They are productive, large landholdings.
5. *Hacienda* owners could choose which land to keep, and always retained the best, that is, land which was irrigated and located near roads, or agro-industrial establishments and other constructions.
6. The state intervened actively in the construction of infrastructure necessary for industry and agriculture, such as communication, electrification and irrigation. Dams were constructed on the most important rivers of the country, and by the end of the Cárdenas presidential period 120 000 additional hectares were irrigated.

References

Barros Nock, M. (1998) 'Small Farmers in the Global Economy, The Case of the Fruit and Vegetable Business in Mexico', PhD thesis, Institute of Social Studies, The Hague, The Netherlands.

Calva Tellez, J.L. (1988) *Crisis Agrícola y Alimentaria en México 1982–1988*, Fontamara, Mexico City.

de Janvry A., Gordillo, G. and Sadoulet, E. (1997) *Mexico's Second Agrarian Reform, Household and Community Responses*, Transformation of Rural Mexico No. 1, Center for US–Mexican Studies, University of California, La Jolla.

de Teresa A.P. and Ruiz, C.C. (1996) 'El agro en México: un futuro incierto después de las reformas', in A.P. de Teresa and C.C. Ruiz (eds) *La Nueva Relación Campo-Ciudad y la Pobreza Rural*, Vol. II INAH, UAM, UNAM and Plaza y Valdés, Mexico City, pp. 17–34.

Escarcega, E. and Botey, C. (1990) *La Recomposición de la Propiedad Social como Precondición Necesaria para Refuncionalizar el Ejido, en el Orden Económico Productivo*, Ceham, Mexico.

Gomez Cruz, M.A., Schwentesius, R. and Merino Sepúlveda, A. (1992) 'Principales indicadores del sector hortícola en México para la negociación de un tratado trilateral de libre comercio', in C. González Pacheco (ed.) *El Sector Agropecuario Mexicano Frente al Tratado de Libre Comercio*, Ciestaam, Unam, Mexico City.

Goodman, D. and Redclift, M. (1981) *From Peasant to Proletarian, Capitalist Development and Agrarian Transitions*, Basil Blackwell, Oxford.

Gordillo de Anda, G. (1985) 'Estado y movimiento campesino en la coyuntura actual', in F. Rello (ed.) *México ante la Crisis*, Siglo XXI, Mexico City.

Gordillo de Anda, G. (1987) *Campesinos al Asalto del Cielo*, Cal y Arena, Mexico City.

Gordillo de Anda, G. (1991) 'Raíz y Razón', *La Jornada*, 8 November 1991.

Harriss, J. (ed.) (1982) *Rural Development: Theories of Peasant Economy and Agrarian Change*, Hutchinson, London.

Hewitt de Alcántara, C. (1976) *Modernizing Mexican Agriculture: Socioeconomic Implications of Technological Change, 1940–1970*, UNRISD, Geneva.

INEGI (1990) *Encuesta Nacional Agropecuaria Ejidal 1988*, Vol. II: INEGI, Ejidos y Comunidades Agrarias, Mexico City.
INEGI (1997) *El Sector Alimentario en México, Edición 1997*, INEGI and CONAL, Mexico City.
Marsh, R.R. and Runsten, D. (1996) 'Del traspatio a la exportación: potencial para la producción campesina de frutas y hortalizas en México', in S.M. Lara Flores and M. Chauvet (eds) *La Inserción de la Agricultura Mexicana en la Economía Mundial*, Vol. 1, INAH, UAM, UNAM and Plaza y Valdés, Mexico City, pp. 167–212.
Morett, J. C. (1991) *Alternativas de Modernización del Ejido*, Editorial Diana, Mexico City.
Myhre, D. (1994) 'The Politics of globalization in rural Mexico: campesino initiatives to restructure the agricultural credit system', in P. McMichael (ed.) *The Global Restructuring of Agro-food Systems*, Cornell University Press, Ithaca, pp. 145–69.
Paré, L. (1991) 'Rezago agrario o rezagados del agro?', *Cuadernos Agrarios, Nueva Epoca*, No. 3: 30–7.
Rello, F. (1985) 'La Crisis Alimentaria', in F. Rello (ed.) *México ante la Crisis*, Siglo XXI, Mexico City.
Robles, R. and Moguel, J. (1990) 'Agricultura y proyecto neoliberal', *El Cotidiano*, No. 34: 3–12.
Salinas de Gortari, C. (1991) *Los 10 Principios Básicos del Liberalismo Social*, Presidencia de la República, Mexico City.
Scott, D.C. (1996) 'El nuevo modelo económico en América Latina y la pobreza rural' in A.P. Teresa and C.C. Ruiz (eds) *La Nueva Relación Campo-Ciudad y la Pobreza Rural*, INAH, UAM, UNAM and Plaza y Valdés, Mexico City, pp. 83–122.
Stanford, L. (1996) 'Ante la globalización del tratado de libre comercio: el caso de los meloneros de Michoacán', in S.M. Flores and M. Chauvet (eds) *La Inserción de la Agricultura Mexicana en la Economía Mundial*, INAH, UAM, UNAM and Plaza y Valdés, Mexico City, pp. 141–66.
Warman, A. (1975) *Los Campesinos, Hijos Predilectos del Regimen*, Editorial Nuestro Tiempo, Mexico City.
Warman, A. (1991) 'Cambio para el campo: la propuesta presidencial', *La Jornada*, 10 November.

10. Global–Local Links in Latin America's New Ruralities

LUIS LLAMBÍ

Introduction

The collapse of the Bretton Woods agreement in 1971, the external debt crisis of Latin America in 1982, the fall of the Berlin Wall in 1989, and the conclusion of the Uruguay Round of the General Agreement on Tariffs and Trade (GATT) in 1994 are all important turning points in the current transition to a new global order. These changes are frequently subsumed under the umbrella of globalization. Equally dramatic but less visible restructuring processes have also been occurring in the productive systems, lifestyles and socio-political dynamics of the rural population, both in the 'First' and 'Third' Worlds. Such changes have recently been seen as the emergence of a 'new rurality' in Europe and Latin America. Our contention in this paper is that globalization processes and structural adjustment programmes are creating the conditions for the emergence of new ruralities and new forms of peasantry in Latin America, as well as the conditions for dissolving former rural social categories.[1]

The academic literature analysing these processes (globalization, rural local restructurings and peasant social differentiation) tends to be compartmentalized by discipline and characterized by a particular macro- or microscopic emphasis which fails to make explicit the multiple connections. The result is a series of shortcomings in the globalization, rural studies, and peasant studies literatures. On the one hand, current theories of globalization tend to exaggerate the homogenizing trends inherent in the current transition and neglect the differentiating effects. On the other hand, rural and peasant studies – both old and new – which emphasize local specificities have tended to underplay the links between these local processes and their national and supranational contexts.

This chapter has two main objectives. Firstly, to propose a macro–micro, global–local approach to an analysis of the links between globalization and the emergence of new ruralities and peasantries in Latin America. Secondly, to illustrate this approach with research findings from a case study of Pueblo Llano, a horticultural community in the Venezuelan Andes.[2] In general, the chapter aims to clarify the relative weight which should be given to local as compared to national and supranational forces in the current agrarian restructuring.

Beyond Globalization Theory

The predominant perspective on the globalization process has produced valuable insights into two important contemporary world restructurings: (i) the gradual integration of markets worldwide and the increasing transnationalization of productive, commercial, service and financial networks (i.e. globalization as an economic restructuring process); and (ii) the continuous negotiation of the rules of the game in the emerging global political and economic order (i.e. globalization as a process of re-regulation and political restructuring).

Globalization, most authors agree, is based on the increasing transnationalization of economic processes as a result of a series of technological and institutional changes which have taken place since the end of the 1960s (Jenkins 1987). In particular, globalization is often regarded as following from the demise of the Fordist regime of accumulation, based on mass production and mass consumption, and from the end of the Keynesian-and-welfare state mode of regulation which prevailed in the industrialized world during the post-war period (Gordon 1988; Kolko 1988). It is argued that the Fordist regime of accumulation entered into crisis at the end of the 1960s and finally collapsed in 1971 with the breakdown of the Bretton Woods agreement. Consequently, the current theoretical and research agenda on globalization is seen to be defined by the need to identify the main traits of a new regime of accumulation and its modes of regulation in the post-Bretton Woods era.

There are several epistemological and theoretical shortcomings of this perspective of the current globalization process, and in recent years a number of authors have contributed to its critique.[3] My objective here is not to reproduce all the arguments but to direct attention to some basic epistemological issues raised in this debate. In a rather schematic way these critiques can be seen as relating to its periodization of history, its morphology, and its insufficient theorization of the causal relationships between agents and structures at different levels of analysis.

Firstly, the Fordist versus post-Fordist divide has been judged to be rather naive, schematic and difficult to sustain empirically. For example, Meegan (1988) points out that Fordist methods of production never predominated in most productive sectors, even in the most advanced industrial countries. Likewise, Whatmore (1994) notes with respect to agriculture that some characteristics, such as flexibility, which are held to typify the post-Fordist regime, have been present for a long time and thus cannot be seen as defining a new regime of accumulation. Van der Ploeg (1992) argues that such an interpretation of globalization only fits into an unilinear deterministic model in which the more advanced forms of the process set the parameters for all others to follow.

In our view, the distinction between Fordist and post-Fordist regimes of accumulation stems from an unidimensional interpretation of the history of contemporary capitalism, which can be traced back to the French regulation school of the 1970s. This school aimed to overcome unilinear Marxist interpretations of history by emphasizing the internal contradictions between so-called regimes of accumulation and modes of regulation. In our view this attempt failed, their interpretation remaining very much concerned with a unilinear Fordist versus post-Fordist interpretation of history. What is proposed here is a multidimensional perspective of the globalization process in which each dimension (economic, political, cultural) has its own specific timing, in which there are multiple connections between dimensions, and in which there is always the possibility of progression and regression. In other words, we view the globalization process as a socially and politically contested terrain rather than as a unilinear process endowed with an underlying logic of development.

In the eyes of most critics, however, the fundamental weakness of the predominant globalization perspective has been its emphasis on homogenizing trends to the detriment of globalization's differentiating tendencies. McMichael, for instance, argues that:

> The essence of global restructuring is precisely this differentiation. That is, if we perceive globalization as the subjection of historically uneven places to internationally competitive forces, where natural regulatory systems have eroded, creating social and economic disjunctures, then it will manifest precisely in a variety of responses (McMichael 1994: 279).

In place of this excessively homogenizing perception, which can be traced back to world systems theory as well as the regulation school, we see the globalization process as a synthesis of multiple and diverse processes, which result partly from local specificities and partly from the intended and unintended actions of individual actors and organizations located at various levels of social analysis and of political and territorial entities (supranational, national, subnational).

Our critique of the predominant globalization perspective also addresses its implicit functionalist and determinist underpinnings. In our view, current globalization–localization processes are endowed not only with their own rationalities but also with their own irrationalities, arising from the contingent and socially contested ways in which these restructuring processes are taking place. Globalization and localization are, among other things, the ways and means by which the rules of a new global economic and political order are in the process of being decided. Yet these rules are the result of a relatively unstable scenario of political forces.

The predominant globalization perspective also assumes the demise of a post-war international political order based on the nation-state, yet this fracture is not sufficiently theorized. Instead of the blanket elimination of the state, assumed by some, we view globalization as a restructuring process in which state power is partially redistributed 'upwards' to supranational institutions and partially 'downwards' to subnational institutions (Llambí and Gouveia, 1994). These different levels of state power have still to be internally disaggregated both in terms of social organizations and individual agents. To assert, for instance, that core states dominate the decision-making processes by which the new rules of the game are enacted, and that non-core states merely react to their initiatives, is inadequate: who is behind these moves and the reasons for them must still be specified.

This leads on to the issue we would like to stress in our empirical analysis: the relative weight to be assigned to local vis-a-vis national and supranational forces in these global-and-local restructurings, and the clear specification of the causal links between agents and social structures at the various levels of analysis. The predominant globalization approach is not very specific about agency. It tends to overemphasize the roles of supranational forces (such as global market trends, transnational corporations, multilateral agents, core states) and downplay the continued relevance of subnational processes and actors in the complex determination of socio-economic and political arrangements. We propose to take seriously the differential capacities of individual agents and social entities located at various levels of analysis (supranational, national, subnational) to support, alter, and even undermine current global trends. This brings us to an explanation of how new ruralities are emerging within this global scenario.

Bringing Rurality Back In

In social science discourse, rurality is usually imagined as being linked to three interrelated phenomena: (i) low demographic density and a dispersed population pattern; (ii) the predominance of agriculture and other primary activities in the productive structure of a locality or region; and (iii) cultural patterns or lifestyles which differ from those of the large cosmopolitan centres. The literature on the new rurality in Europe is an attempt to answer the question of what constitutes rurality in a society in which: (i) there is an accelerated process of suburbanization or counter-urbanization arising from the increased consumption of rural space by the construction, tourism, recreational and environmental industries; (ii) the occupational structure of small population centres is transformed as primary employment shrinks and secondary and tertiary employment swell; and (iii) rural cultural patterns and lifestyles – frequently perceived as backward – have been rapidly transformed by the penetration of values linked to modernity and the adoption of urban lifestyles (Lowe et al. 1993, Whatmore 1994, García Bartolomé 1996). All these processes can be seen as linked to post-rural social structures and post-peasant livelihoods.

In Europe the academic discourse links the emergence of a new rurality to two large sets of transformations. Firstly, the technical and socio-economic restructuring of agricultural spaces in response to the crisis of large agri-food complexes which emerged from the European Community's Common Agricultural Policy and the protectionist policies of the Scandinavian nations. These policies have tended to be replaced by a new regulatory framework attuned to the principles of international competitiveness adopted by GATT and the current European Union. Secondly, the emergence of new activities, new social agents and new regulatory entities in spaces previously dedicated to agricultural activities has resulted in more socially differentiated rural environments and more heterogeneity between rural spaces. This conclusion contradicts the predominant version of the globalization approach which assumes a general trend towards the homogenization of economic, political and cultural conditions worldwide.

Debate about the emergence of new ruralities is also taking place amongst Latin American academics, some of whom frame this within the current transition to a neoliberal, outward-oriented growth model (Giarraca 1993, Murmis 1993, Kay 1994, Rubio 1998). The Latin American debate also draws attention to aspects of the globalization–localization process which are frequently ignored by the predominant globalization approach, such as the impact of changes induced by the International Monetary Fund (IMF) and the World Bank's structural adjustment policies on productive strategies and techniques of production, and on the environmental conditions and quality of life of the rural population.

Contrary to the emphasis placed on global forces by the predominant globalization approach, we also take into account the differential 'room for manoeuvre' which rural communities and agricultural producers have to shape or resist global trends. However, it is also clear that the study of rural/agricultural restructurings and the analysis of rural social agents' strategies cannot be isolated from such global–regional–national forces as trade negotiations, free-trade agreements, or major shifts in agricultural and macro-economic policies.

Bringing Peasants Back In

From classical political economy to the recent present, 'peasant' and the 'peasantry' have been regarded as indispensable social categories in the social sciences. The early political economists regarded the peasantry as a multi-faceted social category, comprising both a variety of dependent labourers (serfs, sharecroppers, renters) and independent smallholding producers. In the late 1970s, however, it became fashionable to reject the category of peasant as being ahistorical and descriptive, a trend aptly termed by Roseberry (1978) as the 'deconceptualization' of the peasantry.

Lenin's historical analyses followed Marx's prognoses of class differentiation, arguing that peasants were destined to fall into one of the two antagonistic classes of capitalism: the bourgeoisie or the proletariat. In so doing, Lenin also abolished the peasantry as a homogeneous entity, splitting it into three categories (rich, middle and poor peasants) according to land area, capital accumulation and wage or family labour.

In my view, the term 'peasant' corresponds not to a single social entity but to several kinds of rural social dwellers. It follows that we must define the links between peasant households and individual agents and between peasantries as historical collective agents in the countryside. Such a procedure should facilitate the analysis of the heterogeneous social processes in which the different peasant social categories are embedded. For example, in twentieth-century Latin America, the category of peasant farmer includes both those independent subsistence farmers formerly relished by Chayanovians and small entrepreneurs embedded in a capital accumulation process. Occasionally, peasant farmers have also variously been sharecroppers on other small or large landowner farms, contract farmers related to agro-industry, or indebted farmers related to merchant and credit agents. In this case, history has seldom been characterized by such an acute polarization of social agents as the dichotomous and discrete categories found in most social theories would lead us to expect. In my view, what unifies these different groups is not an immanent 'peasantness' common to all so-called peasant enterprises, but the multiple social relations linking them to the historical projects of a collective peasantry.

To speak of 'peasants' or 'the peasantry' in general runs the risk of reification, giving agency to an abstract category at a time when current social theory is concerned to bring back the social agents involved in these processes. For this reason, it is important to analyse the differential impact of globalization processes and structural adjustment policies on the different types of 'peasant' farmers. In other words, the kinds of incentives or disincentives created by macro-structural change will translate into different productive, technical and market decisions according to the type of farm and the social status of the household.

Briefly stated, the social heterogeneity of farming is conceived as a filter which sets limits to the ways in which social agents can respond and adapt to changes in their economic, political and natural environment or to their attempts to modify or even subvert those 'external' changes which affect them negatively.

The Pueblo Llano Case Study[4]

Pueblo Llano in Venezuela constitutes the pilot study of an ongoing comparative research project of four municipalities, two in Colombia and two in Venezuela, which are variously linked to rapidly globalizing commodity circuits. These four municipalities are taken to illustrate the effects of globalization processes and structural adjustment policies on the agricultural restructuring and changing livelihoods of rural communities.

The research project was designed to test an interdisciplinary model linking variables located at three levels of analysis: global, national and local. The global level aimed to identify new forms of investment, trade, and multilateral regulatory mechanisms shaping the insertion of Colombia's and Venezuela's agrifood sectors into the emerging global market. The national level aimed to assess the impact of supranational forces, such as the differential presence of multilateral agencies (the World Bank and the IMF) and the 1992 Colombia–Venezuela free trade agreement, on the evolution of each country's agri-food policies and selected commodity circuits. The local level aimed to identify the links between changes occurring in local agri-food systems, the shifting working and living conditions of local populations, and the responses of local agents to these changes.

Pueblo Llano was selected for a number of reasons. Firstly, it is a municipality whose agrarian structure is linked to rapidly globalizing horticultural commodity circuits in which Venezuela is said to possess 'natural' comparative advantages. Secondly, it is a smallholder rural society in which apparently there are relatively low (by Venezuelan standards) poverty rates as reported by official statistical data. Thirdly, the Pueblo Llano municipality is Venezuela's main producer of potatoes, making it particularly vulnerable to the economic opening with Colombia, also a large potato producer. Over and above these reasons, Pueblo Llano was selected as a pilot study to test (in Popperian terms) the hypothesis that structural adjustment policies have a negative impact on agricultural production and on the working and living conditions of rural populations. Available statistical data showed that local farming was experiencing an economic boom and that average income was rising as a result of the implementation of neo-liberal policies, despite the general economic crisis experienced by the country at large and the negative performance of the agricultural sector in particular. All indications were that horticultural production in Pueblo Llano was increasing and benefiting from 'natural' comparative advantages within the current outward-oriented economic model.

Before examining the process of restructuring of Pueblo Llano's rurality, however, we shall briefly set out the national context in which this restructuring is taking place.

The National Context: Transition to an Outward-oriented Regime

In 1989, Venezuela shifted from an explicitly inward-oriented economic growth model to an outward-oriented model based on orthodox IMF-sponsored shock therapy. The cornerstone of the adjustment package was the devaluation and floating of the national currency. The depressive nature of this package contributed to a deterioration of real incomes, had a regressive effect on the distribution of income, and led to a sharp increase in unemployment. The announcement of the first measures of this package in February 1989 led to four days of rioting and looting in Venezuela. Continued political instability produced a partial reversal in June 1991 when some price regulations and direct food and medicine subsidies were re-established.

In January 1992 Venezuela and Colombia entered into a bilateral free trade agreement and shortly thereafter signed a framework agreement with the USA in preparation for joining the North American Free Trade Agreement (NAFTA). Since 1992 trade between the two countries has more than doubled.

In June 1993, the Venezuelan Congress appointed an interim President following the Supreme Court's decision to suspend and judge the former President on grounds of corruption. A 'bottom-up' version of the adjustment programme ensued, calling for a selective and negotiated opening-up of the economy and more state guidance of domestic market mechanisms. Although the new government, elected in December 1993, established temporary exchange-rate controls, it did not basically alter the process of economic opening, and the emphasis given to economic integration with Colombia remained unchanged.

Despite various shifts in public policy after 1989, four basic features of the outward-oriented economic model have been unaltered: (i) a redefinition of the role of the nation state in economic growth as the promoter of market forces; (ii) the high priority accorded to macro-economic stability in order to reduce inflation; (iii) the increased economic opening to external trade and financial flows in order to re-insert the national economy within the emerging global economic order; and (iv) the enactment of 'compensatory' policies to reduce or control the increase in absolute poverty and thereby the risks of social and political instability.

The New Rurality in Pueblo Llano

This section begins by examining the 'top-down' mechanisms through which global and national forces impinge on local restructurings; and follows with a 'bottom-up' analysis of the local responses and organizational capacities which may alter – and even subvert – policy initiatives and regulatory agendas generated at both national and supranational levels. Three main issues are addressed in this section: the impact of structural adjustment policies on agricultural restructuring; the shifting working and living conditions of the rural population; and the response of local agents to the changing global and local scenario.

The impact of structural adjustment programmes

During the 1960s and 1970s the high valleys of the Venezuelan Andes experienced an economic boom. Several factors explain this trend. On the supply side, there was the introduction of high-yield potato varieties from Canada, the construction of irrigation systems by the Regional Development Corporation of the Andes which enabled year round horticulture, and the arrival of Canary Island immigrants who brought with them their knowledge of irrigation technologies suitable for horticultural production. On the demand side, there was the steady and increasing national demand for horticultural products. In a few decades, potatoes and carrots replaced wheat, maize and vegetables oriented to family consumption (Rhoads 1994).

In the 1990s the area has undergone a process of agricultural intensification which includes (i) increased horticultural specialization despite a reduction in yield per hectare and (ii) the development of a new technical pattern of production. In general, the trend towards product specialization (potatoes and carrots) can be seen as the direct result of macro-economic policies which increased the profitability of these products relative to other crops, amidst crises within the agricultural sector generally.

By contrast, the development of a new technical pattern in horticultural production has to be explained by different factors. Horticultural production has been highly labour-intensive since it was first introduced to the area by Canary Island immigrants in the 1960s. Since then, there have been labour shortages arising from historical patterns of out-migration by the native population to other areas of the country in search of better standards of living. In addition, the area's topography (high slopes and a stony topsoil) hampers the introduction of labour-saving technologies for soil preparation and harvesting.

The intensification in land use is explained by the limits posed by physical geography on the use of arable land – a relatively constant resource – and by the increased pressures of demography and market incentives which led to the further colonization of the higher basin. New technology also implied an intensification in the use of some capital inputs, in particular organic fertilizers and agrochemicals. Organic fertilizers (goat and chicken manure) subsequently replaced chemical fertilizers whose price became prohibitive due to the removal of subsidies.

The adoption of new agrochemicals can be related to the opening up of the economy to Colombian suppliers following the 1992 bilateral free trade agreement. Pesticides became essential for sustaining yields and combating new pests and diseases arising from the liberalized trade regime, less stringent phytosanitary controls along the border, and the increased resistance of native pests to previous chemicals.

By contrast, a feature of the new potato technology adopted is the extensive use of non-certified seed potatoes, which are reproduced by the farmers themselves. From the 1960s onwards the purchase of imported seeds from Canada formed the single most important item in the cost structure of potato farms, following the adoption of the technical package based on high-yield varieties. The quadrupling of the price of this input since 1989 forced farmers to substitute domestically grown seed potatoes for the imported hybrids. Consequently, this gave rise to decreasing returns despite rotating plots where the seeds are sown.

One of the most visible impacts of structural adjustment in the area has been increased environmental degradation. This general trend is linked to (i) the increasing deterioration of soil and water resources as a consequence of erosion and increased deposits on the watershed; (ii) the declining quality of water and soil as a consequence of the intensified use of agrochemicals; and (iii) the growing contamination of horticultural products as a result of the increased faecal and chemical residues they contain.

However, not all farmers share the same economic position or the same pattern of land tenure. These structural characteristics determine the differing productive and technical strategies adopted, as well as the different economic outcomes. On the one hand, there is a clear trend amongst some groups towards product specialization (potatoes and carrots) which is explained by the impact of economic policies on non-tradable products, in the context of relatively stable and growing markets and by the accumulation of technical knowledge by farmers in the production of these horticultural products. On the other hand, there is a trend towards horticultural diversification among smaller farmers. Their strategy of diversifying production aims to increase flexibility and thereby offset the high volatility of horticultural market prices.

Changing working and living conditions of the rural population

An unexpected finding of the Pueblo Llano fieldwork was the relatively high morbidity index due to gastrointestinal diseases and high infant mortality rates in the municipality, comparable to those of Haiti in Latin America. These results are in striking contrast to official statistical reports of higher income levels and increased satisfaction of basic needs.

One factor which apparently impinges on health conditions is the increased use of organic fertilizers, such as goat and chicken manure, which caused a proliferation of flies. Flies, however, are only a health hazard when associated with lack of sanitation, and in particular the absence of sewers and septic tanks, as was the case. Another determining factor is the reduced scope of the water-supply system and the lack of a used-water treatment system in the area. Yet another factor is human poisoning arising from the misuse of pesticides by farmers. Finally, the relationship between environmental degradation and the deterioration of health conditions is also linked to a curative rather than a preventive approach to health among local medical doctors.

Under structural adjustment policies, farmers have not received any technical assistance relating to the proper use of chemical inputs or the development of alternative means of control. The Ministry of Agriculture, which was formerly responsible for this task, abolished all agricultural extension services as part of its general austerity drive. Farmers were left to rely on the recommendations of the agrochemical corporations, who are more interested in raising profits than in reducing the health risks of their customers. In addition, the state has neglected to control those highly toxic pesticides now entering the country under the open-border policy following the free trade agreement with Colombia.

The link between the deterioration of sanitary conditions and access to public health services is also differentiated. Although the deterioration of health services affects all social categories of the rural population, those who suffer most are those who cannot afford to pay for health services.

Responses of rural local agents

What initiatives, strategies and forms of organization have local agents adopted to cope with changes in their working and living conditions? In particular, in the context of an outward-oriented economic model, what institutional frameworks have they had to address? And what is their 'room for manoeuvre' in this shifting scenario?

Structural adjustment has meant not only neo-liberal macro-economic policies but also state reforms, and particularly political and administrative decentralization. In Venezuela, the creation of the *municipio* (municipality) created a political entity which is closer to the people.[5] In 1990 the valley of Pueblo Llano, originally administered from the distant town of Timotes, became an independent municipality whose inhabitants gained the right to elect their own mayor and municipal councillors. Local governments and institutions have gradually become a more meaningful arena for rural agents to participate in decision-making. Yet, given the increasingly open economy and the redistribution of some state functions to supranational arenas (for instance, multilateral agencies or supranational institutions engendered by free trade agreements), the responses of local actors cannot be reduced to the local scenario.

During the 1960s agricultural co-operatives formed the backbone of local institutions in the Venezuelan Andes. Over time, however, they have been reduced to simply supplying inputs to farmers, abandoning their former goal of commercializing horticultural production and protecting farmers from middlemen's high profit rates in the national horticultural circuits. Since 1989, the co-operatives have consciously reviewed their goals. In 1993, co-operatives from all the potato-growing areas of the country joined together in a second-tier organization to combat the threat posed by the economic opening with Colombia. Following the 1991 Free Trade Agreement with Colombia, potato imports from Colombia escalated from almost nothing to 30.5 million kilograms in 1992. The Venezuelan potato growers' first response was to lobby the national government in Caracas to impose a ban on the import of potatoes. They were unsuccessful. Facing imminent bankruptcy they took the unprecedented step of directly contacting Colombian growers' organizations and negotiating an agreement within the newly created common market. As a result, in July 1993 both countries informally agreed to manage jointly the enlarged binational market, along the lines of a former agreement between Colombian and Venezuelan farmers' associations.

However, small-scale peasant farmers are not the only agents in this new rural scenario. Sharecropping is the most frequent contractual arrangement in Pueblo Llano's agricultural system. Protracted labour shortages over many years had created a sellers' market in which some Colombian immigrants came to control the supply of the labour force. Most Venezuelan small landowners are thus forced to look for Colombian sharecroppers in order to gain access both to the sharecroppers' labour and to a labour force in general. A turning point was the creation of an Association of Colombian Immigrants in Pueblo Llano in 1992. In 1993 Colombian immigrants, exercising the right to vote which the 1960 Constitution gave foreigners after five years' residence, were decisive in the municipal elections. Their actions bordered on a civil rights movement since they demanded the right to be included in local house-construction plans, to be protected by the municipal council against expulsion, and to have the right to participate in local decision-making.

The return migration of a young and more qualified generation, having become disenchanted with the increased violence and lack of economic opportunities in the urban areas, has also resulted in some young farmers occupying the political spaces opened up by the decentralization process and playing an increasing role in local civil society: the Ateneo (the local cultural forum), the sports clubs, and a local TV station.

Conclusions

The Pueblo Llano case study demonstrates that globalization processes and structural adjustment policies have had varied and contradictory effects at the micro level, both in the agricultural sector and in rural localities. Although the incomes of most peasant farmers improved as a result of the adoption of an open economy and deregulation, intensification of production led to greater environmental degradation and a general deterioration in the health conditions of their rural community. Yet structural adjustment programmes have also been associated with cuts in state expenditures, thereby reducing the scope and quality of rural public services.

The study also showed that structural adjustment programmes have not had a uniform impact on all social categories. The incentives and disincentives created by these policies resulted in producers pursuing different productive strategies, depending on farm size and land tenure. Those who were in a better position to profit from the opportunities offered by the economic transition increased the area under cultivation, thereby raising their incomes and cushioning the impact of inflation. Others, however, were obliged to reduce their land area or to pool their costs and profits with others so as to minimize risks. They were unable to withstand the highly volatile prices of the two major crops of the area (potatoes and carrots) and pursued a strategy of crop diversification to survive.

The study also showed that political decentralization, a component of state restructuring policies, created openings for Colombian immigrants, partly owing to their control over the labour market in a context of acute labour shortages in the high valley area. In addition, the Pueblo Llano case study points to the increasing role played by a better qualified and younger generation of peasant farmers and rural dwellers, whose strategies and political responses differ greatly from those of their predecessors.

Finally, but not least, this case study leads us to question who are 'the peasants' in Pueblo Llano? Are they the small land-owning farmers embedded in a capital accumulation process as a result of deregulation under structural adjustment? Or are they the Colombian sharecroppers struggling for their social and political rights in the new context opened up by state restructuring processes, which also form a component of structural adjustment programmes? The case study illustrates the different responses of these various social agents to changes in their living and working conditions. Depending on the differential 'room for manoeuvre' of each sector of the population, responses are directed toward different levels of decision-making: supra-national political entities, the nation-state, and the local authorities.

In the context of an increasingly open economy, nation-states are no longer the privileged locus of decision-making and problem solving. Even where the national government still regulates or intervenes, problems are often beyond the capability of the state to tackle, and solutions may only be achieved at the supranational level. The global nature of the problems arising from the process of economic opening have meant that most local producers have to organize beyond their local arena. On the other hand, decentralization policies have transformed subnational political entities such as the *municipio* into a relevant locus of decision-making for addressing the social and economic dilemmas of most rural dwellers. Moreover, within this local scenario, old and new social categories have made use of the increased 'room for manoeuvre' afforded by state decentralization.

Market globalization and structural adjustment programmes are ongoing processes, yet their impact is clearly visible in Latin America in the emergence of new ruralities. These new ruralities are in no way similar to those which have emerged in Europe. There is always the risk of elevating a term and concept coined in Europe into an 'ideal type' and using it as a yardstick to measure similar developments all over the world. The emergence of new ruralities in Latin America is not comparable with the blurring of the rural–urban continuum as in Europe, although it is taking place within the parameters set by previous processes of accelerated urbanization. The emergence of new ruralities in Latin America has enhanced the value of spaces neglected by the previous model of inward-oriented industrialization and downgraded those spaces valued by this model. In these shifting scenarios, new social agents and organizations are emerging which will define present and future struggles.

We would like to end on a cautionary note. There is the danger of stressing the homogenizing effects of globalization processes and to regard these as the sole source of change in Latin American rural communities. A global–local theoretical and methodological approach is needed to emphasize the links between globalization processes, structural adjustment programmes and contemporary rural restructuring, but this only makes sense when accompanied by a deep historical knowledge of these changes focusing on what is old and what is new in each case study, and on how to theorize rupture and continuity in the current transition.

Notes

1. Llambí (1991) has argued elsewhere that different 'regimes of accumulation' create the conditions for the emergence of specific peasantries as well as for the dissolution and/or transformation of former rural social categories.
2. Pueblo Llano is one of the case studies in a comparative research project entitled 'Beyond NAFTA: Global–Local Links in the Restructuring of Colombian and Venezuelan Agrifood Systems'. This project is financed by the North–South Center of the University of Miami, with the collaboration of the Department of Sociology of the University of Nebraska at Omaha, the Pontificia Universidad Javeriana de Santafé de Bogotá (Colombia) and the Department of Anthropology of the Instituto Venezolano de Investigaciones Científicas.
3. Among the contributors to this debate are Meegan (1988), Goodman and Watts (1994, 1997), McMichael (1994, 1996), van de Ploeg (1992, 1993), Whatmore (1994).
4. This part of the chapter is based on the results of a seven-month period of field work in Pueblo Llano. Field work research methods included a socio-economic survey of 58 small-scale farmers randomly selected from a universe of about 800, and in-depth interviews of landowning farmers, sharecroppers, farm wage workers, commercial middlemen, government officials, local politicians and grass-roots leaders.
5. The Venezuelan nation-state is divided into 23 states (or provinces) and 330 *municipios* (or counties). The 1961 Constitution conceives the *municipio* as a relatively autonomous political entity.

References

García Bartolomé, J.M. (1996) 'Los procesos rurales en el ambito de la Union Europea', in Hubert C. Grammont (ed.) *La sociedad rural mexicana frente al nuevo milenio*, Vol. II, Plaza y Valdes-UNAM, Mexico.

Giarraca, N. (1993) 'Los pequeños productores en la nueva ruralidad: procesos y debates', paper presented to the XIXth Congress of the Latin American Association of Sociology, Caracas, 30 May–4 June 1993.

Goodman, D. and Watts, M. (1994) 'Reconfiguring the rural or fording the divide? Capitalist restructuring and the global agro-food system', *Journal of Peasant Studies*, 22(1): 1–49.

Goodman, D. and Watts, M.J. (eds) (1997) *Globalising Food: Agrarian Questions and Global Restructuring*, Routledge, London and New York.

Gordon, D. (1988) 'The global economy: new edifice or crumbling foundations?', *New Left Review*, No. 168, 24–64.

Jenkins, R. (1987) *Transnational Corporations and Uneven Development: The Internationalization of Capital and the Third World*, New York, Methuen.

Kay, C. (1994) 'Exclusionary and uneven development in rural Latin America', paper presented to the XVIIIth International Congress of the Latin American Studies Association (LASA), Atlanta, Georgia, 10–12 March 1994.

Kolko, J. (1988) *Restructuring the World Economy*, Pantheon, New York.

Llambí, L. (1991) 'Latin American peasantries and regimes of accumulation', *European Review of Latin American and Caribbean Studies*, No. 51, 27–50.

Llambí, L. and Gouveia, L. (1994) 'Nation-state restructurings and theories of the state: lessons from the Venezuelan case', *International Journal of Sociology of Agriculture and Food*, 4, 64–83.

Lowe, P., Murdock, J., Marsden, T., Munton, R. and Flynn, A. (1993) 'Regulating the new rural spaces: the uneven development of land', *Journal of Rural Studies*, 9(3): 205–22.

McMichael, P. (ed.) (1994) *The Global Restructuring of Agro-Food Systems*, Cornell University Press, Ithaca.

McMichael, P. (1996) *Development and Social Change: A Global Perspective*, Pine Forge Press, Thousand Oaks, USA.

Meegan, R. (1988) 'A Crisis of Mass Production?', in J. Allen and D. Massey (eds) *The Economy in Question*, London, Sage.

Murmis, M. (1993), 'Algunos temas para la discusión en la sociología rural latinoamericana: reestructuración, desestructuración y problemas de excluídos e incluídos', paper presented to the XIXth Congress of the Latin American Association of Sociology, Caracas, 30 May–4 June 1993.

Rhoads, R. (1994) 'Farm, family and the new rurality among vegetable farmers of the Venezuelan Andes', PhD thesis, University of Kentucky, Lexington, USA.

Roseberry, W.(1978) 'Peasants in primitive accumulation: Western Europe and Venezuela compared', *Dialectical Anthropology*, 3(3): 243–60.

Rubio, B. (1998) 'De explotados a excluidos: los campesinos latinoamericanos frente al nuevo milenio', paper presented to the symposium on Globalization and Agro-Food Systems, Caracas.

van der Ploeg, J.D. (1992) ‘The reconstitution of locality: technology and labour in modern agriculture’, in T. Marsden, P. Lowe and S. Whatmore (eds) *Labour and Locality: Uneven Development and the Rural Labour Process*, David Fulton, London, pp. 19–43.
van der Ploeg, J.D. (1993) ‘Rural sociology and the new agrarian question’, *Sociologia Ruralis*, 33(2): 240–60.
Whatmore, S. (1994) ‘Global agro-food complexes and the refashioning of rural Europe’, in N. Thrift and A. Amin (eds) *Holding down the Global*, Oxford University Press, Oxford.

11. Structural Adjustment, Peasant Differentiation and the Environment in Central America

KEES JANSEN

Introduction

Environmental degradation may weaken the resource base of peasant production and threaten the survival of peasant households. Environmental degradation, however, does not affect all peasant households in the same way. Hecht (1987) suggests linking the literature on agro-ecology (a more technical account of how smallholders practise agriculture and use their environment) with the literature on the peasant question. The latter addresses processes of social differentiation, unequal distribution of the means of production, and who wins and loses from agricultural modernization. As the prime focus of this literature is on social relations, changes in the natural environment are of secondary interest, if studied at all. This, however, does not make this body of literature less relevant to current debates on the environmental effects of socio-economic change. Its central concern with social differentiation is the starting point for understanding why producers use their environment for different purposes and in different ways. Changes in the economic sphere can be expected to produce divergent effects in land use, owing to differing and contrasting patterns of social relations (Jansen 1998).

The most important changes in the economic sphere in the past two decades are closely linked to structural adjustment programmes and the liberalization of markets. With respect to the environmental effects of structural adjustment (Reed 1996), in Central America three different views can be discerned: the political economy view; the agro-populist view; and the neo-liberal view. This chapter explores how these three views examine the environmental effects of structural adjustment policies and how they investigate any divergent effects arising from the social differentiation of rural producers.

It is argued here that each of these views neglects social differentiation, local conflicts, and social struggles within rural populations, despite coming to divergent conclusions about the environmental effects of liberalization, and that a much stronger input from the literature on social differentiation is required. The question of changing or disappearing peasantries requires an understanding of both the dynamics of social relations and the changing conditions of the natural environment.

This chapter draws on a case study of peasant differentiation in Honduras. A short description of recent structural adjustment policies affecting peasant production and peasants' use of the environment is followed by a section on the social differentiation of the Honduran peasantry. The following section sets out the different interpretations of the environmental effects of adjustment policies and goes on to argue that adjustment policies may have more contradictory outcomes than anticipated by these interpretations. This argument is developed by drawing on the situation of a differentiated peasantry. Finally, the chapter concludes that a more dynamic approach, which takes into account variations in regional political economies and contradictions within differentiated peasantries, is needed to understand the possible environmental effects of macro-economic agricultural policies.

Neo-liberal Policies and Peasant Production

In the 1980s many Latin American countries confronted economic crises. The import-substitution models, which had informed policy thinking in most countries, had not generated satisfactory economic growth nor articulation between economic sectors. The structural adjustment policies adopted in line with the worldwide shift towards neo-liberalism combined short-term interventions to stabilize the balance of payments with a longer-term strategy to re-activate the national production system by reducing the economic role of the state, privatizing state enterprises and liberalizing markets. In general, the intention was to stimulate export production. External pressure to implement these policies in Central America during the 1980s was relatively low as foreign interests privileged political–strategic objectives above direct economic interests, such as debt repayment in countries involved in civil wars. Honduras did not implement the most severe adjustment measures until the late 1980s, despite facing problems of foreign debt, stagnating economic growth, a deficit on the trade balance and fiscal deficits. In the conflict between the USA and the Sandinista government in Nicaragua, substantial sums of aid money were pumped into the Honduran economy to reduce opposition to the Contra presence. It was not until the Callejas administration (1990–93), following the defeat of the Sandinistas in elections in Nicaragua, that major structural adjustment policies were announced.

The Agricultural Modernization Law was passed in 1992 and became the legal framework for adjustment measures in the agricultural sector (Honduras 1992). It typically combined (i) getting the prices right, (ii) institutional reforms, and (iii) the propagation of individual property rights on land (Thorpe 1995a). The local currency was devalued, export taxes were reduced, sale taxes increased from 5 to 7 per cent, subsidized agricultural credit was eliminated, and price control of agricultural products was abolished (Thorpe et al. 1995, World Bank 1995). As a consequence of adjustment, input prices (fertilizers, pesticides) soared, producer prices for grains rose (Thorpe 1995b)[1], and interest rates increased. The institutional reforms entailed the privatization of the state marketing board and research and extension activities; other state agencies faced severe budget cuts. The propagation of individual property rights over land put an end to the redistributive approach of land reform and redirected state intervention to land titling and the development of a land market (Sandoval Corea 1992, Jansen and Roquas 1998).

The Agricultural Modernization Law does not take into account the existence of structural difference, contradictions and conflict among producers. In the neo-liberal view, each producer is considered to be an individual entrepreneur whose decision-making is based on universal economic calculations. Differences between rural people stem from differences in factor endowments. A World Bank mission to Honduras (World Bank 1995) proposed targeting rural credit programmes, education and health services, and social protection activities to the rural poor, arguing that agricultural policy in the 1980s had only subsidized rich producers. The mission welcomed the rise in producer prices as a source of poverty alleviation, and considered land-tenure policies which focus on land titling as the main way of eliminating discrimination against poor producers and women.

This neo-liberal shift to 'getting the prices right' and individual land titling implied a departure from previous agricultural policies which, to a certain extent, had given special treatment to the peasant sector, for example by organizing peasants on a group basis such as in co-operatives. Throughout the 1960s and 1970s, land-reform projects in many Latin American countries had aimed, at least ideologically, to give land to the tiller, the poor peasant (Barraclough 1973, Thiesenhusen 1989). The land reform process had a relatively large impact in Honduras in the 1970s and a substantial amount of land was redistributed to the peasant sector (Del-Cid 1977, Posas 1979). The question of co-operative development dominated agrarian political debates in the 1970s and 1980s (Posas 1996, Ruben 1997). The redistributive land-reform project focused on structural constraints for peasant production, defining unequal land distribution and the related power structure as the underlying cause of rural poverty. By contrast, the neo-liberal defines poverty as an individual attribute to be alleviated by policies such as individual land titles.

Differentiation of the Peasantry in Honduras

The latest agricultural census lists 317 999 producers in Honduras, of whom a considerable percentage are smallholders (72 per cent have holdings smaller than five hectares and 83 per cent have holdings smaller than 10 hectares: SECPLAN 1994). Historically, smallholders live in the mountainous areas of Honduras and mainly cultivate maize and beans for subsistence and coffee as a cash crop. Subsistence crops are grown on marginal soils on steep slopes, with few or no soil improvements, and therefore yields tend to be low.[2]

In an earlier study, I analysed the process of social differentiation in a typical coffee municipality in mountainous Honduras (Jansen 1998). At the beginning of the twentieth century, access to land in the research area was not a constraint for the development of peasant farming.[3] Differences between rural people were mainly based on other types of capital (cattle, sugar mills); access to labour (mainly family labour); and participation in commercial activities. It was relatively easy to obtain land by buying it (land prices were low), by requesting access to a piece of *ejido* land, or by occupying land which was not being used by other people.[4] In the second half of the twentieth century, land gradually became scarce as the population grew and many cattle owners expanded their holdings. Differential access to land became closely linked with social differentiation. The expansion and intensification of coffee cultivation was another crucial economic development. Those producers who had sufficient access to labour and capital invested in this activity. In the research area, 50 per cent of the producers cultivated coffee. Coffee production was increasing at a time when mean farm size was decreasing sharply (Jansen 1993).[5] These economic changes led to growing inequality between producers. The category of large producers, who operate as entrepreneurs with farms fully based on wage labour and market criteria of profitability, form an important economic group. Cattle raising is a central activity of these producers, who also tend to grow considerable quantities of coffee.

Producing households, falling under the general umbrella of *campesinos* (peasants), can be differentiated into three categories based on the form of labour which dominates. The first is the family labour farm in which the means of production, primarily land, are obtained through inheritance, by using common land or by renting land. Farms on inherited land may be relatively large in size even in the case of poor producers. Family labour is central although casual labour may be hired and household members may work for other producers for a daily wage. The main crops are maize and beans, if possible combined with low-input coffee cultivation.

The second category is that of petty commodity producer. Family labour is important but an adequate supply of cheap seasonal wage labour is essential for this category of producer to exist. Given a certain initial level of means of production (obtained through inheritance, commercial activities, off-farm labour outside the village, or successful accumulation through agriculture), investments in cash-crop production can be made and sustained. High-input coffee production is the backbone of this sector.[6] The level of household consumption determines the share of profits to be re-invested. The tendency to increase consumption often keeps production at a certain level, as profits are not used to further capital accumulation, for example by buying land.

A last category is that of producer–proletarian, whose small maize field is insufficient to guarantee family livelihood. To survive, the producer–proletarian has to work as a farm worker. Patronage relations may provide access to land for subsistence crops. Cultivation tends to be suboptimal; for example labour obligations may lead to late sowing or weeding. In contrast to family labour producers, who aim to secure sufficient food by making their maize fields as large as possible, producer–proletarians rely on employment to prevent food shortages.[7]

These structural differences illustrate the range of farm types which may be grouped under the term *campesino* or peasant. The term *campesino* can be considered as equivalent to how the term 'peasant' is often used.[8] The notion of social differentiation within rural populations proposed here is neither new nor substantially different from previous analyses of peasant differentiation (Djurfeldt 1982, Kearney 1996). Nevertheless the focus on a differentiated peasantry is absent from much of the literature on the agrarian structure in Honduras (Villanueva 1968, Del-Cid 1977, Posas 1979, Williams 1986, Brockett 1988, Puerta 1990) which tends to define *campesinos* as poor rural people who lack capital for technological innovation and are stuck with low levels of production.[9] The depiction of '*el campesino*' or 'the farmer' and 'the community' in this body of literature as a homogeneity of producers disregards local contradictions in social relations of production and the fierce competition for land and labour among *campesinos*. It thereby obscures the internal dynamics of the *campesino* sector.

If we examine the processes of social differentiation in Honduras, two alternative views come to the fore. The first view is the notion of a regional nickel-and-dime capitalism rather than that of a nationwide *latifundio–minifundio* capitalism. 'Nickel-and-dime capitalism' implies the existence of social relations between people in a regional society which are exploitative, but which appear insignificant to outside observers who focus on larger processes of capital accumulation and labour exploitation, and more obvious forms of opposition and polarization.[10] The second view is the notion of multiple livelihoods in place of the dualist emphasis on (export) market-oriented production versus subsistence production.

At the local level, social relations of production are determined not by corporate capital, but by relations between the different types of peasant producer households identified above and between them and a few entrepreneurial agricultural producers.[11] Coffee production is a major economic activity which binds together the different *campesino* types. Petty commodity producers employ producer–proletarians; family labour producers employ other family labour producers and producer–proletarians. They are all involved in (small) debt relations, patronage and political clientelism, and competition for land. The notion of nickel-and-dime capitalism (Jansen 1998: 160–1) is appropriate to represent these multiple forms of exploitative relations. Some peasant producers control more means of production than others and can employ labour to accumulate resources or increase consumption. In other words, they improve their situation, accumulate capital and ensure their reproduction at the cost of others who face increasing problems in securing their livelihoods. Apart from small but crucial differences in control over the means of production, differences in knowledge and in the capability to draw on and define rules and resources of non-commodity relations (such as patronage, kinship, gender, friendship and household relations) are important. Social differentiation at the regional level conditions everyday experience. Analytical emphasis should be placed on how such apparently small differences in control over resources shape the everyday social behaviour of rural people, without denying that people merge into larger systems of production of value and the differential distribution and consumption of that value.

The prevalence of a market or subsistence orientation is not what differentiates these producers. All the producer types are structured by household needs and consumption patterns; all are involved in a variety of relations with external capitals; and all combine livelihoods and decision-making criteria in a dynamic way. Their decisions are based on what is needed for household consumption, on what opportunities are available for cash-crop production (in this case the export crop coffee), and on the expectations they have of alternative livelihoods such as wage labour or commercial activities. All categories consider both subsistence (household needs) and market criteria. For example, petty commodity producers whose main economic activity (in terms of profits generated) is coffee, continue to grow maize for household consumption even if its profitability in terms of labour and capital investment is relatively low. The producer–proletarian continuously weighs up the amount of money which can be earned by selling labour power on a labour market, and the amount of food that this labour can produce if used for subsistence production. The idea of multiple livelihoods of peasant producers, in which coffee production figures centrally, and the existence of a regional nickel-and-dime capitalism, have implications for interpreting the environmental effects of adjustment.

Environmental Effects of Adjustment Measures

This chapter does not aim to review fully the effects of adjustment measures on the environment, mainly because the data needed to do so are not available for Central America.[12] Instead, it explores three contrasting interpretations: (i) the political economy view which mainly perceives an adverse relationship between adjustment policies and environmental conservation; (ii) a neo-populist view which rejects the neo-liberal promotion of large-scale export agriculture but recognizes opportunities in adjustment policies for smallholder development; and (iii) a neo-liberal view which argues that the invisible hand of the market (freed from state-imposed constraints) will lead to efficient and sustainable resource use.

The political economy view is mainly voiced by critical North American scholars who are concerned about the consequences of capitalist development in general and the role of US foreign policy in particular. The neo-populist view is put forward by some non-governmental organizations (NGOs) and academics who are involved in developing technology for smallholder agriculture. The neo-liberal view is particularly defended by the World Bank and related financial institutions.

The political economy model argues that the dominant economic model which focuses on agro-exports is the underlying cause of crisis and political conflict in Central America. The agro-export model dispossesses the peasantry of (high-quality) land and induces capitalist enterprises to pollute the environment with high levels of biocide use (Faber 1993, Murray 1994).[13] The model is supported by an agrarian bourgeoisie, national élite groups, and foreign development interventions (Carrière 1991, Weinberg 1991). The expansion of cotton and cattle has attracted most criticism. Williams (1986) describes how the expansion of cotton on the plains of the Pacific Coast in El Salvador, Nicaragua and Honduras led to social dislocation and environmental deterioration in the 1960s and 1970s. The best soils were sown with cotton by entrepreneurial farmers. Tenants who cultivated food crops on this land were removed. A few years later severe outbreaks of plague led to increased pesticide spraying, until a point was reached at which the costs of pest control exceeded profits and cotton cultivation was abandoned altogether. The cattle boom which restructured agrarian relations in Central America after World War II profited from low land values and was similarly driven by the growth of export opportunities. According to the political economy view, smallholders were dispossessed of the most fertile lands which landlords then turned over to pasture for cattle (Brockett 1988, Williams 1986, Howard-Borjas 1995). Only a small élite profited from the cattle boom, which generated unemployment and soil degradation on the marginal soils where peasants moved to. It added only little value per unit of land.

In the political economy view, structural adjustment policies perpetuate the agro-export model by restructuring the macro-economic conditions that sustain it. Adjustment advocates give high priority to the growth of the agro-export sector (Torres 1996). Structural adjustment aims to create favourable conditions for the cultivation of new agro-export crops such as melon, mangoes and citrus in Honduras (World Bank 1995). Political economists argue that these development strategies are biased against small-scale producers and generate ecological disruption. The most profitable activities are taken over by transnational corporations while the local population suffers from ecological disruption, and new pest and pesticide problems (Murray 1991, Stonich 1991, Murray and Hoppin 1992).[14]

By contrast, a neo-populist view argues the opposite: that structural adjustment policies can provide opportunities for a more sustainable development of peasant production. This view considers the bureaucratic developmentalist state as the enemy of peasant production because its interventions support large-scale, entrepreneurial agriculture and discourage grassroots participation, innovations based on local knowledge systems, and smallholder development (Bunch 1982, Puerta 1990, Cox 1992, Smith 1994, Toledo 1995). Accordingly, support has been given to structural adjustment policies which remove the subsidies for fertilizers and biocides which encouraged their over-use and led to environmental pollution. For example Hruska (1990), whose interpretation shares several insights of neo-liberal ideology, argues that between 1985 and 1988 the Nicaraguan government subsidized input use in two ways: (i) through the maintenance of an extremely favourable exchange rate; and (ii) through *de facto* negative interest rates for agricultural credits.[15] The consequence was a dramatically high use of agrochemical inputs as well as their waste and misuse. In 1988 the Sandinista government of Ortega announced structural adjustment-style economic changes. The local currency was drastically devalued, the preferential exchange rate for imports of agrochemicals was abandoned, and a new interest rate structure suspended cheap agricultural credits. Input prices rose to world market prices, and dissatisfied producers began to cut inputs and look for ways of reducing the use of pesticides. They became interested in integrated pest management and demanded that unnecessary insecticides be removed from the technological recommendations which accompanied credit supply. Likewise, Repetto (1985, 1989) is a proponent of policies to change incentive structures in order to remove market distortions. Changes in financial incentives (by making inputs more expensive) would lead to more efficient use of fertilizers and biocides and of water on farms, lower levels of mechanization, higher levels of rural employment, and more reliance on the self-regulating capacities of ecosystems rather than compensating possible losses with chemical inputs. Repetto pleads for policies that promote more self-generative patterns of agricultural production. This fits in with approaches that advocate technology development based on local knowledge, small-scale production, and support from a network of NGOs (Kaimowitz et al. 1992).

The third view is the neo-liberal view. Central American governments that implement structural adjustment policies do not aim to reduce agricultural inputs. Should this occur, it is seen as the unintended consequence of these policies. Structural adjustment policies in Honduras aim to increase agricultural production by enabling a higher level of inputs through the joint investments of co-operative members turned into smallholders and agri-business capital (Honduras 1992). Joint investment, contract farming and market-led credit programmes are proposed as options for the survival of smallholders, allowing them to become commodity producers who are incorporated into high-value export-crop production. For such schemes to succeed, clear individual property rights and security of land tenure are generally seen as crucial conditions. According to a recent neo-liberal view, pre-adjustment policies depressed land prices and agricultural profitability. Consequently, returns on investment were depressed and farmers' incentives to practise soil conservation were lowered (Repetto 1989: 71). Land titling programmes along neo-liberal imperatives aim to raise land prices and improve security of tenure. This would provide incentives and opportunities for landowners to invest in productivity and soil conservation and related practices of sustainable land use (Atwood 1990, Strasma and Celis 1992, Wachter 1994). If imperfections in land markets were removed, the mobility of land would increase and fall into the hands of the most efficient and productive users (Melmed-Sanjak 1993).

Neo-liberal positions have gradually shifted from an exclusive concern with macro-economic policies to considering ways in which structural adjustment influences the quality of the natural environment (Kutsch Lojenga 1995, Warford et al. 1997). Possible negative impacts of economy-wide reforms are acknowledged but it is assumed that these can be monitored and mitigated. In his review of neo-liberal economic strategies in the agricultural sector in various Latin America countries, Torres (1996) concludes that these strategies are more likely to resolve environmental degradation than inward-oriented policies. He argues that most environmental problems originate from economic distortions which can be removed by outward-oriented policies and liberalization.

Peasant Differentiation and Environmental Change

The three interpretations discussed above analyse the environmental consequences of structural adjustment policies by posing the question of what it means for agricultural modernization. This section explores the extent to which they have a notion of the linkages between agricultural modernization and the social differentiation of the peasantry as outlined earlier.

Political economy

One underlying reason why structural adjustment leaves the agro-export model intact, as political economists argue, is that it does not modify the agrarian structure. The existing agrarian structure is often conceptualized in terms of functional dualism (de Janvry 1981). In this model, after World War II an emerging labour surplus in the countryside in Latin America reshaped the social relations of production. A mass of semi-proletarianized peasants appeared alongside a capitalist agricultural sector. A functional dualism emerged between the latter, which produces commodities on the basis of hired semi-proletarian labour, and the peasant sector, which provides that cheap labour. The below-subsistence wage levels paid by this sector are made possible by the complementary subsistence production in the peasant sector on the basis of family labour (de Janvry 1981: 84, de Janvry et al. 1989). In exploring the contradictions of this functional dualism, de Janvry points to the collapsing resource base controlled by peasants. Land accumulation by capitalist producers has relegated peasant agriculture to the least fertile and resilient soils. The lack of adequate technological innovation results in low productivity. The destruction of the few productive resources available augments as poverty increases: 'soil mining' takes place and soil fertility declines (de Janvry 1981: 86–7).

Faber (1992, 1993) uses this model to explain environmental deterioration in Central America and argues that disarticulated development not only '*produced* severe ecological exploitation but *depended* on it for the subsidised reproduction of semiproletarian labor and generation of a larger mass of surplus value' (1992: 27, italics in original). In this model, capitalist forms of land use which hire semi-proletarian labour produce pollution and deforestation as labourers are left with marginal, over-exploited lands which are subject to soil erosion. According to this view, there exists a functional relationship between these two practices.

This approach usefully documents how the continuing deterioration of natural resources is not only a product of misuse, mismanagement or overpopulation, but is intrinsic to the model of accumulation and the domestic power constellation associated with it. It is less useful when assuming a linear relationship between the form of control over the means of production and the pattern of environmental deterioration: semi-proletarians = hillside erosion, and capitalists = pollution. The Honduran study (Jansen 1998) raises two problems for this approach: (i) the dichotomy which Faber observes in patterns of social relations does not fit the complexity of peasant differentiation in rural Honduras; and (ii) the suggested linear relation between control over the means of production and environmental deterioration does not cover the variety of phenomena and relationships actually existing in Honduras.

The division of rural people into capitalist landowners and land-poor semi-proletarians in Faber's model makes the issue of land distribution central. I have shown elsewhere (Jansen 1998) that unequal land distribution cannot be conceptualized in terms of two categories. Land distribution in Honduras is not simply bimodal. Furthermore, while farm size is important it is not the only determinant of the dynamics of production. Mediating institutions (such as personal relations, markets and the state) shape production, and not necessarily along farm size classes. Likewise, trajectories of technological change do not follow a bimodal pattern, i.e. a capitalist sector characterized by the use of industrial inputs in cash crops, and a subsistence sector of semi-proletarians or peasants using traditional technologies. This is clearly expressed in the remarkable percentage of coffee produced by smallholders. Many of these producers have less than one hectare devoted to coffee and only a small amount of land for other crops. Agro-export production is thus to an important extent in the hands of peasants. The existence of a differentiated peasantry as outlined above invalidates the functional dualism model adopted by Faber. The concept of nickel-and-dime capitalism is a more faithful representation of social relations in many regions of rural Honduras. It implies that rural society cannot be analysed in terms of a simple dualism between a modern and a peasant (semi-proletarian) sector.[16]

A second flaw in Faber's model concerns the linear relationship between relations of production and resource use. Erosion patterns do not simply reflect power relations: no one side of a power relation is exclusively associated with a specific type of erosion. Small and large producers, capitalists and semi-proletarians (or rather, in the terms discussed above, entrepreneurial farmers, family labour producers, petty commodity producers and producer–proletarians) all provoke soil degradation, deforestation and pollution with pesticides. They all cultivate hillsides (soil erosion) and use herbicides in maize production (pollution).[17] Agro-export coffee production, for example, can be undertaken by petty commodity producers on small farms, often with low levels of biocide use but sometimes with high levels. Large landowners can use hillsides in a soil-destructive way for cattle or protect a forest area in order to safeguard crucial water sources. There are no grounds for assuming a simple linearity between type of producer (social structure) and environmental deterioration. This does not mean that there is no relation whatsoever between socio-economic variables and agricultural practices. In an earlier publication (Jansen 1998) I describe a case in which most people who cultivate maize on their own land do not burn to clear their field, while people who rent land or who cultivate common land do. The point is that social relations create conditions which influence agricultural practices but do so without predetermining the specific outcome. The form of land use emerges from a multi-faceted set of social and biophysical variables. This also implies that the final destination of the product, household consumption or export market, does not necessarily reflect the specific social type of producer nor define the related pattern of environmental deterioration.

The argument that functional dualism in political–economic relations determines environmental deterioration is a gross over-simplification. Consequently, the argument that structural adjustment supports the agro-export growth model, and thereby perpetuates the poverty of the peasant sector and upholds environmental deterioration of a particular kind, is short-sighted. Specific forms of growth of Honduran coffee production may provide the economic basis of important sectors of the peasantry, and offer more opportunities for environmental conservation than growing maize for household consumption where innovation is difficult.

Agrarian neo-populism

Neo-populism shares the neo-liberal view that the influence of the state in the management of natural resources and the development and transfer of technology should be reduced. However, unlike neo-liberal ideologies it prioritizes endogenous technology development by peasants over exogenous technology development by science and agri-business. The higher prices of external inputs resulting from structural adjustment are regarded as a very positive effect, as this spawns technology development which makes use of local resources. The question is, however, whether this development benefits all peasant producers equally. In the case of a differentiated peasantry, producers may have different reasons for using specific technologies and experience differences in the availability of labour needed to replace the external inputs.

One problem of higher input prices is that these may directly affect subsistence production as well as production for the market. Producer-proletarians, for example, earn some money from wage labour to buy fertilizers and herbicides to sustain maize yields rather than to increase production. Diminishing soil fertility is being tackled with fertilizers, and increasing infestation with grass weeds and reduced labour availability is tackled with herbicides. Increased input prices thus endanger the possibilities for these producers to produce enough subsistence crops for household consumption. It is still doubtful whether so-called 'alternative technologies' can provide reasonable alternatives to these external inputs, at least in the short term, since they generally require an increase in labour input which is not feasible for the poor in most cases.[18] If input prices rise, the producer–proletarian may have to work longer for others in order to obtain the inputs to sustain subsistence production at the same level. It is not certain whether a lowering of external inputs will affect the poorer producers even when they only produce for subsistence.

The assumption that a lowering of external inputs can be substituted by an increase in labour use makes the question of which peasant types are in a position to mobilize such extra labour crucial. Jansen (1998: 90) describes a family labour producer who worked for more than 2000 hours in the field in 1994, even though he was ill for 65 days of the year. His two sons both worked more than 2300 hours in the field (without counting the many tasks at home). This amount of labour produced just enough for household consumption while a little extra income from coffee was spent on daily household needs, medical care, and small home improvements. No labour was available to carry out planned tasks such as extending their coffee field. This example reflects the situation of many other peasants in Honduras, who tend to use all their available labour already. As a pool of labour is not generally available, reduction of inputs often cuts into subsistence crop yields. Extra labour needs to be hired just to sustain production levels but there is no extra income to pay for this labour. The neo-populist view that wrong technology or wrong mentality (Smith 1994), and not labour, is a problem for peasants, does not correspond to the situation of many peasants in Honduras.

The latter observation has implications for 'sustainable technologies' such as soil conservation techniques and organic farming methods of soil fertilisation and pest control. With current developments only peasants of the petty commodity-producer type, and not the very poor, will be able to invest (hire labour) in soil conservation practices and develop long-term sustainability strategies. They will do so by hiring other, poorer peasant producers such as the producer–proletarian. Any supposed positive effects of adjustment policies, such as fewer inputs and more intensive and sustainable production systems, will thus not be evenly distributed over the peasantry. Whether effects are positive or negative will depend on the exploitative character of labour relations and on who can marshall the labour of others in the new situation of fewer inputs. One cannot assume that adjustment policies will generate a sustainable agriculture for all peasants because external inputs will become more expensive. In the context of a differentiated peasantry, the final outcomes of adjustment policies will be contradictory and will not simply lead to the use of more sustainable technologies by all producers. A full understanding of these outcomes requires more intellectual and political effort than that offered by the neo-populist view.

Neo-liberalism

In the neo-liberal view, differences between rich and poor are gradual in the sense that poorer producers lack resources and therefore tend to over-exploit the few available natural resources. The need to support a family absorbs all resources and limits prospects for capital accumulation and investment in the sustainable reproduction of agricultural resources. The poor's lack of resources is interpreted in terms of market constraints. To overcome the difference between poor and rich, all producers should have equal access to transparent markets. Once constraints have been removed and the right incentives provided, the poor will have access to markets and thus to credit and land to produce in a more capitalized form, which enables investment in soil conservation and other aspects of sustainable agriculture (World Bank 1995).

This explanation presents the problem of lack of resources as one of market access of individual producers. Little attention is paid to how resource distribution is produced and reproduced through social structures, or to the fact that people can also be excluded from access to resources in a free market context. A second problem is that better access to resources does not necessarily lead to investment in environmentally friendly practices. Rationality in economic terms does not necessarily mean a rational use of resources in ecological terms. This is well illustrated by the environmental problems of high-input farming by well endowed producers in many parts of the world. Poverty limits investment in the environment, but affluence does not necessarily lead to agricultural systems which are environmentally friendly.

The statement that market liberalization leads to investment by smallholders in environmentally friendly agriculture may serve a legitimizing function rather than forming an objective in neo-liberal practice. The land titling programme in Honduras in the early 1980s was designed to improve security of tenure for smallholders. Only years later was the argument presented that land titling also aimed to increase investment in soil conservation and other environmentally friendly practices (Wachter 1992). In their review of the Honduran land titling programme, Jansen and Roquas (1998) found no clear links between land titling and capitalization of peasant farmers (through improved credit supply), nor between land titling and investment in soil conservation. The land titling programme did not create a free land market as expected, nor did it recognize the importance of forms of land transactions which did not fit into the programme's legalistic definitions. No attention was paid to the way in which insecurity of land rights are embedded in local systems of property relations and power. Furthermore, the titling programme had no effect at all on soil conservation practices.

Even if a free land market were to be created, this would result not in land for the poorest producers, but rather in dispossession of many peasants from their land. Land titling proponents predict that land titling will lead to higher land prices (to be further raised through taxation) and a shift in land ownership from inefficient to efficient producers (Stanfield 1992, Strasma and Celis 1992). According to this view, poor producers such as producer–proletarians do not till the land efficiently, and with higher land prices they will find it even more difficult to obtain access to land.[19] With higher land prices, it is not the producer–proletarians whose access to resources will benefit from a free land market, but the richer petty commodity producers and entrepreneurial farmers, notwithstanding the rhetoric that land titling will also improve the lot of the poor tiller. Producers with coffee or similar sources of profits will become the main buyers of land. Poor people will be even less able to compete in the land market, and rents for the land they farm will rise. Those producers who have been ousted may be pushed onto marginal or uncleared land so that the concomitant type of unsustainable resource use will continue.

A further neglect of structural difference within the peasantry is present in the idea that higher product prices will stimulate agricultural production and reduce rural poverty (World Bank 1995). Accordingly, higher maize prices will benefit the poor producer.[20] However, a substantial part of the peasantry is not able to cultivate enough food for family survival, and prior to harvest many have to buy maize from local shops. In some parts of the country this is due to the small size of plots, low soil quality, or a shortage of labour in the household (Jansen 1998). In other parts of Honduras, different types of producers sell part or all of their harvest to pay off debts, even though they have to purchase maize at higher prices later (Johnson 1997). A rise in the market price of maize may benefit larger producers (petty commodity producers and entrepreneurial farmers) but undermines the food security of producer–proletarians. The effect of structural adjustment policies on the peasantry is thereby differentiated.

Conclusions

Existing evaluations of the environmental effects of structural adjustment policies in Central America, be it from a political economy perspective, a neo-populist perspective, or a neo-liberal perspective, overlook the existence of a differentiated peasantry. The political economy critique of the agro-export model and the supposed environmental consequences do not take into account the fact that peasants may participate substantially in agro-export production. Furthermore, agro-export production does not necessarily lead to more severe or different environmental consequences than food-crop production. Neo-populist support for adjustment policies which reduce fertilizer and biocide use underestimates their possible negative consequences for sections of the peasantry. Neo-liberal assumptions that 'getting prices right' and individual land titling will lead to free markets and higher product prices, and thus to more rational, efficient and sustainable production and less rural poverty, does not take into account the negative consequences of these developments for sections of the peasantry. Some will be less able to obtain access to land or buy food, and will not acquire the resources to develop sustainable forms of agriculture. Recent shifts in World Bank thinking (Warford et al. 1997), to the effect that some structural adjustment policies may lead to location-specific environmental degradation and thus need complementary and compensatory programmes, remain problematic. This thinking still does not recognize that exclusion from resources is institutionalized in the so-called free market, whether on a global or local scale.

Analysis of the impact of economic change on the environment in the field of agricultural production requires an approach which can explore the multiple ways in which social relations mediate economic change, as well as the resulting differential strategies in land use. It cannot be assumed that macro-economic stability and smoothly functioning markets have benign environmental effects as a matter of course. The erosion of ecological rationality by a free market economy and the continuing process of exclusion require new forms of organization and state regulation which are at odds with central neo-liberal dogmas. Whether adjustment policies have positive or negative consequences for the environment and peasant producers is an empirical question, but in most cases the effects will be differential. An understanding of peasant differentiation is required to know who will be the winners and losers in processes of economic change. We can retain from the political economy approach the notion that marginalization in Central America is strongly related to the alliance between agrobusiness capital and national élites. We have to add, however, the notion that contradiction and small-scale exploitation exist within the peasantry, shaping their daily lives and their participation or non-participation in political organizations. This calls for more detailed research into the different regional economies (i.e. below the national level). This has to be linked up with the study of the manifold ways in which peasants are involved in processes of technological and environmental change, including local knowledge generation – issues which have received ample attention from more populist perspectives. It is a challenge to link these questions to social differentiation, state–peasant relations and wider political and economic contexts. A more dynamic understanding will evade such generalizing statements as are contained in the anti-agro-export views. The production of export crops should not be discarded as a viable option for rethinking opportunities for sustainable agricultural production by peasants.

Notes

1. According to the World Bank (1995) real prices of agricultural products dropped by 37 per cent between 1978 and 1988.
2. The mean maize yield of Honduran producers with a farm size smaller than 10 hectares is about 1.2 metric tons per hectare (calculated from SECPLAN 1994). In the research area practically all maize was cultivated on hillsides and the mean maize yield was less than 0.9 metric tons per hectare (Jansen 1998).
3. Land access was not a fundamental constraint for the peasantry until a few decades ago. During the first half of the twentieth century, land was available for peasant farming to develop alongside large landholdings. Conflicts over land, which have always been present, were mainly about access to good quality soil and other favoured attributes, rather than about space as such (Jansen 1998).
4. *Ejido* land is national land designated to the municipality by the central government. The municipality has the authority to grant individual usufruct rights to *ejido* inhabitants.
5. The mean farm size in the research area declined from 13.6 hectares in 1952 to 4.0 hectares in 1993; coffee cultivation expanded from 236 to 375 hectares and its productivity increased from 0.19 to 0.86 metric tons per hectare.
6. Petty commodity producers are politically represented by AHPROCAFE (Asociación Hondureña de Productores de Café), the Honduran Organization of Coffee Producers, which sees itself as an organization of small- and medium-sized producers.

7. There is an analogy with the category of semi-proletarian here. However, the semi-proletarian is generally conceived as a transitional category, which will disappear in a process of full proletarianization. The category of producer–proletarian is not necessarily transitional. Furthermore, the concept of semi-proletarian suggests an opposition to the capitalist who hires wage labour and thus determines conditions of existence. In the case of the producer–proletarian, the employer may not be a typical capitalist enterprise but a family labour farm or a petty commodity producer. The producer–proletarian has some room for manoeuvre in 'choosing' between wage labour and working on the common land (albeit with lower returns to labour given the low yields on these marginal soils). Nevertheless this producer is generally in a subordinate position. The term producer–proletarian focuses on the fact that labour power is sold to others and on the nature of the agricultural activities carried out by the producer.
8. Several definitions of 'peasant' exist. The Spanish term *campesino* generally adopts a broad definition, i.e. producers who have access to land (be it owned or rented), who cultivate this land with family labour or with a combination of family and hired labour, and who define production primarily in terms of household needs. This means that subsistence production usually forms a substantial part of total production and helps determine the production rationale, even where cash-crop production is an important activity.
9. Notable exceptions are Boyer (1984) and Johnson (1997).
10. The concept of 'penny capitalism' coined by Tax (1953) similarly refers to a society which is 'capitalist' on a microscopic scale. However, it is not adequate here as it refers to 'undeveloped communities' which will (and must) change. For Tax, the difference between poor and rich is a difference between modern economies and primitive underdeveloped societies. Unlike 'penny capitalism', 'nickel-and-dime capitalism' does not mean that everyone is self-employed but refers to the exploitative labour relations between rural people.
11. The concept of entrepreneurial producer refers to farmers who are completely based on wage labour. It is preferred to the concept of capitalist producer as this mistakenly suggests that other producer types are not capitalist.
12. Apart from lack of verifiable data, other factors hamper a thorough assessment of the environmental effects of structural adjustment policies in Central America. Mearns (1991: 23) rejects the general notion that relationships between structural adjustment policies and the environment are 'causal, linear and implicitly measurable'. Adjustment measurements interact with complex and dynamic social and economic processes and it is extremely difficult to analyse cause–effect relationships, let alone to predict outcomes of adjustment policies (Kutsch Lojenga 1995: 27–8). Evaluations of structural adjustment policies do not succeed in separating the effects of these policies from, for example, the effects of trade cycles (such as world market coffee prices) or unknown economic processes (such as the investment of drug trade profits or foreign donations to the *Contras* in the 1980s).
13. This argument builds on earlier critiques of the agro-export model in Central America developed by, amongst others, by DeWalt (1985), Williams (1986), Brockett (1988), and Stonich (1989).
14. A similar analysis has been made of the growing shrimp-farming sector in the Golfo de Fonseca (Stonich 1991).
15. Similar types of subsidies are found in Honduras (Farah 1994).
16. However, the dualist model cannot simply be replaced by one of 'diversity' among producers as this may reintroduce 'homogeneity' through the back door by disregarding structural contradictions between producers. The community is not composed of homogeneous, poor, hillside producers.

17. This does not exclude the possibility that similar practices may stem from different strategies. Entrepreneurial farmers spray herbicides to increase productivity or reduce labour costs, while producer–proletarians use herbicides mainly to offset the labour crisis which results from selling their own labour power.
18. This is a very general statement; some alternative technologies, for example the use of velvet bean (*Mucuna pruriens*) as a green manure crop, may in some situations reduce labour requirements. Velvet bean, however, seems to be an exception. Its potential to reduce labour requirements may explain why it is spreading successfully compared to other alternative technologies, such as compost-making or conservation of physical soil structures. This remark does not imply that experiments with alternative technologies are useless, but does suggest that these do not offer at this moment a simple alternative to external inputs.
19. The Agricultural Modernization Law (Honduras 1992: Art. 69) makes provision for a Land Bank Fund to give loans to smallholders to buy land up to 10 hectares. This appears as a compensation for the fact that the market itself will never redistribute land to poor producers. This fund, however, when set up, can never hope to provide all poor producers with land.
20. The World Bank (1995) mentions in a separate box that maize and beans generate only one-fifth of the net income of the smallest producers, contrary to popular thinking. The document refers to maize that is cultivated for household consumption and not for the market. Nevertheless, the rest of the document reproduces the traditional image of smallholders as producers of commercialized maize in Honduras. Higher maize prizes which (supposedly) result from adjustment policies do not contribute to substantially higher incomes for poor producers, contrary to what the document suggests.

References

Atwood, D.A. (1990) ‘Land registration in Africa: the impact on agricultural production’, *World Development*, 18(5): 659–71.

Barraclough, S. (1973) *Agrarian Structure in Latin America*, Lexington Books, Lexington, Massachusetts.

Boyer, J.C. (1984) ‘From peasant ‘economía’ to capitalist social relations in southern Honduras’, *South Eastern Latin Americanist*, 27(4): 1–22.

Brockett, C.D. (1988) *Land, Power and Poverty: Agrarian Transformation and Political Conflict in Central America*, Unwin Hyman, Boston.

Bunch, R. (1982) *Dos Mazorcas de Maíz*, World Neighbours, Oklahoma City.

Carrière, J. (1991) ‘The crisis in Costa Rica: an ecological perspective’, in M. Redclift and D. Goodman (eds) *Environment and Development in Latin America, The Politics of Sustainability*, Manchester University Press, Manchester, pp. 184–204.

Cox, S.B. (1992) ‘Citizen participation and the reform of development assistance in Central America’, in S. Annis (ed.) *Poverty, Natural Resources and Public Policy in Central America*, Transaction Publishers, New Brunswick and Oxford, pp. 59–83.

Del-Cid, J.R. (1977) *Reforma Agraria y Capitalismo Dependiente*, Editorial Universitaria, Tegucigalpa.

de Janvry, A. (1981) *The Agrarian Question and Reformism in Latin America*, Johns Hopkins University Press, Baltimore.

de Janvry, A., Sadoulet, E. and Wilcox Young, L. (1989) ‘Land and labour in Latin American agriculture from the 1950s to the 1980s’, *Journal of Peasant Studies*, 16(3): 396–424.

DeWalt, B.R. (1985) 'Microcosmic and macrocosmic processes of agrarian change in southern Honduras: the cattle are eating the forest', in B.R. DeWalt and P.J. Pelto (eds) *Micro and Macro Levels of Analysis in Anthropology, Issues in Theory and Research*, Westview Press, Boulder, Colorado, pp. 165–86.

Djurfeldt, G. (1982) 'Classical discussions of capital and peasantry: a critique', in J. Harriss (ed.) *Rural Development: Theories of Peasant Economy and Agrarian Change*, Routledge, London, pp. 139–59.

Faber, D. (1992) 'Imperialism, revolution, and the ecological crisis of central America', *Latin American Perspectives*, 19, 1: 17–44.

Faber, D. (1993) *Environment under Fire, Imperialism and the Ecological Crisis in Central America*, Monthly Review Press, New York.

Farah, J. (1994) *Pesticide Policies in Developing Countries: Do they encourage excessive use?*, World Bank Discussion Paper No. 238, World Bank, Washington, D.C.

Hecht, S.B. (1987) 'The evolution of agroecological thought', in M. Altieri (ed.) *Agroecology, The Scientific Basis of Alternative Agriculture*, Westview Press, Boulder, pp. 1–20.

Honduras, República de (1992) 'Ley para la modernización y el desarrollo del sector agrícola', *La Gaceta*, 6 April, Decreto 31–92.

Howard-Borjas, P. (1995) 'Cattle and crisis: the genesis of unsustainable development in Central America', in Agrarian Questions Organising Committee (ed.) *Agrarian Questions: the Politics of Farming anno 1995: Proceedings*, Wageningen Agricultural University, Wageningen, pp. 617–46.

Hruska, A.J. (1990) 'Government pesticide policy in Nicaragua 1985–1989', *Global Pesticide Monitor*, 1(2): 3–5.

Jansen, K. (1993) 'Café y formas de producción en Honduras', *Revista Centroamericana de Economía*, 14(41): 58–96.

Jansen, K. (1998) *Political Ecology, Mountain Agriculture, and Knowledge in Honduras*, Thela Publishers, Amsterdam.

Jansen, K. and Roquas, E. (1998) 'Modernizing insecurity: the land titling project in Honduras', *Development and Change*, 29(1): 81–106.

Johnson, H. (1997) 'Food insecurity as a sustainability issue: lessons from Honduran maize farming', in J. de Groot and R. Ruben (eds) *Sustainable Agriculture in Central America*, Macmillan, Basingstoke, pp. 89–107.

Kaimowitz, D., Erazo, D., Mejía, M. and Navarro, A. (1992) 'Las organizaciones privadas de desarrollo y la transferencia de tecnología en el agro Hondureño', *Revista Centroamericana de Economía*, 12(37): 46–88.

Kearney, M. (1996) *Reconceptualizing the Peasantry: Anthropology in Global Perspective*, Westview Press, Boulder.

Kutsch Lojenga, R.F. (1995) Structural adjustment programmes and the environment in Costa Rica, MA thesis, Free University, Amsterdam.

Mearns, R. (1991) *Environmental Implications of Structural Adjustment: Reflections on Scientific Method*, Discussion Paper No. 284, Institute of Development Studies, University of Sussex, Brighton.

Melmed-Sanjak, Y. (1993) 'Proyecto de titulación de tierras', paper presented at Seminar on Land Titling Research Project, POSCAE, Tegucigalpa, 1993.

Murray, D.L. (1991) 'Export agriculture, ecological disruption, and social inequity: some effects of pesticides in southern Honduras', *Agriculture and Human Values*, 8(4): 19–29.
Murray, D.L. (1994) *Cultivating Crisis, The Human Cost of Pesticides in Latin America*, University of Texas Press, Austin.
Murray, D.L. and Hoppin, P. (1992) 'Recurring contradictions in agrarian development: pesticide problems in Caribbean Basin nontraditional agriculture', *World Development*, 20(4): 597–608.
Posas, M. (1979) 'Política estatal y estructura agraria en Honduras (1950–1978)', *Estudios Sociales Centroamericanos*, No. 24, pp. 37–116.
Posas, M. (1996) 'El sector reformado y la política agrario del estado', in E. Baumeister (ed.) *El Agro Hondureño y Su Futuro*, Guaymuras, Tegucigalpa, pp. 131–66.
Puerta, R.A. (1990) *El Pequeño Agricultor en Honduras: Situación y Perspectivas de Desarrollo*, Instituto de Investigación y Formación Cooperativista and Fundación Friedrich Naumann, Tegucigalpa.
Reed, D. (1996) *Structural Adjustment, the Environment, and Sustainable Development*, Earthscan, London.
Repetto, R. (1985) *Paying the Price: Pesticide Subsidies in Developing Countries*, Research Report No. 2, World Resources Institute, Washington, D.C.
Repetto, R. (1989) 'Economic incentives for sustainable production', in G. Schramm and J.J. Warford (eds) *Environmental Management and Economic Development*, Johns Hopkins University Press, Baltimore, pp. 69–86.
Ruben, R. (1997) Making co-operatives work, contract choice and resource management within land reform co-operatives in Honduras, PhD thesis, Free University, Amsterdam.
Sandoval Corea, R. (1992) 'La ley para la modernización y el desarrollo del sector agrícola y sus efectos en el proceso agrario Hondureño', in H. Noé Pino, A. Thorpe and R. Sandoval Corea (eds) *El Sector Agrícola y la Modernización en Honduras*, CEDOH/POSCAE, Tegucigalpa.
SECPLAN (Honduras, Secretaría de Planificación, Coordinación y Presupuesto) (1994) *IV Censo Nacional Agropecuario 1993*, Graficentro Editores, Tegucigalpa
Smith, K. (1994) *The Human Farm, A Tale of Changing Lives and Changing Lands*, Kumarian Press, West Hartford, Connecticut.
Stanfield, D. (1992) 'Titulación de tierra: alternativa a la reforma agraria en un contexto de ajuste estructural', in H. Noé Pino and A. Thorpe (eds) *Honduras: El Ajuste Estructural y la Reforma Agraria*, CEDOH-POSCAE, Tegucigalpa, pp. 181–206.
Stonich, S.C. (1989) 'The dynamics of social processes and environmental destruction: a central American case study', *Population and Development Review*, 15(2): 269–96.
Stonich, S.C. (1991) 'The promotion of non-traditional agricultural exports in Honduras: issues of equity, environment and natural resource management', *Development and Change*, 22(4): 725–55.
Strasma, J.D. and Celis, R. (1992) 'Land taxation, the poor, and sustainable development', in S. Annis (ed.) *Poverty, Natural Resources and Public*

Policy in Central America, Transaction Publishers, New Brunswick and Oxford, pp. 143–69.

Tax, S. (1953) *Penny Capitalism, A Guatemalan Indian Economy*, Institute of Social Anthropology Publication No. 16, Smithsonian Institution, Washington.

Thiesenhusen, W.C. (1989) 'Introduction: searching for agrarian reform in Latin America', in W.C. Thiesenhusen (ed.) *Searching for Agrarian Reform in Latin America*, Unwin Hyman, Boston, pp. 1–41.

Thorpe, A. (1995a) 'Agricultural modernisation and its consequences for land markets in Honduras', in Agrarian Questions Organising Committee (ed.) *Agrarian Questions: the Politics of Farming anno 1995: Proceedings*, Wageningen Agricultural University, Wageningen, pp. 1673–96.

Thorpe, A. (1995b) 'Adjusting to reality: the impact of structural adjustment on Honduran agriculture', in J. Weeks (ed.) *Structural Adjustment and the Agricultural Sector in Latin America and the Caribbean*, Macmillan, London, pp. 205–28.

Thorpe, A., Noé Pino, H., Jiménez, P., Restrepo, A., Suazo, D. and Salgado, R. (1995) *Impacto del Ajuste en el Agro Hondureño*, POSCAE/Guaymuras, Tegucigalpa.

Toledo, V. (1995) 'Agricultural technology in peasant dominated areas: a Third World perspective', in Agrarian Questions Organising Committee (ed.) *Agrarian Questions: the Politics of Farming anno 1995: Proceedings*, Wageningen Agricultural University, Wageningen, pp. 1703–20.

Torres, J. (1996) 'Agricultural modernization and resource deterioration in Latin America', in M. Munasinghe (ed.) *Environmental Impacts of Macroeconomic and Sectoral Policies*, ISEE, World Bank/UNEP, Washington, pp. 257–87.

Villanueva, B. (1968) The role of institutional innovations in economic development of Honduras, PhD thesis, University of Wisconsin, Madison.

Wachter, D. (1992) 'Die Bedeutung des Landtitelbesitzes für eine nachhaltige landwirtschaftliche Bodennutzung, eine empirische Fallstudie in Honduras', *Geografische Zeitschrift*, 80(3): 174–83.

Wachter, D. (1994) 'Land titling: possible contributions to farmland conservation in Central America', in E. Lutz, S. Pagiola and C. Reiche (eds) *Economic and Institutional Analysis of Soil Conservation Projects in Central America and the Caribbean*, World Bank Environment Paper No. 8, World Bank, Washington, D.C. pp. 150–6.

Warford, J.J., Munasinghe, M. and Cruz, W. (1997) *The Greening of Economic Policy Reform*, The World Bank, Washington, D.C.

Weinberg, W. (1991) *War on the Land, Ecology and Politics in Central America*, Zed, London.

Williams, R.G. (1986) *Export Agriculture and the Crisis in Central America*, University of North Carolina Press, Chapel Hill.

World Bank (1995) *Honduras, Memorando Económico y Evaluación de la Pobreza*, Report No. 13317-HO, Oficina Regional para América Latina y el Caribe (translation of Country Memorandum/Poverty Assessment 1994).

PART FOUR: ASIAN PEASANTRIES

12. Changing Peasantries in Asia

JOS MOOIJ[1]

ASIA IS, AND HAS BEEN, a peasant continent *par excellence*. To think of the Asian peasantry is to conjure up images of large, green plains or river valleys; of peasant women standing knee-deep in water planting rice; of men ploughing the fields with buffaloes. The landscape appears as a patchwork of small plots punctuated by canals, with forests and plantations covering the distant hills. The people live in small settlements in simple dwellings built from local materials such as bamboo, palm leaves or cow dung.

This idyllic picture of a timeless Asian peasantry, while clearly a misrepresentation, does capture something of the reality. Rice is the most important staple food in Asia, and the peasant household is, and has been, the main unit of agricultural production for several millennia. Many Asian countries are still predominantly rural, with almost three-quarters of the population living in rural areas, and around 65 per cent of the population being employed in agriculture.

However, the Asian continent is large and diverse so that the relative importance of the agricultural sector varies from country to country. Even excluding the Middle East and the Asian part of the former Soviet Union, there is still a wide spectrum, with such highly developed economies as Japan, Korea and Taiwan at one end, and the south Asian subcontinent with the highest concentration of extreme poverty in the world at the other. In south Asia agriculture contributes 25–30 per cent to gross domestic production; in the Philippines and China just over 20 per cent; and in Japan only 2 per cent. In the two largest countries – India and China – around 65 to 70 per cent of the population are economically active in agriculture; in Pakistan and Indonesia the corresponding figure is around 50 per cent; in Korea 18 per cent; and in Japan only 7 per cent (World Bank 1997: Tables 4 and 12). Apart from rice, other major crops are maize, sugarcane, cotton, coffee, tea, rubber, oilseeds and tobacco, some of which are produced mainly by smallholders and others by large estates.

The role of peasant agriculture in the national economies of Asia varies due to different agro-ecological conditions and to distinct, but sometimes similar or interconnected, economic and political processes. It is not possible within the limits of this chapter to examine these natural characteristics and social histories in any detail. Instead we shall make a few general points about Asian peasantries which draw out the comparison with their African and Latin American counterparts.

Peasants, whose labour power or products were appropriated by landlords, priests, the state, traders or others, have existed for a very long time in large parts of Asia. In south Asia 'peasants, as producers of surplus, emerged as a distinct socio-economic group in India during the agricultural revolution in the Indian civilization' (Jha 1997: 1), that is, between 2600 and 1800 BC. After the 'Aryans' came to the subcontinent around 1300 BC., they established a highly stratified society, with peasants cultivating the land and owning cattle. These agriculturalists had to pay both the warriors, who often held power, and the priests. In China, 2000 years ago it was the state which subjugated the peasants. 'The state of Ch'in, which unified China for the first time in 221 BC, . . . pioneered legislation that made peasant owners of their land, in return for taxes, corvées, and military service paid directly to the state rather than to some intervening noble' (E.R. Wolf 1982: 54).

Many Asian societies underwent a high level of technological development, both in and outside agriculture. During the European Middle Ages, parts of Asia had achieved a much higher level of wealth and development (Frank 1998). The extensive and detailed study of Chinese science and civilization undertaken by Needham (1954) shows just how technologically advanced China was as compared to Europe. In her contribution to this *magnum opus*, Bray (1984) shows the skill-oriented nature of many technological innovations in agriculture, particularly in rice production. For millennia, Chinese peasants had been improving their agricultural techniques and their seed to develop a highly efficient agriculture.

Elaborate social, ideological or political structures emerged in many early Asian peasant societies. The caste system in south Asia is a social and ideological system which defines not only the social division of labour but also the social hierarchy between groups of people (castes and sub-castes). In Japan, India and China there had existed powerful dynasties with large empires, highly developed court cultures and elaborate systems of surplus appropriation.

Accordingly, when European colonialists arrived in the sixteenth and seventeenth centuries, they found peasantries which had already been subjected and integrated into wider networks of production and surplus appropriation. In the early phases of colonialism, the European powers collaborated with local rulers, making agreements regarding the commodities (mainly spices) they wanted to 'buy'. Later, as they became interested in gaining control over territory, they started to become more directly involved with production relations. In south Asia, for instance, the British colonial government imposed a new system of land ownership. It converted the existing *zamindars*, chiefs of lineages who held a right to receive tribute from a given area, into owners of the land. Generally, the *zamindars*-turned-landlords did not cultivate the land themselves, but employed middlemen to extract revenue from the tenants. In Indonesia, the Dutch colonial government introduced the Cultivation System, a system of forced cultivation whereby the peasants did not pay taxes in coin but in kind. These policies intensified social differentiation, leading to the concentration of wealth on the one hand and the growth of landlessness and deprivation on the other.

In the second half of the twentieth century, following the withdrawal or expulsion of the colonial powers, Asian countries have followed different paths of development. Some implemented land reforms, while others did not. The east Asian tigers, as well as several other countries in south-east Asia, became firmly integrated into the world market. By contrast, India partly shut itself off and restricted agricultural imports in order to protect its agriculture. China, too, under the Communist leadership, was cut off from the world market. In the course of time, however, both countries have opened up. In China this process began in 1978, and in India market reforms were introduced in 1991. Although this opening resulted in part from the pressure of international financial institutions, the influence of these institutions on national economic policies is relatively limited. Structural adjustment policies are affecting rural and urban livelihoods in Asia, but not as dramatically as in many African countries.

The variation and complexity of agrarian relations make it difficult to generalize about Asian peasantries. Nevertheless, some historians and social scientists have tried to do this and their attempts are briefly described below. This section is followed by a discussion of some recent developments affecting peasant livelihoods in Asia, and their involvement in wider economic and political processes. These include the green revolution, peasant rebellions and revolutions (notably in China and Vietnam), and the increased importance of rural non-farm activities. The overall objective of this chapter is not to produce a comprehensive overview, but to give some idea of the debates on Asian peasantries and of current developments affecting peasant life in Asia.

What Kind of Peasantry?

A few key themes have tended to dominate the literature on Asian peasantries. These include (i) the presumed static and backward character of peasant production; (ii) the small scale of peasant production, especially in rice-producing areas; (iii) the special features of social differentiation within the peasantry; and (iv) the relationship between the peasantry and the state. This section reviews the main contributions to these debates, especially those which adopt a general Asian perspective rather than focusing on an individual country or region.

The notion of an 'Asiatic mode of production', first introduced by Marx, has been widely discussed and contested in both the Marxist and non-Marxist literature. Although the concept is no longer used, some of its attributes still figure in academic and policy debates. The main characteristics of the Asiatic mode of production are 'first, that it is the state which extracts the surplus-product, there is no exploiting class independent of the state; second, that there is an absence of private property in land, the land is state property; and, third, that non-commodity production in agriculture is the dominant form of production' (Hindess and Hirst 1975: 184). The Asiatic mode of production was seen as static and unchanging. While political structures and dynasties change continuously, the 'structure of the economic elements of society remains untouched by the storm-clouds of the political sky' (Marx 1867: 338–9, also quoted by Hindess and Hirst 1975: 201). There is no division of labour between communities, and the division of labour within communities is so rigid that there is no possibility for development or change (Hindess and Hirst 1975: 201).

This interpretation of the Asian peasantry does not differ markedly from the conventional non-Marxist interpretation, as reflected in the work of colonial historiographers. The conventional perspective also emphasized the static character of the agrarian structure, the isolation of and social homogeneity within villages, and the superimposition of a remote state, which was exploitative but did not really affect agrarian social relations at village level (Breman 1988). From this perspective, colonial intervention was a progressive force, bringing an end to an unchanging order and leading to modernization.

The concept of the Asiatic mode of production has not survived the ravages of time. It played only a limited role in the subsequent Indian mode of production debate (Thorner 1982; Patnaik 1990). The concept was deemed to be both theoretically inadequate and empirically inaccurate for describing and explaining the societies in question (Byres 1985: 12). Pre-colonial agriculture was far from stagnant, as Needham and Bray have documented for China. Nor were Asian peasant communities so economically independent and isolated as has been assumed. Many centuries ago there was long-distance trade in commodities such as spices, cottons and silks as well as manufactured products. Medieval India, for instance, had achieved high levels of urbanization. Peasants produced cash crops for urban consumers and paid revenue to the rulers (Alavi 1989: 6). Rural communities were far from homogeneous. Social differentiation already existed in pre-colonial Asia, as did landlessness, although in a different form than occurs today (Breman, Chapter 13 in this volume).

The Asiatic mode of production's conceptual framework reappears in the work of Wittfogel (1957), who was particularly interested in the form of the state. In his attempt to understand past agrarian societies, he developed the concepts of 'hydraulic society' and 'Oriental despotism'. This totalitarian state form, according to Wittfogel, emerged in many pre-capitalist societies, particularly where agrarian production depends on large-scale irrigation works which require administration, coordination and control on a scale far beyond the capacity of individual or collective agriculturalists. In his view, hydraulic societies consist of two main classes: the rulers and the ruled. The rulers are part of the state apparatus (which controls water), while the ruled are the rather undifferentiated commoners or peasants. Slaves are, by and large, absent in hydraulic societies (Wittfogel 1957: 301–24). Wittfogel also fell into the trap of conceptualizing Asian peasant societies as stagnant and relatively undifferentiated but, unlike others, he emphasized exploitation and control by a despotic state.[2]

Rather than irrigation works, Bray (1983) stresses the influence of wet rice, a relatively high-yielding food crop, to explain the distinct patterns of the agrarian structure in Asia. According to Bray:

> wet-rice cultivation is not, like the farming system of Northwest Europe, subject to economies of scale, nor does it respond positively to the centralisation of management (Bray 1983: 19).

> Even where single-cropping is practised a farm of two hectares will support a family (Bray 1983: 9).

There are various ways in which producers can raise yields through intensification, such as by double cropping, transplanting, seed selection and the use of fertilizers. Extensification is less attractive as it involves high initial investment in time and labour and produces lower yields on newly worked fields. Most improvements through intensification are scale-neutral or relatively cheap. Thus:

> in wet-rice societies there is little trend towards the consolidation of holdings and the polarisation of rural society into managerial farmers and landless labourers. Units of management remain small, usually at the scale of the family farm, and the producers are not separated from control of the means of production (Bray 1983: 13).

Even in modern commercialized rice farming, this system of production persists. But Bray's theory has not gone unchallenged; as White states:

> wet rice is . . . not the only . . . crop regime in which polarization in pure form has not emerged . . . and we may wonder whether Bray is correct in focusing on the characteristics of the crop itself as the cause of [the relative absence of polarization] in Asian wet-rice-growing societies. Besides that, large mechanized wage-labor rice farms do exist, and not only in the United States or Australia . . . even though in Asia they coexist with smaller owned or tenanted 'family farms' (White 1989: 23).

In addition to these attempts to generalize about Asian peasantries, there are a wealth of studies dealing with peasantries in particular regions or countries.[3] This literature is vast and varied, dealing with different countries and themes and adopting different theoretical interpretations. Researchers close to the government have usually stressed the backwardness of agriculture and the enduring importance of tradition in the lives of rural people. Marxists have stressed class differences within the peasantry, while (neo)populist authors have emphasized the relative homogeneity of the peasantry and their opposition to an outside élite or state.[4]

The relevance of these positions goes beyond academia. Different conceptual interpretations give rise to divergent political positions and policy recommendations. The interpretation of the peasantry as stagnant and backward tends to justify outside intervention, be it of the colonial state or of post-colonial development agencies. An emphasis on social differentiation points to the need for the radical redistribution of assets, while an interpretation of the peasantry as relatively homogeneous and oppositional to the state often forms part of a critique of the presumed urban bias in state policies, and of proposals to channel more funds to the (undifferentiated) countryside.

Recent Trends

The green revolution, the rise of peasant movements and revolutions, and the trend towards income diversification have altered the key parameters of the agrarian structure since the second world war. The green revolution was more than a change in technology; it affected both commercialization and the labour process. Peasant movements, and especially the peasant revolutions in China and Vietnam, have altered political formations and peasants' access to political power. Rural non-farm activities have the potential to change the structure of surplus creation, accumulation and investment. These three developments, discussed in turn below, affect what Byres refers to as the three problematics in 'the agrarian question': production, politics and accumulation. The production problematic is about 'the extent to which capitalism has developed in the countryside, the forms that it takes, the barriers which may impede its development' (Byres 1991: 9); the politics problematic focuses on the way in which the peasantry can be, and has been, involved in emancipatory political formations; and the accumulation problematic refers to the contribution of agriculture to accumulation in general (see also Bernstein 1996, Akram-Lodhi 1998).

Green revolution

The green revolution, beginning in Asia in the mid-1960s, introduced a package of new, high-yielding seeds, irrigation, cheap credit, chemical fertilizer, and pesticides to boost agricultural production. In Asia, the green revolution mainly involved rice in south and south-east Asia and wheat in north India. The strategy entailed considerable government involvement in the form of cheap credit provisions, input subsidies and food-pricing policy. At the time of introduction, the green revolution was seen by many as a technological solution to the problems of large-scale food insecurity, poverty and deprivation of the peasantry. It was a strategy which transformed 'traditional' agriculture without addressing the problem of unequal land distribution and tenancy relations.

The green revolution has had a considerable impact on rural class relations. In India it dealt a severe blow to landlordism.[5] In key areas of India, a class of capitalist farmers became dominant, while non-cultivating landlords almost disappeared. At the bottom of the agrarian hierarchy, it led to the casualization of labour and immiseration (Breman, Chapter 13 in this volume). The green revolution accelerated rural differentiation, but did not lead to full proletarianization and the disappearance of the peasantry. Indeed, some authors writing at the beginning of the 1980s concluded that the new technology converted middle and rich peasants into capitalist farmers and small ones into landless labourers (see Omvedt 1983, or Byres for a cautious version of this argument). However, more recent micro-studies show such generalizations to be unfounded. Harriss (1992: 195), for instance, concludes that a universal process of dispossession/de-peasantization and proletarianization is unlikely and that, on the contrary, the tendency towards landlessness may have declined. At the same time, however, many households with marginal holdings have increasingly come to depend on casual wage labour in or outside agriculture, both for their livelihood and for retaining their small property (Harriss 1992: 205; see Rigg 1997: 189 for the same argument in relation to south-east Asia).

In other parts of Asia, too, the green revolution forestalled land reform[6], and likewise benefited larger peasants more than smaller ones. In Java, where all holdings are small in absolute terms, the green revolution intensified the differences between larger farm households employing wage labour and the near landless. In particular, the former type of peasants who had access to credit and other subsidies were able to accumulate, while the near-landless benefited less and were excluded from local power structures (Hüsken and White 1989: 253–8).

Apart from class effects, the green revolution also influenced gender relations in agriculture. Among the landless and the marginal peasantry, there has been an increase in the number of women who hire themselves out to work as wage labourers.

> The new technology package requires additional labour for tasks such as transplanting and weeding (normally women's work) but it is not clear

> that this has kept pace with the increase in the numbers of women seeking such work. Other activities, particularly harvesting, threshing and grain-processing, have been subject to substantial mechanization, reducing the opportunities for poor women. The widespread adoption of grain processing mills has vastly reduced women's employment in de-husking of rice, for example (Pearson 1992: 304, referring to Agarwal 1985).

While women in small- and middle-peasant households tend not to engage in wage labour, their work burden on their own farms has often intensified. Women belonging to the rich peasantry share in the greater incomes accruing to these farming households. This often means that they are withdrawn from agricultural production and may become more secluded within the household (Pearson 1992: 306).

All over Asia, the green revolution went together with state intervention. Reviewing evidence from much of south-east Asia, Elson (1997: 67) states that 'increased production could not have occurred without the elaboration of physical and administrative infrastructure'. Governments were involved in the provision of inputs, the procurement of commodities, road construction, research and extension. All this 'represented – and itself further facilitated – a massive increase in the control of the village by the state' (ibid.: 67).

The political effects of state intervention, and the green revolution generally, have been huge. In Indonesia, larger landholders, who were patronized by the state, were more or less loyal to their patron, and 'participated in the "self-policing" of rural areas' (Hüsken and White 1989: 254). In Thailand, the omnipresence of the state is mirrored in the growth of a large number of 'similarly intrusive but frequently oppositionist non-government organisations' (Elson 1997: 68). In India, the class of capitalist farmers, which emerged in the wake of the green revolution, has developed into an important political actor, which strives for higher agricultural prices and a continuation of government subsidies.

Ironically, farmers' movements in India, which are dominated by capitalist farmers or rich peasants, have had the effect of strengthening peasant identities. This is because the movements' ideology stresses the homogeneity and the peasantness of the rural people: village inhabitants who care for the environment and embody the 'traditional and enduring cultural/religious values' (Brass 1995a: 47). Some parts of the farmers' movements oppose large-scale industrial development and advocate a Gandhian type of development based on decentralization, cottage industries, local self-sufficiency and less foreign influence (Brass 1995b: 12).[7] In this way, the green revolution has not only brought capitalist relations of production to the Indian countryside, but has also contributed to a rural consciousness centring around a peasant identity and a peasant way of life.

Peasant movements and revolutions

The farmers' movements, which emerged in the wake of the green revolution, are 'new' in the sense of being based on relatively new rural class configurations rather than that of being the first agrarian movements in India. Indeed, many agrarian/peasant movements arose in India and elsewhere long before the advent of the green revolution.

China, in particular, has a long history of peasant rebellion, the most dramatic being the struggle of the Red Army, mobilized by the Chinese Communist Party from 1927 onwards, which culminated in the establishment of the People's Republic of China in 1949 (Moore 1966). The Chinese Revolution differs from other major revolutions, such as the French or the Russian, as it was based largely on a peasant movement unlike the urban movements of Bolsheviks in Russia and the Jacobins in France (Skocpol 1979: 242). Peasant support and participation under the leadership of Communist cadres was also the key to revolutionary struggle in Vietnam (Migdal 1974, LeVan 1991).

The impact of the Chinese revolution on peasant livelihoods was considerable. A land reform, introduced at the end of the 1940s, resulted in a fairly even distribution of individual landholdings. From the middle of the 1950s onwards, private ownership of land was abolished. In the 'Great Leap Forward', agricultural production was collectivized and rural communes were institutionalized (Riskin 1995). This system endured until the end of the 1970s, when decollectivization was introduced and peasant smallholdings reappeared (see Bramall and Jones, Chapter 15 in this volume). The 'Great Leap' coincided with a famine of calamitous proportions (Riskin 1995: 437). After this set-back, agricultural production started to improve in the mid-1960s, accompanied by rising levels of health and nutrition. In terms of these development indicators, China has done much better than India which had a similar low level of economic and social development at the end of the 1940s (Drèze and Sen 1989: 204–25).

The peasant wars in China and Vietnam triggered off an interesting discussion among western social scientists as to why and under what conditions peasants rebel. After all, as E.R. Wolf (1971: 49) argues, 'it is not easy for a peasantry to engage in sustained rebellion'. Peasants often work alone on their own land in competition with each other, and their lives are controlled by the rhythm of the seasons as well as by local landlords or other powerful people. They form communities and belong to social networks which cross-cut class segmentation, and their lack of political participation has made them unaware of some forms of political action.[8]

Nevertheless, as the Chinese and Vietnamese examples show, peasants have been crucial to some of the great revolutions of the twentieth century. Wolf's own answer to this dilemma is that the land-owning middle peasantry or the poor-but-independent peasantry are willing and able to rebel. Other categories among the peasantry have too many vested interests or are too dependent upon landlords to become involved. Wolf's views have been contested. Paige (1975) concludes that it is the landless, rather than the smallholders, who become revolutionary because they are the ones who can develop a proletarian consciousness. From a very different perspective, Scott (1976) argues that it is not material conditions but perceptions which matter. When peasants perceive that the traditional moral order has been violated, they are likely to rebel. Skocpol's (1982) analysis of 'what makes peasants revolutionary' emphasizes the break-down of an old regime, the international and geo-political dimensions as well as socio-cultural factors.

In recent years, large-scale revolutionary peasant struggle in Asia has subsided, although various kinds of rural-based movements continue to exist: to mention only a few examples, the Naxalites' struggle against oppressive agrarian relations in India; the Philippine peasant movement's struggle for land reform; and the resistance of part of the Indian farmers' movement to the penetration of foreign capital in Indian agriculture. Irrespective of whether there have been major upheavals or not, the rural population in large areas of Asia can no longer be seen as marginal in political terms. In China, the Revolution placed peasants in the forefront of the political process (at least for a while); in some other countries universal franchise and competitive democracy, introduced after independence, have resulted in the 'empowerment of the countryside' (Varshney 1993: 177).

Rural non-farm activities

Although rural non-farm activities are not new, their importance has steadily increased in recent decades (Islam 1987, Alexander et al. 1991, Slater 1991; Koppel et al. 1994). The contribution of agriculture to GDP has decreased as increasing numbers of peasants have become involved in non-farm activities. According to Islam (1987), at the beginning of the 1980s around 50 per cent of the Malaysian rural labour force was engaged in non-farm activities; in Sri Lanka 46 per cent; in Java 38 per cent; in the Philippines 32 per cent; and in India 19 per cent. These activities account for a considerable proportion of rural incomes. Koppel and Hawkins (1994: 9) estimate that between 30 and 40 per cent of farm household incomes in Asia stem from off-farm sources. For landless labourers this percentage is even higher.

Non-farm income is of different kinds. Ellis (1998: 5) mentions five different categories: (i) non-farm rural wage employment; (ii) non-farm rural self-employment; (iii) property incomes (rents, etc.); (iv) urban remittances within national boundaries; and (v) international remittances from cross-border and overseas migration. It is important to point out that the distinction between local rural and urban wage employment has become increasingly blurred as several large export-oriented factory enterprises have moved into rural areas, leading to an 'expansion of the city into rural areas', or 'industrial villages' (Rigg 1997: 178, referring to D. Wolf 1992).

Both rich and poor are involved in rural non-farm activities but in a different way. Many poor people hope to obtain some additional income through non-farm activities. These are often of a part-time, seasonal and gendered nature, sometimes involving women more than men. This type of work is one of the ways in which poor rural households attempt to survive on a permanent basis or overcome seasonal problems and calamities (Agarwal 1990; Breman, Chapter 13 in this volume). While under-employment and lack of income are problems of the poor, under-utilization of capital is the concern of the rich. As Saith (1991: 471) writes, in many developing countries 'there are strong limits to the capacity of the agricultural sector to absorb additional heavy doses of investments at farm level within the existing infrastructural and technological development'. Investment in non-farm rural activities can offer much higher returns to capital and is therefore a frequently pursued strategy.

Kapadia's case study (Chapter 14 in this volume) suggests that the poor are drawn into non-agricultural work under very unfavourable conditions. They have little choice and scant opportunity to improve their structural position through non-agricultural work. Women are worse off than men. By contrast, the employers thrive and benefit from extremely exploitative labour relations. One of the interesting things about this case study of rural industry in south India is that it illustrates how 'old' processes of social differentiation (along class, caste or gender lines) persist in new forms in the non-farm economy.

In addition to differentiating the participation of poor and rich households in rural non-farm activities, some authors distinguish two types of non-farm sector. The first includes enterprises which operate on a more-or-less stable basis, have a certain degree of technical sophistication, use hired labour, and pursue surplus generation and growth. The second category is run solely with family labour, uses rather primitive technology, and responds more to the supply side of the market than to market demand (Harriss 1991: 430, drawing on Mukhopadhyay and Lim 1985). The first category is more prevalent in east Asia, while the second seems to predominate in south Asia.

It is difficult to draw general conclusions about the impact of non-farm activities on income levels and income inequalities. As Ellis (1998: 17) states, one might expect income diversification to lessen the risk of general income failure and to reduce both intra-year and inter-year income variability. Although these effects apply to both poor and rich alike, they are 'particularly important for poor families that have little or no margin to withstand unexpected shortfalls in the annual level of income required for survival' (ibid.: 17). With regard to income distribution, some scholars conclude that diversification increases inequality, while others claim that diversification equalizes income distribution (Ellis 1998: 18–19).

The relationship between non-farm activities and the wider economy can be explored in two ways. Firstly, there is the linkage between non-farm activities and agricultural growth. For example, Mellor (1976) and Hazell and Roell (1983) have argued that agricultural growth leads to higher incomes and, insofar as this accrues to richer households, this means increased demand for non-agricultural commodities and services. This, in turn, leads to more non-farm employment opportunities, more income for the poorest households and more demand for food. In short, there is a positive relationship between agricultural growth and non-farm activities. Ellis (1998: 20) refers to studies in Asia which 'concluded that $1 extra value added in agriculture created $0.80 additional non-farm income'.[9] This growth-linkage model is criticized by others. Hart (1998), for instance, referring to Malaysia, Taiwan and China, stresses that the way in which the agricultural surplus is consumed or invested depends crucially on the existing social relations of production and the exercise of power. With regard to India, Chandrashekar (1993) emphasizes that diversification into non-farm activities can also result from agricultural stagnation and under-employment as well as from growth.

A second linkage is that between non-farm activities and overall industrialization. With respect to European development/industrialization, non-farm artisan and cottage industries have sometimes been interpreted as 'proto-industrialization': a transitional stage between peasant agriculture and modern industry. During this stage, the necessary primitive accumulation of capital from the agricultural sector can be realized and subsequently invested in industrial activities (Saith 1992: 17). In many Asian countries, however, rural industrialization could not play this role. The process was blocked by trade with the more industrialized colonial powers, and the result was de-industrialization and under-development, rather than (proto) industrialization.

To conclude, throughout Asia non-farm activities are becoming increasingly critical for rural livelihoods. These activities, however, vary by region, are shaped by different context-dependent processes, and are likely to generate different effects on peasant livelihoods, social differentiation and the overall structure of the economy.

Conclusions

What has been the impact on the Asian peasantry of these three developments – new agricultural technology, the greater involvement of peasants in political processes and the increased importance of non-farm activities? Do they mean that Asian peasants have lost their peasant characteristics and turned into different kinds of rural-based producers? With respect to south-east Asia, Elson (1997) answers in the affirmative, claiming that superficially south-east Asia may appear rural, but that economic diversification and cultural changes are leading to the disappearance of the peasantry.

> [Rural people] still grow rice, but they grow it more quickly, more often, and according to the template of modern agricultural science, and they grow a great variety of other cultigens as well. They sell the great bulk of what they produce, they produce it to sell, and they purchase the great bulk of what they use. They live in villages, but those villages are administrative creations which look upward and outward, not inwardly oriented local communities. They work outside the village, in a great range of specific and enduring occupations, in rhythms dissociated from those of rural production and at extremes of distance that would both frustrate and bewilder their predecessors. They move about with a facility and alacrity their forebears might both fear and envy. Their culture is not just that of a village but of the nation and the world, relayed to them through schools, newspapers, magazines, CDs, and the electronic media (Elson 1997: xxii).

Elson represents what might be characterized as a strong de-peasantization argument, in which the peasantry remains in name only: their farming activities have become increasingly marginal, their welfare relative to urban dwellers has improved, their family cohesion weakened, and their physical isolation evaporated.

Other authors are more cautious. Whilst agreeing that important transformations are taking place, they observe that small and marginal peasants often actively struggle to retain land and, to a greater or lesser extent, remain peasants albeit less dependent on agriculture. This argument is made, for instance, by Harriss (1992) in relation to India, Rigg (1997) in relation to south-east Asia, and Bramall and Jones (Chapter 15 this volume) in relation to China.

Furthermore, experiences in Asia show that modernization has contradictory effects and does not necessarily mean that peasant identity and the peasant way of life become a thing of the past. The Indian farmers' movements, referred to earlier, cultivate an image of rural India as primarily populated by undifferentiated peasants, living a 'traditional' peasant life. A different example is given by Knight (Chapter 16 this volume) who discusses the emergence of new peasants in Japan. Often from an urban background, these new cultivators are more 'peasant-like' than their long-standing farming neighbours, cherishing traditional practices, organic farming and a peasant lifestyle. These new 'peasants' demonstrate the appeal which peasanthood continues to exert in a global industrial world. These developments, and the fact that peasants are reappearing in large numbers (especially in China after 1978) as well as disappearing, underline the need for caution. Certainly, there have been fundamental changes in rural livelihoods, but the effects are varied and contradictory. In large parts of Asia, 'the end of the peasantry' (as Elson claims for south-east Asia) is far from certain. Whether history will bear out this claim still remains to be seen.

Notes

1. In addition to the two co-editors of this book, I would like to thank Haroon Akram-Lodhi, Henry Bernstein and Peter Mollinga for their comments on an earlier draft of this chapter.
2. For a critique see Hindess and Hirst (1975).
3. For instance, there are extensive debates about involution and differentiation in Indonesia (Geertz 1963, Kahn 1985, White 1976), about modes of production in agriculture in India (Thorner 1982, Patnaik 1990), and about peasant resistance and differentiation in the Muda region of Malaysia (Scott 1984, Brass 1991, Hart 1991).
4. To give some examples, Lipton is an important author within the neo-populist stream. Lipton (1977) formulated the idea of 'urban bias': that most state governments tend to favour the urban population and the industrial sector at the expense of agriculture and the rural population. Byres (1979) provides a forceful Marxist critique. Another influential populist writer is James Scott (1984) who developed the concept of the 'weapons of the weak'. He argued that in general peasants do not organize revolutions but oppose their oppressors in more subtle ways, such as engaging in petty theft. See Brass (1991) for a critique from a Marxist perspective.
5. That is, in those areas where it was implemented. There are many regions in India where the new technologies have not been implemented and where non-capitalist forms of production such as landlordism and exploitative share-cropping relationships persist.
6. This is not to suggest that land reforms have failed all over Asia. In east Asia and China, land reforms have been implemented to a much greater degree than, for instance, in south Asia.
7. Evidently Indian farmers' movements are not homogeneous and different positions are taken on the Gandhian model of development and the liberalization of agricultural markets (Brass 1995a).
8. This argument, made by Wolf, clearly echoes that of Marx and Engels, who also grappled with the possibilities and difficulties of involving peasantries in a revolutionary movement (see Chapter 1 in this volume).
9. The studies referred to are Bell et al. (1982), Hazell and Ramasamy (1991).

References

Agarwal, B. (1985) 'Women and technological change in agriculture: the Asian and African experience', in I. Ahmed (ed.) *Technology and Rural Women: Conceptual and Empirical Issues*, Allen and Unwin, London, pp. 67–114.

Agarwal, B. (1990) 'Social security and the family: coping with seasonality and calamity', *Journal of Peasant Studies*, 17(3): 341–412.

Akram-Lodhi, A.H. (1998) 'The agrarian question, past and present', *Journal of Peasant Studies*, 25(4): 134–49.

Alavi, H. (1989) 'Formation of the social structure of south Asia under the impact of colonialism', in H. Alavi and J. Harriss (eds) *Sociology of 'Developing Societies' – South Asia*, MacMillan, London, pp. 5–19.

Alexander, P., Boomgaard, P. and White, B. (eds) (1991) *In the Shadow of Agriculture: Non-farm Activities in the Javanese Economy, Past and Present*, Royal Tropical Institute, Amsterdam.

Bell, C., Hazell, P. and Slade, R. (1982) *Project Evaluation in Regional Perspective*, Johns Hopkins, Baltimore.

Bernstein, H. (1996) 'Agrarian questions then and now', in H. Bernstein and T. Brass (ed.) *Agrarian Questions: Essays in Appreciation of T. J. Byres*, Frank Cass, London, pp. 22–59.

Brass, T. (1991) 'Moral economists, subalterns, new social movements, and the (re-)emergence of a (post-)modernised (middle) Peasant', *Journal of Peasant Studies*, 18(2): 173–205.

Brass, T. (1995a) 'The politics of gender, nature and nation in the discourse of the new farmers' movements', in T. Brass (ed.) *New Farmers' Movements in India*, Frank Cass, Essex and Portland, pp. 27–71.

Brass, T. (1995b) 'Introduction: The new farmers' movements in India', in T. Brass (ed.) *New Farmers' Movements in India*, Frank Cass, Essex and Portland, pp. 3–26.

Bray, F. (1983) 'Patterns of evolution in rice-growing societies', *Journal of Peasant Studies*, 11(1): 3–33.

Bray, F. (1984), Biology and biological technology: agriculture, in J. Needham (ed.) *Science and Civilisation in China*, Vol. 6, Part II, Cambridge University Press, Cambridge.

Breman, J. (1988) *The Shattered Image: Construction and Deconstruction of the Village in Colonial Asia*, Comparative Asian Studies 2, Foris Publications, Dordrecht.

Byres, T.J. (1979) 'Of neo-populist pipe dreams: Daedalus in the Third World and the myth of urban bias', *Journal of Peasant Studies*, 6(2): 210–44.

Byres, T.J. (1981) 'The new technology, class formation and class action in the Indian countryside', *Journal of Peasant Studies*, 8(3): 405–54.

Byres, T.J. (1985) 'Modes of production and non-European pre-colonial societies: the nature and significance of the debate', *Journal of Peasant Studies*, 12(2–3): 1–19.

Byres, T.J. (1991) 'The agrarian question and differing forms of capitalist agrarian transition: an essay with reference to Asia', in J. Breman and S. Mundle (eds) *Rural Transformation in Asia*, Oxford University Press, New Delhi, pp. 3–76.

Chandrashekar, C.P. (1993) 'Agrarian change and occupational diversification: non-agricultural employment and rural development in West Bengal', *Journal of Peasant Studies*, 20(2): 205–70.

Drèze, J. and Sen, A. (1989) *Hunger and Public Action*, Clarendon Press, Oxford.

Ellis, F. (1998) 'Household strategies and rural livelihood diversification', *Journal of Development Studies*, 35(1): 1–38.
Elson, R.E. (1997) *The End of the Peasantry in Southeast Asia, A Social and Economic History of Peasant Livelihood, 1800–1990s*, Macmillan and St Martin's Press, London and New York.
Frank, A.G. (1998) *Asian Age: Reorient Historiography and Social Theory*, The Wertheim Lecture, Centre for Asian Studies, Amsterdam.
Geertz, C. (1963) *Agricultural Involution, The Process of Ecological Change in Indonesia*, University of California Press, Berkeley.
Harriss, J. (1991) 'Agriculture/non-agriculture linkages and the diversification of rural economic activity: A south Indian case study', in J. Breman and S. Mundle (eds) *Rural Transformation in Asia*, Oxford University Press, Delhi, pp. 429–547.
Harriss, J. (1992) 'Does the "depressor" still work? Agrarian structure and development in India: a review of evidence and argument', *Journal of Peasant Studies*, 19(2): 189–227.
Hart, G. (1991) 'Engendering everyday resistance: gender, patronage and production in rural Malaysia', *Journal of Peasant Studies*, 19(1): 93–121.
Hart, G. (1998) 'Regional linkages in the era of liberalization: a critique of the new agrarian optimism', *Development and Change*, 29(1): 27–54.
Hazell, P. and Ramasamy, C. (1991) *The Green Revolution Reconsidered: The Impact of High-Yielding Rice Varieties in South India*, Johns Hopkins, Baltimore.
Hazell, P. and Roell, A. (1983) *Rural Growth Linkages: Household Expenditure Patterns in Malaysia and Nigeria*, International Food Policy Research Institute, Washington, D.C.
Hindess, B. and Hirst, P. (1975) *Pre-capitalist Modes of Production*, Routledge and Kegan Paul, London.
Hüsken, F. and White, B. (1989) 'Java: social differentiation, food production, and agrarian control', in G. Hart, A. Turton and B. White (eds) *Agrarian Transformations: Local Processes and the State in Southeast Asia*, University of California Press, Berkeley, pp. 235–65.
Islam, R. (ed.) (1987) *Rural Industrialisation and Employment in Asia*, International Labour Organisation, Asian Employment Programme, New Delhi.
Jha, P. (1997) *Agricultural Labour in India*, Vikas Publishing House, Delhi.
Kahn, J.S. (1985) 'Indonesia after the demise of involution: critique of a debate', *Critique of Anthropology*, 5(1): 69–96.
Koppel, B. and Hawkins, J. (1994) 'Rural transformation and the future of work in Rural Asia', in Koppel, Hawkins and James, loc. cit.
Koppel, B., Hawkins, J. and James, W. (ed.) (1994) *Development or Deterioration? Work in Rural Asia*, Lynne Rienner Publishers, London and Colorado.
LeVan, H.J. (1991) 'Vietnam: revolution of postcolonial consolidation', in J.A. Goldstone, T. Robert Gurr and F. Moshiri (ed.) *Revolutions of the Late Twentieth Century*, Westview Press, Boulder, pp. 52–87.
Lipton, M. (1977) *Why Poor People Stay Poor, A Study of Urban Bias in World Development*, Temple-Smith, London.

Marx, K. (1867) *Capital*, Vol. 1, Progress Publishers, Moscow (1954 edition).
Mellor, J. (1976) *The New Economics of Growth*, Cornell University Press, Ithaca, New York.
Migdal, J.S. (1974) *Peasants, Politics and Revolution: Pressures towards Political and Social Change in the Third World*, Princeton University Press, Princeton, New Jersey.
Moore Jr, B.(1966) *Social Origins of Dictatorship and Democracy*, Penguin, Harmondsworth.
Mukhopadhyay, S. and Lim, C.P. (1985) *Development and Diversification of Rural Industries in Asia*, Asian and Pacific Development Centre, Kuala Lumpur.
Needham, J. (1954) *Science and Civilisation in China*, Cambridge University Press, Cambridge.
Omvedt, G. (1983) 'Capitalist agriculture and rural classes in India', *Bulletin of Concerned Asian Scholars*, 20(2): 14–23.
Paige, J.M. (1975) *Agrarian Revolution, Social Movements and Export Agriculture in the Underdeveloped World*, Free Press, New York.
Patnaik, U. (ed.) (1990) *Agrarian Relations and Accumulation, The Mode of Production Debate in India*, Oxford University Press, Delhi.
Pearson, R. (1992) 'Gender matters in development', in T. Allen and A. Thomas (eds) *Poverty and Development in the 1990s*, Oxford University Press in association with the Open University, Oxford, pp. 291–312.
Rigg, J. (1997) *Southeast Asia: The Human Landscape of Modernization and Development*, Routledge, London and New York.
Riskin, C. (1995) 'Feeding China: the experiences since 1949', in J. Drèze, A. Sen and A. Hussain (ed.) *The Political Economy of Hunger, Selected Essays*, Clarendon Press, Oxford, pp. 401–44.
Saith, A. (1991) 'Asian rural industrialization: context, features, strategies', in J. Breman and S. Mundle (eds) *Rural Transformation in Asia*, Oxford University Press, Delhi, pp. 458–89.
Saith, A. (1992) *The Rural Non-farm Economy: Processes and Policies*, International Labour Office, Geneva.
Scott, J.C. (1976) *The Moral Economy of the Peasant: Rebellion and Subsistence in Southeast Asia*, Yale University Press, New Haven.
Scott, J.C. (1984) *Everyday Forms of Peasant Resistance*, Yale University Press, New Haven.
Skocpol, T. (1979) *States and Social Revolutions*, Cambridge University Press, Cambridge.
Skocpol, T. (1982) 'What makes peasants revolutionary?', *Comparative Politics*, 14(3): 351–75.
Slater, R. (1991) *From Farm to Firm: Rural Diversification in the Asian Countryside*, Avebury, Aldershot.
Thorner, A. (1982) 'Semi-feudal or capitalism? Contemporary debate on classes and modes of production in India', *Economic and Political Weekly*, 17, Nos. 49–51: 1961–8, 1993–9, 2061–6.

Varshney, A. (1993) 'Self-limited empowerment: democracy, economic development and rural India', *Journal of Development Studies*, 29(4): 177–215.

White, B. (1976) 'Population, involution and employment in rural Java', *Development and Change*, 7(3): 267–90.

White, B. (1989) 'Problems in the empirical analysis of agrarian differentiation', in G. Hart, A. Turton and B. White (eds) *Agrarian Transformations: Local Processes and the State in Southeast Asia*, University of California Press, Berkeley, pp. 15–29.

Wittfogel, K.A. (1957) *Oriental Despotism*, Yale University Press, New Haven (1981 edition).

Wolf, D. (1992) *Factory Daughters: Gender, Household Dynamics and Rural Industrialization in Java*, University of California Press, Berkeley.

Wolf, E.R. (1971) 'Peasant rebellion and revolution', in N. Miller and R. Aya (eds) *National Liberation: Revolution in the Third World*, Free Press, New York, pp. 48–67.

Wolf, E.R. (1982) *Europe and the People without History*, University of California Press, Berkeley.

World Bank (1997) *World Development Report 1997*, Oxford University Press, Oxford.

13. Labour and Landlessness in South and South-East Asia

JAN BREMAN

Introduction

A central theme of Kautsky's classic analysis of agrarian dynamics in Europe at the end of the nineteenth century is the impact of the capitalist mode of production on rural class formation.[1] According to Kautsky, capitalist penetration differentiated what had been a more or less homogeneous peasantry in the *ancien régime* and gave rise to a class of landless labourers. In colonial Asia the emergence of a landless class of agricultural labour has likewise conventionally been explained with reference to the penetration of capitalism into the rural economy. This chapter critically evaluates these interpretations of European and Asian rural development, and argues that landlessness existed in Asia long before agriculture became organized along capitalist lines.

A second argument developed in this chapter relates to the different trajectories of capitalism in Europe and Asia. In Europe a large part of the rural proletariat became both industrialized and urbanized in the course of the eighteenth to twentieth centuries, whilst in Asia the rural underclass remained dependent on agricultural work and income. It is only during the second half of the twentieth century, following political independence, that the rural economies of Asia became more diversified.

This chapter begins by discussing Kautsky's views on the development of rural capitalism in Europe in more detail. The focus then shifts to Asia, and a discussion of the extent to which landlessness already existed in precolonial and colonial south and south-east Asia. I argue that a distinct underclass existed in much of rural Asia, even before the advent of colonialism, just as had been the case in Europe before capitalism started to penetrate rural life. This underclass is, however, difficult to define precisely because it varied according to time and place and because the boundary between land-poor and landless was often blurred. I then go on to describe the development of the rural underclass in the decades following political independence. In particular the diversification of the rural economy, increased labour mobility and the casualization of employment will be examined. The paper concludes by highlighting the different impacts of capitalist development in Asia and Europe, particularly on the most marginal segments of the peasantry.

The problem addressed in this chapter arises out of two considerations. The first refers to the interest shown by Marx and his followers in the agrarian situation of Asia in particular. As Banaji (1976: fn. 8) notes,

European marxists of Engels's and Kautsky's generation showed little awareness of colonial questions, and their reflections on the 'Asiatic mode of production' were speculative and based on weak empirical evidence. My purpose here is to draw renewed attention to this weakness. Furthermore, having engaged in historical and anthropological research in rural Asia, notably India and Indonesia, for the past 40 years, I am struck by the need to take into account the highly variable nature of the agrarian question, a subject which also formed the focus of Kautsky's analysis.

The Agrarian Question in Europe

According to Kautsky, a protracted process of economic differentiation ended the once homogeneous composition of the European peasantry. In medieval Europe, the peasant family

> composed an economic society that was entirely, or almost entirely, self-sufficient, a society that produced not only its own food, but built its own home, furniture and utensils, forged its own implements of production, etc. Naturally the peasant went to market, but he sold only his surplus produce, and bought only trivialities, except for iron, which he used only sparsely (Kautsky in Banaji 1976: 3).

Uniformity at the base of rural society was accompanied by the subordination of the agricultural workforce to feudal landowners. This implies that, in Kautsky's scheme of development, pre-capitalist society was stratified into two groups: the élite and the masses. The landlord–peasant relationship was the organizing principle of the feudal mode of production and a separate class of landless labourers did not exist.

According to Kautsky, the penetration of capitalism transformed this self-reproducing rural economy, which combined agricultural and artisanal production, in two ways. Firstly, the growth of urban industry and trade deprived the peasantry of its composite resource base. Loss of all-round self-sufficiency forced peasants to become exclusively agrarian producers and to sell their crops for cash to meet their non-agrarian needs. The division of labour between town and countryside gradually subjected the peasant masses to market mechanisms over which they had no control. Secondly, exploitation by mercantile capital meant indebtedness and later alienation from the means of production, leading to progressive economic differentiation.

The emerging process of commoditization in agriculture resulted in a large part of the rural population becoming almost or totally landless. Kautsky relates this slipping down the agrarian ladder to imbalances in the annual cycle of peasant labour. The decline of home industry made it necessary to reduce the household size. Peasant families began to expel some household members, either temporarily or indefinitely. These people had to find alternative sources of employment. The introduction of a new, machine-based technology had a similar impact. At the same time, the remaining workforce was insufficient to meet agricultural needs at peak times of the agricultural calendar. This shortfall was met by hiring seasonal workers, mostly from peasant families seeking supplementary incomes for the surplus labour of adult members or children.

In his subsequent analysis, however, Kautsky rejected the orthodox Marxist thesis of concentration and accumulation, and emphasized the preservation of petty commodity production in agriculture. That preservation took the form of the subordination of the peasant (pseudo-)proletariat to the urban–industrial economy. Only through the sale of labour power, both within and outside agriculture, could the final eclipse of the agrarian family enterprise be prevented.

According to Kautsky, the resulting social formation illustrated the co-existence of agrarian capitalism with pre-capitalist production relations. Petty cultivators, who were unable to consolidate their position as marginal peasants, notwithstanding the sale of their labour power, abandoned the countryside and became fully proletarianized industrial workers. This explains why the landless underclass, which was assumed to be almost non-existent under Europe's *ancien régime*, showed only a moderate increase as capitalism advanced in agriculture.

As pointed out by Banaji (1990: 289), Kautsky's view of the historical evolution of capitalism has no conception of an internal development of agriculture prior to the growth of modern industry in the nineteenth century. By ignoring the history of agriculture (in contrast to Weber), Kautsky greatly underestimated the extent of market relationships in the pre-industrial world. Banaji rejects the notion of a sudden development of commodity production in the countryside and draws attention to widespread practices of waged labour in Europe much earlier than Kautsky acknowledges.

Almost 100 years after Kautsky wrote *Die Agrarfrage*, similar interpretations can still be found. For example, Hobsbawm and Rudé (1973) imply that rural landlessness was alien to the peasant landscape in earlier times[2], and de Vries and van der Woude (1995) adopt a similar position with respect to Dutch agriculture. As long as new land was available for cultivation, agricultural work remained embedded in the peasant household. Proletarianization took place only when the peasant resource base was exhausted and the emergence of larger holdings stimulated demand for hired labour. The transition to a situation of closed resources came about only at the beginning of the nineteenth century (de Vries & van der Woude 1995: 642–3).

The fact that Kautsky's views on the late origin of a landless class of agrarian labour continue to find strong support among agrarian historians of Europe may have something to do with the perspective adopted. In an authoritative work on Europe's agrarian history, Slicher van Bath (1960) argues that studies which take land ownership as their point of departure tend to focus on the upper class and neglect the lower classes who are just as significant for understanding rural society. Drawing on research in the eastern Netherlands, Slicher van Bath concludes that wage labourers and marginalized peasants increased in number during the 1800s, but that signs of a pauperized residual class could already be found at the beginning of the century (ibid.: 340–56). More attention to labour migration could form a significant starting point for a reappraisal of the debate on the agrarian question in Europe.[3]

Landlessness in Colonial Asia

Official interpretations of landlessness in colonial Asia tend to emphasize the closed character of the pre-colonial economic and political system. Alongside the increasing exposure of the Asian population to colonial rule during the nineteenth century came a growing need for the colonial state to gather knowledge on the nature, shape and management of the Asian agricultural economy. In the vast terrain, mapped principally by government officials, the village community was deemed to be the cornerstone of the social order (Breman 1988: 1–9). In descriptions of that institution as a microcosmos, emphasis was placed on the closed character of the local economy, its considerable degree of political autonomy and organization as a collectivity, and on the elementary division of labour between agriculture and industrial manufacture.

Not only were these characteristics seen to be the cause of economic and social stagnation, they were also regarded as distinguishing Asian pre-colonial society from European pre-capitalist society. While Kautsky and his contemporaries perceived the landlord–peasant configuration in Europe as a linkage transcending the locality, in Asia no such configuration seemed to exist. Indeed, the concept of the Asiatic mode of production was developed by Marxist and non-Marxist theories to emphasize the differences between Asian and European pre-capitalist rural life.

According to conventional wisdom, there was no evidence of a distinct landless class of subaltern peasants, although individual sources sporadically refer to landlessness or vagrancy. Van Vollenhoven, architect of customary law in the Netherlands Indies, divided the rural population into three categories: descendants of the village founders who shared fully in communal land ownership; cultivators who were given rights of usage but had no hereditary claim on the land; and the landless who were attached as farm servants to the households of more substantial peasants. Van Vollenhoven added that the boundary between these three groups was fluid, movement between them being dependent on age and status in the local community (Breman 1988: 5).

The creation of a class of landless labourers in British India was held to be the outcome of commercialization and monetarization which, in the late colonial period, led to a radical shift in the social relations of agrarian production. As expressed by Patel in the early 1950s:

> In pre-nineteenth century India there were domestic and menial servants; but their numbers were small, and they did not form a definite group . . . The large class of agricultural labourers represents a new form of social relationship that emerged during the late nineteenth and early twentieth centuries in India (Patel, 1952: 32).

More recent research, however, has led to a fundamental reappraisal of the course of rural transformation in Asia during colonial rule. In a pioneering study of early colonial society in south India, Kumar (1965) refers to a sizeable landless segment, which she estimated to constitute 10–15 per cent of the total population. Her findings are supported by my own historical research in west India which found that the forefathers of the present agrarian underclass were employed as attached labourers by landowning households at the beginning of the last century (Breman 1974). This earlier underclass consisted of tribals, who until the arrival of caste Hindus had made their living as hunters and gatherers or, more often, as shifting cultivators. Their gradual insertion into the larger Hindu society was accompanied by a loss of control over the territory where they lived and over their means of subsistence. The confinement of what were originally outsiders to the bottom rung of a more complex agrarian hierarchy was due to political domination – the exercise of coercive force – rather than economic regression.

Elsewhere in India tribals were incorporated – and subordinated – into the expanding caste society (Prakash 1990). A determining structural feature of Hindu civilization forbade members of high castes to cultivate the land or, more generally, to engage in hard physical labour. By assigning these unclean activities to a clientele especially maintained for the purpose, the rural élite reinforced their claim to a high position in the ritual order. I regard this culture-specific interpretation as a variation of the explanation of the bonding of labour in terms of political economy.

In an ethnological study published in 1910, Nieboer argued that slavery occurs in situations of open resources (Nieboer 1910). This thesis was later extended by Kloosterboer (1954) to refer to forced labour in general. Whenever land is, in principle, freely accessible to all, people will only make their labour power available to others if extra-economic force is brought to bear. However, when land is a scarce commodity – in other words, when resources become closed – force becomes unnecessary. In such circumstances, landlessness is due not to the imposition of power but to the effect of economic differentiation combined with rising population pressure, ultimately resulting in the creation of a voluntary labour supply. This perspective explains both the practice of bonded labour in the countryside of early colonial British India, and its subsequent erosion (Breman 1974, 1983).

Colonial literature in British India did not give proper consideration to the existence of an unfree, landless class. Only very occasionally did its magnitude come to light, as for example during the debate on the abolition of slavery, when the British Parliament demanded an official report from its colonies on the phenomenon of agrarian bondage. Such stocktaking did not lead to their shackles being removed, however. The priority given to the levying of taxes prevented any more radical government interference in the social organization of peasant production. Consequently, the rural landless remained largely invisible to colonial authorities and commentators.

Accounts of the Javanese countryside, dating from the beginning of the nineteenth century or earlier, also reported a sizeable and internally differentiated underclass that was denied access to land. These subordinate workers were employed as sharecroppers or as farm servants by an upper segment of the peasantry. I have emphasized elsewhere the bonded status of these landless clients who, individually or together with their families, belonged to the household of their land-owning patron. Rather than adhering to the conventional wisdom of a homogeneous village community, I consider these corporate and internally differentiated peasant households as having been the primary social formation in Asia's pre-capitalist regime (Breman 1980, 1983).

Others have also argued that there was social differentiation in colonial Java. Boomgaard (1989) concludes from an analysis of available sources that the landless section of Java's rural population was very considerable in the early nineteenth century, though with substantial local variations (ibid.: p. 60). On the basis of detailed archival research, Elson (1994) also reports that landlessness was very common. He connects this phenomenon with the arrival of outsiders who had fled an uncertain existence elsewhere.

> Those newly arrived might have no option but to enter dependency relationships with more established and prosperous peasants which precluded them from holding land; in the absence of alternative means of sustenance, they might find themselves in a permanently servile condition which allowed their patrons correspondingly to enhance their wealth and power through the shrewd deployment of their clients' labour power (Elson 1994: 20).

The introduction of a forced cultivation system on Java in 1830 initiated an agrarian policy which aimed to accelerate Java's integration into the world economy. People were forced to set aside a considerable part of their arable land and their labour power for the cultivation of export crops such as coffee, indigo and sugar. In order to broaden the taxable basis, the colonial government granted members of the landless underclass access to the expanding agricultural resource base. However, this attempt to communalize peasant ownership and production was only moderately successful, as the established land-owning class resisted the redistribution of agrarian property. Only by holding fast to their exclusive rights could heads of the corporate peasant households meet the exorbitant levies imposed on the rural economy by the colonial government. In short, land remained concentrated in the hands of the rural élite.

A distinct yet difficult-to-define underclass

The image of a landless class tied in bondage to peasant households is difficult to reconcile with early colonial reports of a proletariat *avant-la-lettre*, which led an extremely mobile existence in the countryside of Java. Early colonial writings frequently describe such people as 'wanderers and vagrants'. Boomgaard (1989) distinguishes between young bachelors who worked temporarily as farm labourers for a local land-owning household, and a class of free and unattached workers who roamed over a larger area in search of a wage. The first form of employment was temporary, being an apprenticeship of a few years which young men served before being admitted to the established local peasantry, with all its rights and duties. It is the second group which Boomgaard considers as belonging to a subaltern class, permanently obliged to depend on casual work, both in and outside agriculture, for its living (Boomgaard 1989: 65–6). In a more cautious assessment of the divergent and partly contradictory source material, Elson suggests that the dividing lines between the various rural classes were quite fluid and that landlessness did not crystallize into a distinct lifestyle which was reproduced across the generations (Elson 1994: 22).

Although Boomgaard and Elson agree that landlessness did exist in colonial Java, they do not regard those peasants who had no direct command over agrarian resources as forming a distinct, let alone proletarianized, social class. One thing that can surely be concluded is that in both south and south-east Asia 'the history of the bottom layers of the (. . .) countryside is obscure, with plenty of room, indeed a crying need, for further research (Moore 1966: 369).

My own view is that peasant work and life under the *ancien régime* cannot be understood within the framework of a static, homogeneous and closed order – the reputed Asiatic mode of production – but needs to be interpreted in a more open and differentiated frontier context. In this shifting landscape, I do not assume that mobility and bondage at the bottom of the agrarian order were mutually exclusive. On the contrary, I argue that their co-existence determined the dynamics of the peasant economy (Breman 1988: 28–37).[4]

At the beginning of the nineteenth century the size of the landless segment in the Asian countryside varied from a fifth to a third of the total rural population. It is unclear whether late colonial policy caused a greater concentration at the foot of the agrarian hierarchy or not. Certainly, increased population density during the late nineteenth and the first half of the twentieth century had a direct influence on the diminishing size of the peasant enterprise. It is more difficult to establish whether a sharp fall down the agrarian ladder took place, in which landowners were downgraded first to tenants and then to landless labourers.

During the last 150 years of colonial rule, sources of employment in the rural economy probably increased very little or even decreased. This is arguably the case in parts of south Asia where, according to the deindustrialization thesis, the loss of artisanal production organized as home industry increased the pressure on employment in the agricultural sector. Whatever the case, there was little sign of any advance of industrial capitalism, such as had absorbed the surplus peasant proletariat in the European rural economy. Insofar as new industries were established in the colonial metropolises of Asia, rural labour was admitted only on a partial and conditional basis: non-working family members had to remain behind in the village and the labourers themselves were only tolerated in the urban milieu for the duration of their working lives. This also applied to the army of landless people who were recruited as coolies for the mines and on plantations in the Asian hinterlands, or were shipped overseas. When the contract period expired most were sent back home or to a place which passed as such (Breman 1990).

The congestion at the bottom of the agrarian economy cannot have escaped the notice of the colonial authorities although they tended to emphasize land fragmentation rather than land alienation. Nevertheless, they made little effort in the direction of land reform in order to free peasant production from its perpetual stagnation. An exception to this non-interventionist policy was the introduction of a floor, a minimum rather than a maximum size of agrarian property, in a region of Java just before the 1920s. Accordingly, land was confiscated from marginal peasants and added to the acreage of their better endowed co-villagers. The stated objective of this experiment was to strengthen the position of the established peasantry. Transition from the marginal to the landless class was regarded as enabling those liberated from the means of production to become more flexible on the labour market. Given that their tiny plots could not ensure subsistence, the measure was said to have been taken for their own good (Breman 1983: 39–71).[5]

This short overview of conditions in late colonial Asia leads me to conclude that it was the combination of economic and demographic changes which resulted in progressive land impoverishment. Land ownership at the village level continued to be highly concentrated, and a growing portion of the agrarian population were denied access, with the result that the landless class expanded. However, adequate and reliable statistics to support this quantitative shift in the class structure of the peasantry are lacking. In addition, it is difficult in practice to distinguish between the class of small landowners and that of agricultural workers. As Thorner comments with reference to small producers in his well known analysis of the agrarian structure in India in the mid-twentieth century:

> Families in this class may indeed have tenancy rights in the soil, or even property rights, but the holdings are so small that the income from cultivating them or from renting them out comes to less than the earnings from field work (Thorner 1976: 11).

Thus, in order to understand the process of (pseudo)-proletarianization in rural Asia, it is imperative not to make a sharp divide between land-poor and landless. It then becomes evident that, in the densely populated rural regions at the end of colonial rule, these two groups combined comprised between a half to about two-thirds of the peasantry.

The Landless in the Transition to Capitalism

Quantitative changes notwithstanding, at the end of colonial rule there was also a qualitative shift in the social relations of production. Life as an agricultural worker became moulded along new lines. This transformation continued in the post-colonial era as capitalism increasingly influenced the rural economy (Byres 1991).

The impact of the green revolution

The much-discussed green revolution of the 1960s which introduced a modernization package consisting of high-yielding seed varieties, fertilizers and pesticides, credit, new technology, agricultural extension services, and better water management, illustrates the growing trend towards capitalism in agriculture. In contrast to east Asia, the transformation in south and south-east Asia was not preceded by a drastic redistribution of agrarian resources. Large, landed estates, where they still existed, were abolished and tenancy relationships reformed with a view to encouraging a capitalist orientation amongst a well established class of owner–cultivators in India, usually drawn from locally dominant castes. This class in particular was charged with the task of increasing production and productivity (Wertheim 1964: 259–77, Myrdal 1968: Vol. II 1366–84; Byres 1981: 423–27, 1991: 63–4).

The shift in the rural balance of power which accompanied the green revolution development strategy caused the vulnerable position of sharecroppers and agricultural labourers to deteriorate further. Even a very moderate land reform was not on the agenda. Myrdal pleaded in vain for the landless to be given

> a small plot of land – and with it a dignity and a fresh outlook on life as well as a minor independent source of income . . . Even in the most densely populated countries of the region it would be possible to give the landless at least small plots on acreages that are now uncultivated waste. In some cases land is available for the landless in the vicinity of existing holdings. The existing pattern of cultivated holdings need not be seriously disturbed – in some places it would not need to be disturbed at all (Myrdal 1968: Vol. II 1382).

Resources still held in common were rapidly privatized and usually fell into the hands of the landowning élite. In Indonesia the military coup d'état of 1965 put an end to efforts initiated from below to introduce an agrarian law which would improve the position of marginal and landless peasants, who formed the majority of people living in Java's countryside (Breman 1983: 122–6).

My conclusion is that the capitalist-oriented agricultural development policy pursued in the post-colonial era has further exacerbated the vulnerability of life at the bottom of the rural economy. Although initial reports of a mass expulsion of labour following the introduction of rationalized and mechanized cultivation methods proved unfounded, the expansion of agricultural employment as a net effect of the green revolution has not kept pace with the growth of the Asian rural population.

The World Labour Report, published annually by the International Labour Organization, shows that self-employment in agriculture is gradually but steadily giving way to waged labour. It would be premature to explain this trend purely as a sign of progressive proletarianization. The replacement of own or family labour by hired workers is also due to the emergence of a different lifestyle, which leads even middle-sized landowners to prefer to hire and supervise outside labour. This trend has been a contributing factor to the creation of a rural labour market in the capitalist sense.

The continuing abject poverty of the great majority of the landless is due to the fact that the supply of labour far exceeds demand. This excess labour supply helps to explain why earlier forms of labour bondage have considerably weakened. After independence, national policy-makers anticipated that the surplus rural proletariat would be absorbed as industrial workers in the urban economy. In these Asian countries, however, the expansion of large-scale industry has been far slower and, above all, far less labour intensive than envisaged. Opportunities to escape to the cities are therefore limited, while emigration overseas is an equally unrealistic option. For the Asian rural surplus there is no New World in which to settle, as there had been for the proletarianized mass from Europe a century earlier.

In sum, Asia's rural proletariat after the colonial era was far greater in size than Europe's rural proletariat had been after capitalism had transformed the *ancien régime*. Furthermore, the sluggish pace of the industrialization process in Asia since the mid-twentieth century, together with a population growth rate which has only recently started to decline, drastically intensified the pressure on those at the bottom of the rural economy.

Diversification, mobility and casualization

It would be incorrect, however, to infer from the above that the nature of the landless existence has changed little since the end of colonial rule. After political independence, capitalist dynamics came to dominate the countryside, causing drastic changes in the social relations of production.

We can distinguish three interconnected processes. The first refers to the diversification of the rural economy. With the growing demand for labour from agro-industry, infrastructural works, trade, transport and the service sector, agriculture has lost significance in the overall rural employment pattern. Such diversification has not occurred everywhere to the same degree, but the trend is unmistakable. In some cases, off-farm employment is an expression of the growing under-utilization of labour in agriculture. In other instances, however, it reflects real growth in peasant production which has an impact on other branches of the economy. In the villages of west India where I did my field work, and in the state of Gujarat more generally, working in the fields is no longer the predominant source of employment and income for the landless. Rural diversification means that work at the bottom of the rural economy is characterized by occupational multiplicity. From having been an agrarian proletariat, this class has remoulded itself into a more general rural proletariat.

A second and related process which has transformed the situation of the landless relates to the increased mobility of labour. Non-agricultural work usually involves work outside the village of residence, and sometimes migration to towns and cities. Although the drift towards urban centres has increased, the majority of migrants have little chance of settling there, being concentrated in the informal sector, which is the greatest reservoir of employment in the urban economy. The informal sector is not a stepping stone towards a better and settled urban life, but a temporary abode for labour which can be pushed back to its place of origin when no longer needed (Breman 1994). This continual movement to and fro between urban and rural sectors indicates the linkage, rather than the rupture, of rural and urban labour markets.

This interconnectedness of urban and rural labour markets is not caused by the unwillingness of the workforce to commit itself to an industrial way of life, as Thompson seems to suggest was the case in Europe (Thompson 1991: 398). Rather, it is the lack of economic and physical space which prevents the army of newcomers from establishing themselves as permanent urbanites.

Labour migrates not only between village and town but also within the rural milieu. In previous publications on intra-rural labour mobility, I stress the connection between massive long-distance seasonal migration and the emergence of a more pronounced capitalist mode of production (Breman 1985). In relation to Java, the transport revolution enabled the rapid and cheap movement of labour so that members of households with little if any land can circulate in a greatly enlarged labour market (Breman 1995: 21–2).

Diversification of the rural economy and increased labour mobility are in turn connected to a third process which has significantly changed the experience of the landless, namely the casualization of employment. The peasant economy shows a tendency for permanent farm-hands to be replaced by daily wage earners and for indefinite employment to be replaced by short-term labour contracts based on the hire-and-fire principle. This form of employment facilitates the hire of outsiders, who are usually cheaper and more docile than local workers. Labour is now paid principally or exclusively in cash rather than in kind, and remunerated on a piecework or contracting out basis rather than on a time-rate basis as before.

This casualization of labour does not mean that production relations have been cleansed of all pre-capitalist elements. Labour's prerogative to hire itself out at any moment and for the highest possible price is subject to many restrictions. Although labour has become abundant, the transition to a situation of closed resources (i.e. land scarcity) has not stopped employers from resorting to new forms of labour bondage. For example, acceptance of a cash advance frequently entails a contract which immobilizes labour power. Employers also defer wage payment as a means of ensuring that the required quantity of labour continues to be supplied.

Nevertheless, the lack of freedom entailed in such bonding mechanisms differs essentially from the coercive regime to which agricultural labour was subjected in the past. I employ the term 'neo-bondage' to refer to the practices adopted by present-day employers to ensure a sufficient and cheap supply of labour. As argued by Miles (1987) among others, these bonding mechanisms which restrict the liberty of the worker do not necessarily diminish the capitalist character of the production process.[6] (See also Kapadia, Chapter 14 in this volume).

Conclusions

Kautksy's view that 'capitalism concentrates the working masses in the towns . . . favouring their organisation, their intellectual development, their capacity to struggle as a class' (Banaji 1976: 47) is not confirmed by the development route followed by various Asian societies. In both India and Indonesia the rural proletariat is still undoubtedly the largest working class. Furthermore, those who have moved to the urban economy lead an extremely fragile existence in the informal sector. Their capacity to take action as a class is seriously hampered by their lack of organization and their low level of literacy. Finally, capitalism's penetration into the countryside has caused a qualitative change in social relations both in and outside agriculture, in ways which show affinity with urban dynamics. The need to be available for employment in diverse branches of industry rather than to specialize, the pressure towards spatial mobility which often takes on the character of circulation, and the casual mode of employment with its corresponding forms of wage payment, are all mechanisms which frustrate collective bargaining and the formation of a common front from this composite underclass. The articulation of class interests finds a weak basis in this milieu. That is why, with rare exceptions, trade unions are absent in the informal sector. Pressure at the bottom of the economy is so great that there is fierce rivalry for any work that becomes available. In a situation of surplus labour, recruitment on the basis of primordial loyalties preserves lines of demarcation other than that of class.

The capitalist development which large regions of Asia are currently experiencing differs drastically from that which took place in western societies. In Europe, capitalist development went together with an enormous expansion of the formal labour market, government intervention to protect labour, trade unionism and a general increase in the standard of living. In much of urban and rural Asia, the pattern of rapid growth during the past few decades is still based on a strongly informalized labour system and government protection is absent or ineffective. Furthermore, previous patterns of care provision within the family or by means of patron–client relations, which went some way to redressing the sharply unequal social distribution, have been eroded without being replaced by more formal and horizontally structured forms of social security. The lack of any organized countervailing power to the commoditization of labour illustrates the extreme vulnerability of the working masses. As yet, capitalist dynamics in Asia's economies appear to be unaffected by the emancipation of labour. The trend is towards a dual social order which excludes a very substantial segment of the world's population from enjoying a secure and decent life.

Notes

1. K. Kautsky, *Die Agrarfrage*, (Dietz, Stuttgart 1899). A French edition of the first volume was published in 1900 and subsequently reprinted by Maspero, Paris in 1970. Jairus Banaji published an English summary of the French translation in *Economy and Society*, 5 (1976) and it is from this that my quotations are taken. An overview of Kautsky's work for English language readers can be found in Hussain (1981). Kautsky's work has subsequently been translated into English by Pete Burgess and published in two volumes by Zwan Publications, London (1988).

2. In their seminal study on agrarian riots around 1830 in south England, however, Hobsbawm and Rudé (1973: 6) are intrigued by the general lack of interest in the agricultural labourer in the agrarian history literature.
3. New historical research on the Netherlands, such as that by Lucassen (1987), shows that landless and land-poor peasants migrated over long distances and frequently for long periods to hire out their labour power. de Vries and van der Woude (1995: 95–6) likewise draw attention to large-scale seasonal migration during an even earlier period than that studied by Lucassen. Extra-economic coercion played an important role in this labour mobility (Jaritz and Müller 1988).
4. A landless underclass was also present in pre-capitalist Europe – Kautsky's image of a fairly homogeneous peasantry firmly embedded in well established villages should be modified.
5. In this respect, the opinion of colonial policy-makers supports the suggestion made by Kautsky, among others, that marginal peasants were actually worse off than free wage labourers (Banaji 1976: 26–7). This assumption is not confirmed by my own field research in west India and Java, which found that the owners of even a small plot of land have a major advantage over landless households (Breman 1993, 1995).
6. The production process is defined as capitalist because production is for the capitalist market. Ultimately, the reproduction of the labour process depends on a generalized system of commodity production.

References

Banaji, J. (1976) 'Summary of selected parts of Kautsky's *The Agrarian Question, Economy and Society*, 5: 2–49.

Banaji, J. (1990) 'Review article – Illusions about the peasantry: Karl Kautsky and the agrarian question', *Journal of Peasant Studies* 17(2): 288–309.

Boomgaard, P. (1989) *Children of the Colonial State; Population Growth and Economic Development in Java, 1795–1880*, CASA Monographs, Free University Press, Amsterdam.

Breman, J. (1974) *Patronage and Exploitation; Changing Agrarian Relations in South Gujarat*, University of California Press, Berkeley.

Breman, J. (1980) *The Village on Java and the Early Colonial State*, Comparative Asian Studies Programme, Rotterdam.

Breman, J. (1983) *Control of Land and Labour in Colonial Java: A Case Study of Agrarian Crisis and Reform in the Region of Cirebon during the First Decades of the Twentieth Century*, Verhandelingen Koninklijk Instituut voor Taal-, Land- en Volkenkunde 101, Foris Publications, Dordrecht.

Breman, J. (1985) *Of Peasants, Migrants and Paupers; Rural Labour Circulation and Capitalist Production in West India*, Clarendon Press/Oxford University Press, Oxford/Delhi.

Breman, J. (1988) *The Shattered Image; Construction and Deconstruction of the Village in Colonial Asia*, Comparative Asian Studies 2, Foris Publications, Dordrecht.

Breman, J. (1990) *Labour Migration and Rural Transformation in Colonial Asia*, Comparative Asian Studies 5, Free University Press, Amsterdam.

Breman, J. (1993) *Beyond Patronage and Exploitation: Changing Agrarian Relations in South Gujarat*, Oxford University Press, Delhi.

Breman, J. (1994) *Wage Hunters and Gatherers; Search for Work in the Urban and Rural Economy of South Gujarat*, Oxford University Press, Delhi.

Breman, J. (1995) 'Work and life of the rural proletariat in Java's coastal plain', *Modern Asian Studies*, 29(1): 1–44.

Byres, T.J. (1981) 'The New Technology, Class Formation and Class Action in the Indian Countryside', *Journal of Peasant Studies*, 8(4): 405–49.

Byres, T.J. (1991) 'The agrarian question and differing forms of capitalist agrarian transition: an essay with reference to Asia', in J. Breman and S. Mundle (eds) *Rural Transformation in Asia*, Oxford University Press, Delhi.

Elson, R.E. (1994) *Village Java under the Cultivation System, 1830–1870*, Asian Studies Association of Australia, Southeast Publications Series, No. 25, Allen and Unwin, Sydney.

Hobsbawm, E.J. and Rudé, G. (1973) *Captain Swing*, Penguin, Harmondsworth.

Hussain, A. (1981) 'Theoretical writings on the agrarian question', in A. Hussain and K. Tribe (eds) *Marxism and the Agrarian Question*, 2nd edn, MacMillan, London.

Jaritz, G. and Müller, A. (eds) (1988) *Migration in der Feudalgesellschaft*, Ludwig-Boltzmann-Institut für Historische Sozialwissenschaft, Campus, Frankfurt/New York.

Kautsky, K. (1899) *The Agrarian Question*, Zwan Publications, London (translated from German by P. Burgess, 1988 edition).

Kloosterboer, W. (1954) *Onvrije arbeid na de afschaffing van slavernij, (Unfree Labour after the Abolition of Slavery)*, The Hague.

Kumar, D. (1965) *Land and Caste in South India: Agricultural Labour in the Madras Presidency during the Nineteenth Century*, Cambridge University Press, Cambridge (reprinted with a new Introduction, Manohar, Delhi, 1992).

Lucassen, J. (1987) *Migrant Labour in Europe 1600–1900: The Drift to the North Sea*, Croom Helm, London.

Miles, R. (1987) *Capitalism and Unfree Labour: Anomaly or Necessity?*, Tavistock, London/New York.

Moore Jr, B. (1966) *Social Origins of Dictatorship and Democracy: Lord and Peasant in the Making of the Modern World*, Beacon Press, Boston.

Myrdal, G. (1968) *Asian Drama: An Inquiry Into the Poverty of Nations*, Vol. II, The Twentieth Century Fund, New York.

Nieboer, H.J. (1910) *Slavery as an Industrial System: Ethnological Researches*, 2nd edn, Martinus Nijhoff, The Hague.

Patel, S.J. (1952) *Agricultural Labourers in Modern India and Pakistan*, Current Book House, Bombay.

Prakash, G. (1990) *Bonded Histories: Genealogies of Labour Servitude in Colonial India*, Cambridge South Asian Studies No. 44, Cambridge University Press, Cambridge.

Slicher van Bath, B.H. (1960) *De Agrarische Geschiedenis van West-Europa (The Agrarian History of Western Europe)*, Aula, Utrecht/Antwerpen.
Thompson, E.P. (1991) *Customs in Common*, Penguin, London.
Thorner, D. (1976) *The Agrarian Prospect in India*, 2nd edn, Allied Publishers, Bombay.
Vries, J. de and A. van der Woude (1995) *Nederland 1500–1815: de eerste ronde van moderne economische groei (The Netherlands 1500–1815: The First Round of Modern Economic Growth)*, Uitgeverij Balans, Amsterdam.
Wertheim, W.F. (1964) *East–West Parallels: Sociological Approaches to Modern Asia*, W. van Hoeve, The Hague.

14. Responsibility without Rights: Women Workers in Bonded Labour in Rural Industry in South India

KARIN KAPADIA

Introduction

Recent research on trends in the Indian economy suggests that rural off-farm employment is growing and becoming increasingly significant for the economy (Bhalla 1997, Sen 1999). The economic reforms initiated in the 1990s have lessened the importance of agriculture and stimulated rural non-farm productive activity (Harriss-White and Janakarajan 1997). Although agriculture still provides the livelihoods of two-thirds of the Indian population, non-agricultural rural activities have become very important to the reproduction of rural society (ibid: 1475).

This paper deals with one example of a rural industry, the synthetic gem-cutting industry in Tamil Nadu, south India. This industry was initially set up in the 1920s in Tiruchi city by wealthy merchants of the Chettiar caste who returned to Tamil Nadu from Burma. These merchants brought with them the technology for making the 'Rangoon diamond', a synthetic diamond for use in artificial jewellery. From the 1920s until 1990 the primary product of the industry was the Rangoon diamond, both in the form of white 'diamonds' and red 'rubies'. These gems were locally called 'hard gems' (*getti kallu*) (Kapadia 1995a). It was especially the red 'rubies' – locally called 'red gems' (*sehappu kallu*) – which were produced, and so the industry itself was sometimes locally referred to as the 'red gem' industry. These synthetic gems enjoyed huge popularity in the jewellery market, especially among the less rich. Usually, the gems are set in genuine, rather than artificial, gold.

This early gem industry, producing 'rubies' on primitive wooden machinery worked by a pedal, quickly spread amongst the villages around Tiruchi city where agriculture was slowly becoming more unreliable. These villages were situated in the drier areas of Tamil Nadu. Today these areas are, in part, quite arid because rainfall has decreased and rainfed crops, such as paddy, are now seldom planted. It is primarily dry crops, especially millet and groundnuts, which are grown. Apart from these dry crops, a little rice is produced in relatively wet years by a few better-off farmers who have sunk deep bore wells.[1] These areas are described by the local phrase 'where the earth looks to the skies', meaning that it is a struggle to earn a living from the land today. However, accounts of the lakes, ponds and tanks which dotted the area some 30 years ago make it clear that the environment and ecology of the area have deteriorated significantly over time. It is possible that the semi-drought conditions are due to (illegal) deforestation which still continues in the Nilgiri mountains.

This chapter focuses on the largest village in the area, Tannirpalli (a pseudonym), which is the local administrative centre for the surrounding villages.[2] In 1981 Tannirpalli, in the subdistrict of Lalgudi Taluk and the district of Tiruchirappalli, had a population of 7429 people living in 1692 households (Census of India 1983). Most people in Tannirpalli belong to the Soliya Vellalar caste, a middle-ranking 'caste-Hindu' caste. The 'caste-Hindus' define themselves in opposition to the so-called 'untouchable' castes, now known as the 'scheduled castes'.[3] This paper focuses on the Soliya Vellalar caste, as this caste is involved in the gem-cutting industry. By way of contrast, at various points in the chapter I refer to the 'untouchable' Pallar caste which I studied in another village in Tamil Nadu (Kapadia 1995b).

The Soliya Vellalars (hereafter SVs) dominate Tannirpalli so completely that the village seems like a one-caste community. Traditionally, the SVs were peasants. The caste name 'Vellalar' denotes a (male) farmer who owns land: in the Tamil context it denotes dignity and status, especially in a historical context where there were many landless groups. Like other middle-ranking Tamil castes, the SVs have a long tradition of women working alongside men in agricultural work on their own family fields. Work was also carried out on the fields of others as a form of labour exchange. There was little hiring of agricultural labour in the region (in contrast to, for instance, the well-watered Kaveri rice-bowl areas).

The increasing aridity of the area may be a central factor explaining the move away from agriculture to gem cutting in Tannirpalli. Indeed, if it were not for gem cutting, it is unlikely that people would be able to derive a living in the area. Most families appear to have been pushed into gem-cutting work because there was no alternative occupation available when crops failed. It thus appears that what started as an additional occupation for small peasants in the 1920s became their sole occupation as rainfall decreased over the decades.

Today most SV families still own a small parcel of land, but these holdings have become entirely uneconomic. Thus the SVs of Tannirpalli can be seen as a paradigmatic 'disappearing' or even a 'disappeared' peasantry: from full-time agriculturalists at the turn of the nineteenth century, they have become almost entirely dependent on non-agricultural work for their living. Very few SVs farm land in addition to doing gem-cutting work. The few who do so are those who have the money to sink bore wells, and these wealthier families also tend to be among the largest gem-cutting workshop owners. The great majority of people are entirely dependent on gem-cutting work. In this sense, the great majority of gem workers have been fully 'proletarianized', even though they may own tiny plots of land.

Proletarianization in the 'traditional'[4] gem-cutting industry generally takes the form of bonded labour. Bonded labour is typical not only of the gem-cutting industry in Tannirpalli, but of the surrounding villages, and of rural industry in other districts of Tamil Nadu (Kapadia, unpublished). Unfree labour also exists in agriculture. Although it is not clear whether it existed in agriculture around Tannirpalli, it was an important phenomenon of the agrarian structure in other parts of Tamil Nadu (Ramachandran 1990).

In investigating bonded labour, it is necessary to examine gender. The analysis of exploitation and of worker consciousness cannot assume that a class analysis alone suffices. Many women workers feel that their treatment by their husbands is far worse than their treatment by their employers. These perceptions are extremely important and cannot be ignored or simply dismissed as 'false consciousness', even though there might be a degree of mystification involved here (Hart 1991). Whether biased or not, women's perceptions of bonded labour are significant for revealing their experiences and pointing to the gendered nature of labour processes in gem cutting.[5]

This chapter is organized into four sections. The first describes the position of women workers in the gem-cutting industry. Although many of women are main household providers, women do not gain any social status from this role. The second section focuses on bonded labour as an instrument for the control of labour by capitalist entrepreneurs. Section three highlights the need for a gender analysis of bonded labour, arguing that the middle-caste Tamil construction of gender relations is crucial to the structure of bonded labour in the gem-cutting industry. In the last section I return to the question of the peasant past of the SV caste and the way in which gender and class consciousness shape perceptions about present-day exploitation.

Women Workers in the Gem-Cutting Industry

Tamil culture is male-biased. By 'male bias' I mean 'a bias that operates in favour of men as a gender, and against women as a gender' (Elson 1991a: 3). However the degree of bias varies significantly by caste and class: male bias tends to be stronger in upper-caste, upper-class society in rural Tamil Nadu and weakest in the poorest, lowest castes. Most women workers in the synthetic gem-cutting industry in Tannirpalli belong to the middle-ranking SV caste. They are far more constrained by hegemonic upper-caste norms than, for example, women from the 'untouchable' Pallar caste who show a much greater ability to reject gender norms. This ability seems closely correlated with their structural position in relation to hegemonic norms. Their position is structurally contradictory, and in the specific Pallar context this enables women to resist vigorously both employers and husbands. Pallar women are equal, sometimes sole, providers for their families. The authority of Pallar husbands is radically weakened by the fact that in this impoverished caste women are major breadwinners (Kapadia 1995b).

The structural position of SV women gem workers is both similar to and different from that of Pallar women workers in Tamil Nadu. It is similar because both groups of women are poor. Soliya Vellalar women work in the gem-cutting industry out of poverty. Even though gem cutting is tedious and painstaking toil, it is preferred to agriculture because of its higher social esteem. However, the gender identities of SV women gem workers and Pallar women workers are very different. Soliya Vellalar women are not defined as workers: they are merely regarded as the ancillary 'helpers' of their husbands or male kin, who give them 'protection' and control their labour. If married, the SV women usually work alongside their husbands; if unmarried they work alongside their fathers or their brothers. It is the male worker who is regarded as the 'main' worker. Independent women workers are very rare indeed; they are an anomaly both in the production system and socially. Neither SV women themselves nor their community appear to regard their identity as workers as salient, in striking contrast to the ways in which the work status of Pallar women is regarded within their caste. Soliya Vellalar women's central identities are related to their roles as wives and mothers, despite the fact that they work (either alongside men or alone) full-time, every day, and that their earnings are absolutely essential to the survival of their impoverished households.

To substantiate this last point, a random survey of 115 households in Tannirpalli found women to be the main providers in 39 per cent of households. This is an astonishing finding for a middle-ranking caste. Whilst the bread-winning role of very low-caste women is gradually being recognized, the Census and most researchers continue to assume that non-scheduled caste rural women in India are only secondary workers. In the remaining 61 per cent of households, women were not the main providers, although their earnings were considerable. Apart from being important earners, women also contribute a far larger percentage of their incomes to their households than do their husbands.[6]

The social contexts in which SV and Pallar women live are very different. The middle castes, such as SV, espouse high-class/caste values in an attempt to emphasize their social superiority. On the one hand they are meat-eaters: this indicates that they are not a ritually high caste, for castes tend to turn vegetarian when claiming high status (though this norm has weakened today with the relative fall in political power and status of Tamil Brahmins). On the other hand, SVs do not allow widows to remarry. This is a classic marker of high-caste/class aspirations. Further, divorce for women is strongly discouraged and hardly exists. All in all, it is likely that the caste was a lower-ranking caste in earlier times, and is now trying to 'urbanize' its social norms in order to catch up with the upper-caste Joneses. The Pallar caste has no such ambitions.

Caste status has been closely bound up with prescribing or proscribing behaviour for women: within their own caste groups lower-caste/poor women have had the greatest freedom and upper-caste/wealthy women the least. Unlike SV women, for instance, Pallar women can freely divorce and remarry, also after being widowed. The 'freedoms' of lower-caste women are closely linked to their obligations. Impoverished women have to engage in daily paid labour because otherwise their households could not survive. Here the upper-caste norm of the male provider is irrelevant: women are expected to contribute to providing for the household. The upper-caste norms of male authority and male superiority rest on the assumption that men provide for dependent women. These norms are clearly remote from the exigencies of lower-caste life and play little part in them. Consequently, Pallar women walk out on husbands who are wife-beaters and do not provide for the household. Crucially, lower-caste women have always been welcomed back to their natal homes, either as regular visitors or after a divorce. Further, such women can remarry easily because they are seen as assets. They are regarded as earners who will benefit any household to which they are attached.

The relation between married higher-caste women and their natal households is very different. Parents from the upper castes and their emulators, such as the SVs, strongly disapprove of their married daughters abandoning their husbands and returning home. Women who leave their husbands for whatever reason incur the strongest possible social condemnation; they are branded as '*valaivetti*', literally 'those who have lost their lives'. The term implies that such a woman might as well be dead and indeed, in social terms is dead, for her husband ought to be the centre of her life. These powerful norms are utterly foreign to Pallar (lower-caste) culture, but they are an integral, and apparently an increasing, part of SV norms. Consequently, SV women workers who are faced with marital crises or with non-contributing husbands cannot just walk away and go back to their natal families. Instead they face enormous social pressure to stay where they are, even in contexts of physical abuse. Only in exceptional cases are women allowed to divorce their husbands and return to their parents. This only happens when the parents are willing to bear the social and financial costs involved.

Compared to the enormous difficulties confronted by SV women in getting divorced, SV men can desert their wives at will. Further, customary law allows men to have two (or more) wives, so they can implicitly divorce first wives by taking a second. In addition to multiple marriage, men are permitted to remarry very shortly after being widowed. Thus, whilst remarriage is entirely prohibited for widows, widowers are actively encouraged to remarry as quickly as possible.

In short, gender relations among the lower Pallar caste and the SV caste are very different. The rights of women and men in SV society are based on hegemonic religious discourses – those of upper-caste Tamil Hinduism – which represent women as intrinsically inferior human beings (Kapadia 1994). It is this symbolic evaluation of women's intrinsically low worth which justifies and legitimates their subordination in all spheres. In these discourses upper-caste women are represented as always requiring control by men, as women are incapable of controlling themselves. Middle-caste women in upwardly oriented castes are defined likewise. Although Brahmin hegemony has been eroded somewhat, these 'Brahminic' values have survived because they have been strongly internalized by other – non-Brahmin – Tamil upper or middle castes.

Male authority in these upper-caste Tamil discourses is legitimated not only through the religious argument that women are an inferior species of human being, but also by the economic argument that men are the providers on whom women rightly depend. This female dependence is reasserted in everyday interactions between women and men. It takes the form of an extreme deference which women 'owe' to men. This female deference to the superior male is enacted when eating, speaking, sitting, standing. Women must eat last, after serving all the men. Women must use the formal, polite form when addressing their husbands, who respond using the informal, 'derogatory' form. Women must never sit if men are standing, and must always sit at a lower level than men. Thus social behaviour (in these castes) is not only deeply gendered but also profoundly hierarchical. The overarching ideological assumption of these everyday acts of deference is the unquestioned authority and superiority of men and the equally unquestioned subordination and inferiority of women. Female deference implicitly acknowledges the legitimacy of male control of female lives.

These representations and practices, relating to the proper form of relations between the sexes, are disturbed when SV women become the main providers, often as a result of their husbands reneging on their obligation to provide for the household. In general, SV women accept their poverty. They do not express resentment at working alongside their husbands but accept this as part of the hardship of being poor. Nor do they expect their husbands to be the sole providers. However, when husbands habitually spend too much of their earnings on themselves and too little on the household, working wives become very frustrated and sharp conflict ensues. They are bitter about such male irresponsibility, which is usually connected with alcoholism.

It is in such situations that cracks appear: women refuse to behave as 'good' wives and refuse to cook for their husbands. They complain loudly to neighbours and friends, and express resentment towards their parasitic or violent husbands who are merely a drain on scarce household resources. Significantly, these women receive remarkably little support from their female neighbours. Most other SV women caution against rebellion because, despite being workers themselves, many also still depend on their husbands' earnings to feed their children. The standard advice to an aggrieved wife is that she should try to be more patient and forbearing – in short, that she should uncomplainingly continue to feed her non-contributing husband and behave like a proper, subservient wife. Men show little concern or sympathy for such aggrieved wives; they tend to support other men, right or wrong. It was older men who told us, quite authoritatively, that marital discord in the SV community began precisely when women entered waged work. In other words, it was entirely women's fault.

Consequently, SV women who become the main breadwinners of their households are placed in an extremely contradictory position. On the one hand, they have to shoulder the responsibility of feeding their families, including their husbands. On the other hand, despite this 'male' responsibility, they confront a range of social restrictions whose logic depends on the assumption of female dependency. This contradiction, already implicit in the lives of women workers who 'assist' in breadwinning, is glaringly explicit in the position of women who are the main, if not the sole, earners, as in this case the hegemonic norms of male authority begin to break down. Nevertheless, these SV women have none of the rights or freedoms enjoyed by lower-caste women in a similar position. Thus those SV women who are the main providers have all the responsibilities of lower-caste women with none of their rights. This contradictory position is gradually becoming typical of SV women's lives, as increasing numbers of men are either withdrawing from bonded gem cutting or reducing their contributions to family income. During our research we came across several women who were in a state of angry despair about this, but who felt powerless to change the behaviour of their husbands.

The Modernity of Bonded Labour

Although gem cutting is a modernizing industry which has rapidly expanded into global markets, it continues to use a system of bonded labour in its traditional sector. Bonded labour is a strategy by which employers seek to reduce the mobility of labour while simultaneously cheapening its price. This suggests that further modernization in the gem-cutting industry will not necessarily lead to the end of bonded labour. A system of debt bondage enables employers to convert wages into debt, with the consequence that workers are represented as repaying their debts through their work, rather than earning wages. This ideological ploy has enormous power; we found many workers who half-believed employers' claims that the reason they are paid very low wages (approximately Rs15 for a day's piecework) is because they have to repay 'interest' on their loans. Thus while all workers complained that they were paid far too little to live on, most seemed to feel that their debt relation – and often kinship relation –

with the workshop owner prevented them from participating in workers' unions or openly resisting owners' demands. Thus employers use loans as a strategy to retain labour, pay exploitative wages and enhance profits. In this way bonded labour in the gem-cutting industry contributes to excellent returns on investments today (Kapadia 1995a).

There are complex socio-cultural reasons for the continued existence of bonded labour in gem cutting. These socio-cultural factors include the ways in which kinship and caste discourses are used by entrepreneurs to appeal for solidarity and harmonious relations within the workshops, relations which clearly benefit employers. Employers use the language of kinship when addressing workers: for example, an older woman worker is addressed as 'elder sister'. Few workers are actually their kin, so for most workers this is a relation of fictive kinship. Workers also use this form of address to try to extract better conditions or various forms of assistance from their employers, but the putative kin relationship tends to benefit employers more as they continue to hold the upper hand (Brass 1986).

In arguing that bonded labour is alive and well in a dynamic, capitalist, small-scale industry, I am not arguing that bonded labour in this case is a semi-feudal production relation, as do Chopra (1985) Patnaik (1985) and Vidyasagar (1985). The profitability of the traditional gem-cutting industry in Tannirpalli is based on the economics of bonded labour, namely on the control of cheap labour. By transforming wages into the 'repayment of debt' and free labourers into bonded workers, employers in Tannirpalli have successfully de-proletarianized their workforce (Brass 1990, 1993). What is relevant to my argument here is the apparent compatibility of unfree labour with burgeoning capitalist small industry in south India today. Indeed, in the case of gem cutting, employers implicitly argue for the necessity of unfree labour in order to maintain their profits. This suggests that Brass (1993: 50) is right to insist on 'the existence of a connection between unfreedom and capitalism'.

The Need for a Gendered Analysis of Bonded Labour

Much excellent work has been done on bonded labour in India (Brass, 1986, 1990, 1993, Prakash, 1992, Lerche, 1995). Remarkably, none of this work is gendered. None of these writers considers the possibility that the axis of gender might be as important as the axis of class (and that of caste) in structuring and facilitating relations of bonded labour. In fact, gender mediates the access that male bonded workers have to the labour and earnings of female workers, it mediates the control that employers exercise over all bonded workers and it helps to explain why employers seek to entrap male workers, in debt. These are just some of the ways in which gender shapes the structures of bonded labour in gem cutting.

On the surface indebtedness has a deceptively simple origin: workers are paid very low wages which force them to take loans. In addition, as earnings are so low, male workers cannot earn a family income, so other family earners are needed as well. When male workers are in debt, workshop owners expect that family labour will be drawn in to help pay off these debts. This is one of the ways in which the gender norms of a male-biased culture work in favour of employers: as male workers have culturally established rights over the labour and earnings of their wives and children, they become the proxy recruiters enabling employers to gain control over the labour of women and children. Thus the specifically middle-caste Tamil construction of gender is absolutely central to the construction of bonded labour in gem cutting.

The deeper reasons for indebtedness are, as already noted, that this strategy enables employers to capture and immobilize a highly skilled workforce which could earn a much higher income if it were free. At the same time, it makes the price of labour as cheap as possible. Hart (1986: 195) reminds us that there is a third, crucial reason why employers seek to indebt workers: 'The employer's concern is not only that of ensuring an adequate labor force, but also a compliant one'. Accordingly, employers are actually seeking not the repayment of debt, but a docile labour force. Here, too, female labour is central because in Tannirpalli most employers regard women as far more reliable and regular workers than men. While men are often recalcitrant and absent, SV women show all the respectful obedience that their 'kinsmen' – employers expect of them. The fact that these women are regarded as 'ideal' employees has a great deal to do with their cultural conditioning. If, for instance, 'untouchable' Pallar women entered gem cutting, it is very unlikely that they would constitute a similarly subdued and docile labour force.

Married men, working with their wives, will normally receive more credit (which turns into debt) than unmarried men. Having a family is not a criterion for obtaining a loan, as single men receive credit too, but the bigger the size of a man's working family, the bigger the loan he can expect to obtain. Loans are given solely to male workers. Women are not allowed to take out loans unless their husbands give the owner explicit permission to extend loans to their wives. Not infrequently, as a result of the harassment of owners, male workers run away. They are usually recaptured quite quickly and forcibly brought back to the village where, after being verbally abused or even beaten by the owner, they are put to work again. However, where the escape is extended, the wife is held responsible for 'repaying' the entire loan through her work. Women and their labour are held as pawns, to be even more severely exploited by irate employers. A woman worker will be asked to produce the same number of gems per week that both she and her husband jointly produced. Thus women have responsibility for household provisioning and for repaying loans thrust onto them, but are denied the privilege of receiving loans, deciding the allocation of loans and earnings or the right to discretionary spending on their own pleasures.

This is not really surprising because it fits in with middle-caste cultural logic. Husbands are assumed to own all the 'resources' of their wives: their bodies, labour and earnings. In this authoritative middle-caste discourse, when a husband disappears, his wife's labour – being the property of her husband – is automatically attached. As these cultural norms emphasize women's supposedly dependent status, their lack of direct access to resources, such as loans, is legitimized. Here we find re-engraved the pattern of the dilemma which characterizes women gem cutters' lives: the paradox of responsibility without rights.

Perceptions of Exploitation: Gender and Class Consciousness

To summarize, the SV were traditionally peasants cultivating their own land with the help of family labour. In the course of this century, this caste became increasingly involved in gem-cutting work for both ecological and economic reasons. Bonded labour now predominates in this industry. Male workers receive loans, and they work along with other family members to repay these loans. In this way employers have access to a cheap and docile labour force.

Although we cannot prove that present-day labour relations in the gem-cutting industry have their roots in past agrarian relations, this is a possibility. Chari (1997) makes exactly this point in relation to the knitwear industry in Tirupur, a town in Tamil Nadu approximately 200 kilometres west of Tannirpalli. According to Chari, the agrarian caste which moved from farms to factories carried with them a set of social relationships from agriculture which they used and transformed when they became industrial entrepreneurs.

In the case of the SV in Tannirpalli, we have no evidence that bonded labour existed prior to the emergence of the gem cutting industry. However, contemporary gender and 'familial' relations among the SVs have their roots in the gender relations of a middle-class peasantry, and it is this form of gender relations that is made use of by employers.

At the same time, the context in which SV women and men live has changed dramatically, and the dominant gender ideology is increasingly at odds with prevailing practices. This makes life for SV women difficult. Men also find the new relations of bonded labour difficult to accept. Soliya Vellalar men were originally peasants, cultivating their plots relatively independently. The bonded labour relations in which many men find themselves today are very different from the labour relations of their peasant past.

It is, therefore, no surprise that both men and women are full of resentment, although this takes different forms. Male workers feel oppressed by their employers. They speak passionately against them and about the humiliations they endure in bonded labour. Women, on the other hand, complain vigorously about their husbands and resent what they perceive as exploitation by them, whilst being unable to do much to resist such male behaviour. They complain far less about their employers.

Although women's perceptions may be biased, they cannot be entirely dismissed as 'false consciousness' or ignorance. On the contrary, we have to recognize that their perceptions are grounded in women's understanding of their position in gem cutting. Women, as noted earlier, are usually not defined as 'main' workers, nor is their central identity that of a worker. They derive their access to gem work, loans and their own earnings (which are paid to their husbands) through their identity as wives. Thus both the problems caused by non-contributing husbands, as well as all the stresses related to work in bonded labour, are associated with their structural position as wives. They have to do bonded labour because they are the wives of bonded labourers. Their identity as gem workers is subsumed by their identity as wives.[7] Thus women gem cutters are not suffering from ideological mystification when they see their husbands as being greater oppressors than their employers. This perception is based on their understanding of who profits most from their labour.

A striking contrast in perceptions of exploitation is offered by our parallel study of women gem cutters in government employment schemes in the neighbouring district of Pudukottai (Kapadia, unpublished). These credit, training and employment schemes were intended to transform poor rural women into gem-cutting 'entrepreneurs'. Women were given training in using new, 'high-tech', semi-automatic gem-cutting machines. These expensive machines (approximately Rs15 000 or £300 apiece) were given to women trainees as loans-in-kind by the nationalized rural banks. The schemes were part of a countrywide Development of Women and Children in Rural Areas (DWCRA) programme, which in turn formed part of the Integrated Rural Development Programme (IRDP). Although the DWCRA programme was intended to benefit women, its material benefits were largely hijacked by men. Men could not appropriate the semi-automatic machines, which were the women's property, but they soon began to appropriate their wives' earnings in the DWCRA schemes.

Alongside this male appropriation of their earnings at home, women were also increasingly exploited by their employers. Initially DWCRA women workers' earnings were high, at around Rs80–100 per day. Consequently their household incomes soared. However, most of the DWCRA women (in the cohorts we studied) were of middle-ranking caste. This meant that, like Tannirpalli's SV women, they were required to observe middle-caste norms of appropriate female behaviour. Amongst other things, this meant that they had very restricted mobility and could not travel around to market their gems by going to nearby villages and towns as male gem cutters did. In rural Tamil Nadu, unconstrained female mobility is often equated with sexually loose and morally degenerate behaviour. Consequently these women were restricted to selling gems to specific local traders. When local gem traders took advantage of this by cutting the prices they paid to these women gem cutters, their earnings nose-dived. These wealthy traders were all of the same (SV) caste and colluded in steadily lowering the prices they paid to the DWCRA workers for their gems. There was very little that the middle-caste women workers could do about this. They were completely vulnerable as they could not leave the village to sell their gems and, in most cases, their husbands could not act as their agents as they were engaged in other (non-gem-cutting) occupations.

The important point here is that although both groups of women were constrained by middle-caste norms, the DWCRA women workers – unlike the women workers in Tannirpalli – were vehement in their condemnation of the local traders who exploited them. Their anger was focused on these men because they realized that the traders' collusion was the crucial reason why their gem prices had collapsed. The fact that their husbands implicitly or explicitly appropriated much of their earnings did not appear to disturb these women gem cutters half as much as their exploitation by the gem traders. This is probably because their sense of identity as workers and wage earners was far stronger than that of the Tannirpalli women gem cutters. This identity was greatly strengthened by the fact that they received their pay directly into their own hands. Further, all DWCRA women were obviously 'main' workers and all greatly valued the chance they had been given to raise both the economic status of their families and their own social status. Their social status did indeed rise in the first successful year of the project, when women workers had received high gem prices and had made extremely good earnings. However, by mid-1994 the economic situation of all DWCRA women workers deteriorated. Some households were in such dire difficulties that the women finally acquiesced to the loans being proffered by the gem traders. They recognized, bitterly, that they had thereby taken the first step towards becoming bonded labourers.

In sum, a gendered analysis of the bonded labour relations entered into by a disappeared peasantry shows firstly, that bonded labour is structured very differently in relation to the sexes, and secondly, that the resentment of female gem cutters is directed primarily against exploitative husbands rather than against exploitative employers. This unfortunate outcome is one of the great ironies of a gendered configuration of production relations which, at the end of the day, benefits employers most.

Notes

1. We were told that the rice crop planted during the monsoon season which ran from October 1993 to January 1994 was the first rice crop in seven years.
2. Tannirpalli was the main village (out of eight) in which I carried out a two-year research project from June 1992 to May 1994 funded by the Economic and Social Research Council, UK. I made subsequent brief research visits in December 1996/January 1997 and in April 1997 (Kapadia 1997).
3. The 'untouchable' castes are called 'scheduled castes' as they are listed in schedules which state their eligibility for affirmative action policies, notably 'reserved' places in higher education and government employment.
4. I use the term 'traditional' to refer to the sector which produced 'Rangoon diamonds'. This constituted the whole industry until around 1990 when the production of an entirely new gem, the 'American diamond' led to major changes in the labour process and in the profile of the workforce. I refer to the 'American diamond' sector as the 'new' or 'modern' sector of the gem industry. See Kapadia (1997) for a discussion of the new sector.
5. There is no perception without socio-cultural mediation. The epistemology underlying this study implicitly acknowledges the subjectivity of the arguments presented both by our informants and by us, their interlocutors, while insisting on the inevitable subjectivity of all investigation. In Hawkesworth's words (1989: 552): 'The goal of transparency, of the unmediated grasp of things as they are is not [possible], for no investigation, no matter how critical, can escape the fundamental conditions of human cognition'. Within these limits, an attempt is made to understand what labour in a bonded rural industry means for the women so employed.
6. This fact has also been reported by others. For Tamil Nadu see Mencher (1985, 1988), Mencher et al. (1979), Saradamoni and Mencher (1985), Kapadia (1992), and for elsewhere see Dwyer and Bruce (1988), Elson (1991a, b).
7. This is in sharp contrast to Pallar women workers whose identity as workers is primary, whose identity as mothers is secondary and whose identity as wives is the least significant (Kapadia 1995b).

References

Bhalla, S. (1997) 'The rise and fall of workforce diversification processes in rural India', in G.K. Chadha and A.N. Sharma (eds) *Growth, Employment and Poverty: Change and Continuity in Rural India*, Vikas Publishing House, New Delhi.

Brass, T. (1986) 'The elementary strictures of kinship: unfree relations and the production of commodities', *Social Analysis*, No. 20: 56–68.

Brass, T. (1990) 'Class struggle and the deproletarianisation of agricultural labour in Haryana (India)', *Journal of Peasant Studies*, 18(1): 36–67.

Brass, T. (1993) 'Some observations on unfree labour, capitalist restructuring and deproletarianization', in T. Brass, M. van der Linden and J. Lucassen (eds) *Free and Unfree Labour*, International Institute for Social History, Amsterdam.

Census of India (1983) *District Census Handbook: Village and Town Directory; Tiruchirappalli District; Tamil Nadu*, Series 20.

Chari, S. (1997) 'Agrarian questions in the making of the knitwear industry in Tirupur, India, a historical geography of the industrial present', in D. Goodman and M. Watts (eds) *Globalising Food, Agrarian Questions and Global Restructuring*, Routledge, London and New York, pp. 79–105.

Chopra, S. (1985) 'Bondage in a Green Revolution area: a study of brick kiln workers', in U. Patnaik and M. Dingwaney (eds), *Chains of Servitude: Bondage and Slavery in India*, Sangam Books, Delhi, pp. 62–86.

Dwyer, D. and Bruce, J. (eds) (1988) *A Home Divided: Women and Income in the Third World*, Stanford University Press, Stanford.

Elson, D. (1991a) 'Male bias in the development process: an overview', in Diane Elson (ed.) *Male Bias in the Development Process*, Manchester University Press, Manchester, pp. 1–28.

Elson, D. (1991b) 'Male bias in macro-economics: the case of structural adjustment', in Diane Elson (ed.) *Male Bias in the Development Process*, Manchester University Press, Manchester, pp. 164–90.

Harriss-White, B. and Janakarajan, S. (1997) 'From Green Revolution to rural industrial revolution in south India', *Economic and Political Weekly*, 32(25): 1469–77.

Hart, G. (1986) 'Interlocking transactions: obstacles, precursors or instruments of agrarian capitalism?', *Journal of Development Economics*, 23: 17–203.

Hart, G. (1991) 'Engendering everyday resistance: gender, patronage and production politics in rural Malaysia', *Journal of Peasant Studies*, 19(1): 93–121.

Hawkesworth, M. (1989) 'Knowers, knowing, known: feminist theory and claims of truth', *Signs*, 13(3): 533–57.

Kapadia, K. (1992) 'Every blade of green: landless women labourers, production and reproduction in south India', *Indian Journal of Labour Economics*, 35(3): 266–76.

Kapadia, K. (1994) 'Impure women, virtuous men: religion, resistance and gender', *South Asia Research*, 14(2): 184–95.

Kapadia, K. (1995a) 'The profitability of bonded labour: the gem-cutting industry in rural south India', *Journal of Peasant Studies*, 22(3): 446–83.

Kapadia, K. (1995b) *Siva and Her Sisters: Gender, Caste and Class in Rural South India*, Westview Press, Boulder, Colorado.

Kapadia, K. (1997) 'Gender, rural industrialization and the politics of production in south India', paper presented to Workshop on *Rural Labour Relations in India Today*, London School of Economics, 19–20 June 1997.

Lerche, J. (1995) 'Is bonded labour a bound category?: reconceptualising agrarian conflict in India', *Journal of Peasant Studies*, 22(3): 484–515.

Mencher, J. (1985) 'Landless women agricultural labourers in India', in IRRI (International Rice Research Institute) (eds) *Women in Rice Farming*, Gower, Aldershot, pp. 351–72.

Mencher, J. (1988) 'Women's work and poverty: women's contribution to household maintenance in south India', in D. Dwyer and J. Bruce (eds) *A Home Divided: Women and Income in the Third World*, Stratford University Press, Stanford, pp. 99–119.

Mencher, J. et al. (1979) 'Women in rice-cultivation', *Studies in Family Planning*, 11: 408–12.

Patnaik, U. (1985) 'Introduction', in U. Patnaik and M. Dingwaney (eds) *Chains of Servitude: Bondage and Slavery in India*, Sangam Books, Delhi, pp. 1–34.

Prakash, G. (1992) 'Introduction', in G. Prakash (ed.) *The World of the Rural Labourer in Colonial India*, Oxford University Press, Delhi, pp. 1–46.

Ramachandran, V.K. (1990) *Wage Labour and Unfreedom in Agriculture: An Indian Case Study*, Clarendon Press, Oxford.

Saradamoni, K. and Mencher, J. (1985) 'Muddy feet, dirty hands: rice production and female agricultural labourers', *Economic and Political Weekly*, 17: A149-A167.

Sen, A. (1999) 'Recent trends in employment, wages and poverty in rural India', in K. Kapadia, J. Lerche, T.C. Byres et al. (eds) *Rural Labour Relations in India Today*.

Vidyasagar, R. (1985) 'Debt bondage in South Arcot District: a case study of agricultural labourers and handloom weavers', in U. Patnaik and M. Dingwaney (eds) *Chains of Servitude: Bondage and Slavery in India*, Sangam Books, Delhi, pp. 127–61.

15. The Fate of the Chinese Peasantry since 1978

CHRIS BRAMALL and MARION E. JONES[1]

THE SCALE OF ECONOMIC and institutional change in China since the late 1970s has been matched by few other parts of the developing world. The changes concern not only the urban industrial and service sectors, but also agriculture. Agricultural output has grown at a historically unprecedented rate. Rural industry has mushroomed and now employs as much as a quarter of the rural workforce.[2] The restrictions imposed on the operation of rural markets during the late Maoist era have largely disappeared and the communes have been dissolved.

According to a number of writers, these processes have led to the disintegration of the Chinese peasantry (Friedman et al. 1991, Zhou 1996: 24, 26). They argue that the Chinese peasantry had been strengthened under the Maoist regime (1955–76). The impact of collectivization in 1955–56, by their account, was to re-create feudalism[3], and thereby a feudal peasantry. De-collectivization and the re-creation of rural markets in the 1980s are seen as a 'second land reform' (Kueh 1985) which brought with it the re-emergence of small-scale independent farmers who, according to some authors, can no longer be seen as peasants. For this chapter, the key characteristics used to identify households as peasant are: small-scale production, limited exposure to the market, and the cultural dominance of the village community. All of these aspects are in the spirit of Marxian definitions of the peasantry.[4]

Our analysis starts with a summary of the institutional changes which swept across rural China in the two decades after Mao's death in 1976. We then proceed with a description of the impact of de-collectivization, set in motion after 1978, on the Chinese peasantry. We argue that the Chinese peasantry was strengthened, rather than weakened, by de-collectivization itself. In the third section we describe developments after 1983, in particular the increasing rural differentiation, and with it a retrenchment of the peasantry. This retrenchment, in our view, is related to the fact that markets are still underdeveloped, as we argue in the fourth section. The fifth section describes the role of local government in supporting the peasantry. The chapter concludes with a brief summary of the main arguments.

Agricultural Growth and Institutional Change since 1978

To provide a context for the discussion of the post-1978 changes, it is useful first to provide a very brief synopsis of rural policy under Mao. During the

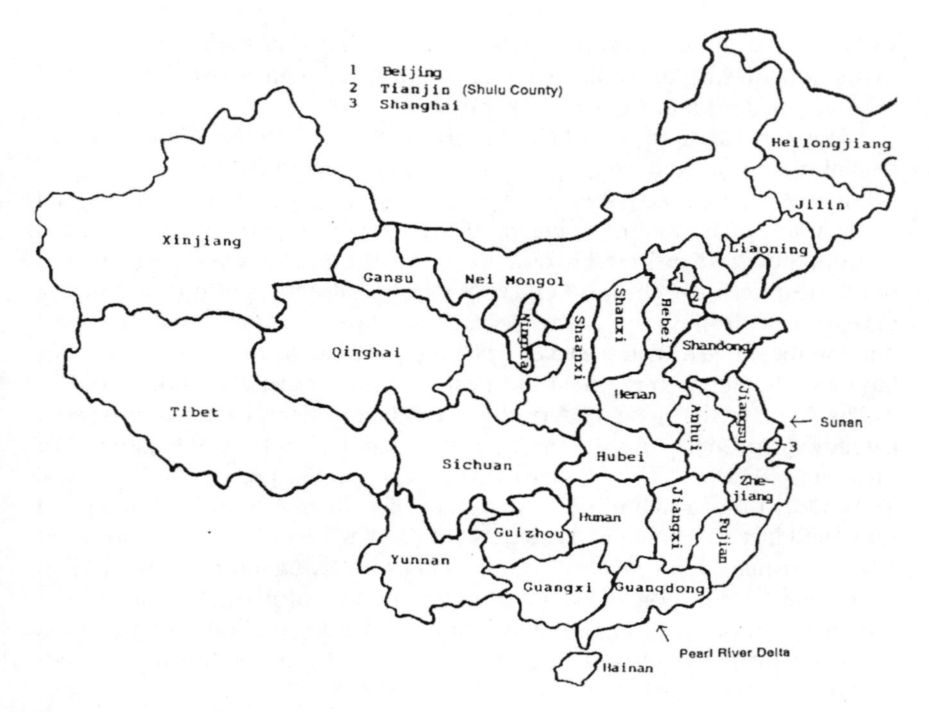

Figure 15.1: Map of China

Revolution and the post-revolution retrenchment (1947–52), land reform was the chief policy of the Chinese Communist Party (CCP). This took the form of highly equitable land reform and class struggle which saw the establishment of an alliance between the party and the classes of the formerly landless, and the small and middle peasants against the large peasant and landlord classes. This alliance continued through to the institutional changes embarked upon in 1978. The period between 1952 and 1955, inclusive, was the high tide of the Chinese peasantry under Mao, where agricultural production was dominated by small-scale, largely subsistence-based farming. This was followed in 1956–7 by the first movements towards the collectivization of agriculture, and rapidly led to the formation of the large communes in a movement that was rarely grassroots in nature. By 1958 the large communes were established[5], and in 1959 the Great Leap policies were implemented. The years 1959 to 1961 were catastrophic for the rural population of China, resulting in a famine which is estimated to have cost as many as 30 million lives (Ashton et al. 1984). Following the famine, the very large communes were divided into smaller units but the fundamentally 'feudal' nature of the production relations continued, with an emphasis on *corvée* labour in the slack season, local grain self-sufficiency in agricultural production and, perhaps most importantly, the extraction of surplus value from agriculture through a disadvantageous relative price set and rigidly stable purchase prices.

The first break in these policies occurred in 1977–78 when some localities in Anhui and Sichuan started experimenting with contracting out responsibility for farming activities to small groups of people or even individual households. This was followed in 1979 by revolutionary changes in agricultural purchase prices, encompassing both enormous increases in the purchase prices for certain key crops (grain, oilseeds, cotton) and also a massive shift in the terms of trade in agriculture's favour to improve production incentives. By the end of 1983, there was *de facto* private control of land and the agricultural means of production for most rural households.

The changes that have occurred in rural China since 1978 fall into three categories: property rights, marketization, and a shift in the pattern of intersectoral flows. The changes to property rights are the best known. They led to the dismantling of a system of collective farming which had remained largely unchanged since its creation in 1958. The most important characteristics of this system were a comparatively egalitarian distribution of income based upon work points[6], the absence of private ownership of the means of production, and restrictions on labour mobility. In a gradual process, which began as early as 1977 in some of China's poorest provinces (Bramall 1995), these collectives were dissolved.[7]

Of equal importance were changes to property rights in the rural non-farm sector, and especially rural industry and commerce.[8] Restrictions on private enterprise imposed under Mao were fully removed by the mid-1980s. This led to the re-emergence of a diversified range of household enterprises by the 1990s. Even more significantly, local government was itself encouraged to set up and to lease out rural industry. Many of these new enterprises were inherited from the communes, when their residual functions were transferred to the newly restored organs of local government after 1983, but the bulk were newly created by the use of surpluses made in agriculture.

The second major change since 1978 has been the growing marketization[9] of the rural economy, a process significant enough to be called the 'third revolution' in the Chinese countryside (Garnault et al. 1996).[10] In rural areas this process started with a removal of prohibitions on private-sector commerce, and by the mid-1980s many of the Maoist controls on wages, prices and commercial transactions had been removed.

Despite this growing marketization, in the mid-1980s there were still two areas in which market forces were not allowed to penetrate fully. Firstly, procurement prices for farm products remained under state control. These prices remained below international levels, although there were increases of over 20 per cent in 1979 and regularly thereafter. Secondly, the price at which procured farm products were sold in urban areas remained well below the procurement price. This meant, in effect, that urban consumers were being subsidized by the state to the extent of the difference between procurement and urban retail prices.

Both issues were tackled during the late 1980s and early 1990s. By 1993 the rationing system for grain and other farm products had been eliminated in urban China, while unified sale/procurement prices were gradually made subject to market forces. As a result approximately 90 per cent of agricultural products was traded at market prices by 1993 (Li 1996: 84), and by 1994 the price of some key grains (rice, wheat and maize) even exceeded international prices (Garnault et al. 1996: 188–90). Although the liberalization of markets is still not fully carried through, it is evident that the 'third revolution' has started China down the road of creating a market-based system of farm price determination.

A third major change relates to the shift in the pattern of intersectoral flows. In the late Maoist era, the main function of agriculture in the national economy was to support 'Third Front' industrialization[11] by supplying low-cost grain to the industrial workforce and by providing surpluses to finance investment. This process of resource extraction was reversed in the late 1970s. A first step towards this reversal was the reduction of compulsory procurement in poor regions. More importantly, central government shifted the intersectoral terms of trade dramatically in favour of agriculture in 1979.[12] In addition, the central government has reduced its emphasis on the need to achieve local self-sufficiency in grain production. As a result, many of the better-placed rural areas have shifted away from grain production and exploited instead their comparative advantage in non-food grain crops and vegetables (Huang 1990). This is illustrated by the fact that grain output increased by only 2.4 per cent per year between 1978 and 1994, while the production of cotton and vegetable oils increased at annual rates of 3.7 and 6.8 per cent, respectively.[13]

Taken together, these changes to property rights, the growing marketization of the rural economy, and the scaling down of the extent of intersectoral resource outflows from agriculture, have brought about a dramatic increase in rural production. Indeed, the actual growth rate of agricultural output exceeded the wildest dreams of the leadership, especially in the period 1978–84 (Table 15.1). The real growth rate for the post-1978 period was much higher than at any other time in the century, and compared favourably with the rates achieved in other developing countries. The sharp rise in labour productivity in the period between 1978 and 1984 is unique.

Despite the pace of economic, institutional and social change in China since 1978, agriculture remains very important in terms of employment. The absolute number of people employed in agriculture has risen. In 1978 some 285 million workers found employment in agriculture; in 1986 this had risen to 305 million (Nongye bu 1989: 15); in 1989 to 324 million (LSTJ

Table 15.1: Chinese agricultural growth in historical perspective

Period	*Net value of agricultural output*[1]	*Net value of agricultural output per capita*[2]	*Labour productivity*[3]
1952–57	4.1	1.7	2.0
1957–78	2.8	0.6	–0.2
1978–94	5.4	3.9	4.3
(1978–84)	7.2	5.8	5.8
(1984–94)	4.3	2.9	3.3

Growth rates of agricultural output at 1990 prices, per cent per annum. All growth rates by ordinary least squares (OLS).

(1)The net value of agricultural output (NVAO) growth before 1978 is based on the standard ZGTJNJ (Statistical Yearbook of China) NVAO data. After 1977 it is calculated by expressing the output value of each subsector at 1990 prices and then re-aggregating; where sideline data are not available (a time series for sidelines is no longer given in the statistical yearbooks after 1992); the growth of the farm sector is used as a proxy.

(2)The population denominator used to calculate NVAO per capita is total population.

(3)The figure for the labour force, used to calculate labour productivity, is the primary sector workforce before 1978; thereafter, it is the rural labour force employed in farming, forestry, animal husbandry and fisheries (ZGTJNJ 1995: 330).

Source: ZGTJNJ 1993: 33–34, 81, 101; ZGTJNJ 1994: 328, 330; ZGTJNJ 1995: 330, 332).

1990: 14); and in 1994 to 327 million (Nongye bu 1995: 7) or 68 per cent of the rural labour force (ZGTJNJ 1995: 329–30). As the way of life of these households conforms to our definition of the peasantry – small-scale production, limited participation in the market, the cultural dominance of the village community (although television ownership is growing quite quickly) and subordination to the holders of power (local and central government) – it is far too early to talk of the 'death' of the Chinese peasantry.

In addition to these developments in agriculture, the rural non-farm sector has also enjoyed spectacular growth. This process was already well under way in the mid-1970s in the more prosperous areas of China such as Sunan, the Pearl River Delta[14] and the suburbs of the main cities, but in other areas this sector grew hardly at all before 1978. In 1978, 28 million workers were employed in commune- and brigade-run industry throughout China (Nongye bu 1989: 286). After 1978, the rural industrial sector grew at a real annual rate of over 15 per cent and, quite remarkably, this level of growth has been sustained into the mid-1990s (the 1989–91 recession apart). An abundance of new jobs has been created. By 1984 employment in the rural non-farm sector had increased to 52 million and by 1994 it accounted for 120 million out of a total rural workforce of nearly 450 million (Nongye bu 1989: 288, 1995: 6, 174).

After this discussion of the changing political and economic context of rural China, we turn now to the impact of these changes on the Chinese peasantry itself. Has the peasantry been strengthened, or is it in the process of dissolution? The following sections show the twin processes of the initial creation of a highly homogeneous peasantry and its subsequent differentiation.

The Impact of De-collectivization on the Chinese Peasantry

As previously mentioned, the rural population in the Maoist period exhibited many of the characteristics of feudalism: strict controls on labour mobility, the considerable power of local cadres, and the use of *corvée* labour. The period of de-collectivization saw the resurgence of independent peasant households. This new peasantry was relatively homogeneous in that income inequalities amongst the rural population were only slight. Although official survey statistics are not especially reliable and probably over-estimate income inequality, the data suggest a Gini coefficient for rural incomes in the late 1970s/early 1980s of about 0.23 (Bramall and Jones 1993: 45). This was low by international standards and would have been lower still but for the existence of substantial regional inequalities. Within China's villages, income differentials were very low. Cadres, to be sure, did better than the average in material terms but overall there was no significant social and income stratification.

The impact of de-collectivization (1978–83) was probably to reduce social stratification even further. Although it differed from place to place, its essential characteristic was the allocation of land-use rights and tools on a per capita basis.[15] In other words, there was no attempt to establish a class of rural capitalist producers or proletarians. The emphasis was on a relatively egalitarian distribution of means of production.[16]

China's land reform resulted in family farms on tiny plots of land. Nationally the average size is a tenth of a hectare, but in most regions south of the Yangzi river it is perhaps a fifteenth. However, this did not lead to proletarianization. This means that it is possible for households in some places to work full time in rural industry and still be able to cultivate the land in their spare time, achieving only semi-proletarianization. Household labour resources are flexible and fungible, often being switched between farm and non-farm activities depending upon the season.

In sum, de-collectivization strengthened the Chinese peasantry, in the sense that independent family farms were created which could reproduce themselves through cultivation and off-farm employment. Much more controversial is the net impact on the peasantry of changes after de-collectivization.

Peasant Differentiation

There is no doubt that differentiation has occurred since 1983 (Wang et al. 1995: 14). This phenomenon is reflected in the academic literature. By the end of the 1980s, articles analysing the differentiation of the peasantry started to appear in China's leading journal on agriculture, *Nongye Jingji Wenti* (*Problems in Agricultural Economics*) (e.g. Lu and Zhang 1990). There have been explicit attempts to divide the peasantry into strata or even classes, as by Lu (1995) or Wang et al. (1995).

The differentiation of the rural population has occurred along the following lines: peasants, proletarians, capitalists and government officials. Peasants remain the largest group in rural China, and comprise the vast majority of the rural population in the non-coastal areas. The peasantry itself can be further subdivided into categories ranging from labour-rich peasant households contracting the land of others, to labour-poor households or those in particularly disadvantaged regions practising little more than subsistence agriculture.[17] In the worst cases, government assistance is necessary for these households to survive.

Proletarians are people who work in non-farm activities either locally or by temporary migration to urban areas. When these people are hired by the private sector (as opposed to the local public sector) there is often harsh exploitation. Capitalists can be subdivided into self-employed entrepreneurs (who have fewer than eight employees), petty capitalists (who have eight or more employees), and township and village enterprise managers (who are notionally public employees). These designations have as much to do with Chinese bureaucratic labels as with significant differences between them, as they all hire and exploit workers. Finally there are the government officials who live in rural areas. The key difference between them and other rural dwellers is that government officials enjoy all the advantages of urban public employees in the form of health, unemployment insurance, and other remunerations in kind which augment their salaries.

The chief difficulty in characterizing rural households is that most combine two or more of these elements.[18] One quarter of the rural labour force is either proletarian or entrepreneurial and not peasant (Lu 1995, 42–3), but many of these people live in households where some members remain peasant producers. It is not easy to identify purely peasant or purely proletarian households in rural China.

The mechanism that has given rise to this situation is de-collectivization. On one hand, as described above, it meant land reform which granted a small acreage to all rural households. However, in most cases this acreage was at best only enough for a subsistence living. On the other hand, the dissolution of the communes in 1983 meant that the vast majority of the rural population lost their rights to social security benefits, including famine relief grain stores, health insurance, unemployment insurance, and state-subsidized education. Since 1983 the role of the state has been severely curtailed in all but the wealthiest and most developmentally oriented areas. As a result, most households have to make use of every option available. It is hence not surprising that they are highly reluctant to part with their contracted land. Instead they either cultivate the land themselves using household labour or they rent out their land during good times when other jobs are plentiful and return to agricultural activities during an economic downturn (Bramall and Jones 1993; Jones 1997).

This risk-averse behaviour on the part of rural households results in barriers to the development of land and labour markets, preventing the emergence of larger-scale, mechanized, 'allocatively efficient' or higher-aggregate-yield farming as well as limiting the spatial mobility of labour (Jones 1997). Labour-market rigidity is also the product of continuing regulation and only partial easing of restrictions on permanent rural–urban migration. In effect, the extremely small size and fragmented nature of holdings permits the 'leisure' time cultivation of these fields and frees up household labour for employment in the non-farm sector. In turn, the cash income from non-farm employment is available for investment in other household productive activities, including green revolution technology and animal husbandry.

The standard view of development processes stemming from the theories of Lewis (1954) and Kuznets (1955) is that the proportion of the population living and employed in the modern, industrial or mechanized sector of the economy increases – usually through urban migration – resulting in the gradual proletarianisation of the population. This is known as modern-sector enlargement growth, and is often crucial to trickle-down theories of development. By contrast, in China's development process the mechanisms at play are largely traditional-sector enrichment growth, through the growth of farm incomes and off-farm employment within rural areas[19], and modern-sector enrichment growth in the urban and industrial parts of the economy. Very little modern-sector enlargement growth has taken place due to labour market rigidities. As expected, this has given rise to considerable increases in income inequality: rural–urban inequality, spatial inequality and intra-local inequality.

When we use the Gini coefficient as an approximation of differentiation, we can observe the process in quantitative terms. There is a sharp rise in the Gini coefficient, up from an average of 0.22 in 1980–82 to 0.32 during 1992–94 (Bramall 2000: Table 2.15). Another study, based on improved if imperfect data, shows rural income inequality at 0.338 in 1988 and rising rapidly to 0.416 in 1995 (Khan and Riskin 1998: 237). Although these figures are not too bad when placed in an international context, it is important to realize that it means a sharp increase in inequality, particularly since Chinese data on inequality still tend systematically to under-report the phenomenon (Bramall and Jones 1993).

This process of differentiation has been driven by changing property relations, markets and terms of trade, and in particular by the growing opportunities for enrichment presented by the spectacular growth of the agricultural and industrial sectors. This process is most advanced in those regions where industry has developed most quickly – the suburbs of the main cities, Sunan, much of Zhejiang and many parts of Guangdong. In these areas one can observe prosperous families living in brick houses stocked with consumer durables and enjoying a modern lifestyle. Here the area under farm crops, especially grain, has declined significantly because of higher returns from activities outside farming. Critically, the growth of rural industry and other non-farm activities has led to the increased proletarianization of some members of rural households, as some underemployed farm workers have abandoned the land in search of high-income jobs, while many others have not given up agriculture completely.

In the literature on China, it is quite common for the process of rural economic development and industrialization to be interpreted as spelling the end of the peasantry. Instead we argue that this is merely giving rise to the greater differentiation of the peasantry and to only very limited proletarianization of the rural population, either through rural–urban migration or by employment shifts within the rural area. The following two sections discuss two key elements in this dynamic: uneven marketization, and the role of the state at various levels. There are vast differences in the experiences of the peasantry in China, and these are distributed along a spectrum from the least to the most developed areas. At one extreme are backward areas with limited differentiation of the peasantry and marketization, both of which are a function of the fewer alternative economic opportunities in these areas. At the other extreme are the highly developed regions, where differentiation is a product of relatively robust markets, considerable growth of rural industry and therefore some proletarianization. Further, these areas are often adjacent to large urban areas facilitating migration. Despite this, people continue to cling to the land to a disproportionate extent.

Uneven Marketization

One important reason why the peasantry remain entrenched is the fact that the reach of the market is far from complete. This statement is true for both product markets and factor markets. Especially in the poor parts of western China, the penetration of the market is limited. Since there are fewer opportunities for off-farm employment and market-led developments in mountainous and ethnic minority areas, the process of dissolution has proceeded least quickly in these regions. Perhaps the best example is the Tibetan border region, encompassing western Sichuan (the old Tibetan province of Kham) and north-western Yunnan, but other examples are parts of Yunnan, Guizhou, Gansu and the mountainous regions of Hunan and Sichuan (see Figure 15.1, page 263).

A weak infrastructure in all these poor areas prevents the development of a proper market economy. Animal husbandry, the production of corn, wheat and tobacco, and forestry remain the bedrock of the local economy. These activities seldom generate enough revenue to allow the local government to play a developmental role, so that little money has been available for education, health care and basic infrastructure in the 1980s. This in turn has meant that economic growth has been slow, and few jobs have been created. There are a significant number of counties in south-west China where average real per capita incomes have not increased at all since the early 1980s (Bramall 2000: Table 2.14).[20] In these areas there is limited marketization and considerable poverty. The able-bodied and educated migrate in growing numbers, leaving behind a poor and comparatively undifferentiated peasantry.

The development of markets is also limited in the eastern provinces of China. Factor markets for land, credit and labour remain underdeveloped. Farmers are generally reluctant to sell their land and become full-time workers or entrepreneurs even when it is possible (Kelliher 1992: 186, Rozelle 1994: 107). This reluctance is partly fuelled by the reliance on land as social security provision. Farmers are aware of the risks involved in business failure arising from competition or recession. In addition, they fear that a change in policy towards a re-emphasis on agricultural production would brand non-agriculturalists as 'capitalists'.[21] Consequently, many people prefer to rent out their land, retaining use rights as insurance, whilst concentrating on their non-farm business.

Initially, during the late 1970s and early 1980s de-collectivization served to entrench the peasantry by establishing a large number of homogeneous, small, family farms. After 1984 the forces of marketization and the strategies pursued by rural households in the face of massive institutional change led to the differentiation of this peasantry. Of particular importance here are the changes in social security provisions, which lead to a consideration of the importance of state institutions in this process.

The Role of Central and Local Government

Some policies pursued by local and central government have served to check the differentiation of the peasantry. Central government has contributed to this by continuing to stabilize agricultural prices, as we have seen. In addition, controls on rural–urban migration, although weakened compared to the pre-1978 period, remained very strict by international standards throughout the 1980s. The role of the central government in rural areas has been significantly curtailed since 1978, with several waves of devolution of power to the provinces and the local government. This process of devolution has left the central government weak both fiscally and in terms of policy implementation. Most 'developmental' activities have devolved to local governments, and are dependent on their political ideology[22] and on their ability to raise revenue to support their programmes.

It is critical to recognize that the dissolution of the communes has not led to the collapse of local government. The new *xiang* (township)[23] governments are far from impotent (Gold 1988, Oi 1990), although some former activities related to overseeing and controlling the agricultural production process have come to an end. In some places – notably the wheat-growing areas of north-east China – they retain an important role in the organization of production (Sicular 1991). In addition, local government continues to restrict the operation of rural markets. For example, land-use rights can be transferred between households, but land ownership cannot easily shift from one person to another. The provision of credit by local co-operatives and branches of the Agricultural Bank of China is also heavily regulated by local government. Local governments often pursued protectionist policies to prevent the free movement of goods across county and provincial frontiers (Kumar 1994, World Bank 1994, Zhou 1996: 97). Finally, some local governments have played an instrumental role in town planning, creating transport and market infrastructure, the regulation of commerce, environmental protection and water conservancy (Blecher and Shue 1996). Whilst not all local governments have acted in this 'developmental' way, one of the paradoxes of the ostensibly market-promoting policies of the 1980s is that the local state has been strengthened by the growth of the rural economy and the tax revenue this provides.

As a result, some local governments have been able to prevent peasant differentiation and to check the growth of income inequalities. Some local governments have seen their role as 'developmental' – that is, as being the promotion of the well-being of the entire community.[24] They have actively intervened in the redistribution of arable land, in particular by securing the property rights of small farmers. They have also diverted resources with the aim of supporting agricultural production, which may not make sense from a narrowly defined efficiency point of view, but which does so in terms of equity. Perhaps even more importantly, they have used tax revenue from rural enterprises to invest in education, health care and infrastructure. In areas ruled by such developmental governments, the system of rural welfare established in the Maoist period has been strengthened, thus providing greater opportunities for socio-economic advancement. Given that rural incomes are positively correlated with educational attainment[25], these actions by local government have been of great importance in checking social differentiation and improving the qualify of life.

Most fundamentally, those parts of China where local government has remained strong have been extremely successful in creating employment in local state-owned industrial enterprises. Where rural industry has developed very rapidly, and especially where local government has controlled pay differentials, peasant differentiation has been checked because these lucrative industrial jobs are open to all.[26]

The 'problem' in much of rural China, however, is that local government is often not developmental. In many areas, local government has abandoned any such ambition and instead relies almost exclusively on market forces, more from a lack of tax revenues than from ideological inclination. In Wenzhou[27] for instance, with little pre-1978 industrial development, local government is weak. The economy is dominated by the private sector, and the local government is unable to enforce taxation effectively and has increasingly abdicated responsibility for welfare and infrastructure. As a result, school fees have risen and school drop-out rates (especially for girls) have spiralled. The incomes of the disabled and the illiterate and those of many elderly dependants have barely increased. Not surprisingly, income inequality increased exceptionally quickly in Wenzhou in the 1980s (Nolan and Dong 1990). In other areas, there is simply no surplus to extract. The local government has no income and spending on infrastructure or welfare is therefore inadequate.

In this respect, there is a marked contrast between the pattern of industrialization in Taiwan (where inequality remained low) and that of China after 1978. This contrast reflects the weakness of the central government in the People's Republic. Unless local government throughout China acts in the same way as it does in much of Sunan and in places such as Shulu, the rapid differentiation of the peasantry is likely to continue on a regional basis. However, this does not mean the disappearance of the Chinese peasantry.

Conclusions

The comparatively homogeneous Chinese peasantry, which emerged in the wake of the de-collectivization settlement of 1982–83, did not endure. Under the twin pressures of rural industrialization and marketization, the peasantry has become rapidly differentiated, but has not disappeared. Most of those working in the new rural industries are essentially semi-proletarians who have retained access to arable land. Rural money, labour and land markets remain under-developed, thus constraining the appearance of a class of capitalist farmers.

In some, mainly affluent, parts of the People's Republic, local government remains strong enough to redistribute income to those poor farmers least able to participate in the market economy. In the poorest regions of the country, the differentiation of the peasantry has proceeded slowly because of the severely limited development of the non-farm sector, hampered as it is by weak transport infrastructure and limited product demand in local markets. Consequently, although employment in the non-agricultural rural economy increased from about 30 million to 120 million workers between 1978 and 1994, in the same period those employed in agriculture also increased by perhaps 40 million, making a total of 327 million people. Unless rapid industrial growth can be sustained for a long period and, more importantly, replicated in those parts of western and central China where the majority of peasants live, the Chinese peasantry is likely to survive well into the next century despite continued rapid economic growth.

Notes

1. We are grateful to Vince Benziger and Alex Kelly for their comments on an earlier draft.
2. The term 'industry' is used throughout this paper to include the entire non-agricultural rural economy.
3. Indeed, the strict controls on labour, the requirement to perform *corvée* labour during the winter months and the absolute authority exercised by local cadres ('little emperors') made the feudalism of the Maoist era more 'authentic' than the feudalism of previous centuries. Nevertheless, in our opinion, the idea that the Maoist regime re-created feudalism in rural China takes the argument a stage too far. If one insists upon adopting a critical stance towards Maoism, it is more sensible to describe the mode of production as 'Asiatic' or as an example of 'hydraulic despotism', given the extensive involvement of central government in the rural economy, especially in the spheres of grain procurement and water management. But in truth neither 'feudal' nor 'Asiatic' makes much sense as a description because the late Maoist economy was characterized by the growth of rural industry, mechanization and the absence of strip farming, the development of primary health care, the rapid growth of literacy and the increasing use of green revolution chemical fertilizers and new seed varieties after 1965, demonstrating just how far removed this era was from the classical late Ming/early Qing China or late Tokugawa Japan examples of Asian feudalism.
4. See for example Marx 1887: 78–9, 714–6.
5. The creation of the communes in 1958 did not signal a decisive break with the past because they were no more than large collectives. Although the egalitarianism of the work-point system and restrictions on the private sector varied over time within these communes, the system of farming remained recognizably collective. The only real change in this period was when some provinces (notably Anhui) effectively restored private farming for a brief period in the early 1960s.
6. Work points were the means of wage accounting on the Chinese communes and were usually based on whether the individual was male or female and the type and duration of the work done.
7. For accounts of decollectivization, see Ash (1988), Potter and Potter (1990), Kelliher (1992), Lin (1996), Zhou (1996).
8. For the growth of local state enterprises in rural China in the 1980s, see Wong (1988), Byrd and Lin (1990), Findlay et al. (1994), Ho (1994), Cheng (1996). For the private sector, see Nolan and Dong (1990), Odgaard (1992).
9. We specifically chose to use the term marketization rather than liberalization as it is a less loaded term. Our preference for marketization rather than commoditization relates to the fact that we wish to emphasize not only that more peasants in rural China are being exposed to the market and are producing for the market, but also that old markets are being re-established in the wake of de-

collectivization and that new markets are being created where none previously existed or where they functioned only sporadically.

10. Land reform (1947–52) and decollectivization (1977–83) were the first two revolutions.
11. The massive programme of defence industrialization was initiated in western China after 1964 in response to what were perceived to be US and Soviet military threats.
12. Since 1979 there have been some marked fluctuations in the terms of trade.
13. These data, however, need to be treated with caution. Official figures on post-1978 growth tend to exaggerate, especially between 1978 and 1984, while pre-1978 output was under-estimated (Stone 1988, Oi 1989). 1984 grain-output data were exaggerated by the manipulation of stocks (Hinton 1990). On average, the weather during 1978–84 was better than in either the early 1970s or the period following 1984 (Kueh 1995). Nevertheless, the acceleration in output growth, particularly outside the grain sector, is undeniable.
14. Sunan is the prosperous region to the west of Shanghai (see Figure 15.1). The Pearl River Delta is close to Hong Kong.
15. This redistribution was seen as desirable in that it offered full employment and a rudimentary form of social security, even though it was regarded as inefficient in purely economic terms.
16. The distribution was not egalitarian in respect of gender, women being treated less well than men in the allocation of factors of production (Judd 1992).
17. The Chinese experience is rather different from the usual perception of rich, middle and poor peasants, but the fragmentation of holdings and their small size has given rise to this unusual pattern, with some households specializing in grain production and others concentrating on non-grain cultivation and animal husbandry, or on becoming semi-proletarianized through participation in non-farm activities.
18. An additional difficulty arises in the Chinese literature, as the Chinese use the term *nongmin*, peasant, to refer to virtually anyone living in a rural area.
19. Township and village enterprises (rural-based industrialization) cannot be counted as part of the modern sector in many respects because the mode of production in these enterprises is heterogeneous, and not homogeneous as one would expect from the Lewis model.
20. This is comparable to the classic Krugman (1991) story in which the poverty of poor regions is locked in by path dependence. High transport costs, limited markets and low agricultural yields limit the revenue of local government and private sector profits. Investment is therefore low and growth is virtually non-existent. Over time, out-migration compounds the problem by reducing market size and labour force quality.
21. Many enterprises folded during the recession of 1989–91. Accordingly, it is more sensible to regard the tendency of the Chinese peasantry to cling to the land as 'rational' rather than 'moral'. As Lenin (1956: 172–73) said of the Russian peasantry: 'Despite the theories that have prevailed here over the past half-century, the Russian community peasantry are not antagonistic of capitalism, but, on the contrary, are its deepest and most durable foundation'. These sentiments are equally applicable to China's farmers.
22. For more on the importance of political ideology, see Mood (1997).
23. With the dissolution of the communes in 1983, a new level of local government was created, the township. The township is responsible for a considerable breadth of local activity, from welfare funds and education to investment and infrastructure. This role has evolved over the past 15 years as the process of devolving power from central to local governments has been extended.

24. For the notion of the 'developmental state', see Johnson (1982), White (1991). Two counties, Shulu and Linyang, represent two very different models of developmental local governments. Shulu county in Hebei has integrated marketization with a developmental state (Blecher and Shue 1996). The quality of the local leadership, with considerable human capital and a well developed 'old-boys' network', key early investments from the 1940s and good transportation facilities, have all helped Shulu to achieve rapid economic development. At the other extreme, is Nanjie township in Linying county, Henan Province, which is famous for having re-collectivized (*Far Eastern Economic Review*, November 17, 1994, p. 32) and for achieving rapid development within a Maoist as opposed to a market socialist framework.
25. In 1983 the average income accruing to households with an upper-middle school education was between 40 and 70 per cent higher than that of illiterate households (Zhonggong Sichuan sheng wei nongcun jingji shehui fazhan zhanlue yanjiuzu, 1986: 671, 720, 721).
26. See Gelb (1990) for some evidence on Jiangsu, and Mood (1996, 1997) for rural Tianjin.
27. Wenzhou is a coastal region in the eastern province of Zhejiang, which lies south of the Yangzi river.

References

Ash, R.F. (1988) 'The evolution of agricultural policy', *China Quarterly*, No. 116: 529–55.

Ashton, B., Hill, K., Piazza, A. and Zeitz, R. (1984) 'Famine in China, 1958–61', *Population and Development Review*, 10(4): 613–45.

Blecher, M. and Shue, V. (1996) *Tethered Deer*, Stanford University Press, Stanford.

Bramall, C. (1995) 'Origins of the agricultural "miracle": some evidence from Sichuan', *China Quarterly*, No. 143: 731–55.

Bramall, C. (2000, forthcoming) *Sources of Economic Growth, 1970–1996*, Oxford University Press, Oxford.

Bramall, C. and Jones, M.E. (1993) 'Rural income inequality in China since 1978', *Journal of Peasant Studies*, 21(1): 41–70.

Byrd, W.A. and Lin, Q. (eds) (1990) *China's Rural Industry*, Oxford University Press, Oxford.

Cheng, H. (1996) 'Promoting township and village enterprises as a growth strategy in China' in M. Guitian and R. Mundell (ed.) *Inflation and Growth in China*, International Monetary Fund, Washington, D.C.

Findlay, C., Watson, A. and Wu, H.X. (ed.) (1994) *Rural Enterprises in China*, Macmillan, London.

Friedman, E., Pickowicz, P.G. and Selden, M. (1991) *Chinese Village, Socialist State*, Yale University Press, New Haven.

Garnault, R., Guo, S.T. and Ma, G.N. (eds) (1996) *The Third Revolution in the Chinese Countryside*, Cambridge University Press, Cambridge.

Gelb, A. (1990) 'TVP Workers' Incomes, Incentives and Attitudes' in W.A. Byrd and Q.S. Lin, *China's Rural Industry*, Oxford University Press, Oxford.

Gold, T.B. (1988) 'Still on the collective road: limited reform in a north China village' in B.L. Reynolds (ed.) *Chinese Economic Policy*, Paragon, New York.

Hinton, W. (1990) *The Privatization of China*, Earthscan, London.
Ho, S.P.S. (1994) *Rural China in Transition*, Clarendon Press, Oxford.
Huang, P. (1990) *The Peasant Family and Rural Development in the Yangzi Delta, 1350–988*, Stanford University Press, Stanford.
Johnson, C. (1982) *MITI and the Japanese Miracle*, Stanford University Press, Stanford.
Jones, M.E. (1997) 'Rising inequality and declining living standards in China since 1983', paper presented at the Association for Asian Studies, and Working Paper No. 75, Department of Economics, University of Regina.
Judd, E.R. (1992) 'Land divided, land united', *The China Quarterly*, No. 130.
Khan, A.R. and Riskin, C. (1998) 'Income Inequality in China,' *The China Quarterly*, No. 154.
Kelliher, D. (1992) *Peasant Power in China*, Yale University Press, New Haven & London.
Krugman, P. (1991) *Geography and Trade*, MIT Press, Massachusetts.
Kueh, Y.Y. (1985) 'The economics of the second land reform in China', *China Quarterly*, No. 101: 122–31.
Kueh, Y.Y. (1995) *Agricultural Instability in China, 1931–1991*, Clarendon Press, Oxford.
Kumar, A. (1994) 'Economic reform and the internal division of labour in China' in D.S.G. Goodman and G. Segal (eds) *China Deconstructs*, Routledge, London and New York.
Kuznets, S. (1955) 'Economic growth and income inequality', *American Economic Review*, March: 1–28.
Lenin, V.I. (1956) *The Development of Capitalism in Russia*, Foreign Languages Publishing House, Moscow.
Lewis, W.A. (1954) 'Economic Development with Unlimited Supplies of Labour', The Manchester School, May 1995.
Li, B.K. (1996) 'Price reform for agricultural products' in R. Garnault, S.T. Guo and G.N. Ma (ed.) *The Third Revolution in the Chinese Countryside*, Cambridge University Press, Cambridge.
Lin, J.Y. (1996) 'Success in early reform: setting the stage' in R. Garnault, S.T. Guo and G.N. Ma (ed.) *The Third Revolution in the Chinese Countryside*, Cambridge University Press, Cambridge.
LSTJ – Zhongguo guojia tongjiju (Chinese State Statistical Bureau) (ed.) (1990) *Quanguo gesheng zizhiqu zhixiashi lishi tongji ziliao huibian* (*Collection of Historical Statistical Materials on China's Provinces, Autonomous Regions and Centrally Administered Cities*), Zhongguo tongji chubanshe, Beijing.
Lu, X.Y. (1995) 'Rethinking the Chinese peasantry', *Chinese Law and Government*, 28, 1: 39–80.
Lu, X.Y. and Zhang, H.Y. (1990) 'Nongmin de fenhua wenti yu duice' (The differentiation of the peasantry: problems and remedies), *Nongye jingji wenti* (*Problems of Agricultural Economics*), No. 1, 16–21 (translated in CAR-90-040, 29 May 1990, pp. 59–67, Washington, D.C.: Joint Publications Research Service).

Marx, K. (1887) *Capital*, Vol. 1, Foreign Languages Publishing House, Moscow, (1961 edition).

Mood, M.S. (1996) 'Political duplications of economic transitions', PhD thesis, Cornell University, USA.

Mood, M.S. (1997) 'Risks and rewards: effects of rural enterprises on work and welfare in rural Tianjin', paper presented at the Association for Asian Studies, Chicago 1997.

Nolan, P. and Dong, F.R. (eds) (1990) *The Chinese Economy and Its Future*, Polity Press, Cambridge.

Nongye bu (1989) *Zhongguo nongcun jingji tongji daquan 1949–1986* (*Complete Statistics on China's Rural Economy*), Nongye chubanshe, Beijing.

Nongye bu (1995) *Zhongguo nongye tongji ziliao 1994* (*Statistical Materials on Chinese Agriculture*), Nongye chubanshe, Beijing.

Odgaard, O. (1992) *Private Enterprise in Rural China*, Avebury, Aldershot.

Oi, J.C. (1989) *State and Peasant in Contemporary China*, University of California Press, Berkeley.

Oi, J.C. (1990) 'The fate of the collective after the commune' in D. Davis and E. Vogel (ed.) *Chinese Society on the Eve of Tiananmen*, Harvard University Press, Harvard.

Potter, S.H. and Potter, J.M. (1990) *China's Peasants*, Cambridge University Press, Cambridge.

Rozelle, S. (1994) 'Decision-making in China's rural economy', *China Quarterly*, No. 137, pp. 99–124.

Sicular, T. (1991) 'China's agricultural policy during the reform period' in Joint Economic Committee, US Congress (eds) *China's Economic Dilemmas in the 1990s*, US Government, Washington D.C.

Stone, B. (1988) 'Developments in Agricultural Technology', *China Quarterly*, No. 118.

Wang, H.S., Cheng, W.M., Yan, X.F. and Yang, W.M. (1995) 'Industrialization and social stratification', *Chinese Law and Government*, 28(1): 9–38.

White, G. (1991) *The Chinese State in the Era of Economic Reform*, Macmillan, London.

Wong, C.P.W. (1988) 'Interpreting rural industrial growth in the post-Mao period', *Modern China*, 14(1).

World Bank (1994) *China: Internal Market Development and Regulation*, World Bank, Washington.

ZGTJNJ – Zhongguo guojia tongjiju, (Chinese State Statistical Bureau) (ed.) (various years) *Zhongguo tongji nianjian* (*Chinese Statistical Yearbook*), Zhongguo tongji chubanshe, Beijing.

Zhonggong Sichuan sheng wei nongcun jingji shehui fazhan zhanlue yanjiuzu, (Research Group for the CCP's Sichuan Committee on the Development Strategy for the Rural Economy and Society) (ed.) (1986) *Sichuan nongcun jintian he mingtian* (*Rural Sichuan Today and Tomorrow*), Sichuan kexue jishu chubanshe, Chengdu.

Zhou, K.X. (1996) *How The Farmers Changed China*, Westview, Boulder.

16. Japan's New 'Peasants'

JOHN KNIGHT

Introduction

The decline of Japanese agriculture has been the object of protracted and intense public debate and media commentary in Japan over recent decades. In the 1990s Japanese agriculture is widely viewed as in a state of crisis, if not in terminal decline. 'Without an increase in young people coming in and taking over, Japanese rice production, and indeed all of Japanese agriculture, is headed for oblivion' (Kubō 1994: 6). The growing international pressure on Japan to liberalize agricultural trade and allow imports of farm products has only heightened this national sense of foreboding. The prospect of the demise of the Japanese farm sector in general, and of rice farming in particular, excites popular fears and political concern about the loss of national food security and its adverse effects on rural livelihoods and the environment.[1]

Another reason for popular concern about the future of farming involves the importance of agrarianist ideas in Japan. There is a long intellectual tradition in Japan according to which farming is viewed as the basis of Japanese civilization.[2] Japanese agrarianists have long idealized peasant farmers for their diligence, frugality, spirit of co-operation, love of the soil, commitment to tradition, and loyalty to the nation. Although first and foremost associated with the pre-war era, agrarianist sentiments are also evident in post-war Japan. Thus, for Kunimoto (1971: 450), the farm village is 'both the womb and the spine of traditional Japanese culture'. The same author warns that agricultural contraction poses 'the danger of Japan's culture degenerating into a shallow modernism that has no nationality', and calls on the government 'to examine the agricultural problem not from the standpoint of policies or economic principles but from the standpoint of the true prosperity of the Japanese race' (ibid.: 450).

The Japanese debate on agricultural liberalization in the 1980s and 1990s shows that rice and other farm products continue to be important symbols of Japanese national identity. One commentator explained Japanese opposition to rice imports in the following way.

> Rice alone is the symbol of a well-fed nation safe from the vagaries of fluctuating international circumstances; no other food or foods could take its place. This is because rice is both the staple food of the Japanese and a food that is more than a food. . . . The mention of rice may bring vivid images to the minds of some Japanese. A steaming bowl of rice, each kernel pristine white. . . . Hot sake that warms the insides in the

cold of winter. Thick braided straw ropes that hang across entryways at Shinto shrines. . . . Paddies, green with nature's bounty, layering mountain slopes. Row upon row of brown sheaves lining paddies after the harvest. The rural ethos and salt-of-the-earth countryfolk (Ni'ide 1994: 20).

In addition to producing the national staple, the Japanese village has played the no less vital role of reproducing the national population. One of the arguments deployed by Japanese agrarianists in the earlier part of the twentieth century was that the countryside was demographically indispensable to the cities (Yokoi Tokiyoshi, in Gluck 1985: 180). But at the end of the century it is the countryside which cannot reproduce itself. The theme of 'the dying Japanese village' (Hiraike 1985) has been a recurring one in post-war Japan. Rural depopulation has led to the abandonment of many villages and to the serious ageing of many more. One observer characterizes the remote villages he visited as 'villages of death' (*shi no shūraku*) and rural depopulation as a form of 'cancer' (*gan*) (Aoyama 1994: 19–20).

This chapter considers an alternative future for the Japanese village, one in which a new generation of 'peasants' is drawn from the cities. Rural resettlement – migration to remote rural areas by idealistic urbanites in order to take up farming – is a phenomenon that has been documented in many urban–industrial societies since the 1970s.[3] In Japan urbanites are also migrating to the countryside to take up farming. One example is given below of such rural resettlement in Japan. Although still a minor trend, rural resettlement gives contemporary expression to the tradition of Japanese agrarianism.

The first part of this chapter gives an overview of the decline of the Japanese peasantry and changes in Japanese agriculture. The second part describes recent rural resettlement in Japan, drawing both on first-hand ethnographic data from the Kii Peninsula, western Japan, and on reports on rural resettlement in other regions.

Disappearing Peasants

In the course of the twentieth century, Japan has changed from a predominantly agrarian society to an urban–industrial society. In 1900, 70 per cent of the Japanese working population were employed in primary industries, mainly agriculture; by 1990 this had fallen to 7 per cent (Kobayashi et al. 1991: 214).

Following the Meiji Restoration of 1868, the Japanese state embarked on a course of rapid industrialization. Japanese industrialization is generally held to have drawn heavily on surplus extraction from agriculture. Calder (1988: 244) notes that for more than three generations after the Meiji Restoration of 1868, agriculture faced strong discrimination from a state apparatus that placed highest priority on industrialization and military security. Only with rising rural unrest in the 1920s did this begin to change and then only marginally.

Pre-war Japanese agriculture, characterized by the existence of a powerful landlord class and a large class of tenants, is often described as 'feudal'.[4]

It was the (Occupation-inspired) agricultural land reform of 1947–50 which broke up large farm landholdings, eliminated tenant farming, and created a new class of small-scale owner–farmers. 'About 2.8 million acres of rice paddies and 1.95 million acres of upland were transferred from 2.34 million landowners to 4.75 million tenants and farmers who possessed less than the legal maximum' (Hane 1982: 249). The reform was inspired by American ideas of 'Jeffersonian agrarianism' which 'emphasized the connection between ownership of private property and independence, liberty, and model citizenship' (Moore 1990: 85–6), and had the political purpose of preventing social unrest and of removing any bases of support for fascism or communism in rural areas.

One of the consequences of the post-war land reform was that it exacerbated the problem of the small scale of Japanese farming and thereby severely circumscribed the competitive potential of Japanese agriculture. Average farm size in Japan is around 1.5 hectares, more than 100 times less than that of the USA, but about the same as the average landholding in India.

In contrast to the post-Meiji period, public policy in the post-war period has been marked by a 'rural bias' (Calder 1988: 231). Considerable resources have been transferred to the Japanese regions through agricultural subsidy, public works programmes and regional policy more generally. This has had the effect of transforming Japanese farming from a labour-intensive activity into a highly mechanized, technologically advanced one. Most farming households own their own farm machines (tillers, tractors, transplanters, harvesters, threshers etc.) and use synthetic fertilizers, insecticides and herbicides on their fields. These new technological inputs have greatly reduced the physical drudgery of agricultural tasks such as transplanting seedlings, weeding, harvesting and threshing.

More generally, this public policy has raised the standard of living in rural Japan to match that of urban areas, has expedited rural industrialization and diversified rural employment, and helped create a new social class in Japan, made up of rural workers who continue to form part of farm households. 'The share of part-time farmers deriving over half their income outside agriculture has risen in Japan to sharply higher levels than in any other major industrialized nation today' (Calder 1988: 241).

The majority of Japanese farm households (around 85 per cent) farm on a part-time basis. In 1990, 65 per cent of total farm household income was derived from non-farm activities (Kobayashi et al. 1991: 216). The stability of part-time farming, facilitated by both farming subsidies and improved off-farm employment opportunities through rural subcontracting of industry, has been until recently one of the chief characteristics of post-war farming in Japan.[5]

In the late twentieth century, this situation is changing. Rural industry in Japan is in decline because of the trend towards industrial relocation to more competitive production sites overseas. Government commitment to agriculture has waned somewhat. Since the early 1970s the Japanese government, faced with an over-production of rice, has encouraged acreage reduction. Pressures for the liberalization of agricultural trade have intensified. In 1993 the Japanese government agreed to a timetable for opening up its rice market to imports, and has also committed itself to the deregulation of the domestic rice market.

Japanese agriculture faces a crisis of reproduction. Agrarian decline has accelerated in recent decades. In 1970 there were 5.4 million farm households in Japan, but by 1990 the number had fallen to 3.9 million (Kobayashi et al. 1991: 214). A major problem is the ageing of the farming population and the small number of young people entering agriculture. 'Over half of all Japanese farmers are over 60, while the 30 000 farmers aged 16 to 29 account for only 3 per cent of the farm population' (Kubō 1994: 6). In addition to the poor prospects of farming as an industry, farming is handicapped by a serious image problem among rural youth, and especially among young rural women from whom the farmers' wives of the future must be drawn. Farming is often characterized in Japan as a '3K' activity – *kusai* (smelly), *kitanai* (dirty) and *kitsui* (exhausting). On account of its physical rigours, Japanese farming has also been portrayed as 'wife-killing farming' (*yomegoroshi nōgyō*). Consequently, males who inherit farms often have difficulty finding brides, and this rural 'marriage problem' is a further reason why young men reject farming.

Rural Resettlement

National, prefectural and municipal governments have responded to the farming crisis in a variety of ways. There are attempts to rejuvenate farming economically by increasing the scale of rice-farming operations (through landholding consolidation and leasing agreements); by promoting the commercial cultivation of new non-rice crops (fruit, vegetables, flowers, bedding plants etc.); and by encouraging technological innovation in farming (such as greenhouse cultivation, biotechnology, and indoor 'soil-less farming').

There are also attempts to recruit new farmers from among the urban population. Regional authorities promote return-migration. Prefectures have opened offices in Tokyo to publicize the 'U-turn' option and to handle inquiries. There have been advertising campaigns, including posters in the Tokyo subway, newspaper advertisements and television commercials, exhorting migrants from the regions to return to their rural home towns. Some rural municipalities even offer monetary incentives to encourage return-migration (Nozoe 1994: 88–9). In 1980 the number of return migrants who resumed or took up farming was over 60 000, nearly two-thirds of whom were aged 50 and over (Uchiyama 1990: 149–51).

In addition to migrants, unrelated outsiders who are willing to take up farming are actively recruited. Prefectures have established offices in metropolitan areas to field inquiries from would-be rural settlers or 'I-turners' (a play on the term 'U-turn'). One example is Nagano Prefecture which has attracted 2000 settlers from the major cities since 1989 (Hidaka 1996: 173). Many prefectures have established assistance and training programmes to attract 'new farmers' to their rural areas. At the national level, the Japanese Ministry of Agriculture has launched a scheme to promote farming-related rural resettlement in remote areas (ibid.: 2). In fact, such policies are in large part a response to existing counter-urbanization trends in Japanese society. According to the official figures published in the Nōgyō Hakusho (based on inquiries to an officially funded information centre and the various prefectural consultancy centres), in 1996 3570 people of urban origin made inquiries about taking up farming in the countryside, and 384 people actually did so (NTK 1998: 174). However, these figures account for no more than a part of the trend towards back-to-the-land farming in Japan, as many of the new farmers take up farming through word-of-mouth connections rather than through these formal channels.

There is considerable dissatisfaction with living conditions among Japanese urbanites and suburbanites. One expression of this is the emergence of 'country living' or *inakagurashi* as a prominent theme in the Japanese mass media. Television programmes on country life appear regularly, while specialist magazines with titles such as *Country Life*, extol the advantages of rural life and list available properties. A 1993 survey of Tokyo dwellers found that 30 per cent would like to move out of the metropolis (KKTK 1994: 45). The main reasons given by Japanese urban dwellers for preferring to live in the countryside include clean air, clear water, fresh food, large houses, short commuting time, neighbourliness and social intimacy, low crime rates, and peace of mind. A 1993 survey of rural incomers found that 43 per cent had opted to leave the city 'in order to live in a rich natural environment' (ibid.: 47). One common perception among rural resettlers is that the countryside is a place of human warmth (*ninjōmi*), in contrast to the loneliness, crime, congestion and preoccupation with money experienced in urban Japan (Kitsu 1993: 10–12).

Modern rural resettlement in Japan dates back to the 1970s.[6] Japanese rural resettlement typically centres on farming, even though settlers have taken up a variety of other occupational activities including woodcrafts, charcoal-burning and forestry (Hidaka 1996: 152–66). One pattern of rural resettlement involves the clustering of new settlers in the same area, forming in effect a network or group,[7] but there are also more scattered patterns of rural resettlement where a single family takes up residence in a village.

Two types of rural resettlement can be distinguished. One takes the form of elderly urbanites who move to the countryside on retiring from their job in the city. There has been a growth of retirement homes in rural Japan. Although these retirees may well cultivate vegetables, this form of rural resettlement can be seen as part of the urban-industrial society and its prescribed life-course. By contrast, the rural resettlers examined here reject urban-industrial society and its salaried occupations, and commit themselves to an alternative, agrarian lifestyle. This rural resettlement is typically inspired by idealistic and utopian currents of neo-agrarian thought and couched in ecological idioms.

One influential figure among idealistic rural resettlers is Fukuoka Masanobu, the well known guru of 'natural farming' (*shizen nōhō*). On the basis of his ecocentric view of farming and his biocentric understanding of human existence, Fukuoka has become a leading proponent of the back-to-the-land idea in Japan. Fukuoka believes that industrial civilization is unstable, destructive and dehumanizing, and that it is destined to collapse under the weight of its multiple contradictions.

> Life in Japan's large cities has reached about the same level of affluence as in advanced Western countries. . . . But all that has really grown is the economy. The inner life of people has become stunted, natural joy has been lost. More and more people have turned to standardized forms of recreation such as television, the pachinko parlour, and mahjong, or seek temporary solace through drinking and sex . . . People no longer tread over the bare earth. Their hands have drawn away from the grasses and flowers, they do not gaze up into the heavens, their ears are deaf to the song of the birds, their noses are rendered insensitive by exhaust fumes, and their tongues have forgotten the simple tastes of nature. All five senses have grown isolated from nature (Fukuoka 1985: 257).

For Fukuoka, Japan has reached a turning point whereby the problems of urban life, generated by the destructive separation of the Japanese people from nature, are finally being recognized and alternative ways of living pursued. He calls for the 'return of all the people to the country to farm and create villages of true men' in order that Japan should once again become a 'society of farmers' (ibid.: 258). In his manifesto for rural resettlement, entitled *Farming for All*, Fukuoka presents a vision of the Japanese people as a whole returning to the land.

> Japan has about 15 million acres of farming land, which works out to about a quarter-acre per adult. If Japan's land were divided evenly

among 20 million households, this would give each household three quarters of an acre of farmland plus two and a half acres of mountain [forest] and meadow land. With total reliance on natural farming, all it takes to support a household of several people is a quarter-acre. On this amount of land, one could build a small house, grow grains and vegetables, raise a goat, and even keep several chickens and a hive of bees (Fukuoka 1985: 260).

The Kumano Settlers[8]

The mass 'return' of the Japanese people to the land envisaged by Fukuoka Masanobu has yet to occur. However, rural settlers influenced by Fukuoka's ideas have emerged in many Japanese regions, including on the southern Kii Peninsula, in the area commonly known as Kumano. Since 1980 around 50 families have come to settle in the Kumano area, where they rent empty houses and unused farmland in remote village settlements. Around 20 of these new families have settled in the upland municipality of Hongū-chō.

Hongū has undergone severe agricultural decline. The area of Hongū farmland has diminished by two-thirds. Some of the former farmland has become housing land, but most of it has been planted with conifer saplings for timber. Despite the fact that more than half the 1960 rice-field acreage has been converted to other uses, in 1995 over a quarter of the remaining Hongū rice land was unused. One of the causes of agricultural contraction in Hongū is out-migration. The municipality lost over half its population in the post-war period. There has also been a repudiation of farming among the remaining residential population. In 1955 two-thirds of the working population of Hongū worked in the primary sector (farming and forestry), but by 1990 this had fallen to 13 per cent. In 1990 it was the tertiary sector (including tourism) which accounted for nearly two-thirds of the Hongū workforce. The combined trends of out-migration and de-agrarianization create deserted villages and overgrown rice fields. It is in these vacated rural spaces that the newcomers have come to settle.

The Hongū newcomers originate, for the most part, from the major cities of Tokyo, Osaka and Kyoto, but some come from the regions (such as Hiroshima, Shikoku and Aomori). They are typically young (in their twenties and thirties) and university-educated, and their previous occupations include company employee, designer, computer programmer, gardener, livestock farmer, baker, Buddhist priest and artist. Most practise organic farming, and rent farmland on which they grow rice, vegetables and fruits, and keep farm animals. Many grow and eat 'natural food' (*shizenshoku*) – and are referred to by locals as 'the natural food people' (*shizenshoku no hito*) – and eat brown rice rather than the white rice preferred by the local people and most Japanese. One or two new families follow a macrobiotic diet.

The settlers tend to be critical of modern urban life more generally. They have migrated to the Kumano region because it is different from Tokyo and Osaka. Many explicitly state that it is 'great nature' (*daishizen*) which has drawn them to Kumano. Some approach nature as an object of worship, and make the notion of 'gratitude' (*kansha*) central to their lives, particularly in relation to the food they grow and eat, and even characterize their new way of life as a form of religious austerity or *shugyō* (Hidaka 1996: 157). A number of the Hongū settlers have visited India, and are influenced by Indian mystical and religious traditions (including Bhagwanism).

The settlers are widely read in the field of alternative and ecological literature, and are familiar with the ideas of such thinkers as Steiner, Schumacher and Capra. Kumano is a mountainous region well known in Japan for its shrines and as a site of medieval pilgrimage. Some of the newcomers have translated this sacred character of Kumano into a global New Age idiom of energy lines, vibrations and meridians. Like Stonehenge and Mecca, Kumano is held to be one of the primary points in the earth's energy system. There is also a keen interest in indigenous cultures such as the Ainu, ancient Celts and North American Indians who stand as exemplars of a simple, natural lifestyle in stark contrast to modern materialism.[9]

For many of the newcomers, the 'peasant', like the indigenous hunter-gatherer before, stands as a symbol of anti-materialism. The newcomers tend to refer to themselves as 'peasants' or *hyakushō*. In Japanese, the term *hyakushō* has certain negative connotations; as a noun it is readily paired with negative adjectives, such as *mugaku na hyakushō* or 'ignorant peasant'. Among Hongū people, the term *hyakushō* is sometimes invoked as a form of self-deprecation. For example, it is used to explain why young people leave the village (to escape 'peasant' life) or why farming sons cannot find brides (because young women refuse to marry into a 'peasant' family). Indeed, among larger farmers there is an effort to escape this 'peasant' imagery and to define farming as a modern occupation. Kelly (1986: 609) describes how a particular part-time farmer 'styles his work identity and routine as a "scientific and rational occupation"', and goes on to stress the importance of new machines in creating a modern image of farm work which will hopefully persuade younger farmers to stay on the farm.

However, the Kumano settlers invoke the term *hyakushō*, with its associations of a simple life of honest toil on the land, with a certain ironic pride. The 'peasant' lifestyle represents the polar opposite to that of the salaried worker which many of them followed. In fact, a common media term applied to rural settlers is *datsusara* or 'salary-shedders', making the point that the new settlers reject the very status and lifestyle of the urban middle-class salaried worker to which most young Japanese (including rural youth) aspire.

For some newcomers, the 'peasant' lifestyle is synonymous with autarky. They pursue a lifestyle of near 'self-sufficiency' (*jikyū jizoku*) in which household food is largely self-produced and participation in the money economy is minimized. Some explicitly eschew the 'money economy' (*kahei keizai*), viewing money as the central symbol of the materialistic society they reject. They occasionally sell their produce for much-needed cash, but do so reluctantly. By contrast, their village neighbours have become absorbed by the cash economy through waged employment. Factory-employed farmers' wives no longer contribute so much labour to growing vegetables and making home-made foods such as *miso* (bean paste), *tsukemono* (pickled vegetables) and *umeboshi* (pickled plums). At a time when the newcomers were moving into the countryside to pursue their goal of autarky, rural families were increasingly 'buying their vegetables in stores instead of growing them and using processed foods instead of preparing them at home' (Nozoe 1981: 224). In addition to their rejection of money, some new families refuse to send their children to local schools. One Hongū family opposes school attendance because it is believed that the schools simply serve to regiment the children and to inculcate the materialistic values of the wider industrial capitalist society.

The settlers' approach to farming differs from mainstream Japanese farming in a number of respects. There is a rejection of synthetic fertilizer, both because it is believed to be harmful to the human body, and because fertility is held to be something which should come from the soil itself. Pesticides are similarly rejected on safety grounds. The newcomers therefore carry out the demanding task of weeding by hand. The newcomers' farming is largely unmechanized, in contrast to the mechanized farming of villagers. In some areas, there are even examples of rural settlers who have revived the old practice of ploughing their fields with oxen (Saitō 1985: 38).

Some newcomers practise a more radical form of alternative farming, informed by the ideas of Fukuoka Masanobu mentioned above. Fukuoka's 'natural farming' method involves the rejection of tillage and weeding. Tillage is eschewed in order to restore the integrity and fertility of the soil by increasing organic matter, and there is no weeding because weeds are seen as beneficial, naturally 'tilling' the soil through their roots and, on dying, providing nutrients to micro-organisms in the soil (Fukuoka 1983: 48–53). According to this method, the farmer does not really 'cultivate' (*tsukuru*) at all, but assists with the crop growth which is generated by the powers of fertility intrinsic to the soil.

Some newcomers fertilize the soil with family waste. At a time when villagers increasingly opt for flush toilets instead of non-flush latrines (a symbol of the 'smelly' and 'dirty' character of the Japanese countryside), the newcomers positively choose the latrine because it allows them to recycle nightsoil as farm fertilizer in the traditional way. Another source of organic fertilizer for their fields comes from the domestic animals which many newcomers keep. Until the 1950s it was common for most farming households to have one or two cows and some chickens. In the past few decades, however, farm animals have largely disappeared from Japanese villages as machines replaced cows for farmwork and synthetic chemical fertilizers replaced animal dung. Among the new farmers, however, chicken, cow and goat droppings are used as farmland manure.

Another feature of 'natural farming' is the linkage of forest and farm. The use of the forest is seen as integral to earlier peasant farming. Mountain forests provided green fertilizer for fields and fodder for animals, as well as food, fuel and timber for building. Fukuoka (1985: 137) suggests that every new farmer should be able to draw on some nearby forest for organic fertilizer. Some new families in Hongū reject the use of modern forms of energy such as electricity and gas, preferring instead candles, oil lamps, and forest fuels such as firewood and charcoal. In this they are imitating the pre-war pattern of energy usage in rural areas.

Many of the Kumano settlers grow distinct rice varieties (such as *koganemasari*) which grow better under chemical-free conditions, and circulate seeds among themselves. Earlier generations of Japanese farmers developed their own family or village rice seed, which was better suited to local conditions, but this has since been replaced by uniform, high-yielding rice varieties scientifically produced by government laboratories and distributed by the Agricultural Co-operative. The newcomers lament this loss of seed variety in rice farming.

In general, the newcomers grow the same range of crops as local families. In addition they grow some crops which have been discontinued by villagers, the prime example being a winter crop of wheat on their rice fields. Again, this 'double-cropping' practice, facilitated by the mild winters of western Japan, is associated with the peasant farming of the past.

Local impact of rural resettlement

Although the newcomers consider their farming to accord with the 'peasant' tradition of the Hongū area, this form of farming is a source of friction with villagers. Adjacent farmers sometimes find that their fields are adversely affected by insects and other pests as a result of the newcomers' pesticide-free rice fields. The newcomers' use of human and animal waste on the fields also leads to complaints about bad smells. The newcomers' farming methods are viewed as inferior. One basis for this perception is the poor harvests of the newcomers, as much as 30 per cent less than other farmers. There are also doubts about the quality of the rice produced. These are expressed in stories circulating among villagers in which wild animals, such as wild boar, eat the crops grown by villagers but tend to shun those of the newcomers.

There is a local perception of the settlers as 'idlers' (*namakemono*). While some perform the demanding task of weeding the rice field by hand, others eschew weeding altogether. As they do not use weedkiller, this means that their fields become riddled with weeds. This is something which offends the villagers' sense of what a field should look like and reinforces the local impression of the settlers as feckless and incompetent. Such misgivings are further fuelled by tales of settlers who, rather than bending down to transplant seedlings in the traditional back-breaking way, opt to scatter the seeds (encased in small clay balls) by hand (Nakamura 1991: 14).

Newcomers find that they have restricted access to certain basic farming inputs. Irrigation is one problem. The direct-seeding methods employed by some newcomers entail a particular timetable for cultivation and specific irrigation requirements. Usually, village farmers co-ordinate seedling transplanting and collectively irrigate their fields. This customary communal control of irrigation channels can lead to disputes with the newcomers whose own farming is hindered by a lack of control over irrigation (Fukuoka 1985: 179). Another problem arises with green fertilizer from the forest. For some newcomers the forest is effectively out of bounds because of village requirements to join the local forest association (*kurinkai*) as a condition of forest access. For many cash-strapped newcomers the cost of doing so is prohibitive.

The new farmers tend to be perceived as impermanent by their village neighbours. Typically, they rent rather than own the land they live on and farm. One reason for renting is the reluctance of rural families to sell land. Land, inherited from earlier generations ('made with the tears and sweat of ancestors'), is regarded as something that a family should pass on to the next generation and never sell. Even when a villager does sell land, other villagers are customarily given first option to buy it. (In fact, in the 1980s and 1990s a proliferation of rural land sales to outside buyers occurred, but this has taken place in the context of large-scale tourist development and inflated land prices.)

A further reason for renting has to do with the settlers' rejection of land ownership and the restrictions on mobility and freedom that it entails. There has been a high turnover of newcomers on the Kii Peninsula and elsewhere in Japan. Some find their new way of life harder than anticipated, and give up after a few weeks or months. Others positively opt for successive migrations, moving on after a number of years to lead the same kind of farming lifestyle in another region. One new family in Fukui Prefecture, for example, referred to themselves as 'guerrilla peasants' (*gerira nōmin*) who must move on in due course rather than stay in one place (Yamashita 1993: 113); others refer to themselves as 'travellers' (*tabi no hito*) or 'ramblers' (*yūhojin*) (Takahashi 1984: 34). The same spirit of adventure that brought them to the region may well lead them out again.

Despite these problems, the new settlers have usually been positively received by the depopulated villages they enter. One effect of rural depopulation is the demoralization of the remaining population, manifested most starkly in the high rates of suicide reported among the rural elderly.[10] In addition to empty village houses, the abandonment and loss of farmland is a source of particular dismay and distress. The original reclamation of arable land is viewed by village descendants as a great ancestral achievement which is the focus of gratitude and a source of pride. 'For generations, farmers had considered it a virtue to reclaim land for paddies, a practice their forebears had begun centuries ago' (Ni'ide 1994: 18). Conversely, farmland that is overgrown or that has reverted to forest is one of the saddest of sights for elderly villagers, and arguably a factor contributing to rural demoralization. The new occupancy of long-vacated houses and the renewed cultivation of fallow rice fields help to offset this despair by suggesting that village decline may not, after all, be inexorable. The arrival of a new family in a dilapidated old village often generates great excitement among the remaining inhabitants. In those remote villages, which had seemed destined to abandonment, the appearance of new settlers offers much-needed hope for the future.

The newcomers can also restore confidence in upland farming, something which has been seriously dented in recent decades. One major problem for Kumano farmers is damage to crops from widlife, a perennial threat to farmland, but one which has greatly worsened with depopulation. Elderly cultivators are sometimes forced to abandon outlying fields in the face of repeated depredations. New settlers likewise suffer such farm damage (despite comments to the contrary of some of their neighbours), and this is one of the reasons why they too may give up farming and leave. In general, however, the presence of the newcomers, farming what is often the most vulnerable farmland by the forest fringe, rekindles villagers' resolve to resist encroachment by erecting or repairing fences and investing in wildlife repellents and scare devices.

In the weeks before harvest, some newcomers physically guard their rice fields against visits from wild boar in the night. Such field-guarding, another revived custom associated with the 'peasant' past, is a clear demonstration of the newcomers' commitment to farming which earns them the respect of their elderly neighbours, many of whom undertook the same task in their youth decades ago. This guarding of vulnerable peripheral fields also tends to elicit a wider local gratitude as it serves to protect village farmland more generally.

The newcomers make other major practical contributions to the villages they enter. They join in collective work tasks and duties of the village (such as path-clearing, fire-fighting drills, funeral preparations, clearing up typhoon damage). As youthful newcomers to what are typically elderly villages, their contribution is often very important and highly valued. Their children boost the numbers enrolled at small village schools, and thereby help the locality to resist the pressure for school closure.

The settlers can also radicalize the villages they enter. The Kumano settlers are often outspoken in their criticism of local industries such as forestry, construction and tourism, and have even become involved in protests against development initiatives such as road construction, dam construction or the establishment of nuclear power stations. This activism can lead to friction with other villagers, especially where the perception is created that the newcomers are not committed to rural development. However, there are clear examples where newcomers, by alerting the local population to the adverse environmental consequences of certain exogenous development plans, such as golf-course construction, have acted as the catalyst for a wider local protest (Moen 1997: 21–2). At a time when 'resort development' is transforming land use in rural Japan on an enormous scale, with metropolitan capital buying up large swathes of the Japanese countryside to build ski-runs, golf courses and condominiums, and encountering little resistance from the dwindling numbers of rural dwellers, the new settlers constitute an important source of resistance.

The new settlers also oppose cultural standardization. They often bring with them a great enthusiasm for local customs, traditions and other aspects of village life and culture which are being discontinued and forgotten. They are keen attenders of village festivals, and some even undertake the documentation of village folklore. Settlers have played an important role in perpetuating or reviving such traditions, and in stimulating renewed local interest in them (Fujimoto 1992: 13).

As mentioned earlier, settlers are often champions of the 'natural farming' lifestyle. There is a certain amount of evangelizing among village neighbours. In Hongū a few local families have emulated their new neighbours and farm without chemicals, and many more have reduced their use of chemicals. To diffuse their ideas more widely, some Kumano settlers have established an induction course – nationally advertised in certain alternative magazines – in which would-be rural resettlers can come and learn how to lead a self-sufficient, organic farming lifestyle. Settlers have also become involved in debates on local development, in some cases forcefully arguing that agrarian revival based on organic farming methods is the only solution to the widespread problem of rural depopulation (Yamashita 1993: 206–8).

Recent trends in the Japanese food sector have tended to facilitate a more positive local reception for the settlers' ideas about farming and food. Organic farming is of increasing commercial importance in Japan. There are widespread consumer concerns about the quality of purchased farm products and the perceived over-use of chemicals by output-maximizing Japanese farmers.[11] One striking expression of such concerns is the rise in membership of consumer co-operatives in Japan. 'In 1996, the 688 primary Seikyo food co-operatives alone had a national household membership of 14 million' (Moen 1997: 14). Many consumer co-operatives subcontract rural producers to grow organic food for their largely urban membership (Inoue 1996b: 62–8). Some rural municipalities offset the decline in mainstream farming by converting to market-directed organic farming (Takeuchi 1993: 117). The appearance of the new 'peasants' in rural Japan coincides with this new consumer trend. Even though the Kumano newcomers are generally not involved in new rural enterprises, their organic farming ideas have had an impact on the development of local commercial products, some of which are marketed nationally as 'chemical-free' (*munōyaku*), 'additive-free' (*mutenka*) 'health foods' (*kenkō shokuhin*).

Finally, the newcomers have attracted enormous mass-media interest. The Hongū settlers have been regularly visited by journalists and filmed by television camera crews. Rural resettlement is a phenomenon which captures the imagination of the wider Japanese society, especially where it involves young, middle-class families willingly embracing the everyday hardships of the peasant past, such as wood-stove cooking and machineless farming. Some Kumano settlers have become minor media celebrities in their own right. This media attention is often encouraged by municipal authorities keen to maximize national publicity for the locality, with an eye to tourist promotion and further settlement.

Conclusions

Japanese farming in the modern era has undergone a number of transitions. One major transition was that from the pre-war era of surplus extraction to the post-war era of subsidized farming. At the end of the twentieth century another transition is evident, from the post-war 'rural bias' to the withdrawal of state commitment to farming, as manifested in the trends of agricultural liberalization, deregulation and even prospective desubsidization. The most emphatic demonstration of this shift – and of the prioritization of Japanese industry over agriculture – came in 1993 when the Japanese government agreed to a timetable for rice imports at the conclusion of the General Agreement on Tariffs and Trade. Although state support for the regions continues in Japan, support for farming lifestyles is effectively being withdrawn.

In the 1990s the future of Japanese farming appears in great doubt. There is a dire shortage of younger farmers, and a shortage of brides for farmers. The Japanese farming sector would appear to be incapable of reproducing itself in the twenty-first century. Some media commentary suggests that agriculture is set to become the next Japanese industry to be relocated to other parts of Asia, with farmers in Thailand, Vietnam and China likely to supply the Japanese food market and become the growers of Japanese japonica rice varieties (Kubō 1994: 8).

The plight of Japanese farming readily accords with modernist expectations of agrarian decline in advanced industrial society, whereby the peasant appears condemned to disappear (Giner and Sevilla-Guzman 1980; Kearney 1996: Ch. 3). This tendency to see the peasant in the past tense has become pronounced in post-war Japan, with its much-vaunted 'economic miracle' and its assumption of 'economic superpower' status.

Yet twentieth-century Japan also provides a clear example of the phenomenon, well documented in other urban-industrial societies,[12] whereby the disappearance of agrarian lifestyles co-exists with the persistence of agrarianist motifs. One of the conspicuous features of Japanese modernity has been the ideological incorporation of peasant motifs and imagery as a central constituent of national identity in the industrial or post-industrial age. Along with the emperor and the family, the peasantry have served as an enduring symbol of cultural continuity and timeless national essence in the course of Japanese modernization. One theme of post-war social science in Japan relates to the continuity of the agrarian past in the urban-industrial present in the form of latent principles of social organization. As Harootunian (1989: 83) points out, post-war Japan represents a prime example of the way in which 'the values of an agrarian order have been made to serve the requirements of a postindustrial society'. This transmutation of the peasantry into an underlying motif of the industrial order legitimates Japanese modernization and, with it, de-agrarianization. Agrarianism in this abstracted form serves 'to sanction, not to resist, the modernizing changes Japan has realized' (Harootunian 1993: 216).

The new 'peasants' of Kumano have an ambivalent relationship to this process of modernist incorporation of the agrarian. On the one hand, they challenge the 'teleologic master narrative' (Kearney 1996: 73) of peasant disappearance in the course of modernization. Rejecting the urban, salaried lifestyle in favour of the 'peasant' farmer, they invert – and potentially de-naturalize – the dominant trend of post-Meiji Japan. Moreover, by physically committing themselves directly to the land, they manifest the possibility of a literal agrarianism – as lifestyle – in late-twentieth century Japan, and thereby challenge the modern appropriation of the agrarian as a legitimating device for the urban-industrial order. As 'salary shedders', they reject Japanese industrialism and, *ipso facto*, any supposed latent agrarian legitimations of it. They embody the possibility of a direct continuation into the present of Japan's 'peasant' past.

Many newcomers consider themselves to be the vanguard of a new trend which will accelerate in the decades ahead, as other urbanites realize the limitations of city life and opt to 'return' to the land. However, statistically, rural resettlement remains a minor phenomenon compared to ongoing agricultural contraction and rural depopulation. Its principal significance is therefore probably not as rural repopulation, at least not on a scale commensurate with rural depopulation, but as a concrete statement of the possibility of an agrarian future for rural Japan.

Nevertheless, the new settlers cannot avoid becoming caught up in the larger ideological process of agrarian symbol-mongering in present-day Japan. Despite the autarkic goals animating much Japanese rural resettlement, in practice, as we have seen, there is a degree of enlistment of the new settlers, along with their ideas and rhetoric, by the host locality to the cause of market-directed rural development. Rural municipalities have become aware of the instrumental potential of agrarian motifs in relation to both commercial product development ('home-town food', organic 'health foods', etc.) and tourism, as is indicated most strikingly by the emergence of what might be called rural tourism.[13] Despite the antipathy to 'industrial society', 'capitalism' and 'materialism' among many of Japan's new rural settlers, in the long run their primary significance may well lie in the way they come to articulate with symbolically infused national markets such as food and tourism, as much as in the establishment of alternative autarkic lifestyles.

Notes

1. The abandonment of upstream agricultural land has long been cited as a cause of downstream flooding (Yūki 1970: 147). More recently, the Japanese Ministry of Agriculture commissioned a study in which the land and environmental preservation function of rice paddies was estimated at ¥12 trillion a year, some three times the total value of rice production. Paddy fields absorb carbon dioxide efficiently, prevent the leaching of nitrogen and nitrogen pollution, and also prevent soil erosion (Tashiro 1992: 42–3).
2. See, for example, Havens (1974), Smethurst (1974), Ogura (1979: Ch. 1), Ohnuki-Tierney (1993: Ch. 6).
3. For examples of rural resettlement in Britain, see Bennett (1993), Coates et al. (1993); for France, McDonald (1989); Leger (1982); for the USA, Berry (1992).
4. The status of pre-war Japanese agriculture – and therefore the character of the Japanese agrarian transition – is something which has been much debated; see Byres (1991) and Smethurst (1986: 6n). The view of pre-war agriculture as a site of feudalism has been challenged by scholars who argue that pre-war rural Japan was a site of capitalism and that the Meiji Restoration was Japan's 'bourgeois revolution'.
5. On the emergence and importance of these farm-based workers, see Prindle (1984), McDonald (1996).
6. The return to the land is a theme of pre-war Japanese agrarianism. There were a number of utopian settlements established in the countryside by Japanese intellectuals, such as the 'new villages' founded by the novelist Mushakoji Saneatsu in 1918 and the Fraternal Village (*Kyōdai Mura*) associated with Tachibana Kōzaburō in 1915 (Havens 1974: 113–14, 236). Other pre-war instances of back-to-the-land movements were religiously inspired and centred on alternative farming (Shimazono 1996: 54–5).
7. Well known examples of new rural settlements include Oak Village in Nagano Prefecture which was established in 1974 by a group of idealistic university graduates. In the north of Wakayama Prefecture a new village, called *Banjirō Mura* (Guava Village), was founded in the mid-1980s.

8. See Knight (1997) for an earlier, extended analysis of rural resettlement on the southern Kii Peninsula.
9. In the late 1980s, a number of the newcomers joined in the Japan leg of the American Indians' 'Run for Peace'.
10. On the demoralization of depopulated rural areas, see MSAS (1988: 71–5). On the high rates of suicide among the rural elderly, see MSAS (1988: 87–9) and Nozoe (1994: 63–6).
11. In a 1991 survey of Tokyo consumers, 84 per cent expressed concern about farm chemicals in fruit and vegetables (Inoue 1996a: 26).
12. See, for example, Rogers (1987), Brass (1997).
13. Rural tourism is another expression of the modernist preoccupation with the agrarian past in Japan. Expressions of the touristic incorporation of pastoral motifs are evident in the proliferation of meadows, ranches and parkland as scenic tourist attractions in rural areas. But the agrarian tradition has been even more directly incorporated into tourism in Japan through the emergence of 'tourist farming' (*kankō nōgyō*) in many rural areas, where urban tourists undertake recreational farming in the form of tea-leaf picking, potato harvesting, rice harvesting and fruit-picking. There are also farm guesthouses where visitors can stay, craft centres and theme parks offering visitors the chance to learn rural crafts, and 'owner' schemes in which urban Japanese families purchase the right to a crop (apples, potatoes, mushrooms etc.) which they harvest themselves.

References

Aoyama, H. (1994) 'Tenryū ringyōchi kara no hōkoku', (A report from the Tenryu forestry region), in Sanson Keizai Kenkyūsho (ed.) *Sanson ga kowareru mae ni, (Before Mountain Villages are Destroyed)*, Nihon Keizai Hyōronka, Tokyo, pp. 15–25.

Bennett, N. (1993) 'A snug little island', in Mike Money (ed.) *Health and Community: Holism in Practice*, Green Books, Dartington, pp. 191–4.

Berry, B.J.L. (1992) *America's Utopian Communities: Communal Havens from Long-wave Crises*, University of New England Press, Hanover and London.

Brass, T. (1997) 'The agrarian myth, the "new" populism and the "new" right', *Journal of Peasant Studies*, 24(4): 201–45.

Byres, T.J. (1991) 'The agrarian question and differing forms of capitalist agrarian transition: an essay with reference to Asia', in J. Bremen and S. Mundle (eds) *Rural Transformation in Asia*, Oxford University Press, Delhi, pp. 3–76.

Calder, K.E. (1988) *Crisis and Compensation: Public Policy and Political Stability in Japan*, Princeton University Press, Princeton.

Coates, C., How, J., Jones, L., Morris, W. and Wood, A. (eds) (1993) *The Guide to Communal Living: Diggers and Dreamers 94/95*, Communes Network, Winslow.

Fujimoto, I. (1992) 'Lessons from abroad in rural community revitalization', *Community Development Journal*, 27(1): 10–20.

Fukuoka, M. (1983) *Wara ippon no kakumei* (*One Straw Revolution*), Shunjūsha, Tokyo.

Fukuoka, M. (1985) *The Natural Way of Farming: The Theory and Practice of Green Philosophy* (translated by F.P. Metreaud), Japan Publications, Tokyo.

Giner, S. and Sevilla-Guzman, E. (1980) 'The demise of the peasant: some reflections on ideological inroads into social theory', *Sociologia Ruralis*, 20(1–2): 13–27.

Gluck, C. (1985) *Japan's Modern Myths: Ideology in the Late Meiji Period*, Princeton University Press, Princeton.

Hane, M. (1982) *Peasants, Rebels, and Outcastes: The Underside of Modern Japan*, Pantheon Books, New York.

Harootunian, H.D. (1989) 'Visible discourses/invisible ideologies', in M. Miyoshi and H.D. Harootunian (eds) *Postmodernism and Japan*, Duke University Press, Durham, pp. 63–92.

Harootunian, H.D. (1993) 'America's Japan/Japan's Japan', in M. Miyoshi and H.D. Harootunian (eds) *Japan in the World*, Duke University Press, Durham, pp. 196–221.

Havens, T.R.H. (1974) *Farm and Nation in Modern Japan: Agrarian Nationalism, 1870–1940*, Princeton University Press, Princeton.

Hidaka, K. (1996) *40 sai kara no inakagurashi* (*Country Life after Forty*), Tōyō Keizai Shinpōsha, Tokyo.

Hiraike, Y. (1985) 'The dying Japanese village', *Japan Quarterly*, 32(3): 316–19.

Inoue, K. (1996a) 'Toshi seikatsusha to guriin tsūrizumu' (Urban dwellers and green tourism), in K. Inoue, O. Nakamura and M. Yamakazi (ed.) *Nihongata guriin tsuūrizumu,* (*Japanese-style Green Tourism*), Toshi Bunkasha, Tokyo, pp. 25–40.

Inoue, K. (1996b) 'Guriin tsūrizumu to chiiki nōgyōzukuri' (Green tourism and the development of regional farming), in K. Inoue, O. Nakamura and M. Yamakazi (ed.) *Nihongata guriin tsūrizumu (Japanese-style Green Tourism)*, Toshi Bunkasha, Tokyo, pp. 59–71.

KKTK (Kasochiiki Kasseika Taisaku Kenkyūkai) (1994) *Kasochiiki kasseika handobukku (Handbook on Revitalization of Depopulated Areas)*, Gyōsei, Tokyo.

Kearney, M. (1996) *Reconceptualizing the Peasantry: Anthropology in Global Perspective*, Westview Press, Boulder.

Kelly, W.W. (1986) 'Rationalization and nostalgia: cultural dynamics of new middle-class Japan', *American Ethnologist*, 13: 603–18.

Kitsu, K. (1993) *Inaka urimasu (Selling the Countryside)*, Daiyamondosha, Tokyo.

Knight, J. (1997) 'The soil as teacher: natural farming in a mountain village', in P.J. Asquith and A. Kalland (eds) *Japanese Images of Nature: Cultural Perspectives*, Curzon Press, London, pp. 236–56.

Kobayashi, S., Morison, J.B. and Riethmuller, P. (1991) 'A review of recent developments in Japanese agriculture and agricultural policy', *Review of Marketing and Agricultural Economics*, 59(3): 208–28.

Kubō, H. (1994) 'Japan and rice: a new vision', *Look Japan*, 40, 465: 4–8.

Kunimoto, Y. (1971) 'Rural communities in northeastern Japan', *Japan Quarterly*, 18(4): 443–51.

Leger, D. (1982) 'Charisma, utopia and communal life: the case of neorural apocalyptic communes in France', *Social Compass*, 29(1): 41–58.
MSAS (Mainichi Shinbun Akita Shikyoku) (ed.) (1988) *Kaso* (*Rural Depopulation*), Mumeisha, Akita.
McDonald, M.G. (1996) 'Farmers as workers in Japan's regional economic restructuring, 1965–1985', *Economic Geography*, 72(1): 49–72.
McDonald, M. (1989) *"We are not French!" Language, Culture, and Identity in Brittany*, Routledge, London and New York.
Moen, D.G. (1997) 'The Japanese organic farming movement: consumers and farmers united', *Bulletin of Concerned Asian Scholars*, 29(3): 14–22.
Moore, R.H. (1990) *Japanese Agriculture: Patterns of Rural Development*, Westview Press, Boulder.
Nakamura, K. (1991) *Hyakushō shigan* (*Peasant Aspirations*), Shizenshoku Tsūshinsha, Tokyo.
Ni'ide, M. (1994) 'Rice imports and implications', *Japan Quarterly*, 41(1): 16–24.
Nozoe, K. (1981) 'At dangerous crossroads, Japan's agriculture and food security', *Japan Quarterly*, 28(2): 217–26.
Nozoe, K. (1994) *Furusato no saisei no michi* (*The Road to the Rebirth of the Hometown*), Ochanomizu, Tokyo.
NTK (1998) *Nōgyō hakusho Heisei 9 nendo* (*Farming White Paper 1997*), NTK, Tokyo (Norin Tokei Kyōkai).
Ogura, T. (1979) *Can Japanese Agriculture Survive?* Agricultural Policy Research Centre, Tokyo.
Ohnuki-Tierney, E. (1993) *Rice as Self: Japanese Identities through Time*, Princeton University Press, Princeton.
Prindle, P.H. (1984) 'Part-time farming: A Japanese example', *Journal of Anthropological Research*, 40(2): 293–305.
Rogers, S.C. (1987) 'Good to think: the "peasant" in contemporary France', *Anthropological Quarterly*, 60(2): 56–63.
Saitō, E. (1985) 'Mo hitotsu no mirai shakai' (One More Future Society), Gendai Ringyō, (*Present-day Forestry*), No. 229, Zenkoku Ringyō Kairyō Fukyū Kyōkai, Tokyo, pp. 34–9.
Shimazono, S. (1996) 'Alternative knowledge movements as religion: an alternative farming movement in Japan', *Social Compass*, 43(1): 47–63.
Smethurst, R.J. (1974) *A Social Basis for Prewar Japanese Militarism: The Army and the Rural Community*, University of California Press, Berkeley.
Smethurst, R.J. (1986) *Agricultural Development and Tenancy Disputes in Japan, 1870–1940*, Princeton University Press, Princeton.
Takahashi, Y. (1984) *Inakagurashi no tankyū* (*Investigating Country Life*), Sōshisha, Tokyo.
Takeuchi, K. (1993) 'Waga machi, mura o utsukushiku' (Making our town/village beautiful), in Tanba no Mori Kyōkai and N. Isao (eds) *Mori-hito-machizukuri* (*Developing the Forest, People and the Town*), Gakugei Shuppansha, Kyoto, pp. 85–120.
Tashiro, Y. (1992) 'An environmental mandate for rice', *Japan Quarterly*, 39(1): 34–44.

Uchiyama, M. (1990) *Gendai nihon nōson no shakai mondai* (*Social Problems of Present-day Japanese Villages*), Tsukuba Shobō, Tokyo.
Yamashita, S. (1993) *Datsusara nōmin wa naze genki* (*Why are New Farmers Doing Well?*), Ie no Hikari Kyōkai, Tokyo.
Yūki, S. (1970) *Kamitsu kaso: yugamerareta nihonrettō* (*Overcrowding and Depopulation: The Distorted Japanese Archipelago*), San'ichi Shinsho, Tokyo.

PART FIVE: CONCLUSION

17. Disappearing Peasantries? Rural Labour Redundancy in the Neo-liberal Era and Beyond

DEBORAH FAHY BRYCESON[1]

TRACING PROCESSES OF peasantization and de-peasantization temporally and spatially, this book has endeavoured to highlight the question of peasants' prospects. The geo-politics and economic significance of peasantries today must be sifted from locationally specific case studies. The preceding chapters have provided a rich array of evidence upon which to base analytical judgements about peasantries' existence and well-being in the foreseeable future.

This chapter ventures to summarize the case-study findings through a schematic examination of the changing nature of peasant negotiating complexes. It then turns to the most salient challenge facing peasantries today, namely their growing labour redundancy in the world market. Peasant responses are outlined before considering the current policy environment and viable policy options. The conclusion returns to the issue of academic bias and the ambiguity of western attitudes more generally towards peasants and their legacy to the world.

Analysis of Peasant Negotiating Complexes

A number of theoretical misconceptions have clouded the perception of peasantries. Far from being 'primarily subsistence producers', their peculiar characteristic is that they combine commodity and subsistence production to varying degrees. Highly differentiated by class, gender, age and locality, peasants do not constitute a homogeneous social grouping. Their differentiation into various class strata renders them particularly elusive as an analytical category. Over time, peasantries have expanded and contracted in size through the elevation and relegation of members of their poor and rich strata.

The instability of a peasantry relates to their involvement in continual negotiations over:

- access to productive resources, i.e. land, labour and capital;
- external extractive claims on their labour product;
- the terms and conditions of production, notably the level of externally provisioned social and productive service infrastructure;
- the amount of production risk they shoulder.

Such negotiations are carried on with some degree of direct access to the means of production, be it family labour and/or land, and greater or lesser degrees of independent production of their subsistence food and other basic needs. The core of any peasantry, the 'middle peasantry', falls squarely within these negotiating parameters. The middle peasantry is readily identifiable as rural household units involved in commodity production mediated by an appropriating class. Rather than forming an immutable category of rural farmers, the middle peasantries and the poor and rich peasant strata they mutate into are an outcome of incessant negotiation over the agrarian labour process.

Along with their elusiveness, peasantries evince an enigmatic dual character as both partially autonomous and highly vulnerable producers. Their vulnerability derives from exposure to external market fluctuations, declining terms of trade, and state taxation, often uncalibrated with their ability to pay. Nonetheless they exercise partial autonomy by virtue of their subsistence production, and their circumvention of land and labour markets through the use of community-held land and family labour. Furthermore, the prevalence of family- and community-centred ideologies has historically buffered them against cultural incursion.

Over the past two centuries, peasantries have endured in Africa, Asia and Latin America on the basis of negotiating positions that draw strength from their enigmatic character. In this chapter, a 'negotiating complex' is defined as a configuration of specific agents, their resource base, asset holdings, bargaining positions, objectives, investment stakes and fall-back options. In a peasant negotiating complex the agents are on the one hand, various peasant strata, and on the other, 'overlords' who vary with respect to the nature and degree of control they exert over peasants.

The wide-ranging case studies in this volume provide an informational basis for discerning broad temporal and spatial patterns in peasant negotiating complexes. Continental comparisons are always at the expense of in-depth understanding of national and local community case-study variation, but nonetheless facilitate the identification of broad trends in this period of heightened globalization. Three major periods have been identified related to the changing nature of domination over peasants exerted by: (i) the colonial state and local rural élites; (ii) the post-colonial centralized state; and (iii) international financial institutions and the global market. Each stage finds peasants faced with progressively more distanced but more sophisticated and insidious power over their labour.

Peasant negotiations with colonial states and local rural élites, 1800–1945

Africa, Asia and Latin America represent three highly contrasting peasant negotiating complexes. Colonial influences between the seventeenth and twentieth centuries have left their mark on both the size and character of these peasantries. During this period, peasants' negotiating positions were influenced by their largely unimpeded access to family labour, whereas their land was frequently subject to colonial confiscation, especially in Latin America. Extractive claims on their labour product tended to be exerted through taxation and various kinds of rent payments. Generally, middle peasantries of any strength had yet to congeal. Taxation was often paid through labour service rather than sale of peasant-produced agricultural commodities. On the colonial side, the level of social and productive service infrastructure was extremely rudimentary. However, famine relief was sometimes provided to reduce peasants' risk of shortfalls in subsistence production.

The early colonial conquest of Latin America resulted in the decimation of local peasantries and their imperial overlords, the Aztec, Inca and Mayan empires. Over the course of the next two centuries, peasants reasserted themselves in the interstices of colonial enterprise. As peasantries, they were not consciously created by the colonial powers, rather they resulted from local rural dwellers' attempts to evade labour control of the large-scale colonial enterprise, be it in the form of mining, plantations or *haciendas*. Rural producers with serf-like relations to large colonial land holdings sought leverage through peasant subsistence production.

Asian peasantries at the time of colonial penetration were more resilient, more numerous in number and subject to élites which often matched the European invaders in military prowess. Gradually, however, through a combination of state and market forces, colonial governments asserted their authority in many Asian countries, sometimes interlocking with existing local élites' methods of peasant surplus extraction.

Nonetheless, it would be highly misleading to assume that colonial Asia could be portrayed as a vast sea of unchanging exploitative rural relations between peasantries and landlord classes. As Breman (Chapter 13 in this volume) demonstrates, colonial exploitation and growing landlessness expanded the size of the rural proletariat. The landless, rather than peasants, occupied the bottom of the rural class pyramid. Most European colonial governments failed to mount 'remedial' policies to curb or contain the growing number of rural landless labourers, so many of whom were entwined in labour bondage to peasants. The landless had virtually no escape. Migration to urban areas was possible only in the short run, as low bachelor wage levels prevailed. Colonial governments, especially in India, China and Indonesia, exported indentured 'coolie' labour to other less densely populated colonial territories of the West Indies, and South and East Africa.

Systems of 'indirect rule' became widespread during the colonial conquest of Africa in the late nineteenth and early twentieth centuries. Indirect rule was a means not only of accessing, but also of creating, peasantries. Colonial government-engineered native authorities operated as agencies for introducing and enforcing the production of cash crops and labour recruitment for colonial enterprise. Chiefs, sometimes with pre-colonial legitimacy but often without, occupied an ambiguous intermediary position (Chapter 5 in this volume). Usually they did not constitute a rural landlord class. They were custodians of community land, not owners. In effect, they were part of the peasantry, rich peasants with labour foreman responsibilities. Under colonial rule, they enjoyed an elevated standard of living in exchange for implementing the colonial state's taxation and peasant labour control policies.

Peasant negotiations with national urban élites, 1945–80

During the period of decolonization, peasantries asserted themselves in the mass politics of the time. Rural élites, on the other hand, namely the large *latifundia* interests of Latin America, rural landlords in Asia, and chiefs in Africa, often found themselves on the defensive. In most areas, peasants' and rural landlords' negotiating complexes were superseded by peasants and national urban élites seemingly in partnership for higher returns. The stakes were raised and negotiations took on the theme of converged interests.

Urban élites, dominating national power in the name of 'modernizing' and 'developing' states, were often willing to meet peasants' demands for land (Moore 1966). Land reform became an important development agenda item, particularly in Latin America, where rural élites had historically monopolized land. This was a step in the direction of 'modernizing' agricultural labour relations as well. With rural élites' grip on land resources loosened, they had less recourse to interlocking land and labour contracts with peasants in the form of sharecropping and land tenancy. Finally, this was the period when nation-states seriously endeavoured to create conditions for peasants to access credit and improved productive inputs. Government measures were taken, often with western donor support, for the provisioning of productive infrastructure and social services.

Naturally, these concessions to peasants were not extended without costs. Peasants were expected to 'pay' in the form of increased agricultural output and commodity sales. Most states had erected price controls and marketing arrangements that were intended to ensure cost recovery of peasant credit and surplus generation for state coffers. Throughout this period, as peasants became increasingly involved in agricultural commodity production tied to loan repayment, their production risks increased. On the other hand, they devised numerous ways of evading credit repayment – seeking other market outlets or diverting crop inputs to subsistence crops – such that their production risk in fact was increasingly shouldered by the nation-state. In an era dominated by the ideology of development, national urban élites had vested resources in the broad masses of rural producers. Their policies tended to support the creation of strong middle peasantries who clearly exhibited that peculiar blend of defining peasant characteristics: partial production autonomy, economic flexibility, and vulnerability to external state and market forces.

In Latin America, which had decolonized centuries earlier, national governments were receptive to peasant demands precisely because they posed a threat to political stability. More equitable distribution of land to peasants was at the expense of the rural landed élites (Chapter 7 in this volume). Cuba and Mexico, for example, experienced violent peasant revolts prompting revolutionary changes to government, followed by widespread equitable land allocation to peasantries (Chapters 8 and 9). In the process, peasant differentiation tended to even out, promoting the consolidation of broad middle peasantries. In some countries land reform progressed to agrarian reform, involving government credit and input-provisioning programmes to capitalize peasant production. However, in many countries landed and plantation interests continued to have the ear of government, generating tensions that sometimes erupted into full-scale civil war. This was especially apparent in Central America, notably Nicaragua and Honduras, where the existence of large-scale, often American-owned plantations blocked peasants' land aspirations. However, Cuba followed a very different path, mirroring China, by replacing local landlords with direct state control of peasant marketed production.

While it is difficult to characterize overall tendencies in Asia, the Chinese revolution stands out as a critical conjuncture that demonstrably altered peasants' negotiating power. Mao had established his original power base in the countryside. Sensitive to rural demands, the revolutionary national government took radical steps to address the country's enormous rural land problem by dispossessing landlords and allocating land to peasant household heads on an equitable basis in the 1950s (Chapter 15 in this volume). Thereafter, the national and regional level of the state subjected peasants to collectivization of their production.

India contrasts markedly with China. Although land reforms were enacted in almost all states, in practice very little was done for the asset-depleted landless whose vast numbers continued to languish in the countryside, unable to secure adequate wages or accommodation through urban migration. In the late 1960s and 1970s, technological rather than political measures were pursued to raise agricultural productivity and rural living standards. The introduction of green revolution technology dynamized local agrarian economies and consolidated middle peasantries who could afford to purchase the improved input packages in climatically favourable regions. In the process, the local hegemony of rural landlords was indirectly challenged (Chapter 12). Generating large grain surpluses, the middle peasantries invigorated local rural markets for producer and consumer goods. Rural wage labour opportunities grew in parts of the country through the expansion of the agricultural and rural industrial sectors. The use of agricultural implements, machinery and the provisioning of productive infrastructure supported continuing improvement in agricultural productivity, though very unevenly spread over the country.

These developments, while facilitating rural labour absorption, did not eliminate the exploitative nature of the landless population's labour contracts. Rich and middle peasants could hire casual labour and dismiss it at the end of the agricultural season. As Kapadia illustrates in Chapter 14 of this volume, rural industries could be established on the basis of bonded labour that used the ideology of caste and family patriarchy to subjugate the labour of women and youth.

Post-independent sub-Saharan states, whatever their political complexion, were interested in wooing the broad masses of the peasantry, often sacrificing support from the chiefly rural élite (Chapter 2). In most countries land reform was not an issue, given the still large expanses of land subject to customary land tenure. The rallying cry was agricultural modernization. Many African states attempted to distribute improved input packages to peasants with limited success (Chapters 3 and 4). The introduction of such packages tended to have a differentiating effect on peasant producers, with poorer peasants unable to benefit to the same degree as middle and rich peasants. African post-colonial states endeavoured to extract surpluses from peasants in the form of food for urban supply and export crops to generate foreign exchange. However, the extractive process was mediated by African state officials who, as first-generation urban dwellers, could still identify with peasant interests. In many countries, the first two decades after independence gave African peasant populations their first real educational opportunities, health facilities, and basic rural infrastructure such as roads and water supplies.

Peasant negotiations with international financial institutions and the global market, 1980 and beyond

Whatever material prosperity peasants had been able to garner in the 1950s and 1960s rapidly evaporated during the 1970s. Jolted by the oil crisis and the dismantling of the Bretton Woods international financial regulatory system, international agricultural commodity markets started slumping. Latin America, sub-Saharan Africa and some Asian governments quickly amassed debts amidst the easy credit of recycled petro-dollars. A spiralling debt crisis ensued during the 1980s. One by one national governments, gripped in debt, became subject to structural adjustment programmes (SAP) and International Monetary Fund (IMF) conditionality. Subsidized, improved agricultural input packages and rural infrastructural building were drastically reduced. As the peasant 'modernization' effort in Latin American and African nations was abandoned, peasant farmers were subjected to the international financial institutions' (IFIs) 'sink-or-swim' economic strategy. National market deregulation pushed agricultural producers into global commodity markets where middle as well as poor peasants found it hard to compete. SAPs and economic liberalization policies represented the convergence of the worldwide forces of de-agrarianization and national policies promoting de-peasantization.

In the negotiating complex, peasants encountered a new but virtually absentee partner who acted through national governments. The World Bank and IMF-enforced policies had profound implications for peasants' access to productive resources. Input credit dried up, and national government-provisioned rural productive and social service infrastructural maintenance and expansion crumpled. Exposed to far greater risks in relation to their commodity and subsistence production, they faced the possibility of harvest failure arising from adverse climatic conditions, as well as wider fluctuations of market prices for their commodities and the full loan servicing on advanced credit. Long-established safety nets were disappearing. The impoverished finances of nation-states made them less able to respond to peasant food shortages and famines (Bryceson et al. 1999).

Declining returns from agricultural commodity production and increased production risks caused profound perturbation amongst peasants who rushed to diversify their income sources to ensure basic livelihoods. The scramble deranged the occupational structures and residential locality of long-standing middle peasantries in both continents (Bryceson and Jamal 1997; Zoomers 1999).

In Latin America, the drive for income diversification had agricultural and non-agricultural directions. New consumer markets were expanding to provide fresh fruit, vegetables and flowers to affluent North American consumers (Chapters 9 and 10). Here, peasant commodity production was giving way to large-scale production of 'just-in-time' and ready-packed shipments to international airports. Exceptionally, good local peasant leadership was far-seeing enough to buck this tendency, as exemplified in Llambí's Colombian/Venezuelan case study (Chapter 10 in this volume). Latin American peasant communities were, however, able to respond to the other booming market – the US$30 billion drug market – precisely because they were remote. High Andean peasants producing coca enjoyed buoyant demand for their product, but were at the mercy of Latin American drug barons, whose profit-making instincts were rarely tempered by benevolent concern for local agrarian communities (Thoumi 1995).

In like manner, North American markets also influenced Latin American rural dwellers' off-farm income diversification. Migrant labour to the USA and Canada resulted in divided families and circular migration patterns that opened peasant communities to a barrage of cultural change. Another migration stream comprised low-paid, female casual labour to job opportunities in the large-scale farming sector (Chapter 9). Cuba provides a remarkable exception to these proletarianization tendencies. From 1993, Cuban government policy has been directed at renewed peasantization by transforming state farms into peasant production co-operatives (Chapter 8).

In sub-Saharan Africa, the decreasing viability of the peasant export crops for which the continent was known, notably coffee, cocoa, tea and oilseeds, led many peasants to turn to quick or year-round maturing crops to provide a more reliable cash flow (Ponte 1997). The dominant tendency was peasant entry into non-agricultural income diversification on a self-employed basis, often straddling both local rural and urban markets (Chapter 2). In many countries, youth were especially attracted to mining, with the hope of striking it rich, digging for gold, diamonds, and precious stones (Chachage et al. 1993). Rudimentary living conditions and highly erratic returns to labour at mining sites usually necessitated miners' own subsistence food production. Similarly, peasants who flocked into non-agricultural trading and service activities attempted to retain their subsistence agricultural base to reduce economic risk and ensure basic survival.

During the 1980s and until very recently, the Asian experience provided stark contrasts with Latin America and Africa. Several countries, including Bangladesh, Sri Lanka, Pakistan and the Philippines, experienced a debt crisis and the imposition of SAP reforms. Other Asian states, however, were not pressurized to implement SAP policies, having embarked on forward-looking economic expansion programmes that had the support of international corporate investors. Asia's historical bane, a vast labour surplus, became its major asset as multinational corporations relocated their factories to the cheap labour zones of east and south-east Asia. The rural poor gravitated to these jobs, which tended to be casual and very low paid (Chapter 13). Young women were especially popular with employers who saw them as cheap, docile labourers who would eventually leave their employment to get married without exerting longer-term worker benefit claims.

The industrial boom was accompanied by growing agricultural markets, as well as major expansion programmes in the production of various tropical products such as cloves, cocoa and natural rubber, encouraged by IFIs such as the World Bank. In many countries, investment was directed primarily at large-scale rather than peasant agriculture, accelerating rural proletarianization and the release of cheap, casual wage labour for an expanding wage labour market.

In China, an opposite tendency was at work. The easing of state control over rural agricultural markets caused a surge of peasant family farming. Peasants, with more autonomy over use of their land, could produce their subsistence and sell their food crops to China's burgeoning urban markets. On the other hand, there were signs that peasants, particularly the youth, were eager to abandon agriculture and seek higher returns in non-agricultural work in rural as well as urban areas (Chapter 15).

The Asian economic crash of the late 1990s has largely halted industrial growth and caused severe foreign capital investment cutbacks. At the time of writing, there is insufficient case-study material to judge what effect the crash has had on Asian peasantries and whether urban dwellers have sought respite in the countryside from the hardships of rampant urban inflation and job redundancy.

Peasant Labour Redundancy amidst Worldwide Agricultural Restructuring: Sectoral and Local Responses

The introductory chapter of this volume refers to the long-term tendency for employment in the agricultural sector to shrink in relation to the industrial and service sectors of national economies. De-agrarianization has accelerated in the past 20 years, and is now propelled by global rather than national markets. Everywhere, including Europe and North America, family farming at small and medium levels of operation is facing the competitive force of large-scale agro-industry. The current crisis of the middle peasantry in Africa, Asia and Latin America is deeply entwined with this tendency.

Agricultural sector shrinkage and the rise of international agro-industry

Several major tropical agricultural commodities, including coffee, cocoa, tea, cotton, oilseeds and sugar, have experienced deteriorating terms of trade since the early 1980s (Sapford and Singer 1998, Gibbon and Raikes 1999, FAO various years). Market decline can be traced back to the 1960s when synthetic materials started replacing natural fibres such as sisal, cotton and jute. Thereafter the oil-price booms of the 1970s and changing lifestyles and tastes of more health-conscious, affluent northern consumers took their toll on peasant-produced export crops such as coffee, sugar and tobacco. At the same time, the export of North America's and Europe's cheap subsidized grain surpluses and food aid to developing countries was undermining peasants' domestic production of wheat, rice and maize.

Many nation-states' marketing policies and subsidies buffered the agricultural production of their peasantries from the full competitive force of these external events and policies. This ceased in the 1980s and 1990s as IFI-enforced market liberalization policies and the Uruguay round of the World Trade Organization's agreement began shifting international trading patterns, with far-reaching consequences for peasantries of the developing world as well as for small- and medium-scale producers in Japan and North America (Chapter 16). The process of subsidy removal has been selective. Grain farmers were more vulnerable than farmers of crops with higher unit value. Major Northern producing countries used their 'legal skills to maintain significant parts of the protective structure intact or to be dismantled at the very end of the ten-year period' (Gibbon and Raikes 1999). Thus, many small- and medium-scale farmers in the North have so far been spared what peasant farmers in Latin America, Asia and Africa already face, namely the competitive edge of agro-industry practised by exceptionally large-scale northern 'farmer–industrialists' and multinational corporations. This was dramatized by the recent 'banana wars' arising from a triangular dispute between the Caribbean banana-producing islands, the USA and the European Union over the World Trade Organization's ruling on the international banana trade (*Financial Times*, 8 March 1999; Godfrey 1998).

But the worst may yet be to come, as highly industrialized 'just-in-time' production of agricultural products using precision farming techniques combines with biotechnological advances (McMichael 1995, Goodman and Watts 1997). The sale of genetically modified maize, tomatoes, soya beans, cotton and rapeseed is already well under way in North America. Current biotechnological research represents a huge investment, primarily on the part of large multinational chemical firms such as Monsanto who are vying to gain patent rights over genetically modified (GM) plants.

Current research has focused on imparting greater pest resistance and herbicide tolerance to plants, which would offer future benefit to farmers in the North and the South. But the existence of 'terminator technology' which genetically renders GM seeds' progeny infertile raises the question of affordability for peasant farmers in the South who are accustomed to saving seeds from the previous harvest for next year's planting (Tripp 1999). Public concern about GM crops is mainly concentrated in the North where consumer organizations and environmental groups have raised questions about food safety and the dangers to biodiversity.[2] Ironically, little has been said about biotechnology's long-term implications for world peasant farming, and the not inconceivable future possibility of GM tropical products being produced within northern market zones much more efficiently than far-flung peasant producers can manage.

As world agricultural production increasingly falls under the sway of agro-industries and multinational chemical corporations, northern supermarket chains have emerged as 'supermarkets' in more than the colloquial sense. A few have consolidated themselves to control enormous national retail markets which now seek to reduce marketing costs through outcompeting middle rungs of the wholesale marketing chain, in favour of direct contract farming with select, large-scale producers in both the North and the South. This is best illustrated in the horticultural market where northern supermarkets buy directly from highly capitalized farmers capable of just-in-time production and product delivery. In many Latin American, African and Asian countries, peasant produce is primarily marketed through medium-scale wholesalers. Their decline has an adverse knock-on effect on peasant producers.

The increasing corporate and industrial character of world agriculture has profound implications for the size of the world's agrarian labour force and the type of labour involved. Agro-industrial corporations' enormous economies of scale, high levels of capitalization, and advanced technology are antithetical to the relatively low-yielding, labour-intensive nature of peasant family farming. Family farms, particularly the very small, undercapitalized peasant family farms of Latin America, Asia and sub-Saharan Africa, are being sidelined rather than incorporated into agro-industry's corporate drive for increasing market share. Environmental and developmental protest may move some agro-industrial corporations to provide 'showcase' smallholder contract farming schemes, but peasant agrarian labour displacement – not absorption – is now the norm. In the words of the historian Eric Hobsbawm:

> The case for maintaining a large peasantry in being was and is non-economic, since in the history of the modern world the enormous rise in agrarian output has gone together with an equally spectacular decline in the number and proportion of agriculturalists; most dramatically so since the second World War (Hobsbawm 1995: 355).

Rural labour's options

Agricultural restructuring has struck at the heart of the middle peasantries' agrarian base. Failure to compete on prices in the world market or meet stringent demands for timely product delivery has made middle peasants' commodity production increasingly untenable. As the middle peasantries' agrarian *raison d'être* in the world market erodes, their resource base similarly erodes and they are faced with an acute crisis. The decline in agricultural productivity that is related to peasants' lack of productive inputs could jeopardize their subsistence food output as well as their commodity production. Some resort to using less than the specified dosages of fertilizer and insecticide, which in the long run can cause plant disease and insect resistance or can undermine soil fertility.

As the middle peasantries' productive base gives way, strong centrifugal forces of economic polarization and class differentiation set in (Chapters 4, 9 and 11), and the middle peasantry starts pulling apart at the seams. A few are able to muster both agrarian and non-agrarian resources to achieve income levels that will afford the purchase of the prescribed agricultural inputs. Their agricultural operations tend to focus on food markets and increases in scale. Larger-scale peasant farmers may be able to retain their role as domestic food producers catering for national markets, either in such bulky, mass-consumption products as grains and starchy root crops, or in perishable horticultural product markets that are not supermarket-driven. Nonetheless, the enforcement of neo-liberal market policies may threaten this through lack of import barriers to give peasant farmers sufficient protection from cheaper food imports, especially of staple grains.

Most middle peasantries, unable to scale up their agricultural production, have responded with a battery of income-diversification coping strategies, usually of a non-agrarian nature. In the process of doing so, they face head-on competition with the already existing casual wage labour force and self-employed income-generating activities of the rural asset-poor and landless population. It is difficult to discern patterns in the scramble for alternative work, let alone identify sectoral tendencies. Nonetheless, it is abundantly clear that there is a strong tendency for peasant agrarian labour time to be redirected to non-agrarian, often service-sector work. The form that this takes varies: it can be one or two members of a peasant household redirecting their energies, or a seasonal concentration of all members of a family on non-agrarian work, or the opportunistic insertion of non-agrarian work here and there by any household member at any time throughout the working day. The term 'sunlighting' rather than 'moonlighting' would encapsulate its nature, for diversified non-agrarian activities are not simply supplementary to peasant agriculture, rather their active pursuit tends partially to replace agriculture, providing a more reliable income stream than would be likely from sole reliance on agriculture. Stretching the analogy, these activities extend income sources like 'energized sunlight' where the darkness of economic despair would otherwise prevail.

In sub-Saharan Africa, recourse to self-employment is very strong and this may allow peasants to remain in their home locality, although they are constrained by extremely low levels of rural purchasing power. In Latin America and Asia, where low-paid, casual wage employment is more likely, peasants' searches for viable livelihoods often take them outside of village settings, usually to national urban centres or even beyond to foreign destinations. Low-paid workers' interests could be well served by mobilization of their numbers and articulation of their grievances. However, the spatial dispersal and erratic nature of the casual labour force precludes such action (Chapter 13). Casual labourers must put their individual livelihood concerns above group interests.

Many migrant labourers retain some semblance of an agricultural fallback. These are different from the 'peasants' in cities depicted by Roberts (1978, 1995) as these migrated with the intention of remaining there. Today's 'vestige peasants' often live in an urban–rural continuum with an indeterminate residential and occupational future, or are part of 'multi-spatial households' in which reciprocal support of members is given across geographical space (Tacoli 1998, Bank 1999).

Rural–urban separations of work and home life are emerging. Elson (1997) records the high incidence of this in south-east Asia. Increasingly, the poor are engaged in time-consuming, long-distance, energy-inefficient commuting patterns. In southern Africa, many urban employees return to their homes in the countryside at weekends or alternatively commute by minibus daily. By contrast, casual workers from some of the poorest neighbourhoods in Latin America's largest cities are bussed to large plantations and rural agri-business sites beyond city boundaries, known in Brazil as the *'boias frias'* because of the cold lunches they take with them to the fields (Stolcke 1988, Redclift 1991). While dispelling rural isolation, these regularized commuting patterns tend to weaken the coherence of rural communities.

The blurring of social identity

As middle peasantries fracture economically, their social cohesion, ideology and identity belie the strain. Post-modernists circumvent the class dynamics of this situation by concentrating on the process of identity loss. They see the 'blurring' of peasantries' social identity as the cumulative outcome of individuals participating in fragmented multiple locational and occupational identities which crowd out their peasant identity and produce a hybrid alternative identity (Kearney 1996). The existentialist flavour of much of the post-modernist literature on identity formation harmonizes with the prevailing economic philosophy of neo-liberalism. Individual choice becomes both an economic and a cultural imperative, with the quest for a globalized western consumption pattern as its driving force.

Another perspective arises from tracing the social re-definition process through intra-familial pressures experienced within the peasant household. Patriarchy has almost invariably served as a peasant family ideology functioning to generate corporate discipline, internal economic coordination and class identity. External extractive agencies have worked through peasant male heads of households, reinforcing the power of patriarchal ideologies. The past 20 years of market liberalization and declining agricultural earnings have been eroding the economic dominance of peasant patriarchs, particularly in sub-Saharan Africa and Latin America. Income diversification has usually involved all adult and youthful household members in the search for work (Bryceson 1999). In many places women, who had hitherto been labelled 'financial dependants' of the patriarch, have been favoured in the labour market much to the chagrin of their fathers, husbands and brothers (Chapter 9).

In the context of external economic and internal social upheaval, many peasants, particularly youth, begin actively to relinquish their peasant identity as a way of distancing themselves from the poor economic prospects of their agrarian homes and the social confines of traditional familial roles. Sometimes they rationalize their movement in western terms, as an escape from the stultifying countryside and 'stupid peasant' ways. The disintegration of peasantries as local communities arises from this ideological fissure between the generations, as well as from the physical departure of its members.

On the other hand, most peasants in transition cannot afford irrevocably to cut the umbilical cord that binds them to their peasant roots. They retain their peasant survival instinct for autonomy in the form of having a subsistence fallback. In so doing, they remain 'peasants' in the absence of a strong communal identity, cultural adherence or family household integrity.

Subsistence fallback: peasants' last stronghold or cheap labour reserve?

Peasants' subsistence production, often considered the hallmark of backwardness by critics, is in fact their major trump card. The fear of 'retreat into subsistence production' was the bane of many colonial officers who viewed it as the peasants' bolt-hole to escape market fluctuations and government demands. How often peasants' 'just walk away' response actually cropped up in past negotiations with their colonial overlords is highly debatable.

Decades have elapsed and few could now exercise such nonchalance and self-assurance about their subsistence fallback. Rural standards of living have drastically altered, and peasants' totally self-sufficient subsistence production of food and non-food items would, more than likely, be considered meagre fare. The utility of subsistence production for peasants now lies in accommodating to, rather than escaping from, the market. In periods of market decline or strong price fluctuations, subsistence production has an essential cushioning function, safeguarding peasant survival in the face of adversity.

The term 'subsistence fallback' refers to the act of producing basic food and non-food for direct consumption and its enabling conditions of production, i.e. access to land and family labour. The existence of the subsistence fallback lends partial autonomy to peasants, provides insurance against risk, and facilitates physical survival. Its value to peasants cannot be overestimated. Even when peasants' command over land or labour is considerably diminished, recourse to their subsistence fallback can give them a negotiating strength and 'staying power' that is not evident amongst fully landless, proletarianized rural populations, as illustrated in Kapadia's Indian case study (Chapter 14).

Nonetheless, for many peasants staying on the land and resorting to subsistence fallback is both a residual and reviled option, as having what Barros Nock refers to as 'no where else to go' (Chapter 9 in this volume). Youth who feel estranged from the culture of the local peasant community, and Latin American peasantries who are exposed to high rates of in and out migration and thereby wide experience of the 'outside world', are especially apt to express this view. As Kay (Chapter 7) observes, returning to one's home area and having recourse to a subsistence fallback is part of an on-going process of semi-proletarianization and structural poverty. The most marginalized have come to be known as *pobretariado*, an amalgam of *pobres* (poor) and *proletariado* (proletariat) whose distinguishing characteristic is not their exploitation as wage labourers – since it is considered unlikely that they will ever find employment in the urban or rural sectors – but their efforts to maintain some marginal land fragment as a means of survival. Peasants' subsistence fallback can be double-edged, strengthening or weakening their negotiating position, depending on employers' strategies, government policies, peasants' own organizational skills and overall levels of labour supply and demand.

In the former colonial economies, peasants' reliance on subsistence production structurally enabled employers to pay low bachelor wages (Chapter 2). Presently, the enormous reservoir of cheap, casual labour in Asia (Chapter 13) as well as Latin America is premised on the employed worker's claim to a subsistence fallback upon return to his or her immediate or extended family. The vast over-supply of labour combined with international migration has brought a new dimension to peasant labour exploitation. Capitalist employers in affluent northern countries are availed cheap labour subsidized by asset-poor peasant families of the South, as illustrated by tens of thousands of Mexican and Central American labourers employed in the USA. As 'international peasants', they participate in a global labour market which is not backed by national or international governmental forces committed to their continuation as a class. The IFIs give precedence to ever-increasing capitalization, not labour absorption or safeguarding local rural communities' livelihood. Thus 'international peasants' exhibit the quintessential class characteristic of peasantries through time – autonomy from and vulnerability to exploitation by external state and market agencies – but as a class, they face proletarianization by the force of global commodity and labour markets combined with governmental indifference.

Most international labour migrants from peasant backgrounds consider themselves the lucky ones who have found paying jobs and are availed a taste of western consumerism. Sub-Saharan African peasants have had comparatively little experience of international labour migration. In some parts of Asia, international migration plays an important role and is especially focused on the Middle East, e.g. Pakistanis in the Gulf States. Similarly in Central America and the Caribbean, Mexicans, Dominicans and Haitians are particularly prominent labour migrants to North America.

Have peasants' negotiating objectives totally reversed? During the colonial period, peasants' ultimate escape was posited as local self-sufficient subsistence production; now the ultimate escape, especially in the minds of more youthful peasants, is employment abroad in the North. The global village of neo-liberalism has arrived. The IFI policies of economic liberalization and structural adjustment had held out the promise that the South could become like the North. Many peasants' wanderlust job-seeking is goaded by their impatience or disbelief that this transformation will ever happen in their home areas.

If peasants' subsistence fallback is as much a curse as a blessing, and if peasants' now seek out western material comfort, has this undermined peasant militancy in the world today? Buijtenhuijs explores this question in Chapter 6 of this volume. There is certainly no shortage of civil disorder, unrest and war in rural areas of Latin America, Asia and Africa, but only a few of these hot spots exhibit coherent peasant organization and political demands. The Chiapas of Mexico stand out in this regard with their desire to gain greater access to land and control over their local affairs. Other rural-based struggles exhibit far more opaque statements of their objectives and often resort to individual terrorist attack rather than group mobilization and protest to make their cause felt. The Tamil Tigers of Sri Lanka, the Shining Path of Peru, and the numerous warlord-led movements in sub-Saharan Africa tend to project an ethnic character. Yet their lack of motivation in winning the broad masses of the target ethnic community to their cause, and various local wealth-depleting methods such as smuggling of valuable raw materials like diamonds, gold, ivory and hard wood, cast doubt on their stated concerns for the ethnic community.

What these more inarticulate and desperate struggles share in common is their occurrence in rural areas where peasantries are in the process of disintegrating, and alternative economic livelihoods are lacking. Under these circumstances, recruitment of young combatants is rarely a problem. Ironically, while never articulating the problem of labour displacement, the war solves it in an immediate sense. A senseless, destructive war from the perspective of the peasant community, the nation-state and the world is totally logical in the minds of the individual combatants. They have a livelihood, and often a lucrative livelihood, as long as the war continues (Peters and Richards 1998).

Filling the Policy Vacuum: Transforming Peasants in the Information Age

The 1995 *World Development Report* (World Bank 1995) highlights that 'workers of the world' are increasingly being channelled into international markets subject to the accelerated flow of information, goods and capital. Estimates suggest that between 1965 and 1995 the global labour force doubled to 2.5 billion people of working age, and will triple in the following 30 years. The greatest increases will be observed in Latin America, Africa and Asia. At the same time, worldwide divergence between rich and poor workers is unfolding, part of a process of unprecedented wealth differentiation that has been taking place over this century. According to the World Bank's (1995) own data, in 1870 the average per capita income in the rich countries was 11 times higher than that of the poorest. In 1960 the ratio rose to 38, and by 1985 it was 52. Peasant labour displacement, on the scale that is now occurring in the poor countries, is contributing to this widening income gap. Yet the World Bank (1995) states that inequality need not grow further if national governments adopt 'good policies' according to neo-liberal prescriptions.

As argued in Chapter 1 of this volume, the neo-liberalist perspective has crowded out debate about peasant transformation. Peasants-cum-smallholders-cum farmers are, like anyone else, expected to meet the challenge of the market. If they fail in the agricultural commodity market, they can resort to the wage labour market or the informal sector and claw their way up the ladder of prosperity. Economic success is up to the individual.

Post-modernists have often reinforced this atomistic, ahistorical approach by focusing on individuals' multiple identities and rejecting what they call 'meta-narratives'. Criticizing earlier western social science's Eurocentric conception of development trajectories, they make many valid points, particularly about the industrialization imperative that blinded so much of development studies in the 1970s and 1980s. However, the drawback of leaving analysis at the level of individual identity and indeterminate direction is that there is little conceptual basis for grounded policy formulation to alleviate the galloping wealth differentiation currently taking place.

The 'new rurality' approach is more practically focused (Chapter 10). It is alert to the group dynamics embedded in new institutions and agencies capable of articulating group interests. It is clear that mobilization of 'peasant interests' in this period of disappearing peasantries is unlikely to take classic forms. As Llambí's case study illustrates, Latin American peasants' demands for land are being replaced by a variety of initiatives including attempts to coordinate production and marketing of crops across national borders, and environmental concerns related to the makeshift dwellings of peri-urban areas rather than permanent village settlements.

International donor agencies have responded to these shifting rural interests, new institutions and economic strategies. Since the early 1980s, development efforts beamed at rural communities have been successively described as supports to 'survival', 'coping' and 'livelihood' strategies, in recognition of the worsening conditions threatening agrarian livelihoods. Presently, a number of donor agencies have adopted a 'sustainable rural livelihoods' approach, which stresses rural risk management directed at 'reducing vulnerability – helping people to develop resilience to external shocks and increase the overall sustainability of their livelihoods' (Carney 1999: 3). The approach aims to be participatory and holistic by taking non-agricultural income-diversifying activities into account, and emphasizing the social as well as economic dimensions of rural life.

The sustainable rural livelihoods approach has surfaced in the context of declining aid flows, the growing importance of the NGO sector with its more restricted financial resources and emphasis on networking, and increasing awareness of environmental degradation. The target population consists of 'rural' rather than 'peasant' or 'agricultural' households. Reference to farmers' means of production – notably land, labour, and capital – has been replaced by a focus on rural dwellers' investment in 'capital assets', defined widely to embrace natural, physical, financial, human and social forms of capital (Carney 1998).

Interestingly, the most nebulous of these capitals, 'social capital', has been accorded the most attention. There are a wide array of interpretations of its meaning (Harriss and De Renzio 1997), with donor agencies such as the World Bank relying heavily on Putnam's (1993) normative interpretation of true 'social capital' as the associational ties built on horizontal cultural norms of identity, trust and reciprocity. Thus, neither the emotional ties of family nor vertical authoritarian or patronage networks of trust or reciprocity count as social capital. This distinction is linked to donors' promotion of 'good governance' and 'democratization'. Horizontal associational ties of trust within the community, i.e. 'civil society', provide the basic trust upon which the 'transaction costs' of everyday economic exchange can be minimized.

Community harmony at the micro-scale is linked to macro-scale civic order and democratic politics. The trust embedded in social capital is considered to be cumulative and path-dependent, bringing about a virtuous cycle of citizens' relationships to the state and market. This is in contrast to the opposite path of vertically channelled, exclusionary clientelist supply of goods and services generating widespread societal distrust and economic and political corruption (Bebbington 1998, Durston 1998). The 'thickening of social capital' is believed to generate improved civic leadership, better information flows within and between networks, more democratic interaction and efficient local economies. Thus investment in social capital within the rural community is seen as a way of individual actors improving their resource access at the same time as they are paving the way for a 'sustainable' enabling environment for their communities. This perspective and its accompanying terminology and optimistic outlook is reminiscent of Adam Smith's 'invisible hand', metaphorically wearing a social rather than an economic glove.

Can the sustainable rural livelihoods and social capital approaches achieve these ambitious aims? With their openness to the complexity of rural life, they pick up the rural development debate where Lipton's (1968) article on peasant logic left off (see Chapter 1). Thirty years on, and in the wake of more than a decade of neo-liberal policy implementation, can a bottom-up perspective and concessions to non-economic disciplinary approaches through the use of participatory techniques, and a focus on the social and political dynamics of the locality, improve the life chances of rural dwellers today?

The sustainable rural livelihoods approach marks a vast improvement over neo-liberal oversight. Its capital asset approach provides a common analytical framework for economists, political scientists, sociologists and anthropologists with respect to understanding peasant populations. It offers a future-oriented investment perspective in place of past emphasis on production. However, this approach has certain theoretical blind spots and internal inconsistencies that could undermine its good intentions. These include:

- The 'rural' nature of the sustainable rural livelihoods approach cannot be taken for granted. The rural–urban continuum in which many 'rural dwellers' conduct their livelihood strategies can render a primarily rural-based approach off-target.
- The applicability of the current concepts of 'civil society' and horizontal 'social capital' must be treated with caution. These terms are normatively defined and highly prescriptive, and may run counter to an appreciation of local rural societies' internal organization and external context.
- Emphasis on building 'social capital' may be counter-productive, representing donors' attempts at making do with declining physical resource transfers, rather than reflective of the actual needs of rural dwellers. The build-up of human capital rather than social capital is the fundamental issue in view of the labour redundancy currently experienced by the world's peasantries.

Questioning rural appearances and peasant identities: taking account of how far de-peasantization has progressed

The past 15 years of neo-liberalism have rendered the rural population in Latin America, as well as many parts of Africa and Asia, both highly differentiated and highly mobile. While the rural livelihoods approach recognizes that individual and group aims of villagers may not be directed at agricultural investment, there is still an implicit assumption that there is a willingness to invest in the rural locality. This may be an unrealistic assumption.

Zoomers' (1999) analysis of the 'point of contact' between farmers' strategies and development interventions in the Bolivian Andes demonstrates some of the limitations of the sustainable rural livelihoods approach in rural areas characterized by high rates of temporary and permanent migration. The variation between peasant families with respect to migration patterns and commoditization of rural-based agricultural and non-agricultural production makes it impossible to assume that rural settlements are 'homogeneous', and population counts may be difficult to determine given the transient nature of village residents. Under these circumstances, adoption of villages as 'target areas' by external intervention agencies could prove to be myopic. The peasants' livelihood strategies embrace far wider geographical terrains than the village, and their working lives are full of contingent rather than permanent aims.

The concept of 'social capital' has provided a multidisciplinary meeting ground for social scientists consciously fostered by the World Bank, but its analytical clarity has suffered from being too widely and variously defined (Fox 1997, Harriss and De Renzio 1997). There seems to be a general consensus that 'social capital' refers to the realm of informal institutions, but there is little agreement on what is included in the informal realm. Often 'civil society' is used to embrace this amorphous realm, laden with a number of implicit conservative assumptions in line with the anti-statist bias of Putnam (1993) and Fukuyama (1995). To date, the concepts of social capital and civil society largely ignore the state's role in creating enabling conditions for social trust to function, while according the family a central role in nurturing such trust (Putzel 1997).

In considering the applicability of the concept of social capital to peasant societies, there is a need to gain greater analytical precision. Social capital's horizontal associational ties cannot be assumed to exist or to be necessarily desirable. Internal organizational features of peasant society have tended to be based on hierarchical and ascriptive relations embedded in differences in age, gender and geneological descent. While many of these vertical organizational features are eroding, they have been doing so at varying rates within different peasantries. To assess how far this process has come, and what potential it gives to the development of social capital, means confronting the vagueness of the term 'civil society' by examining individual agents' and peasant family units' actions *vis-à-vis* the 'community' or 'communities' that they interact with. The 'community' refers to localities with dense concentrations of interpersonal relations and commonly held behavioural norms based on a shared identity, associational ties and mutual support. As peasant mobility and exposure to outside value systems increase, the likelihood grows of being entangled in conflictual norms. Quite apart from the effects of enhanced mobility, the intensified interaction of peasant households and communities *vis-à-vis* wider state and market processes can engender such conflictual norms that could serve to undermine rather than promote social trust within the community.

The 'social capital' literature argues for the superiority of horizontal over vertical associational ties. It sees the former as more altruistic, open and democratic by nature, compared to vertical ties of family and clientage networks which are characterized as exclusionary and less accountable to the wider society. Putzel (1997) challenges the view that horizontal ties escape exclusionary practices, since most are based in one form or another on a group identity that distinguishes outsiders from insiders. Sometimes, such group identity is formulated on the basis of fictitious kinship, something that could be expected to be prevalent amongst people with peasant origins. By contrast, Durston (1998), citing the example of a Guatemalan peasant society, accepts the dichotomy between horizontal and vertical ties, but argues that 'traditional peasant' vertical ties are basic building blocks for creating more democratic horizontal associational ties.

The issue of external agency intervention to promote social capital formation within peasant communities echoes modernization assumptions. Most often, the outside agency is an NGO, whose role is to dynamize local people through leadership training and networking. The aim is to develop functional horizontal associational ties within the community, then scale up and 'thicken social capital' by linking their efforts to levels of the state and market operating beyond the community, to improve local access to resources (Bebbington 1998, Bebbington and Perreault 1998, Durston 1998). The optimism of this literature is tempered by Fox (1997) who cautions against the assumption that external agency intervention will improve local resource access. On the contrary, externally instigated projects may serve to dismantle rather than build local social capital by introducing new, highly coveted resources that devalue existing resources, thereby narrowing the peasant community's resource base and generating intensified resource competition.

Investing in human capital: strategic timing and targeting of social groups

Localized in focus, the sustainable rural livelihoods approach is liable to be criticized for not confronting the incompatibility between its stated local sustainable rural livelihood objectives and the priority IFIs place on the global market's labour allocative function. Furthermore, its emphasis on enhancing access to social capital could be interpreted as simply tinkering with the symptoms of peasant labour displacement without acknowledging or facing the challenge it poses.

If poverty alleviation is the main objective of this approach, then the issue of rural labour displacement with all its occupational and spatial implications cannot be avoided. The rural poor of Latin America, Africa and Asia are being progressively marginalized from commercial agricultural production while trying to maintain food self-provisioning and rural subsistence as fall-backs. The neo-liberal era has been a critical turning point for them. Agricultural development efforts to raise their standard of living will no longer suffice. Their future lies increasingly in labour-force participation outside rural agriculture. They need literacy, numeracy, knowledge of the national language, and various occupational and computer skills, that will give them the means to command sufficient income for themselves and their families, as well as to raise the overall level of labour productivity in their respective countries. Capability enhancement through human capital investment is vital (Sen 1997).

Enhancing the employment chances of the enormous pool of ever-more-marginalized rural peasant farmers is an enormous developmental task that requires clearly specifying target groups, activities and timing. The sustainable rural livelihoods approach is open-ended and participatory, and 'sustainable' rather than 'strategic' planning objectives could merely amount to time-consuming discussions and activities at the local level, failing to mobilize sufficient decision-making power or to generate the sense of direction needed to advance the economic prospects of the rural people involved.

In this period of extremely rapid change, there is a need to match target groups with activities more precisely. This could be facilitated by abandoning the fixation on adult target groups, in preference to youth and children. Rural children's access to primary schooling is a foundational requirement. The importance of resuscitating primary school education programmes where they have deteriorated under SAP public-spending cutbacks cannot be over-emphasized (Watkins 1999). Participatory discussions that pivot on realistic assessments of villagers' agrarian/non-agrarian prospects in relation to local and global markets are vital. Such discussions could be more focused and useful if they involve groups distinguished on the basis of gender and age cohorts. The prospects of young women aged 15–20 would be very different from that of their mothers or even boys their age, while efforts were made to steer away from gender stereotyping which could prejudice the welfare of either sex. On the basis of such discussions, village non-agricultural specializations could be identified. Those discussion groups which are already formed could provide a platform for mobilizing skills training and marketing, and for providing infrastructure for villagers' economic activities.

Rural poverty-alleviation projects tend to target the poor on the basis of the size of their land holdings, and command over agrarian capital stock or wage labour. Reliance on these discrete, easily defined criteria may now be a misleading basis for identifying the poor. Small land holdings no longer necessarily pinpoint the poorest of the rural community (Zoomers 1999). Unless external intervention agencies have intimate knowledge of the local community they are likely to misread the ostensive wealth indicators. For this reason, and given the extremely heterogeneous nature of the community, it is often better for project interventions to avoid rigid income-group targeting, and target either age groups or activities which are self-selecting in terms of villagers' interest and time availability.

In rural areas, where labour migration strategies are not so pronounced and where rural purchasing power affords a local market in goods and services, there is scope for improvements in rural dwellers' income diversification. Donor interventions in this area are difficult. Every villager has a different work portfolio that is intricately suited to the individual's needs. Whatever activity is targeted, the intervention is likely to affect other activities in the portfolio, usually by diverting the labour of the portfolio-holder. Assisting villagers with their portfolios would entail attention to short-term labour time management, and longer-term capital investment and career planning. Time management is not just about dovetailing daily or seasonal activities. A sense of direction is vital for optimizing portfolio-holders' labour, providing the focus that the sustainable rural livelihoods approach largely circumvents, that of rural dwellers' long-term agrarian prospects.

The ephemeral quality of living conditions in the countryside and farmers' lives could render the search for 'sustainable solutions' unrealistic (Zoomers 1999). Farmers are interested in adaptation and flexibility, whereas project planners pursue sustainability and permanent solutions. The dynamics of farmers' lives lead them to regard sustainability as a low priority. Farmers may view projects without lasting results – despite their brief duration – as beneficial to progress if some community members' life chances are improved. Thus temporary help at the right time can enable rural dwellers to achieve lasting improvements in their lives. Emphasis should be placed on finding critical 'target moments', related to decision-making associated with life-cycle transitions. Rural families in the Bolivian Andes still operate as family support units, despite high rates of out-migration. They, like peasant families in Africa and Asia, see their children's education as a long-term family investment. An offspring's eventual job acquisition represents fulfilment of family project objectives, and it is immaterial whether it is in the village or not.

Forward-looking considerations are often antithetical to the opportunistic, sometimes desperate, activity selection process that most rural dwellers have followed by default over the past two decades. In a simply reactive way, the poor have pursued an assemblage of 'last-resort' activities given their restricted access to capital. The sustainable rural livelihoods approach has dignified this process by arguing that all income diversifiers draw on a range of 'capitals'. While marking a step forward in inter-disciplinary analysis, it does raise the analytical problem of incomparability. The poor will be very poor in financial capital and possibly not so poor in social or cultural capital, but such distinctions should not detract from the critical point that the poor 'lack sufficient' capital to afford them activity choice.

Zoomers (1999) warns against accepting the 'average conditions' assumption implicit in the risk calculations that the sustainable rural livelihoods approach posits on peasant decision-makers. Peasants' accommodation to climatic variation through time, and their heavy exposure to market fluctuations more recently, renders the notion of 'average conditions' misleading. Peasants are in the habit of keeping the 'worst-case scenario' uppermost in their minds. Under the circumstances, any search by external agencies for 'sustainable solutions' may meet with wide disbelief or cynicism on the part of peasants. In some parts of Africa, where war and famine are a daily reality, this attitude is especially justified. Donor agencies tend to deal with these areas as 'humanitarian' rather than 'development' project areas, overlooking that the difference between the two is generated by quantitatively, not qualitatively, different forces. Peasants, feeling the forces of disintegration within their communities, are perhaps justified in expecting the worst at any moment.

Academic Fashion versus Enduring Peasant Legacies

> The most dramatic and far-reaching social change of the second half of this century, and the one which cuts us off for ever from the world of the past, is the death of the peasantry . . . Only three regions of the globe remained essentially dominated by their villages and fields: sub-Saharan Africa, South and continental South-east Asia, and China . . . Admittedly these regions of peasant dominance represented half the human race at the end of our period. However, even they were crumbling at the edges under the pressures of economic development . . . on the whole, the countries of the Third World . . . no longer fed themselves, let alone produced the major exportable food surplus that might be expected from agrarian countries . . . (Hobsbawm 1995: 289–92).

Do peasants matter any more? The term 'peasant' has had a derisory connotation for a very long time. The English words 'boor', meaning clumsy or ill-bred person, and 'bore', a tiresome dull person, are related to the Dutch and German words for farmer, '*boer*' and '*bauer*'. In fact, in English the term 'peasant' is distinguished from 'farmer' as a more backward agricultural producer. Despite their enduring backdrop role in history, peasants' image has been on a slippery slope, Marx's nineteenth century 'sack of potatoes' has been demoted to a 'not really worth mentioning' status as the twenty-first century dawns. Current avoidance of the term comes from modernist development economists and post-modernist social scientists, both uneasy with its associated connotations in western culture. In the process, peasants have become invisible. The recent banana wars were reported in the western press as a confrontation between two super trading powers, the European Union and the USA. Commentators largely disregarded the original issue, that of the competition between Caribbean peasants producing bananas and US-owned banana plantations in Central America (*Economist*: 6 March 1999, *Financial Times*: 8 March 1999). The inevitability of de-peasantization was simply taken for granted.

It is indeed strange that western social science has abandoned the project of tracing peasantries' historical encounter with industrial and post-industrial societies just when this encounter seems to have reached its most critical juncture – when peasants' continuing existence is at stake. Is this the fickleness of academic fashion or an evasive guilt complex – or worse, indifference moulded by the global economy of the affluent? In the words of Castells (1998: 5):

> The flexibility of this global economy allows the overall system to link up everything that is valuable according to dominant values and interests, while disconnecting everything that is not valuable, or becomes devalued. It is this simultaneous capacity to include and exclude people, territories and activities, that characterizes the new global economy as constituted in the information age.

On the other hand, this seeming indifference towards peasantries may hide an ambivalent love–hate relationship deeply buried in the psyche of industrial and post-industrial societies. Peasant influences live on in the daily life of the industrialized population. The values of peasant communities are enshrined in the world's main religions. The world's cultural and literary traditions are encrusted with peasant perspectives. Some choose to ignore these reminders, whereas others seek solace in them. The industrial world's ecology movement draws heavily on peasant conceptions of the environment. In Chapter 16, Knight provides a vivid example of Japanese utopian environmentalism. The 'back-to-the-countryside' movement in Japan, albeit small, demonstrates the value urbanites still place on being part of a bounded community, and espousing a work ethic and concern for the physical environment not just as a recreational resource, but as an object of one's labour, 'tilling the land'. The irony in this example is that born-again peasants are embracing such values at a time when long-standing Japanese farmers' are delighting in labour-saving devices and materialist accumulation.

The ambivalence of western discourse about peasants is more reflective of the confused, uncertain identity of the post-modern world, than indicative of the intrinsic nature of today's peasantries. The labels and connotations that peasants are lumbered with have unfortunately clouded the significance of their current predicament. The evidence in this book suggests that they are the losing partners in an on-going labour negotiating process with international capital. The global market is blind to their dissolution, and IFIs have not seriously addressed their plight with any measures other than highly localized poverty-alleviating projects. In this post neo-liberal era, the national governments of Asia, Latin America and Africa are largely powerless to implement policies to ensure peasants' survival as agrarian producers. Thus as the processes of de-agrarianization and de-peasantization combine, the vulnerability of peasantries deepens. Peasantries are disappearing, more rapidly than before.

Nonetheless, as long as peasant families retain their subsistence fallback and strong networks of support emanating from their natal communities, they partake in what we in the post-industrial world can only imagine or try to reconstruct – the 'world we have lost' (Laslett 1965). It is anybody's guess how long they will cling to their peasant subsistence fallback, before they are geographically dissipated by policy neglect and out-migration or physically disseminated by civil war and famine.

Whatever the outcome, the social and political legacy of peasant culture is bound to endure long after peasant economies disappear. Today's indifference will inevitably become romanticized nostalgia and regret. There is even the possibility that future global identity crises will be resolved by drawing on the world's peasant legacy. Modernity's victims may become its saviours. Time will tell – second thoughts are always deeper thoughts, but they tend to come far too late.

Notes

1. I am indebted to my co-editors for their comments and suggestions on this chapter, but I alone take responsibility for the views expressed here.
2. However, various Indian farmers' movements and African NGOs are vigorously protesting against the introduction of GM seeds and field experiments planned by Monsanto (Maathai 1998).

References

Bank, L. (1999) *No Visible Means of Subsistence: Rural Livelihoods, Gender and De-agrarianisation in the Eastern Cape*, Afrika-Studiecentrum Working Paper, Leiden.

Bebbington, A. (1998) 'Sustaining the Andes? Social capital and policies for rural regeneration in Bolivia', *Mountain Research and Development*, 18(2): 173–81.

Bebbington, A. and Perreault, T. (1998) 'Social Capital and Political Ecological Change in Highland Ecuador: Resource Access and Livelihoods', University of Colorado at Boulder, Department of Geography, unpublished mimeo.

Bryceson, D.F. and Jamal, V. (ed.) (1997) *Farewell to Farms*, Ashgate, Aldershot.

Bryceson, D.F., Seppälä, D.F. and Tapio-Bistrom, M.-L. (1999) 'Maize marketing policies in Tanzania, 1939–98: from basic needs to market basics' in T. Dijkstra, L. van der Laan and A. van Tilberg (eds) *Agricultural Marketing in Tropical Africa*, Ashgate, Aldershot.

Bryceson, D.F. (1999) 'African Rural Labour, Income Diversification and Livelihood Approaches: A Long-Term Development Perspective', *Review of African Political Economy*, No. 80, 171–89.

Castells, M. (1998) 'Informational capitalism and social exclusion', *UNRISD News*, No. 19.

Carney, D. (ed.) (1998) *Sustainable Rural Livelihoods: What Contribution Can We Make?*, Department for International Development, London.

Carney, D. (1999) 'Approaches to sustainable livelihoods for the rural poor', *ODI Poverty Briefing*, January 1999.

Chachage, C.S.L., Ericsson, M. and Gibbon, P. (1993) *Mining and Structural Adjustment: Studies on Zimbabwe and Tanzania*, Research Report No. 92, Uppsala.

Durston, J. (1998) 'Building Social Capital in Rural Communities (Where It Doesn't Exist)', paper presented at the Latin America Studies Association, Chicago, September 1998.

Elson, R.E. (1997) *The End of the Peasantry in Southeast Asia: A Social and Economic History of Peasant Livelihood, 1800–1990s*, Macmillan, London.

FAO (various years) *Food and Agriculture Trade Yearbooks*, Food and Agriculture Organization of the UN, Rome.

Fox, J. (1997) 'The World Bank and social capital: contesting the concept in practice', *Journal of International Development*, 9(7): 963–71.

Fukuyama, F. (1995) *Trust: The Social Virtues and the Creation of Prosperity*, Pergamon, London.

Gibbon, P. and Raikes, P. (2000) 'The current restructuring of African export crop agriculture in a global context', *Journal of Peasant Studies*, Vol. 27, No. 2.

Godfrey, C. (1998) *A Future for Caribbean Bananas: The Importance of Europe's Banana Market to the Caribbean*, Policy Department, Oxfam UK and Ireland, Oxford.

Goodman, D. and Watts, M.J. (ed.) (1997) *Globalising Food*, Routledge, London and New York.

Harriss, J. and De Renzio, P. (1997) '"Missing link" or analytically missing? The concept of social capital: an introductory bibliographic essay', *Journal of International Development*, 9(7): 919–37.

Hobsbawm, E. (1995) *Age of Extremes: The Short Twentieth Century, 1914–1991*, Abacus, London.

Kearney, M. (1996) *Reconceptualising the Peasantry: Anthropology in Global Perspective*, Westview Press, Boulder.

Laslett, P. (1965) *The World We Have Lost*, Methuen, London.

Lipton, M. (1968) 'The theory of the optimizing peasant', *Journal of Development Studies*, 327–51.

Maathai, W. (1998) 'The link between patenting of life forms, genetic engineering and food insecurity', *Review of African Political Economy*, 25(77): 526–31.

McMichael, P. (ed.) (1995) *Food and Agrarian Orders in the World Economy*, Praeger, London.

Moore, B. (1966) *The Social Origins of Dictatorship and Democracy: Lord and Peasant in the Making of the Modern World*, Beacon Press, Boston.

Peters, K. and Richards, P. (1998) 'Jeunes combattants parlant de la guerre et de la paix in Sierra Leone', *Cahiers d'Etudes africaines*, 150–152, XXXVIII-2–4: 581–617.

Ponte, S. (1997) 'Get Your Cash Fast: Rural Households' Adaptations to Liberalized Agricultural Markets in Two Tanzanian Districts', paper presented at the African Studies Association Conference, Colombus, USA, November 1997.

Putnam, R. (1993) *Making Democracy Work: Civic Traditions in Modern Italy*, Princeton University Press, Princeton.

Putzel, J. (1997) 'Accounting for the "dark side" of social capital: reading Robert Putnam on democracy", *Journal of International Development*, 9(7): 939–49.

Redclift, M. (1991) 'Land, hunger and power: the agrarian crisis in Latin America', in CEDLA (ed.) *The Crisis of Development in Latin America*, CEDLA, Amsterdam, pp. 23–52.

Roberts, B. (1978), *Cities of Peasants*, Edward Arnold, London.
Roberts, B. (1995), *The Making of Citizens: Cities of Peasants Revisited*, Edward Arnold, London.
Sapford, D. and Singer, H. (1998) 'The IMF, the World Bank and commodity prices: a case of shifting sands?', *World Development*, 26(9): 1653–60.
Sen, A. (1997) 'Editorial: Human capital and human capability', *World Development*, 25, 12: 1959–61.
Stolcke, V. (1988) *Coffee Planters, Workers and Wives: Class Conflict and Gender Relations on Sao Paulo Plantations, 1850–1980*, St Martin's Press, New York.
Tacoli, C. (1998) *Bridging the Divide: Rural–Urban Interactions and Livelihood Strategies*, International Institute for Environment and Development, London.
Thoumi, F.E. (1995) *Political Economy and Illegal Drugs in Colombia*, Lynne Rienner Publishers, Boulder.
Tripp, R. (1999) 'The Debate on Genetically Modified Organisms: Relevance for the South', *ODI Briefing Papers* 1999(1): 1–4.
Watkins, K. (1999) *Education Now: Break the Cycle of Poverty*, Oxfam, Oxford.
World Bank (1995) *World Development Report 1995: Workers in an Integrating World*, Oxford University Press, New York.
Zoomers, A. (1999) *Linking Livelihood Strategies to Development: Experiences from the Bolivian Andes*, Royal Tropical Institute/Centre for Latin American Research and Documentation, Amsterdam.

INDEX